Proto Witotoan

Summer Institute of Linguistics and
The University of Texas at Arlington
Publications in Linguistics

Publication 114

Editors

Donald A. Burquest
University of Texas
at Arlington

William R. Merrifield
Summer Institute of
Linguistics

Assistant Editors

Rhonda L. Hartell

Marilyn A. Mayers

Consulting Editors

Doris A. Bartholomew
Pamela M. Bendor-Samuel
Desmond C. Derbyshire
Robert A. Dooley
Jerold A. Edmondson

Austin Hale
Robert E. Longacre
Eugene E. Loos
Kenneth L. Pike
Viola G. Waterhouse

Proto Witotoan

Richard P. Aschmann

A Publication of
The Summer Institute of Linguistics
and
The University of Texas at Arlington
1993

Cover sketch and design by Hazel Shorey

Copies of this and other publications of the Summer Institute of Linguistics may be obtained from

International Academic Bookstore
7500 W. Camp Wisdom Road
Dallas, TX 75236

Contents

Foreword

Richard Aschmann's Witotoan book is an excellent example of the kind of work that is now needed in historical linguistics, both for its methodology and for its results.

The methodology applied in historical linguistics has been developed largely on the basis of investigation of the Romance and the Germanic subgroups of the Indo-European language family. For the Romance languages we have the source, as well as a large amount of data; for the Germanic languages we have extensive documentation of the several subgroups over a period of a thousand years and more. Accordingly, linguists have been able to draw their conclusions without examining all of the available materials. Moreover, stages in each of the languages have been determined largely on nonlinguistic grounds.

By contrast, in determining the relationships among the Witotoan languages and in reconstructing Proto Witotoan, Aschmann must rely entirely on linguistic evidence. Examining this thoroughly, he carefully reconstructs the proto forms of languages attested only today. Having arrived at two protolanguages for the two subgroups of Proto Witotoan, he reconstructs the ancestral language. His procedure is comparable to an undertaking that would reconstruct Middle English, Middle Frisian, and so on by examination of English and Frisian dialects spoken today, rather than to produce grammars on the basis of the texts that have survived from earlier periods. Since such a procedure would be salutary for all languages, Aschmann's book will serve as guide for studies in historical phonology of even well-studied languages.

The book is also highly recommended in a period when distant comparison has caught the imagination of leading linguists and especially of specialists in palaeo-sciences. Rather than relying on likeness among words for which cognates are not found in each language of a proposed family, Aschmann practices the rigorous comparison of phonological elements that has been a fundamental procedure since its application by Jacob Grimm in 1822 to the Germanic consonants. Aschmann's careful use of the comparative method achieves assurance for his conclusions, and provides another forceful demonstration of its central role in historical linguistics.

We may hope that Aschmann's book will serve as model, as well as inspiration, for further such careful studies. Linguistics enjoys a unique role in attention to earlier periods of societies for whom only the languages of today are known; unlike archaeological materials, its data alone can be assuredly associated with a given people. All scholars concerned with accurate historical reconstruction of earlier societies as well as of their languages must assign highest priority to linguistic evidence, which is especially valuable when determined with the care and authority exhibited by Richard Aschmann.

Winfred P. Lehmann
The University of Texas at Austin

1

Introduction

The purpose of this book[1] is (1) to demonstrate the genetic relationship between the two Boran languages—Bora[2] and Muinane—and to reconstruct Proto Bora-Muinane (PBM); (2) to demonstrate the genetic relationship between the four Huitoto-Ocaina languages—Nɨpode Huitoto, Mɨnɨca Huitoto, Murui Huitoto, and Ocaina[3]—and to reconstruct Proto

---

[1]This book began as a result of a comparative linguistic workshop conducted by Winfred Lehmann of the University of Texas for the members of the Colombia branch of the Summer Institute of Linguistics, held at Lomalinda, Meta, Colombia in 1987.

[2]Miraña is a dialect of Bora (Grimes 1988), and the data demonstrate that Miraña and Bora are extremely close. A dialect-intelligibility test conducted by Van Otterloo and Peckham (1976) indicate 94% intelligibility between Bora and Miraña. Miraña, however, exhibits certain conservative features which it shares with Muinane. I, therefore, refer to it occasionally in this study although I have not included Miraña data in the wordlist.

[3]Nɨpode is also commonly called Muinane Huitoto, and Murui is called Búe. Minor (undated A) uses the terms Nɨpode, Mɨnɨca and Búe; nɨpóde, mɨnɨ́ka and bu.e are the words these three groups use respectively to say 'What is it?' (see word 259 in the wordlist) and are often used by the Huitotos themselves as terms for the various groups. I use Nɨpode in this study to distinguish this language from Muinane.

Throughout this study I use the term Huitoto to refer to Nɨpode, Mɨnɨca, and Murui, exclusively, since these are commonly called Huitoto. I use the term Witotoan, on the other hand, to refer to the entire language family.

These six languages are spoken by small groups in the Colombian Department of Amazonas and in neighboring regions of Colombia, Peru, and Brazil. Approximate populations and locations are: Bora, Colombia-Peru border, mostly in Peru (Miraña dialect in Brazil and in northern Amazonas in Colombia), 2000–2500; Muinane, eastcentral Amazonas, 150; Mɨnɨca, Río Igaraparaná in Amazonas and points northwest, 2500; Murui, Río Putumayo on Colombia-Peru border, 2000–2800; Nɨpode, scattered, mostly in Peru, 50–100; Ocaina, mostly in Peru, 150–250 (these data are primarily from Grimes 1988, most of them ultimately from SIL sources; the Nɨpode figure is an estimate by Eugene Minor).

1

Huitoto-Ocaina (PHO); and (3) to demonstrate the genetic relationship between these two groups of languages as members of the Witotoan language family and to reconstruct Proto Witotoan (PW). Purposes one and two are accomplished conclusively; three has also been accomplished to the author's satisfaction in spite of the lower demonstrated cognate count.[4] This study is the first detailed reconstruction of Proto Witotoan carried out to date.

Greenberg (1987:385), Key (1979:104ff), Grimes (1988), and Tax (1960:433) maintain that the Bora-Muinane and Huitoto-Ocaina families constitute a Witotoan stock, although this has been doubted by Tovar (1961:145) and by Loukotka (1968:187–191).

Some have maintained that Ocaina is more closely related to Bora and Muinane than to Huitoto (Mason 1950:245); others accept the closer affinity to Huitoto (Tovar 1961:146) demonstrated here. Tovar (1961:150) is uncertain as to whether to classify Muinane with Bora or with Huitoto. This may be due to the naming confusion between Muinane Huitoto (Nɨpode) and Muinane proper. Muinane is unquestionably closer to Bora, as demonstrated here.

A number of claims have been made concerning membership in larger units, the best consensus being Macrokariban (Kaufman 1990:57). The most conservative conclusion, however, is that the Witotoan stock is an isolate (Grimes 1984; Kaufman 1990:43).

Concerning other languages considered Witotoan, some have claimed that Orejón is related to Bora or Huitoto (Tovar 1961:146; Loukotka 1968:188). According to Mason (1950:246), "the name [Orejón] seems to be applied to two adjacent groups . . . One group . . . is southern *Witoto* and apparently extinct. Another . . . is the *Coto* . . . of *Tucano* affinity." The latter is a Western Tucanoan language (Grimes 1988; Waltz and Wheeler 1972; Wheeler in preparation). Others have claimed that Andoke is Witotoan (Grimes 1988; Tax 1960:433; Mason 1950:246, with disclaimer; Kaufman 1990:43, tentatively). Andoke, however, is generally accepted as an isolate (Tovar 1961:150; Witte 1981:1; Grimes 1984).[5]

---

[4]Data for this study are taken primarily from a 375-word comparative wordlist, based on the Swadesh-Rowe wordlist. The author found that Bora and Muinane have between 73% and 76% cognates (between 275 and 285 words); Huitoto and Ocaina have between 42% and 50% (between 159 and 187 words); and Proto Bora-Muinane and Proto Huitoto-Ocaina have between 25% and 35% cognates (between 92 and 131 words). The lower figure in each case indicates reasonably certain cognates, whereas the higher figure includes uncertain cognates. The wordlist, including all reconstructed words, is included as chapter 6 in this book.

[5]It is unclear why Grimes changed her mind between her 1984 and 1988 editions. Witte (1981:1) states, '. . . se ha comprobado que definitivamente no se trata de una lengua huitoto . . .', although he does not state where or by whom this was proven. I

On a more rigorous level, others have claimed a relationship with Resígaro (Tax 1960:433). Allin (1975:495) maintains that Resígaro is related to Witotoan and to Arawakan; he therefore concludes that Witotoan is a branch of the Arawakan phylum. Payne (1985) has demonstrated through further analysis of Allin's data, however, that the apparent relationship of Resígaro to Witotoan is the result of borrowing and he, therefore, rejects any connection between Arawakan and Witotoan, leaving Resígaro squarely in the Arawakan family. For this reason, Resígaro is not included in this analysis.

Grimes (1988) lists Nipode as a dialect of Minica. This must be an error, however, since Nipode is, phonologically at least, much more different from either Minica or Murui than these are from each other. Eugene Minor, who worked for many years in both Nipode and Minica, confirms this (personal communication).

The reconstruction is strictly phonological and lexical; no comparison of the grammatical systems of these languages is attempted in this book.[6]

---

had access to an incomplete Andoke wordlist containing only items 1 through 86 (Minor, undated B) and was able to find only 7 words which appeared to be even potential cognates. I, therefore, conclude that Andoke cannot be demonstrated to be a Witotoan language.

[6]Data for this analysis were obtained from the following sources: For Bora, from Allin 1975:497–527, from Thiesen in preparation, and from Thiesen 1978; Miraña data (not included in the wordlist, but referred to in the text) from Smith 1990 and from Van Otterloo and Peckham 1976. For Muinane, from Walton in preparation, and from Walton, Hensarling, and Maxwell in press. For Nipode Huitoto, from Minor (undated A) and from Minor and Minor 1971. For Minica Huitoto, from Minor (undated A) and from Minor and Minor 1987. For Murui Huitoto, from Minor (undated A) and from Burtch 1983. For Ocaina, from Leach 1971.

All of the data in the sources except for that in Minor (undated A), Walton, Hensarling and Maxwell (in press) and Van Otterloo and Peckham 1976 were written in the orthographies used for printing literature in these languages. In these orthographies, the following conventions are used: c or qu (the latter only before /e/ and /i/) for /k/, except that Bora uses c and k respectively; more recently k has been used in Bora material; ts for /ts/; ds for /dz/; ch for /č/; ll for /ỹ/; y for /ỹ/ (more recently y has been used in Huitoto); h for /ʔ/; pb for /b̃/; td for /d̃/; f for /ɸ/; s (Murui) or z (Minica) for /θ/; s for /s/; sh for /š/; v for /β/; ñ for /ñ/ or /ny/; m̃, ñ, ñ for /m̃, n̥, ñ̥/; y after a consonant for palatalization; ng for /ŋ/; an acute accent over a vowel for accent or high tone (in early material in Nipode and Minica the acute accent is not indicated if it falls on the first syllable, the most common position; in later material the Spanish conventions are used, i.e., accent is marked except when penultimate); a grave accent over a nonsyllabic vowel to indicate a one-syllable vowel cluster (diphthong) in Huitoto (although in later literature this is not generally written, at least in Minica); in all Huitoto and in Ocaina, j for /h/ and x for /x/; in Bora and Muinane, j for /x/; in all Huitoto, i for /ɨ/; in Bora and Muinane, i for /ɨ/; in Ocaina and Bora, u for /ɨ/; in Muinane and all Huitoto, u for /u/. Nasalization of vowels in Ocaina is indicated with an n after the vowel (e.g., jinñóónhfu for /hĩñóóʔɸɨ́/). In the Bora orthography, unaspirated stops are

A description of the phonologies of the six languages follows, showing the phoneme inventory and the symbols that are used here to represent them.[7]

In all six of the languages, /e/ and /o/ are typically realized phonetically as [ɛ] and [ɔ], respectively. In apparently all of the languages, vowel-initial words have a phonetic [ʔ] before the vowel. In all of the languages except Bora this word-initial glottal is fully predictable and does not contrast with its absence; for this reason linguists have treated it as nonphonemic. In a few cases the glottal is retained when a prefix is added, in which case it becomes phonemic. In Bora the word-initial glottal stop is obligatory only in utterance-initial position; in utterance-medial position it is contrastive with its absence. For details, see §1.1.

The numbers in the phoneme charts accompanying each phoneme indicate the relative frequency of the phoneme by percentage of occurrence. These were determined separately for consonants and vowels by adding up the total number of vowels or consonants and then taking the percentage of occurrence for each individual phoneme. For Ocaina the oral vowels were counted separately from the nasal vowels. Double (long) vowels were counted as two separate vowels. In Ocaina and Bora, syllable-initial and syllable-final glottals are counted separately, since they have separate reflexes in the other languages; syllable-initial and syllable-final /x/ are counted separately in Bora for the same reason.

Those phonemes marked with a dagger (†) in the phoneme charts are in general extremely rare and do not appear to be a reflex of any proto-phoneme. A few phonemes are marked with a dagger when the relationship to the protolanguage is confusing or peculiar, e.g., the /ɓ/-/p/ correspondence between Nípode and Murui, which is rare when it logically should not be, or /č/ in the Huitoto languages.

In five of the six languages, the form of the adjectives and verbs in the wordlist (based usually on the citation forms chosen to include in the dictionaries) carry standard suffixes that significantly skew the phoneme count for the phonemes they contain. For example, more than half of the occurrences of /d/ in Huitoto in the wordlist are in the adjective-verb suffixes /-de/ or /-re-de/. I have excluded these suffixes in making the

represented as voiced (*b d ds ll g* for /p t ts č k/), and aspirated stops as voiceless (*p t ts ch c* or *k* for /pʰ tʰ tsʰ čʰ kʰ/). /kʷ/ is written *w* in Bora. Miraña uses the same orthography as Bora. Payne (1985) was apparently not aware of these spelling conventions when he rewrote Allin's Bora data phonemically.

[7]Phonological descriptions of the six languages were obtained from the following sources: for Bora, from Thiesen and Thiesen 1975; for Muinane, from Walton and Walton 1972 and Walton, Hensarling, and Maxwell in press; for Nípode Huitoto, from Minor 1956; for Minica Huitoto, from Minor and Minor 1976. For Murui Huitoto, from Burtch 1975 and Burtch 1983. For Ocaina, from Agnew and Pike 1957 and from Leach 1971:66, 163–164.

phoneme counts and totals, since they would obscure the historical correspondences, although I have included in the charts in parentheses the additional percentage these phonemes would have had if I had included the suffixes (all percentages, including those for the suffixes, are based on totals without the suffixes). The suffixes in question are indicated in (1).[8] The total counts of consonants and vowels in the wordlist (excluding the suffixes in (1)) are given for reference at the bottom of each phoneme chart with totals including the suffixes placed in parentheses.

(1)   Murui   *-de, -te, -re-de*
       Minica   *-de, -te, -re-de, -re-ra*
       Nɨpode   *-de, -de, -re-de*
       Muinane   *-no, -ño, -ne, -ñe, -ʔi*
       Bora   *-ne(e), -nʸe(e)*

1.1 Bora

Bora has twenty-eight consonants (not including /ʔy/), six vowels, and two tones. These are presented in (2). The consonants are in two series, nonpalatalized (15) and palatalized (13, excluding /ʔy/). Each nonpalatalized phoneme except /kʷ/ has a palatalized counterpart, with the following clarifications: (a) I analyze the palatalized counterpart of /ʔ/ as a cluster /ʔy/, not a unit /ʔʸ/;[9] (b) the palatalized counterpart of /r/ is /y/; (c) /kʷ/ has no palatalized counterpart, resisting all of the palatalization rules affecting the other consonants. All of these pairs of consonants experience morphophonemic alternation in Bora, with the palatalized phonemes occurring almost exclusively after /i/ and /a/.

---

[8]The suffixes in (1) for Murui, Minica, and Nɨpode occur with adjectives and verbs. Those for Muinane and Bora occur only with adjectives, with the exception of -ʔi in Muinane, which occurs only with verbs.

[9]I am treating /ʔy/ as a sequence because it simplifies the consonant inventory. Thiesen and Thiesen (1975:1) analyze this sequence as a unit phoneme, although they admit (note 4) that since it never occurs either word initially or word finally, and since word medially it only occurs in environments in which sequences of glottal stop plus consonant are permitted, it could be analyzed as a sequence. They are inconsistent in their representation: usually they write /ʔʸ/, a unit phoneme, but on page 8 they list *ʔimíʔye* 'good' as an example of the sequence /ʔy/. (My decision concerning the treatment of /ʔy/ is based on phonological, not grammatical criteria; there is no doubt that /ʔy/ does vary morphologically with /ʔ/ in a number of cases.)

This sequence also occurred in Proto Bora-Muinane, which is not the case for the other palatalized consonants. Most cases of Bora /ʔy/ derive from palatalization of PBM *ʔ, but there are clear cases which are derived from *ʔy.

The other palatalized segments in Bora cannot be treated as a sequence of consonant plus /y/ because to do so would introduce an otherwise nonexistent syllable structure,

6 Proto Witotoan

The palatalized phonemes were not in Proto Bora-Muinane, but were formed by a palatalization process, followed by loss of the conditioning environment.

The phoneme /kʷ/ varies phonetically between [kʷ] and [kᵖ], a double stop; the variation appears to be more dialectal than allophonic: [kᵖ] is by far the most frequent allophone in Bora proper, whereas [kʷ] is more frequent in Miraña (Wesley Thiesen, personal communication). The phonemes /k/ and /kʸ/ are extremely rare. There are only three examples of /k/ in the wordlist used for the present study—none of which is cognate with a known Muinane form, and no examples of /kʸ/. Thiesen (in preparation) has a few examples of each.

Bora /r/ is described by Thiesen and Thiesen (1975:3) as a voiced alveolar trill, but my observation is that it tends to be a voiced retroflexed alveolar fricative.

Bora contrasts glottal-initial and vowel-initial stems. This is not apparent in isolation, however, since all vowel-initial stems have glottal in utterance-initial position. The contrast is, nevertheless, clearly discernible in utterance-medial position and when prefixes are present. These two groups of stems have different sources. In Proto Bora-Muinane the sources of vowel-initial forms had an initial *x,[10] which was regularly lost in this environment in Bora, whereas the sources of glottal-initial forms had an initial vowel, with probable glottal onset.[11]

Thiesen and Thiesen (1975) indicate that words may end in /ʔ/. They also specify (1975:5), however, that all vowel-final words have a phonetic [ʔ] in utterance-final position. In the dictionary (Thiesen in preparation), there are no examples of word-final glottal,[12] and in fact it is never written in the Bora

---

CCV. These palatalized segments occur word initially (unlike /ʔy/) and can occur following /ʔ/ and /x/ in word-medial position (e.g., 4 aʔtiiʔtʸo 'tooth', 295 axtʰʸïβa 'green'), both of which are otherwise true only for unit consonants.

A possible third alternative would be to treat /y/ as a suprasegmental phoneme. However, its distribution is somewhat dependent historically on the consonant with which it occurs, and for some of the consonants (*ts g r with nonpalatalized Bora reflexes /tsʰ kʷ r/) the palatalization has completely merged with the consonant, producing an alveopalatal consonant indistinguishable from others derived from other sources (i.e., /čʰ č y/). In light of this, I conclude that palatalization does not function synchronically as a suprasegmental, but instead as an integral part (or feature) of the consonant.

[10]Proto Bora-Muinane and Proto Huitoto-Ocaina forms are marked with a single asterisk, and Proto-Witotoan forms with a double asterisk.

[11]I have not reconstructed a phonemic glottal in Proto Bora-Muinane in word-initial position, since it probably did not contrast with its absence at that time. It would almost certainly have been phonetically predictable in that position, as is the case now in all of the Witotoan languages except Bora.

[12]The word-initial contrast between glottal-initial and vowel-initial words is clearly indicated in the dictionary, although some inconsistency is notable in the rough draft to which I had access.

(2)   Bora phonemes

p^h	t^h	ts^h	k^h				i	$ɨ$	$ï$
4.5	3.9	5.1	11.2				12.2	9.3	20.7
p^{hy}	t^{hy}	$č^h$	k^{hy}				e	a	o
0.1	1.6	1.4	1.3				17.6 (1.6)	26.8	13.4
p	t	ts	k	k^w	$ʔ$				
5.1	2.4	0.3	0.1	6.4	5.0 Init.				
					6.3 Final				
p^y	t^y	$č$	k^y†	$(ʔy)$					
0.4	0.04	2.8	0.0	0.8					

x high tone (acute accent)
5.8 Init.   low tone (unmarked)
6.2 Final

x^y
1.3

$β$
3.8

$β^y$
0.4

m n
8.8   7.5 (1.6)

m^y n^y
0.3   1.8 (0.2)

        r
        4.1

        y
        1.3

2502 (2545) consonants, 3057 (3105) vowels.

orthography. According to Wesley Thiesen, however, word-final glottal is contrastive in phrase-medial position in the same way that word-initial glottal is, but because of literacy considerations the Thiesens have chosen not to write it in the practical orthography (personal communication). Thus information on word-final glottal stop is not available in the data.[13]

---

[13]The only example I have (Wesley Thiesen, personal communication) is the word *imíʔ* 'good' (see wordlist item 224), which according to Thiesen retains its final glottal in phrase-medial position, and which when followed by the suffix *-re* (meaning unknown) produces *imíʔ-ye* (the /r/ being palatalized to /y/). However, the glottal is apparently not retained before some or all consonant-initial suffixes, as is evidenced by the (diminutive?) form 224. *imí-kwɨ* 'good'. Therefore the status of word-final glottal seems tenuous at best.

The syllable structure of Bora, like that of the other five languages, generally permits no consonant clusters or syllable-final consonants, with the exception that /x/ and /ʔ/ may occur in syllable-final position. /ʔ/ may occur freely before any consonant and word-finally (though as mentioned, the latter are not written in the data). Syllable-final /x/ normally occurs only before aspirated stops,[14] thus creating preaspirated stops, which are reflexes of Proto Bora-Muinane geminate stops. I am not treating preaspirated stops as unitary phonemes in Bora, however, even though they derive from specific protophonemes, since syllable-final /x/ is not currently restricted to prestop position in Bora. Preaspirated stops occur both word-medially and word-initially, but in the latter case the preaspiration is only realized in phrase-medial position, as the word-final [x] of a preceding word (§2.2).

Bora appears, at first glance, to have the usual six-vowel system common to languages in northwestern South America, with one notable difference: it has /ï/ instead of /u/, thus having a contrast between three high unrounded vowels, /i/, /ɨ/ and /ï/ (according to Thiesen and Thiesen 1975). This is an extremely unusual system, in that /ɨ/ and /ï/ do not normally contrast in natural language. Ladefoged (1971:76–77) in fact states, "I cannot find any clearcut cases of three vowels within a language which contrast just by being front, central, and back, with all other features remaining the same."

Upon further observation, however, Ladefoged appears to be vindicated, in that the Bora /ɨ/ does not appear to be pronounced at the cardinal position for [ɨ]. In fact, Michael Maxwell (personal communication), after listening to a native speaker, concluded that this /ɨ/ was not a high central vowel, but a high open front vowel [ɪ]. Upon subsequent listening, however, I personally conclude that this vowel is neither front nor central, but at the midpoint between these two positions. Its vertical positioning appears to be high open, i.e., at the same height as [ɪ]. Smith (1990) describes this vowel in Miraña (a dialect of Bora) as a "high unrounded slightly front of central vowel, somewhat more fronted than the traditional [ɨ]." Its acoustic characteristics are distinct from those of [ɪ], as is further confirmed by the fact that Van Otterloo and Peckham (1976), in the wordlist of Miraña they recorded while conducting a dialect survey of Colombian languages, totally failed to discern the phonetic distinction between /ɨ/ and /ï/, although Smith (1990) verifies that these phonemes do contrast in Miraña (a dialect of Bora). As native speakers of English, Van Otterloo and Peckham would not be expected to make this error if the /ɨ/ vowel sounded like an [ɪ]. This error is further explained by another fact: the Bora /ï/ is slightly farther forward than the cardinal position for [ï].

---

[14]/x/ occasionally occurs before unaspirated stops, before /n/ and word-finally (not necessarily followed by an aspirated stop in the next word). There are a handful of examples in Thiesen and Thiesen (1975), in Thiesen (in preparation) and in Allin 1975.

The phonetic locations of Bora vowels, represented in (2) give the appearance of a system in flux. Of the six vowels, only the high vowels /i/ and /ï/ appear to have the same height, and only the front vowels /i/ and /ɛ/ appear to have the same degree of backness (the vowel /ɛ/ is written /e/ for simplicity in (2) and throughout the remainder of this book).

If Ladefoged is right, a feature system with other than the two degrees of height and three degrees of backness represented in (3) must be proposed to account for this unusual system. The simplest alternative would probably be a system with three degrees of height and two degrees of backness. The real answer, however, is probably that we have a system in flux, not easily reducible to a simple set of features.

(3)   Phonetic locations of the Bora vowels

    i   ï

      ɨ

                 o

  ɛ

      a

I consider the source of Bora /ɨ/ to be Proto Witotoan **e, from a split into Proto Bora-Muinane *e and *ɨ. If this is correct, the current phonetic positions of Bora /e/ and /ɨ/ are not surprising since they would have drifted from a common point between their current positions. Current Bora vowel positions are probably essentially unchanged from those of Proto Bora-Muinane.[15]

1.2 Muinane

Muinane has twenty-six consonants, six vowels and two tones. These are listed in (4). One special feature of Muinane is that voiceless stops have contrastive geminate forms, which, as is common with geminate consonants, apparently occur only word-medial.[16]

---

[15]This is discussed further in §2.6.

[16]Walton and Walton (1972) are apparently unaware that these geminate consonants are contrastive with their nongeminate counterparts. They observed the feature (Walton and Walton 1972:50), describing it as a 'pause' preceding the voiceless stops in word-medial position, but they apparently thought that it occurred obligatorily in that position and was therefore subphonemic. During a writer's workshop conducted in Colombia in January 1989 which included Muinane speakers, however, Wesley Thiesen first identified this feature as phonemic and observed that it tended to occur in precisely those words whose Bora cognates had preaspirated stops. This was later

(4)   Muinane phonemes

	tt	tt^y	čč	kk		i	ɨ	u
	1.0	0.5	0.3	3.8		20.1 (3.9)	17.3	13.9
p†	t	t^y	č	k		e	a	o
0.4	4.6	0.3	0.8	7.5		14.0 (0.5)	26.0	8.8 (3.0)
b	d	d^y	ǰ	g	ʔ			
7.7	2.8	0.1	1.2	10.9	8.6 (5.2)			
ɸ	s		š	x				
4.4	6.5		0.2	11.1				
β								
2.9								
m	n		ñ					
10.1	8.0 (4.2)		1.2 (0.5)					
	r	r^y						
	3.0	0.2						
		y						
		2.0						

high tone (acute accent)
low tone (unmarked)

1473 (1619) consonants, 1999 (2145) vowels.

As in Bora, there is a palatalization process, but it only affects the alveolar consonants. /tt t d r/ are phonetically palatalized; /s n/ become alveopalatal. The palatalized members of these pairs, /tt^y t^y d^y š ñ r^y/, occur in the wordlist only after /a/ and occasionally after /i/ (in the case of /ñ/, occasionally after /ai/).[17] The palatalized consonants experience morphophonemic alternation with their nonpalatal counterpart. As is shown in §2.1, the five palatalized phonemes were not present in Proto Bora-Muinane, but were formed by the same palatalization process that

---

confirmed through investigation with two Muinane speakers by Michael Maxwell and this author. When asked to specify which words in the wordlist had 'double' /p/, /t/, /k/ or /č/ and which did not, the native speakers were able to do so with little hesitation, much more easily than they could identify the tone patterns for these words, thereby confirming the phonemic status of gemination.

I am treating these as separate phonemes rather than as consonant clusters, since the syllable structure of Muinane has no consonant clusters or syllable-final consonants—not even glottal stop, as does Bora. The argument could be made that since geminate stops apparently occur only word-medially, they should not be treated as separate phonemes. Not investigated here is whether they occur contrastively in some words word-initially when they are phrase-medial, as is the case for their Bora counterpart, preaspirated stops.

[17]There are a miniscule number of examples in the Muinane dictionary of these phonemes in other environments.

produced the palatalized phonemes in Bora, with subsequent loss of the conditioning environment in most cases.

Muinane /r/ is described by Walton and Walton (1972:45) as a voiceless alveolar trill, but my observation is that it tends to be a voiceless retroflexed alveolar affricate.

1.3 Nɨpode Huitoto

Nɨpode Huitoto has eighteen consonants, six vowels and one accent, which are presented in (5). It is phonologically the most conservative of the three Huitoto languages, and its phonological structure is essentially unchanged from that of Early Huitoto, the mother language of the three Huitotos.

(5)   Nɨpode Huitoto phonemes

p	t	čɨ	k	ʔɨ	i	ï	u
7.7	4.7	1.1	13.2	0.2	17.2	20.0	7.0
b	d	j	g		e	a	o
5.7	7.4 (8.3)	5.1	3.7		12.6 (7.7)	24.0	19.2
ɓɨ	ɗ						
0.2	3.3 (1.2)						

h
9.3

β
0.6

accent system (with complex patterning on geminate vowels only)

m	n	ñ	ŋ
9.8	13.3	2.2	1.2

r
11.2(1.7)

937 (1042) consonants, 1370 (1475) vowels.

The most interesting feature of Nɨpode Huitoto is the relative frequency of the two voiced implosives, /ɓ/ and /ɗ/. /ɗ/ is fairly common, whereas /ɓ/ is extremely rare. This frequency is an apparent exception to the rule given by Greenberg (1970:127f) who states that "injectives tend to have front articulation" and that "if a language has one injective obstruent, it is ʔb; if it has two they are ʔb and ʔd (the most common pattern)."[18] If this generalization were true for Nɨpode, /ɓ/ and /ɗ/ would be expected to be

---

[18]Greenberg writes his implosives as preglottalized stops, for the reason given in the next paragraph.

at least equally common, or else /ɓ/ to be more common than /ɗ/. Instead, the reverse is true. The possibility of proposing that these phonemes were originally (voiceless) ejectives does not improve the situation as far as Greenberg is concerned. He does indeed say that "a gap in the class of ejectives at the bilabial point of articulation is found in a number of world areas," but he also states that "ejectives [tend] to have back articulation" (1970:127). The many languages he gives as examples all have a velar ejective, which is certainly not the case with Nɨpode.

Greenberg states that "There is ... no evidence, as far as can be seen, of phonologically distinctive contrast among laryngealized, preglottalized, and implosive obstruents" (1970:125). Indeed, the source of /ɗ/ in Nɨpode proves to be *ʔt (with an intermediate stage of *ʔd; see §3.1). Nɨpode /ɓ/ is rare, and its early history is unclear; the only cognate, 377, has apparently lost the (assumed) Proto Huitoto-Ocaina glottal in Ocaina and become /β/. I can therefore only posit the origin of /ɓ/ as being *ʔb, by analogy with /ɗ/.

The /p/ phoneme has a "freely variant fricative allophone [ɸ] after e, a, and o" (Minor 1956:133). This is significant, since this phoneme has the reflex /ɸ/ in all environments in the other two Huitoto languages and in Ocaina.

The /r/ phoneme in the Huitoto languages and in Ocaina is a voiced alveolar flap, unlike the corresponding phonemes in Bora and Muinane.

The glottal phoneme is extremely rare. As is shown later (§3.1), all glottals in Proto Huitoto-Ocaina were lost in Huitoto, and the few in modern Huitoto were apparently derived from word breaks. In Minica, glottal is listed as a phoneme (Minor and Minor 1987), but there were no examples in the wordlist. It is not phonemic in Murui.

The three Huitoto languages have the peculiar feature that there is contrast between one-syllable vowel clusters (diphthongs[19]) and two-syllable vowel clusters. For example, áɨkɨ is the name of a certain type of insect larva in Minica, whereas á.ɨkɨ means 'flying monkey' (Minor and Minor 1987). One-syllable clusters (diphthongs) always contain a high vowel (with the exception of /ae/ mentioned in Minor (1956) and possibly /ao/ as in Nɨpode 158, although since Minica and Murui both have /a.o/ for this item, this is doubtful); geminate vowels are always two syllables. This system is fully explained in Minor 1956. Syllable breaks between vowels in Huitoto are marked in this study with a period.

---

[19]Throughout this book, I do not use the word diphthong to mean a single phoneme composed of a phonetic vowel sequence. My usual use of the term is to refer to a one-syllable sequence of vowel phonemes as opposed to a two-syllable sequence, as in the above discussion. If this distinction does not always appear clear in later sections, this is simply due to the difficulty in establishing the syllabification of the protolanguages.

Such an analysis is rather unusual, since it requires positing a phonemic syllable break; but the reconstruction supports it. As is shown later, vowels separated by a syllable break usually resulted from loss of a consonant, notably Proto Huitoto-Ocaina glottal, which was lost in all cases, or from a morpheme break. Proto Huitoto-Ocaina *h, *β and *y were also lost in certain environments. Monosyllabic diphthongs are not usually the result of consonant loss, and do not contain morpheme breaks between the vowels.

For a discussion of accent on geminate vowels, see §1.7.

1.4 Minica Huitoto

Minica Huitoto has eighteen consonants, six vowels and one accent. These are listed in (6). Unlike Nipode, Minica lacks implosives, but has two additional voiceless fricatives, /ɸ/ and /θ/; the same is true for Murui. These fricatives are reflexes of Nipode /p/ and /t/, which should therefore be missing in Minica and Murui. Minica and Murui /p t/ turn out, however, to be reflexes of Nipode /ɓ d/. Like the Nipode /ɓ/, /p/ is extremely rare in Minica and Murui, even more rare than Nipode /ɓ/.

(6)   Minica Huitoto phonemes

p†	t	č†	k	ʔ†	i	ï	u
0.3	3.7 (1.4)	0.9	14.5	0.0	17.9	20.3	6.6
b	d	ǰ	g		e	a	o
5.2	5.7 (7.0)	4.8	3.7		14.3 (6.4)	21.8	19.2
ɸ	θ			h			
8.5	4.6			9.3			
β							
0.1							

accent system (with complex patterning on geminate vowels only)

m	n	ñ	ŋ
9.4	13.1	2.2	1.8
	r		
	12.4 (1.4)		

969 (1065) consonants, 1457 (1550) vowels.

1.5 Murui Huitoto

Murui Huitoto has sixteen consonants and six vowels. These are listed in (7). The only differences in phonological structure between Minica and

Murui are cases of loss: Murui lacks Minica phonemes /ŋ/ (which is realized as /ñ/), glottal, and accent.

(7)   Murui Huitoto phonemes

pʈ	t	čʈ	k		i	ï	u
0.2	3.1 (1.7)	0.3	14.4		18.5	19.3	7.9
b	d	ǰ	g		e	a	o
5.2	6.1 (7.3)	5.4	4.2		12.9 (7.1)	22.7	18.8
ɸ	θ		h				
7.0	5.8		8.5				

β
0.2

m   n   ñ
10.3   13.3   3.4

r
12.5 (1.7)

(no accent system;
noncontrastive stress on first
syllable)

967 (1070) consonants, 1449 (1552) vowels.

1.6 Ocaina

Ocaina has twenty-six consonants, nine vowels, and two tones in a basic pitch-accent system with minor complications. These are listed in (8).

There are several differences between Ocaina and the other languages. It has a series of nasalized vowels, which none of the others have. Furthermore, instead of the six-vowel system the others have, it has, for all practical purposes, only a four-vowel system (/e/ is extremely rare, has only one cognate with Huitoto, and has no nasalized counterpart).

Ocaina has two contrastive series of nasals, a fortis series (written /m n ñ/) and a lenis series (written /m n ñ/). Fortis nasals are often realized phonetically as long nasals. Lenis nasals are described by Leach (1971:164) as being without closure, i.e., as nasal fricatives. These two series do not contrast word-initially. It is unclear, however, which series occurs word-initially or whether neutralization occurs. Agnew and Pike (1957:26) state that fortis nasals do not occur word-initially. But the dictionary (Leach 1971) lists only fortis nasals word-initially.[20] It may be that word-initial nasals share features of both series; they may be like lenis nasals in

---

[20]It is possible, of course, that this is merely an orthography convention, using the simpler symbol in word-initial position, since there is no contrast in this position.

shortness, but like fortis nasals in closure. I have followed the dictionary and assume that word-initial nasals are fortis.

In addition to nasals, there are three other phonemes which do not occur word-initially, /r š y/ (Agnew and Pike 1957:26).[21] As is shown below, /r/ resulted from a word-medial allophone of *d. Ocaina has /dy/ but no /d/.

The most common consonant phoneme of all in Ocaina is glottal, which can occur freely before vowels, before consonants, and in final position. It is the only consonant that can occur in syllable-final position since, due to its syllable structure, Ocaina (like the other five languages) otherwise has no consonant clusters or syllable-final consonants.

In spite of the apparent similarity between the phoneme charts of Ocaina and of Bora and Muinane, Ocaina is closer to Huitoto. Phonemes (/p s š e/) have an obscure origin, most cases possibly having resulted from borrowing, some from Bora and Muinane. Ocaina may in some sense form a bridge between Huitoto and Bora-Muinane.

(8)   Ocaina phonemes

p†	t	tʸ	ts	č	k		i		ï
0.9	4.3	5.6	2.1	0.9	3.6		14.2		13.6
b		dʸ	dz	ǰ	g	ʔ	e†	a	o
2.6		2.6	1.7	0.6	1.6	5.3 Init.	0.9	35.1	36.2
						11.9 Final			
ɸ			s†	š†	x	h			
6.6			0.9	0.2	8.3	12.7			
β							ī		ĩ
4.0							16.9		12.6
m	n			ñ				ā	õ
4.6	2.9			3.2				26.2	44.4
m̄	n̄			ñ̄					
2.3	3.0			2.2			pitch-accent:		
	r			y			high tone (acute accent)		
	4.9			0.9			low tone (unmarked)		

1288 consonants, 1330 oral vowels, 390 nasal vowels

1.7 Accent and Tone

The pitch-accent system of Ocaina is in a sense intermediate between the tone systems of Bora and Muinane, on the one hand, and the accent

---

[21]Agnew and Pike found no examples of these three phonemes word-initially, but there is one word-initial example each of /r/ and /š/ in the dictionary (Leach 1971).

system of Huitoto, on the other. In Bora and Muinane, the tone is a syllable-level feature, each syllable in a word being either high or low tone.[22] In Nɨpode and Minica, only one syllable in each word may be accented (with accompanying high pitch).[23] Murui lacks contrastive accent altogether.

In Ocaina, there is normally only one syllable in a word which has high tone, except that geminate vowels often have high tone on both vowels (this does not appear to happen with nongeminate vowel clusters, and there are even a few cases of geminate vowels with one high and one low tone). However, a word may also have no high tones. There are a number of minimal pairs for this case (e.g., ñonǒǒha 'achiote pods', ñonōōha 'wood worms'; φɨɨ́xo 'axe', φɨ́ɨxo 'your axe' (Agnew and Pike 1957:26).

There is one group of words in Ocaina which can have more than one high-tone syllable, those containing the second-person-singular morpheme, which is not a prefix like the other persons, but instead is simply high tone on the first syllable of the word. If the root word has high tone on a syllable other than the first, both high tones are retained. (e.g., hɨmāʋ́áʋ́oφo 'pencil', hɨ́māʋ́áʋ́oφo 'your pencil', amɨ́ɨ́ʔka 'shirt', ámɨ́ɨ́ʔka 'your shirt'; Leach 1971:165).

It seems probable from comparison with Huitoto that Proto Huitoto-Ocaina had an ordinary accent system, which has become slightly more complicated in Ocaina.

---

[22]According to Michael Maxwell (personal communication) tone is morphologically predictable in Muinane, and there are significant restrictions on allowable tone patterns (e.g., a low tone may not precede a high tone except for a handful of low-tone prefixes, and diphthongs such as /ai/ always have uniform tone). Nevertheless, on a strictly phonological level tone is apparently not fully predictable.

[23]Minor (1956:132) claims that geminate vowels (which are analyzed as two syllables) may have four patterns in Nɨpode: V.V, V́.V, V.V́, V́.V́. However, V.V́ appears to be quite rare, and I question whether V́.V́ exists at all.

Both Minica and Nɨpode have numerous cases of V.V and V́.V (e.g., items 111, 44, 283), but the only case of V.V́ that I could find in Minica (in either dictionary or wordlist) was 183. da.ámani 'three', which in Murui is treated as two separate words. The Nɨpode dictionary (Minor and Minor 1971) yields a few additional examples of V.V́ (e.g., hɨ.íčikairo 'type of worm', hu.úku 'small porcupine'), but in each case the Minica cognate has V́.V.

There are no examples of V́.V́ in the wordlist, and I could find none in either the Minica or Nɨpode dictionary. Only two examples were given in Minor (1956:132), both complex forms which could not be verified from the dictionary to see if further study had supported his analysis. Therefore the existence of V́.V́ does not seem to be well established, and does not provide evidence that Proto Huitoto-Ocaina had anything more complex than a simple accent system.

2
Proto Bora-Muinane

I propose a reconstruction of Proto Bora-Muinane (PBM) that includes twenty-one consonants, six vowels and two tones. The consonant system is simpler than in either of the daughter languages, since several processes were active which produced phoneme splits. Although the vowel and tone systems survived with the same inventory in both languages, the vowel correspondences are quite complex because of a massive vowel rotation which took place in Muinane, followed by significant vowel harmony changes. Both Bora and Muinane have two-tone systems but tone patterning appears to be very different. A comparison of the two systems was not done in this study.

A chart of proposed PBM phonemes is presented in (9). Relative frequencies have been calculated for the protophonemes, and these are indicated in (9) as in earlier phoneme charts. They were calculated on the basis of reconstructed words in the wordlist. The values match up well with the expected values from the sound change rules (especially for consonants). Frequencies are given with half a percentage point of precision for consonants[24] and a whole percentage point for vowels.

Of the words in the list, approximately 60% (about 226 out of 375) are cognates between Bora and Muinane. The relationships are therefore quite clear. These two languages are much closer to each other linguistically than is the case for Huitoto and Ocaina.

In what follows I occasionally refer to Miraña (Mr), a dialect of Bora which shares certain conservative phonological features with Muinane.

---

[24]Except for *čč, which was so rare I estimated its frequency as .3.

(9)   Proto Bora-Muinane phonemes

$*pp$	$*tt$	$*tts$	$*\check{c}\check{c}$	$*kk$		$*i$	$*ɨ$	$*ï$
1	1	1.5	.3	3.5		18	9	17
$*p$	$*t$	$*ts$	$*\check{c}$	$*k$		$*e$	$*a$	$*o$
4	5	4	1	9		18	25	13
$*b$	$*d$		$*\check{j}$	$*g$	$*ʔ$			
6	2.5		1	9.5	6.5 Init.			
					5 Final			
				$*x$				
				9				
$*\beta$								
3								
$*m$	$*n$							
9.5	12.5							
	$*r$		$*y$			two tones		
	4		1					

2649 consonants, 3612 vowels.

2.1–5 Consonant Reflexes

2.1. The palatalization process. PBM had a very common diphthong
(vowel sequence) *ai* which accounts for about 20% of all occurrences of
a and 33% of all occurrences of *i* reconstructed in the protolanguage. It
appears that, not long before the separation of Bora and Muinane,[25] this
diphthong caused the palatalization of a following alveolar consonant (*t*,
ts, *d*, *n*, *r*). (In certain environments a preceding *i* also caused this
palatalization.) Subsequent to this process (or simultaneously), *ai* was
reduced to /a/ when followed by one of these palatalized alveolar consonants, thus effectively phonemicizing these consonants through loss of
the conditioning environment. I am not including these palatalized
phonemes in the list of Proto Bora-Muinane phonemes, however, prefer-
ring to show the earlier, simpler stage.

---

[25]The palatalization of alveolars caused by *ai* resulted in a contrast between *ts^y*
and *č* in late Proto Bora-Muinane. It seems unlikely that these two consonants could
remain contrastive for a long period without either dissimilating in some way or
coalescing. In Bora they coalesced, whereas in Muinane they dissimilated, the former
first becoming a fricative *s^y* (parallel to the change of its nonpalatalized counterpart
ts to /s/) and subsequently becoming an alveopalatal /š/. Hence, the palatalization of
alveolars must have occurred not long before the Bora-Muinane split.

(10) The effects of palatalization in Bora, Miraña, and Muinane

PBM	standard reflex			after *ai			after *i		
	B	Mr	M	B	Mr	M	B	Mr	M
*pp	xp^h	xp^h	ϕ	xp^{hy}?			xp^{hy}		
*p	p^h	p^h	ϕ	p^{hy}			p^{hy}		
*tt	xt^h	xt^h	tt	xt^{hy}	xt^{hy}	tt^y	xt^{hy}	xt^{hy}	
*t	t^{hy}	t^{hy}	t	t^{hy}	t^{hy}	t^y	t^{hy}	t^{hy}	
*tts	xts^h	xts^h	s	$xč^h$	$xč^h$?	$š$	$xč^h$	$xč^h$	
*ts	ts^h	ts^h	s	$č^h$	$č^h$?	$š$?	$č^h$	$č^h$	
*čč	$xč^h$	$xč^h$	$čč$						
*č	$č^h$	$č^h$	$č$						
*kk	xk^h	xk^h	kk	xk^{hy}			xk^{hy}		
*k	k^h	k^h	k	k^{hy}		?	k^{hy}		
*b	p	p	b	?			p^y		
*d	t	t	d	t^y	t^y?	d^y	t^y	t^y?	
*ǰ	$č$	$č$	$ǰ$						
*g /__e,i	$č$	$č$	g	$č$	$č$				
*g /__i	ts	ts	g	$č$?					
*g /__o,ï	k	k	g	$č$					
*g /__a	k^w	k^w	g						
*ʔ /__V	$ʔ$	$ʔ$	$ʔ$	$ʔy$			$ʔy$		
*x	$x,\emptyset$	$x,\emptyset$	x	x^y	x^y		x^y		
*β	$β$	$β$	$β$	$β^y$			$β^y$		
*m	m	m	m	m^y	?		m^y		
*n	n	n	n	n^y	n^y	$ñ$	n^y	n^y	
*r	r	r	r	y	r^y	r^y	y	r^y	
*y	y	y	y						

Abbreviations used: B Bora, Mr Miraña, M Muinane, PBM Proto Bora-Muinane.

After the separation of Bora and Muinane, this palatalization process continued to spread to other consonant phonemes in Bora, but not in Muinane. It eventually affected every single consonant in Bora except /kʷ/. All Bora consonants except /kʷ/ thus have a palatalized counterpart, all but one being unit phonemes. (I consider the palatalized counterpart of /ʔ/ to be the two-phoneme sequence /ʔy/.) In addition, the palatalization process was extended to apply in many more environments after *i (encompassing in the end all consonants except reflexes of *g), as well as always occurring after *ai. Following this, all cases of *ai were reduced to /a/ in Bora, in all environments, even word finally (there are a tiny handful of examples of /ai/ in Bora today).[26] Thus, the inventory of consonant phonemes in Bora is nearly double that of PBM.

In Miraña (a dialect of Bora), the palatalization did not go nearly as far as it did in Bora proper, but it went somewhat farther than it did in Muinane. Specifically, the only phoneme which underwent palatalization in Miraña besides the alveolar phonemes is /x/. However, the alveolars also underwent palatalization after *i in Miraña, whereas in Muinane they only did so after *ai. The palatalized counterpart of /r/ is /rʸ/ in Miraña, just as it is in Muinane, whereas in Bora it is /y/.

Interestingly, palatalization in Bora (and Miraña) appears to be blocked if the phoneme is followed by /i/ for /pʰ tʰ kʰ p t? ?? x? β? m n?/ no matter what precedes them (those with question marks yielded no examples). These are precisely the phonemes for which the palatalization process would have produced simple palatalization if it had applied, rather than a shift in point of articulation to alveopalatal. Apparently palatalization is not contrastive before /i/ in Bora (probably because it would be hard to hear).

A summary of the effects of the palatalization process is presented in (10). Examples are presented later in §§2.8–13.

2.2. Aspiration and devoicing of stops in Bora. A major phonetic change which did little to change the actual phonological system was the aspiration and devoicing of stops in Bora. All voiceless stops (*p *t *ts *č *k) became aspirated in Bora (or were already aspirated subphonemically in the protolanguage), and the geminate stops (*pp *tt *tts *čč *kk) became preaspirated. Subsequently, all voiced stops (*b *d *ǰ *g) lost their voicing. As a result, there are no voiced stops in modern Bora.

I am proposing that PBM had a geminate stop series, as does modern Muinane. Phonetically, however, these could have been fortis stops, preaspirated stops, or even preglottalized stops.[27] In Bora, these PBM geminates are realized as preaspirated stops.

2.3. Fricativization in Muinane. Two PBM voiceless stops, *p and *ts, became fricatives /ɸ/ and /s/ in Muinane. Their geminate counterparts *pp and *tts did the same and, in the process, lost their gemination. Bora thus

---

[26]Phonetically there are still traces of the *ai diphthong in certain environments, according to Wesley Thiesen (personal communication): e.g., 40 kʷače 'woman' is realized phonetically as [kᵖaⁱče?]. The offglide, however, is phonologically predictable in present-day Bora, and thus subphonemic.

[27]This is discussed further in §4.1.

provides the only evidence for these two geminate stops in PBM. A similar process occurred in Huitoto and Ocaina (3.1), but I assume that the process occurred independently in the two halves of the family.

As a result, /p/ is very rare in Muinane. There are only four examples of Muinane /p/ in the data, none of which has a cognate—list items 53 (= 54), 113, 144, and 261 (= 342).

2.4. Loss of glottal. Bora has glottal in syllable-final position, whereas Muinane does not. I assume that this is a case of loss in Muinane, rather than of generation of some sort in Bora, since syllable-final glottal clearly contrasts in Bora with its absence, and I discern no pattern. Glottals are retained before vowels in Muinane. Again, a similar loss of glottal occurred in Huitoto (§3.5), but I assume that it occurred independently.

2.5. Reflexes of PBM *g. One protophoneme underwent changes independently of the others in Bora, namely *g, which split into the five phonemes /kʷ č ts k kʸ/, depending primarily on the following vowel. It underwent the palatalization rule mentioned in §2.1, with the reflex /č/, but only after *ai. A preceding *i had no effect in this case. The most frequent reflex by far is /kʷ/; /k/ and especially /kʸ/ are very rare. There are only three examples of Bora /k/ in the wordlist (221, 276, 351), none of which has a cognate, and no examples of /kʸ/. There were no examples of either in the wordlist prepared by Allin (1975:497–527). The only example of each in Thiesen and Thiesen (1975:1) has no Muinane cognate. There are a few examples in the dictionary (Thiesen in preparation), but very few cognates can be found.[28]

The reflex /ts/ occurs before /ɨ/. This may seem unexpected, but there are other cases in natural language in which a high central vowel produces an alveolar sibilant reflex, notably Japanese, whose /u/ vowel (which is actually a high central rounded vowel) produces a [ts] allophone of a preceding /t/. In Mandarin Chinese, the vowel /ɨ/ only occurs after alveolar sibilants.

Interestingly, one of the reflexes of PBM *g, /ts/, filled a hole in the Bora phoneme chart, increasing the symmetry of the Bora phoneme system. On the other hand, the addition of /kʷ/ (and the extreme rarity of /k/ and /kʸ/) contributed to its asymmetry, leaving the symmetry of the system about equal.

---

[28]Details are given in §2.9.

2.6–7 Vowel reflexes

2.6. The vowel rotation. A rotation of four of the PBM vowels occurred in one of the two daughter languages. Early in the analysis it was
unclear which way the rotation went, i.e., which daughter language has the
rotated system and which has the protosystem. The situation was further
obscured because Muinane has undergone a number of vowel-harmony
processes in addition to vowel rotation.

Based on several criteria, however, mainly the effects of PBM *i on the
split of PW **t into PBM *t and *ts (§4.3) and the relatively high degree
of correspondence between the Bora and Huitoto vowels (§5), I conclude
that the rotation was counterclockwise, Bora having the protoystem and
Muinane the rotated system.[29]

The rotation was thus ï > i > e > o > u as indicated in (11), with *i and *a
not being involved in the rotation. The rotation is thus a closed circle
(ignoring the difference in rounding between [u] and [ï]), with the starting
and ending points of the chain shift remaining unclear.

The one clue we have about a possible starting point for the rotation
was mentioned in some detail in 1.1, namely, that PBM, like modern Bora,
had an inherently unstable vowel system which was unlikely to be stabilized
by any kind of clockwise rotation of /i/ and /ï/. The probable starting point
was thus the slightly lower and fronted PBM *i moving down to /e/, and
the ending point the slightly fronted PBM *$ï$ moving into the position
vacated by *i. It is interesting that the inherent instability in the Bora (and

---

[29]Michael Maxwell, who read and critiqued the first draft of this study and who has
done extensive study of Muinane, proposed just the opposite after studying my
analysis—that the rotation was counterclockwise, and that Muinane has the protovowel
system. He, in fact, proposes a seven-vowel system of *i *t *e *a *o *u *$ï$ for PBM
(his /ɨ/ in lieu of my lowered fronted /i/), and incorporates some of my proposed
Muinane vowel harmony processes into the earlier vowel shifts. An approximate
comparison of Maxwell's rules with mine follows: Both Maxwell and I propose that
PBM *a > **B** a, **M** a; **PBM** *i > **B** i; and **PBM** *$ï$ > **B** $ï$, **M** i. But (1) where I propose
that **PBM** *e > **B** e, **M** o (> e, u in certain environments), Maxwell proposed that
PBM *e > **B** e, **M** e and that **PBM** *o > **B** e, **M** o (> e, u in certain environments);
(2) where I proposed **PBM** *i > **B** i, **M** e (> i in certain environments), Maxwell
proposed that **PBM** *t > **B** i, i, **M** e and that **PBM** *i > **B** i in certain environments;
and (3) where I proposed **PBM** *o > **B** o, **M** u, Maxwell proposed that **PBM** *u
> **B** o, **M** u.

This analysis has much merit, and handles a few things mine does not. It avoids
proposing that *e became /o/ in Muinane and then /e/ again in a number of cases by
a vowel harmony rule. The net result, however, does not seem to me to be more
efficient; it adds a PBM vowel, producing a system even less symmetrical than the one
I propose.

PBM) vowel system shown in (3) would most easily be resolved by precisely the sort of rotation proposed in (11). The former system already gives
the appearance of being partly rotated (though it was not historically
produced from such a rotation according to my reconstruction, but instead
from a vowel split of Proto-Witotoan **e).

(11)   PBM vowel rotation to Muinane

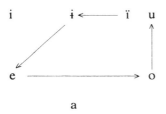

Thus, nearly all of the changes in the vowel system occurred in Muinane,
and Bora has apparently undergone no vowel system changes from PBM
except the reduction of *ai to /a/.[30] Details and examples are presented in
§2.14.

2.7. Vowel harmony in Muinane. There are four vowel harmony rules
in Muinane, two of which are cases of /i o/ becoming /e/ in the environment of a front vowel and two of which involve raising of /e/ and /o/. The
pattern is not particularly symmetrical. It seems that all of the vowel
harmony took place subsequent to the completion of the vowel rotation.
One of the rules reverses the change from /e/ to /o/ in the vowel rotation,[31]
and another of the rules moves the resulting /o/ on around to /u/ (§2.15).

2.8–15 PBM sound changes

The following eight sections present detailed discussion of and evidence
for the sound changes proposed between PBM and the daughter languages
Bora and Muinane, beginning one-by-one with six classes of consonants—

---

[30]After all of these changes, the vowel inventory of Muinane is structurally the same
as that of the protolanguage, if we ignore details of phonetic positioning, except for
the rounding of the high back vowel, which would be expected since it came from *o.

[31]Another alternative is to assume that the two processes took place around the
same time and that the vowel harmony rule blocked the action of the rotation in these
cases. This, however, presents a more complicated process.

voiceless stops (§2.8), voiced stops (§2.9), glottal (§2.10), fricatives (§2.11), nasals (§2.12), and liquids (§2.13)—and proceeding first with a discussion of early vowel changes (§2.14) followed by a discussion of later vowel changes (§2.15).

A few general remarks need to be made concerning conventions.

First concerning the restricted environments in which certain changes took place, in a sound change expressed as **PBM** *p/i_a > **M** ϕ, **B** p^h, the environment i_a is at the PBM horizon. Most of the restricted environments are at this horizon. In fewer cases, the change occurs within a restricted context at a later horizon and not in all daughter languages. In such cases, the restricting environment is associated with the daughter reflex, as in **PBM** *$V\!?V$ > **M** $V\!?V$, **B** $V\!?V/\_r,\#$, which indicates that the named Bora reflex is found only in word-final position or precedes r at the Bora horizon.

PBM material in parentheses is only attested in one or the other of the languages. Because of this the reconstruction of some of this material may be doubtful. Empty parentheses (), indicate that the reconstruction in question is incomplete. Slashes between examples indicate alternate forms. When exceptions are given, I normally specify which language has the exceptional reflex; the exceptional reflex is usually specified in parentheses. Not all examples of a phoneme or rule have been given, since these would be too numerous. All clear exceptions to the rules are listed.

Those items marked ?* are uncertain reconstructions; those marked ??* are very uncertain. When the phrase *no cognate* occurs, it usually means that there is no cognate at all between Bora and Muinane for that word, but it may also mean that only the portion of the word in question for that rule does not appear to have a cognate, even if other parts of the word are clear cognates.

The Miraña cognate is not normally given. This means either that the Miraña and Bora forms are identical or that the Miraña form provides no additional insight into the rule. The Miraña form is only listed, therefore, in rules for which it differs from Bora and provides further insight into the historical process. In these rules the comment *Miraña lacking* means that no cognate for the Bora item was found, not that no Miraña form with the specified meaning was available.

In some cases of change in restricted environments, rules are listed even though no cognate sets are known. This is done when, in the absence of a counterexample, a strong inference from analogy can be drawn and the assumption made that data are simply lacking from our sample. Thus, **PBM** *$pp/ai\_$ > **M** p^h, **B** xp^{hy}? is proposed as an analogy with **PBM** *$p/ai\_$ > **M** p^h, **B** p^{hy}, even though unsupported directly by a known cognate set. Such rules are often flagged with a phrase like *no examples of *$aipp$ except $\_i$.

2.8. Voiceless stops. This section presents the rules for the PBM geminate stops **pp, *tt, *tts, *čč,* and **kk,* and their simple PBM counterparts **p, *t, *ts, *č,* and **k.*

PBM **pp /ai__* > M ϕ, B *xpʰʸ?*
No examples of **aipp* except */__i.*
PBM **pp /i__e* > B *xpʰʸ.*
The following item is the only example in the Bora dictionary of /xpʰʸ/:
*ímippéde 'be well'. B *ímixpʰʸéte.*
PBM **pp /i__a* > B *xpʰ?*
PBM **pp /__i* > M ϕ, B *xpʰ.*
  38 = 39 **gai-ppi* 'man'. M *gái-ϕi.* B *kʷa-xpʰi.*
  307 **tsi-ppi* 'other (masc)'. M *sí-ϕi.* B *tsʰi-xpʰi.*
    Noncognate examples:
  64 **kóoxí-e(ppi) nïʔï-ba* 'sun'. M *(kúuxe-o) níʔi-ba.* B *nïʔ-pa (kʰóóxí-expʰi).*
  65 **pékkó-e(ppi) nïʔï-ba* 'moon'. M *(ϕúkkuo) níʔi-ba.* B *nïʔ-pa pʰéxkʰó-expʰi.*
PBM **pp /VV__i* > M ϕ, B *pʰ.*
  39 **tsaa-ppi* 'one-male'. M *sáa-ϕi.* B *tsʰaa-pʰi.*
  38 **míámĭnáa-ppi* 'man'. M *míyáminaa-ϕi.* B *míamĭnáa-xpʰi (xpʰ* exception).

For a complete discussion of the last rule, see **kk* in the environment /VV__; the rule for **kk* has many examples and has no exceptions. Because the evidence for the gemination was lost in both languages in this environment, we should not even have been able to reconstruct this geminate. We were able to do so morphologically, however, because items 38 (the exception), 39, and 307 in the preceding rule contain the same suffix **-ppi,* meaning 'male'.

PBM **pp /__* > M ϕ, B *xpʰ.*
  14 **(mé)-ppíiï-xi* 'chest'. M *ϕéeyi-xe* B *(mé)-xpʰíï-xi.*[32]
  15 **(mé)-mĭppaine* 'breast'. M *míϕaño.* B *(mé)-míxpʰanʸe.*
  48 **nĭ-ppaiko* 'water'. M *ϕaiʔu, nĭ-ϕáiʔu.* B *nĭ-xpʰakʰʸo.*
  294 **tĭ-ppai-ne* 'red'. M *tíϕai-ño.* B *rʰíxpʰa-nʸe.*
  319 **mĭppáine-ppáiko* 'milk'. M *míϕaño-ϕái?u.* M *míxpʰánʸe-xpʰákʰʸo.*
    Noncognate examples:
  33 = 266 **tĭĭ-(ppaiko)* 'blood'. M *tíí-xóʔo.* M *rʰĭ-xpʰakʰʸo.*
  157 **ĭmeʔé-(ppáiko)* 'sap'. M *ímoʔo tíí-xoʔo.* B *ĭmeʔé-xpʰákʰʸo.*
PBM **p /ai__* > M ϕ, B *pʰʸ.*
The following item is the only example in the Bora dictionary of /apʰʸ/.
*áipíxakóóβe 'smell'. B *ápʰʸíxakʰóóβe.*
PBM **p /i__e* > M ϕ, B *pʰʸ* (Mr *pʰ*).
  228 **dí-pe* 'go!' M *di-ϕó.* B *tí-pʰʸe* (Mr *tí-pʰeé*).

---

[32]The Bora prefix *me-* 'our' was included on a number of body parts in the wordlist the author used. I have not removed these, one reason being that they provide useful information about word-initial glottal stop, which contrasts with its absence in Bora. See discussion and examples with **ʔ* in §2.10 and **x* in §4.6.

120 *gi?pe 'mouse'. M gíiɸo. B čí?pʰʸe (Mr čí?pʰe).
PBM *p /i__a > M ɸ, B pʰ.
148 *níipa-xɨ 'chigger'. M níiɸa-xe. B níipʰa-xɨ.
PBM *p /__i > M ɸ, B pʰ.
351 *piko 'throw'. M ɸíkú-?i. B pʰikʰʸo.
PBM *p /__ > M ɸ, B pʰ.
68 *pekko 'night'. M ɸúkku. B pʰexkʰo.
87 *pííkkɨ-gai 'fishhook'. M ɸííkkɨ-gai. B pʰííxʸɨ-kʷa.
99 *típáí?oó(ï) 'puma'. M tíɸai?ui. B tʰíĩpʰá?yoóï.
116 *páápaiba 'white-lipped peccary'. M ɸááɸaiba. B pʰáápʰapʸa.
128 *páá(i)bɨ(?o) 'hummingbird'. M ɸááibe. B pʰáápɨ?o.
136 *pííkaxɨ 'guan'. M ɸéékaxe. B pʰíikʰaxɨ.
146 *píime(ba) 'ant'. M ɸíimo. B pʰíímʸepa.
147 *páaga-xɨ, *paagá-(yï) 'spider'. M ɸáaga-xe. B pʰaakʷá-yï, pʰáákʷa-xɨ.
163 *píikkaá 'cassava'. M ɸéekka. B pʰíikʰaá.
190 *pa-?ottsɨɨ-kkï(-neβa) 'ten'. M ɸa-?úsee-kki. B pʰa-?óxtsʰɨ-kʰɨ̃-neβa.
205 *mï?-pɨ 'we (f.d.)'. M mí-ɸe. B mï?-pʰɨ.
206 *ámïï?-pɨ 'ye (f.d.)'. M amíí-ɸe. B ámï?-pʰɨ.
207 *dii-t(é)-pɨ 'they (f.d.)'. M díítɨ-ɸe. B tiitʰʸé-pʰɨ.
342 *(p)(ai)rïïkí-ne 'smooth'. M párʸíiki-no (p exception doubtful). B pʰɨrïïkʰɨ̃-ne.
Many more examples.
PBM *tt /ai__ > M ttʸ, B xtʰʸ.
277 *aittími 'see'. M áttyíme-?i. B axtʰʸími.
295 *aittíβá-ne 'green'. M attyíβa-no. B axtʰʸíβa, axtʰʸíβá-ne.
PBM *tt /i__ > M tt, B xtʰʸ.
164 *íttáko-gííxï 'cassava flour'. M íttáku. B íxtʰʸákʰo-číxʸï.
313 *nittí-(kï) 'wash'. M nítti-?i. B nixtʰʸï̃-kʰï.
358 *aakí(t)te 'fall'. M áákétte-?i. B aakʰítʰʸe (tʰʸ exception).
269 *(óka)-(x)ítto 'horn'. M íttu. B ókʰa-xíxtʰo (xtʰ exception).
Noncognate examples:
20 *(mé)-nékkï-(gai)-(étsitto) 'upper arm'. M nókkɨ. B mé-néxï-kʷa-étsʰíxtʰʸo.
240 *(mé)-nékkí-(gatsítto) 'lower arm'. M nókkɨ. B (mé)-néxɨ̃-kʷatsʰíxtʰʸo.
PBM *tt > M tt, B xtʰ.
29 *(mé)-ttí-?aáí 'foot'. M tí-?ai. B (mé)-xtʰíĩ?aá.
30 *(mé)-ttí-gaáí 'toe'. M tí-gai. B (mé)-xtʰɨ̃-kʷaá.
191 *(it)tï(k)kénï 'first'. M íttikoni. B tʰïxkʰénï.
Noncognate example:
299 ?*pá(tté)ï 'round'. M ɸáttíyï. B pʰaï.
PBM *t /áí__ > M ttʸ, B tʰʸ.
42 *taxi, *áí-táxɨɨ, *áíxïï 'husband'. M áttʸaxe, táxe, aixi. B tʰaxi, áxʸïĩ, átʰʸáxɨɨ.
43 *taába, *áí-táabaá 'wife'. M táaba, áttʸáaba, B tʰaápa, átʰʸáápaá.
PBM *t /ai__ > M tʸ, B tʰʸ.
214 *táí-tïïbo-ga 'my bow'. M ta-tʸííbu-ga. B tʰá-tʰʸípoo-kʷa.
Noncognate examples:
258 ?*ka(aité?a)-xaa- 'who'. M ká-xáá-nɨ, ká-xáá-mo. B kʰaatʰʸé?a-xa.
PBM *t /i__a,o > M tʸ, B tʰʸ.
220 *mita-ne 'big'. M mítʸa-no. B mitʰʸa-ne.
262 *míta-(ne) 'many'. M mítʸáá-bo B mítʰʸane.
132 *(pi?)tói(?o) 'parakeet'. M tʸúi?u B pʰi?tʰʸói.

PBM *t /i__e,ɨ > M t, B tʰʸ.
207 *dii-te 'they (pl)'. M díí-to. B tií-tʰʸe.
207 *dii-t(é)-tsi 'they (m.d.)'. M díítɨ-si. B tiitʰʸé-tsʰi.
207 *dii-t(é)-pɨ 'they (f.d.)'. M díítɨ-ɸe. B tiitʰʸé-pʰɨ.
213 *díí-te-ʔóttsɨ-ne 'their hands'. M díí-to-ʔuse-ne. B tií-tʰʸe-ʔóxtsʰɨ-ne.
225 *ími-tíí-ne 'bad'. M ímɨ-tɨ-no. B ímɨ-tʰʸíí-ne.
     Noncognate examples:
366 *igí 'fear'. M ígɨ-ʔi. B iči, ičí-tʰʸe.
PBM *t /__ > M t, B tʰ.
  5 *tíxɨ-ʔo, tíxɨ-ʔ(exɨ) 'nose'. M tíxɨ-ʔu. B tʰíxɨ-ʔo, tʰíí-ʔexɨ.
33 = 266 *tíí-(xéʔe), *tíí-(ppaiko) 'blood'. M tíí-xóʔo. B tʰíí-xpʰakʰʸo.
 42 *taxɨ, *áí-táxɨɨ, *áíxɨɨ 'husband'. M áttʸaxe, táxe, aixɨ. B tʰaxɨ, áxʸíí, átʰʸáxɨɨ.
 43 *taába, *áí-táabaá 'wife'. M táaba, áttʸáaba. B tʰaápa, átʰʸáápaá.
 49 *teé-ʔi 'river'. M téé-ʔi. B tʰeé-ʔi.
 71 *tíí-ʔi 'rainbow'. M tɨɨ-ʔi. B tʰíí-ʔi.
94; 95 *tíïbó-ga 'bow, arrow'. M tɨɨbú-ga. B tʰɨpóó-kʷa.
 99 *tɨpáíʔoó(ɨ) 'puma'. M tíɸaiʔui. B tʰíípʰáʔyoóɨ.
109 *tooʔxɨ 'anteater'. M túuxe. B tʰoʔxɨ.
110 *takkɨ 'paca'. M tákkɨ. B tʰaxkʰɨ.
167 *dóoto- 'gourd'. M dúutuʔu. B toórʰo, tóórʰo-ɨ.
     Many more examples.

*t and *tt never occur before *ɨ and only once before *i in any reconstructed word. In every case, Muinane /te/ (the expected reflex of *tɨ) derives (or could derive in the case of noncognates) in every case from earlier /to/ (PBM *te) or /tɨ/ (PBM *tɨ) by vowel harmony (49, 332, 358). The only apparent case of *tti is Muinane 299 ɸáttíyɨ, whose Bora cognate is missing the syllable containing the *tt. This word could be derived from *páttéï. I therefore conclude that *t and *tt never occurred before *ɨ or *i in PBM.

On the other hand, *ts only occurs once before *e, in 355 *tseeʔdi. It is therefore probable that *ts did not normally occur before *e in the protolanguage. Before *a, *o and *ï, however, *(t)t and *(t)ts contrast fairly well and must therefore be posited as separate phonemes in PBM. As indicated in §§4.1 and 4.3, however, I posit that PBM *(t)t and *(t)ts were the result of phoneme splits at an earlier stage in Proto Witotoan.

PBM *tts /ai__ > M š, B xčʰ.
308 *(áx)áittso-(ne), ?*(gaʔ)áittso-(ta) 'few, soon'. M áxášu-no. B kʷaʔáxčʰo-tʰa.
PBM *tts /i__ > M s, B xčʰ.
 69 *()tsittsi 'thunder'. M sísi. B čʰixčʰi.
 96 *gittsíí-xï 'blowgun'. M gisɨ-xɨ. B čixčʰíí-xï.
283 *ittsi 'swim'. M ísi-ʔi. B ixčʰi.
356 *tsíttsɨ 'tie'. M sísɨ-ʔi. B čʰíxčʰí.
365 *gittsíí-(kï) 'blow'. M gísɨ-ʔi. B čixčʰíkʰï.
PBM *tts /__ > M s, B xtsʰ.
 22 *(mé)-ʔóttsɨɨ 'hand'. M úse. B (mé)-ʔóxtsʰɨɨ.

159 *battsó-() 'seed'. M basúta. B paxts^{h}ó-k^{w}a, paxts^{h}ó-ï.
309 *(o)ttso-(ï) 'fog'. M súi. B oxts^{h}ó-tí.
335 *íttsi-(ne) 'thin'. M ísi-no. B ïxts^{h}i.
360 *íttsam(áá)i, *itts(o) 'think'. M ésámáái-?i. B ïxts^{h}améi, ïxts^{h}o.
361 *mattsí-βa 'sing'. M másíβa-?i. B maxts^{h}í-βa.
362 *ottsó-?i 'smell'. M úsu-?i. B oxts^{h}ó-?i.
365 *boottsó-(kï) 'blow'. M búúsu-?i. B poxts^{h}ók^{h}ï.

In addition to the above examples, all of the following contain some
form of 22 'hand': 23, 24, 185, 186, 187, 188, 189, 190, 208, 209, 210, 211,
212, 213, 271.

PBM *ts /ai__ > M š?, B č^h.
288 *ka?ts(ïï)βe, (čai)?ts(ii)βe 'sit'. M kásííβe-?i. B k^{h}árárixííβe, č^{h}a?č^{h}ííβ'e.

There are no good cognates for this rule. In the example given, the reflexes
of *ts are probably cognate, but the preceding vowel is probably not (the /k/
and /č^h/ do not match), which is why the Muinane form does not appear to
follow the rule. I am, however, proposing this rule by analogy with the same
rule for *tts. There are only two examples of Muinane /š/ in the data,
308 = 221 and 119 (see *tts and next rule, respectively).

PBM *ts /i__ > M s, B č^h.
69 *()tsittsi 'thunder'. M sísi. B č^{h}ixč^{h}i.
229 *dí-tsaa 'come!'. M di-sáá. B tí-č^{h}a.
356 *tsíttsï 'tie'. M sísi-?i. B č^{h}ixč^{h}ï.

The following example, which would be an exception in Muinane, is
unlikely to be a cognate since it is borrowed from Spanish, which almost
certainly did not come into contact with these languages until after Bora
and Muinane split (§5).

119 *míítsii 'cat'. M mííši. B mííč^{h}ii.

PBM *ts /__ > M s, B ts^h.
39 *tsaa-ppi 'one-male'. M sáa-ɸi. B ts^{h}aa-p^{h}i.
46 *tsíimene 'baby, infant'. M séemene. B ts^{h}íimene.
86 *ts(í)nïkó?o 'fish net'. M síni-ku?u. B ts^{h}ínïí, ts^{h}ínï-k^{h}óó?o, ts^{h}ínï-k^{h}óó?a.
89 *n(ii)ts(í)ga-(gayï) 'knife'. M níísúga. B nïits^{h}ík^{w}a-(k^{w}ï).
104 *tsokko 'otter'. M súkku. B ts^{h}oxk^{h}o.
150 = 161 *tsókkómïxi 'grass'. M súkkumexe. B ts^{h}óxk^{h}ómïxi.
181 *tsaane 'one'. M sááno. B ts^{h}a-ne.
205 *mï?-tsi 'we (m.d.)'. M mí-si. B mï?-ts^{h}i.
206 *ámïï?-tsi 'ye (m.d.)'. M amíí-si. B ámï?-ts^{h}i.
207 *dii-t(é)-tsi 'they (m.d.)'. M dííti-si. B tiit^{hy}é-ts^{h}i.
222 *tsiïko 'cold'. M síiku. B ts^{h}iïk^{h}o.

226 *tsítsįį-ne 'white'. M sééé-ne. B tsʰítsʰįį-ne, tsʰįtsʰį.
69 *()tsittsi 'thunder'. M sísi. B čʰixčʰi (čʰ exception).
356 *tsíttsï 'tie'. M sísɨ-ʔi. B čʰíxčʰï (čʰ exception). Many more examples.

The preceding two items are probably the result of assimilation of the word-initial consonant in Bora. Item 69, however, may have had a preceding *i at one stage; see item 69 under **PW** **ï in §4.9.

Contrast between *(t)ts and *(č)č is not excellent, but is sufficient to require reconstructing separate phonemes. When palatalized, these pairs of phonemes fell together in Bora. Parenthesized PBM items below could be derived from either *(t)ts or *(č)č.

PBM   *čč > M čč, B xčʰ.
230 *maččoó 'eat!'. M maččú. B maxčʰoó.
244 *(mé-ke)-máčč o-(ï), *maččo-(xota) 'stomach'. M mačču-xuta.
    B mé-kʰe-máxčʰo-ï.
275 *maččo 'eat'. M máčču-ʔi. B maxčʰo.
323 *-ʔaččíixï 'if'. M -aččixɨ. B -ʔaxčʰíixʲï.
    Items without cognates, both ambiguous as to source:
351 (íččiβétso, íttsiβétso) 'cause to leave'. B íxčʰiβʲétsʰo.
368 (maittsótso, maččótso) 'feed'. B maxčʰótsʰo.

The first four examples of *čč above are all preceded by /a/. These could also have been *ai, which was always reduced to /a/ before palatalized consonants. There are three factors, however, which prevented me from reconstructing the forms listed for *č and *čč from *(t)ts: (1) item 308 (cited above under *tts) shows that *(t)ts became Muinane /š/ when palatalized, whereas *č became Muinane /č/. (2) *č is found in word-initial position (see examples under */č/ below, the best one being item 125); this is not a possible palatalizing environment, since the palatalization process depended on a preceding vowel. (3) Analogy with its voiced counterpart *ǰ, whose existence is less questionable.

PBM   *č > M č, B čʰ.
125 *čiráágai 'coral snake'. M čiráágai. B čʰiiyákʷa.
353 *gá(č)ére(á)ko 'split'. M gájéréku-ʔi (ǰ exception). B kʷáčʰéreákʰo.

The following are without cognates but are apparently unambiguous as to origin, since the fact that they occur word-initially would seem to eliminate the possibility that they could have been derived from *ts. In some cases, however, a possible (sometimes distant) Muinane cognate is given to show that another analysis is conceivable:

53 (čooróga) 'spring of water'. M píisírí-gai? B čʰoorókʷa (**Mr** lacking).
127 (čeʔréï) 'species of bird'. B čʰeʔréï (**Mr** lacking).

193 *(čeʔkéï)* 'rattle'. **B** *čʰeʔkʰéï* (**Mr** *tʰéʔkʰéï*).
221 *(čoʔxï)* 'small'. **M** *áxášu-no?* **B** *čʰoʔxï* (**Mr** lacking).
288 **kaʔts(ïï)βe, *(čai)ʔts(ii)βe* 'sit'. **M** *kásïïβe-ʔi.* **B** *kʰárárixïïβe, čʰaʔčʰïïβʸe* (**Mr** lacking).
308 *(čóʔxíné-re)* 'few, soon'. **M** *áxášu-no?.* **B** *kʷaʔáxčʰo-tʰa, čʰóʔxíné-re* (**Mr** lacking).
341 *(čáxaaβé-né)* 'rotten'. **B** *čʰáxaaβé-né* (**Mr** lacking).
    Items without cognates, ambiguous as to source:
183 *(pápiʔtsíï, pápiʔčíï)* 'three'. **B** *pʰápʰiʔčʰíï* (**Mr** lacking).
305 *(ítsii, íčii)* 'here'. **B** *íčʰii.*
313 *(gáitsáitsaʔxíkï, gáčáčaʔxíkï)* 'wash'. **B** *kʷáčʰáčʰaʔxíkʰï* (**Mr** lacking).
348 *(pítsítsiʔíkï, píčíčiʔíkï)* 'rub'. **B** *pʰíčʰíčʰiʔyíkʰï* (**Mr** lacking).
366 *(ápiitsóge, ápiičóje)* 'fear'. **B** *ápʰiičʰóče* (**Mr** lacking).
367 *(páitsíïʔxáko, páčíïʔxáko)* 'squeeze'. **B** *pʰáčʰíïʔxákʰo* (**Mr** lacking).
PBM   **kk /ai__ >* M *kk* **B** *xkʰʸ* (**Mr** *xkʰ*).
139 **gáíkkoxɨ* 'piranha'. **M** *gáíkku-xe.* **B** *kʷáxkʰʸoxɨ* (**Mr** lacking).
249 **gáíkkoʔai* 'corn field'. **M** *gáíkkuʔai.* **B** *kʷáxkʰʸoʔa* (**Mr** lacking).
158 **ba(i)(k)ké-(ʔeke), *bá(i)(k)keé* 'root'. **M** *bakó-ʔoko* (*k* exception). **B** *páxkʰʸeé* (**Mr** *páixkʰeé*).
PBM   **kk /i__ >* M *kk*, **B** *xkʰʸ* (**Mr** *xkʰ*).
61 **níkke-xɨ* 'sky'. **M** *níkke-xe.* **B** *níxkʰʸe-xɨ* (**Mr** *níxkʰe-xɨ*).
362 **xïgíkk(o)* 'smell'. **M** *xígíkku-ʔi.* **B** *íčíxkʰʸï, íčïïkʰï* (**Mr** *ítsixkʰï/*).
368 **ikka(ne)* 'hold'. **M** *ikka-ʔi.* **B** *ixkʰʸa* (**Mr** lacking).
78 **ikka-ga* 'seat, stool'. **M** *íkka-ga.* **B** *ixʸa-kʷa* (*xʸ* exception) (**Mr** *íxa-kʷa*).
87 **píikkɨ-gai* 'fishhook'. **M** *φíïkkɨ-gai.* **B** *pʰíïxʸï-kʷa* (*xʸ* exception) (**Mr** *pʰixí-kʷa*).
    Noncognate example:
296 **gíí-()-ne* 'yellow'. **M** *gíí-giβa-no.* **B** *čí-xkʰʸá-ne-íβí.* (**Mr** *čí-xkʰa-ne*).

The following rule, in which Bora loses the expected /x/ before /kʰ/, reflecting loss of the assumed PBM gemination, is precisely the same rule that applied in several Indo-European languages, notably Latin and Old English, namely, that a long vowel could not precede a geminate consonant or consonant cluster. In several cases the Muinane examples appear to have lost the long vowel, or else the Bora example has transferred the length from the consonant to the vowel (items 182, 223, 340, 362).

The same rule applied to **pp* (see example under **pp*) and probably also to the other voiceless stops. **tt* and **čč* yield no examples of this rule, but neither are there any counterexamples with Bora /xtʰ/ or /xčʰ/ after long vowels. **tts* yields no examples because the rule would eliminate all evidence for the gemination in both languages; the same is true for **pp*, but one example was reconstructible based on morphological information.

The Bora dictionary does yield a number of examples of preaspirated stops after long vowels, one of them being 38 *míamĩnáa-xpʰi* 'man', the exception under the **pp* rule for this environment. This is therefore clearly not a synchronic rule in Bora, but must have applied at some point in the past. Item 31 *tsʰaa-pʰi* 'one male' is apparently a more common term for 'man' than *míamínáa-xpʰi* 'male being' which resisted regularization of the suffix after the rule ceased to apply. In light of the fact that this rule is no longer active, it is noteworthy that we have no other exceptions to it among the cognates listed for any of the aspirated stops.

PBM   **kk /VV__ > M kk, B kʰ.*
163   **píikkaá* 'cassava'. M *ɸéekka*. B *pʰíikʰaá*.
182   **míinéékkiї́* 'two'. M *míinokkɨ*. B *mínʸéékʰïї́*.
190   **pa-ʔottsɨɨ-kkï(-neβa)* 'ten'. M *ɸa-ʔúsee-kkɨ*. B *pʰa-ʔóxtsʰɨ-kʰї́-neβa*.
223   **áɨgookkó-né* 'hot'. M *áɨgúkku-no*. B *ačóókʰó, áčookʰó-né*.
287   **(tó)-g(ɨ)ɨ́-kkïnɨ́* 'lie down'. M *gɨ́ɨ-kkɨ́nɨ-ʔi*. B 287 *tʰó-tsɨ́ɨ́-kʰïnɨ́*.
288   **(ak)ïɨ̈́-kkïnï* 'sit'. M *gɨ́ɨ-kkɨ́nɨ-ʔi*. B *ákʰïɨ́kʰïnï*.
340   **ɨ́diikk(o-ne)*, **ɨ́díikk(ïї́)* 'dirty'. M *ɨdíkku-no*. B *ɨ́tíɨ́kʰʸ̈ï*.
354   **kápáítïї́kkï-nï* 'pierce'. M *káɸátʲʸïkkɨ-ʔi*. B *kʰápʰátʰʸïї́kʰï-nï*.
362   **xïgíkk(o)* 'smell'. M *xïgíkku-ʔi*. B *ičíxkʰʸї́, íčïɨ́kʰï* (Mr *ítsixkʰï*).
PBM   **kk /__ > M kk B xkʰ.*
12   **xɨ́kk(e)ʔ(ai)* 'beard'. M *xɨ́kkoʔai*. B *íxkʰaʔe*.
32   **bákkïї́* 'bone'. M *bákkɨ*. B *páxkʰïї́*.
65   **pékkó-e(ppi) nïʔï-ba* 'moon'. M *(ɸúkkuo) níʔɨ-ba*. B *nïʔ-pa pʰéxkʰó-expʰi*.
68   **pekko* 'night'. M *ɸúkku*. B *pʰexkʰo*.
104   **tsokko* 'otter'. M *súkku*. B *tsʰoxkʰo*.
110   **takkï* 'paca'. M *tákkɨ*. B *tʰaxkʰï*.
150 = 161   **tsókkómïxɨ* 'grass'. M *súkkumexe*. B *tsʰóxkʰómïxɨ*.
290   **akkï* 'give'. M *ákkɨ-ʔi*. B *axkʰï*.
343   **tsa-tïkkeβe* 'straight'. M *sá-tíkkoβo*. B *tsʰatʰïxkʰe-βe*.
350   **(k)átḯ(kkaáï)ro, ?*(g)átḯ(xɨ)ro* 'push'. M *gátíxeru-ʔi* (x exception).
        B *kʰátʰïxkʰaáʸo*.
191   **(it)tï(k)kéni* 'first'. M *íttɨkoni* (k exception). B *tʰïxkʰénï*.
241   **(mé)-ʔótsɨ-(k)kéxɨ* 'wrist'. M *úse-kexe*. B *(mé)-ʔótsʰɨxkʰéxɨ*.
173   **bá(k)ke(tamï)*, **(né)ba(k)ke* 'Banisterium'. M *bákotamɨ*. B *népaxkʰe*.
19   **(mé)-nékkï-gai* 'arm'. M *nókkɨ-gai*. B *(mé)-néxï-kʷa* (x exception).
20   **(mé)-nékkï-(gai)-(étsitto)* 'upper arm'. M *nókkɨ*. B *mé-néxï-kʷa-étsʰïxtʰʸo* (x exception).
240   **(mé)-nékkɨ́-(gatsítto)* 'lower arm'. M *nókkɨ*. B *(mé)-néxḯ-kʷatsʰíxtʰʸo* (x exception).

As the last three exceptions in **B** show, **PBM** **kk* sometimes (exceptionally) became /x/, presumably by reduction of earlier **xkʰ*, whereas **PBM** **k* never did. (See also palatalized examples 78 and 87 in an earlier rule.)

297   **gaʔape-né*, **gáʔap(é)(k)kïnɨ́-né* 'full'. M *gáʔáɸo-no, gáʔáɸɨkkɨnɨ-no*.
        B *kʷaʔpʰe, kʷáʔpʰé-kʰïnɨ́né* (kʰ exception).

The following item is apparently only a Bora exception because of loss of the vowel which separated the **ʔ* from the **kk* followed by simplification of an impossible Bora sequence **ʔxkʰ* to /ʔkʰ/.

366 *?*(ai)n(ó)ï?(i)kko() 'fear'. **M** ñí?ikku-?i. **B** nóï?kʰóče, nï?néβe.

The only examples of Bora /kʰʸ/ after *ai* that have clear cognates are the noun classifier *xpʰakʰʸo* 'liquid' (33 = 266, 48, 157, 266, 319, 324, 325), with Muinane *ɸáí?u*. The following rule seems rather odd, but it cannot really be characterized as a doubtful rule, since the form is otherwise well established, and there are no counterexamples. However, the PW reconstruction casts doubt on this rule. Items 59 and 247 probably have the same suffix, but I have reconstructed it in these with *? because of the corresponding Ocaina form. The Muinane form in the three 'noncognate' examples 33 = 266 and 157 may be a mangled form of the same morpheme. Item 123 (specifically the Bora form) may possibly be related also; the Muinane form has lost the syllable containing *k.

PBM *k /ai__ > **M** ?, **B** kʰʸ (**Mr** kʰ).
48 *nï-ppaiko 'water'. **M** ɸaí?u, ní-ɸáí?u. **B** ní-xpʰakʰʸo (**Mr** ní-xpʰaikʰo).
319 *mïppáíne-ppáiko 'milk'. **M** míɸaño-ɸáí?u. **B** míxpʰánʸe-xpʰákʰʸo
(**Mr** míxpʰánʸe-xpʰaikʰo).
Noncognate examples:
33 = 266 *tïï-(xé?e), *tïï-(ppaiko) 'blood'. **M** tíí-xó?o. **B** tʰï-xpʰakʰʸo
(**Mr** tʰï-xpʰaikʰo).
123 *íígai(ko) 'anaconda'. **M** ígáíβatï. **B** ííkʷakʰʸo (**Mr** lacking).
157 *íme?é (tïï-xe?e), *íme?é-(ppáiko) 'sap'. **M** ímo?o tíí-xo?o. **B** íme?é-xpʰákʰʸo
(**Mr** lacking).
PBM *k /i__ > **M** k, **B** kʰʸ (**Mr** kʰ).
351 *piko 'throw'. **M** ɸíkú-?i. **B** pʰikʰʸo (**Mr** lacking).
Noncognate examples:
70 (róri?kó) 'lightning'. **M** (no cognate). **B** róri?kʰʸó (**Mr** róri?kʰoó).
79 *kïgá-(taxi), *kïgá-(í?ki) 'mat'. **M** kíga-taxe. **B** kʰïkʷá-í?kʰʸï (**Mr** lacking).
81 *kïgá-ííxi, *kïgá-(taxi), *kïgá-(í?ki) 'bed'. **M** kíga-íixe, kíga-taxe.
B kʰïkʷá-í?kʰʸï, kʰíkʷa-ííxí (**Mr** kʰíkʷa-ííxí).
PBM *k /__i > **M** k **B** kʰ.
This overrides the above rule, and presumably also the second one above, though no examples appear to exist of *aiki.
103 *kíkiixe 'bat'. **M** kíkíxe. **B** kʰíkʰíix'e.
242 *(mé)-tákki-(ï) 'lower leg'. **M** tákkiyï. **B** (mé)-tʰáxkʰii.
329 *ki-(?da?íni) 'cut'. **M** kí-tti-?i. **B** kʰí-?t'ja?íni.
358 *aakí(t)te 'fall'. **M** áákétte-?i. **B** aakʰít'hʸe.
PBM *k /__ > **M** k, **B** kʰ.
9 *ímiko 'forehead'. **M** ímeku. **B** ?ímikʰo, ?ímíkʰo-ï.
52 *(ípá)-káa-xa-(neba), *káa-(mi) 'swamp'. **M** káa-me, íɸá-káa-xa.
B kʰááxánepa.
56 *kííxi-gai 'fire'. **M** kííxi-gai. **B** kʰííxï-kʷa.
58 *kííxí-gai-(kko) 'charcoal'. **M** kííxi-gai-kku. **B** kʰííxí-kʷa-yï.
60 *koó- 'firewood'. **M** kúúxo-?o. **B** kʰoó-kʷa, kʰoó-i.
64 *kóoxí-e(ppi) nï?ï-ba 'sun'. **M** (kúuxe-o) nï?i-ba. **B** nï?-pa (kʰóóxí-expʰi).
66 *mííkïrï-gai 'star'. **M** méékiri-gai. **B** mííkʰïrï-kʷa, míík'hïrï.

67 *kóoxɨɨ 'day'. M kúuxe. B kʰóóxɨɨ.
75 *káamée-xa 'house'. M káamooxa. B kʰáámée-xa.
79 *kɨ̈gá-(taxɨ), *kɨgá-(íʔkɨ̈) 'mat'. M kɨ́ga-taxe. B kʰɨ̈kʷá-íʔkʰʸɨ̈.
81 *kɨ̈gá-ɨ̈xɨ, *kɨgá-(taxɨ), *kɨ̈gá-(íʔkɨ̈) 'bed'. M kɨ́ga-íixe, kɨ́ga-taxe. B kʰɨ̈kʷa-ɨ̈íxɨ́,
  kʰɨ̈kʷá-íʔkʰʸɨ̈.
84 *kóomɨɨ 'village'. M kúumɨ. B kʰóómɨɨ.
289 ?*(í)xo(k)ɨ̈́ɨ̈́βe 'stand'. M xújééβe-ʔi (ĵ exception). B íxʸokʰɨ̈́ɨ̈́βe. Many more
  examples.

*k and *kk seem not to occur before *ɨ. Muinane (k)ke (the expected
reflex of this) derives in every case in the wordlist from earlier (k)ko (PBM
*(k)ke) or (k)ki by vowel harmony (e.g., 61, 358). Why this is so is unclear.
Comparing Proto Huitoto-Ocaina does not help to clarify this, since PBM
*ɨ resulted from a split of PW *e into PBM *e and *ɨ (see §4.9).

2.9. Voiced stops. This section presents the rules for the PBM voiced
stops *b, *d, *ĵ, and *g.

PBM *b /i__e > M b, B pʸ (Mr p).
202 *dií-be 'he'. M díi-bo. B tií-pʸe (Mr tií-pe).
PBM *b /i__a > M b, B p.
  3 *(mé)-xɨ́-niba 'lip'. M xí-niba. B (mé)-ɨ́nipa.
  16 = 244 = 245 = 272 *(mé)-ɨ̈íʔbá(ɨ̈) 'stomach'. M ɨ̈iba. B íʔpáɨ̈, mé-ʔpáɨ̈́.
111 *niʔiba 'crocodile'. M níʔiba. B niʔpa.
102 *xiíbai 'deer'. M xííbai. B iipa.
105 *kɨ̈ʔĵíba 'cebus monkey'. M kɨĵíba. B kʰɨ̈ʔčípa.
PBM *b /i__i > M b, B p.
172 *xíibɨ̈ɨ̈-(ʔe) 'coca'. M xííbi-(ʔo). B ɨ̈ípɨ̈ɨ̈.
PBM *b /__ > M b, B p.
  18 *(mé)-xɨ́xɨ-ba(ɨ̈) 'shoulder'. M xíxe-baɨ. B mé-ɨ́xɨ-pa.
  32 *bákkɨ̈ɨ̈ 'bone'. M bákkɨ. B páxkʰɨ̈ɨ̈.
  34 *(mé)-xɨ̈ibɨ̈ɨ̈ 'heart'. M xéebɨɨ. B (mé)-ɨ̈ɨ̈pɨ̈ɨ̈.
  43 *taába, *áɨ̈-táabaá 'wife'. M táaba, áttʸáaba. B tʰaápa, átʰʸáápaá.
  57 *báɨ̈-gɨ̈íxɨ 'ash'. M bai-gíɨ̈xɨ. B pá-čiɨ̈xʸɨ̈.
  62 *níixa-ba 'rain'. M níixa-ba. B níɨ̈xʸa-pa.
  64 *kóoxɨ́-e(ppi) nɨ̈ʔɨ̈-ba 'sun'. M (kúuxe-o) níʔɨ-ba. B nɨ̈ʔ-pa (kʰóóxɨ́-expʰi).
  65 *pékkó-e(ppi) nɨ̈ʔɨ̈-ba 'moon'. M (φúkkuo) níʔɨ-ba. B nɨ̈ʔ-pa pʰéxkʰó-expʰi.
  80 *gaáɨ̈-ba 'hammock'. M gááɨ̈-ba. B kʷaá-pʸa, kʷaá-pa.
  91 *boʔódó-ga 'paddle'. M búʔúdú-ga. B poʔtó-kʷa, poʔtó-xɨ.
  94; 95 *tɨ̈ɨ̈bó-ga 'bow, arrow'. M tɨ̈ibú-ga. B tʰɨ̈póó-kʷa.
111 *meeʔdóba 'crocodile'. M méédúba. B meʔtópa. Many more examples.
PBM *d /(a)i__ > M dʸ, B tʸ.
  No cognates:
155 (táɨ̈-deeka-no) 'my flowers'. M tá-dʸeeka-no.
265 *(táɨ̈)-do 'my flesh'. B tʰá-tʸo. (Compare this example with 265 in the next
  rule.)
329 *kɨ́-(ʔdaʔɨ̈nɨ̈) 'cut'. M kí-tti-ʔi. B kʰɨ́-tʸaʔɨ̈nɨ̈, kʷá-ʔtaʔɨ̈nɨ̈.

There are no examples of Muinane /dʸ/ in the entire Muinane dictionary (Walton in preparation, searched by computer). Muinane /dʸ/ only occurs in words with the first person singular prefix *tai, which is realized as Muinane /ta/ in all cases (exceptionally, presumably from levelling by analogy) and as Bora /tʰa/. In Bora, /tʸ/ is somewhat more common than its Muinane reflex /dʸ/.

PBM *d /__ > M d, B t.
  91 *boʔódó-ga 'paddle'. M búʔúdú-ga. B poʔtó-kʷa, poʔtó-xɨ.
 111 *meeʔdóba 'crocodile'. M méédúba. B meʔtópa.
 166 *xáʔadi 'cotton'. M xáʔadi. B aʔti.
 167 *dóoto- 'gourd'. M dúutuʔu. B toótʰo, tóótʰo-ï.
 171 *díí-ʔoï 'chili pepper'. M déé-ʔuɨ. B tɨɨ́, tɨɨ́-ʔoï.
 202 *dii-be 'he' (see also 203, 207, 209). M díi-bo. B tii-pʸe.
 228 *dí-pe 'go!' M di-ɸó. B tí-pʰʸe.
 229 *dí-tsaa 'come!' M di-sáá. B tí-čʰa.
 231 *d-ádoó 'drink!' M d-adú. B t-átoó.
 265 *doó-(xeʔe) 'flesh'. M dúú-xoʔo 'edible' B toó.
 267 *díïrïba 'grease'. M díïriba. B tíïrïpa.
 274 *ado 'drink'. M ádu-ʔi. B ato.
 275 *doó-(ʔi) 'eat meat'. M dúú-ʔi. B toó.
 276 *ïiʔdo 'bite'. M éédu-ʔi. B iʔto.
 340 *ïdiikk(o-ne), *ïdíikk(íḯ) 'dirty'. M ídikku-no. B ítíïkʰʸïḯ.
 355 *tseeʔdi 'dig'. M séédi-ʔi. B tsʰeʔti.
 356 *doʔxín(ï) 'tie'. M dúxéne-ʔi. B toʔxíní.
 302 *mïʔ(j)ï, *mïʔ(d)ï 'how'. M míjɨ (j̃ exception). B mïʔtï.
PBM *j̃ > M j̃, B č.
   6 *(me)-ʔáájïï 'eye'. M áájɨ̈, B (me)-ʔáčïï.
  82 *gírí-ʔijo 'cooking pot'. M gírí-ʔiju. B číyi-ʔčo.
 105 *kïʔjíba 'cebus monkey'. M kɨjïba. B kʰïʔčípa (Mr lacking).
 352 *íjaáyo 'hit'. M íjáyu-ʔi. B íčaáyo (Mr lacking).
        Unambiguous noncognate examples:
 131 (joóra) 'parrot'. B čoóra (Mr yoóra).
 198 (j̃ïïβáábeé) 'medicine man'. B číïβáápeé (Mr lacking).
 313 (íjoáko) 'wash'. B íčoákʰo (Mr lacking).
 349 (tájári(ʔx)ïkï) 'pull'. B rʰáčári(ʔxʸ)ïkʰï (Mr lacking).
 347; (47) (kíjaʔo-te) 'old man'. M kíjaʔu-to.
 107 (xíbííjaxɨ) 'spider monkey'. M xíbíïjaxe.
 128 (róóbíjï) 'hummingbird'. M rúúbéjɨ.
 160 (jári-ga) 'stick'. M jári-ga.
 169 (jíróómïba) 'sweet potato'. M jínúúmɨba.
 192 (ájïba-) 'last'. M ájiba-ri, -tɨ, -anɨno.
 357 (pájóó) 'sew'. M ɸájúú-ʔi.

Contrast is not excellent between *j̃ and *d or between *j̃ and *g, but it is sufficient to require reconstructing them all as separate phonemes. When palatalized, PBM *j̃ and *g fell together in Bora. Most occurrences of Bora /č/ are either clearly derived from *g or are ambiguous as to source, the items listed above being an exhaustive list of those which clearly derive from *ǰ. For ambiguous noncognate examples, see the examples for *g below.

PBM   *g /ai__o,e,i,(i̵?),(i̵?) > M g, B č (Mr k /__o,(i̵?),č /__e,i).
223   *áígookkó-né 'hot'. M áígúkku-no. B ačóókʰó, áčookʰó-né (Mr áikookʰó-ne).

The preceding example is the only one to which the /__e,i rule below did not also apply. Apparently in Miraña the preceding *ai has no effect, but only the following vowels.

40   *gai-ge 'woman'. M gáí-go. B kʷa-če (Mr same).
57   *báí-giíxi̵ 'ash'. M bai-giíxi̵. B pá-čiíxʸï (Mr same).
291 *xi̵ïb(ái)ge 'tell'. M xíïbege-ʔi, xíïbogoo-bo. B ïïpáče (Mr lacking).
     The following example was added from the dictionaries:
     *aige 'rain'. M áige-ʔi. B ače.
     Noncognate examples for Bora (ambiguous as to whether *g or *ǰ):
17   (má-ʔaǰï, má-ʔaigï) 'back'. B má-ʔačï (Mr lacking).
137 (gáǰerááʔe, gáigerááʔe) 'hen'. B kʷáčerááʔe (Mr lacking).
290 (éxekkáǰo, éxekkáigo) 'give'. B éxexkʰáčo (Mr lacking).
PBM   *g /ai__a > M g, B kʷ.
     There were no examples of this environment in the wordlist, which is surprising, since the sequence *ga is extremely frequent (see the rule for the environment */__a below). The example given is from the dictionaries, and shows that *g resisted palatalization in this environment in Bora, becoming labialized instead, just as it did in the sequence *iga (see below). There were other examples of /aiga/ in the Muinane dictionary, but this was the only one for which I could find a cognate:
     *áiga 'fast, diet'. M áiga-ʔi. B akʷa.
PBM   *g /__e,i > M g, B č (Mr č).
44   *giʔí-ro(bi) 'father'. M gíʔí(rubi). B čiʔí-yo, čiʔí-ï.
77   *gééʔo-ga 'doorway'. M gúʔú-ga. B čééʔo-kʷa.
82   *gíri-ʔiǰo 'cooking pot'. M gírí-ʔiǰu. B číyi-ʔčo (Mr číri-ʔčo).
96   *gittsí-xi̵ 'blowgun'. M gisí-xi̵. B čixčʰí-xi̵.
100 *geéï 'armadillo'. M góóï. B čeéï.
120 *giʔpe 'mouse'. M gíiɸo. B čiʔpʰʸe (Mr číʔpʰe).
130 *ni̵ge 'toucan'. M ni̵go. B niče.
203 *dii-ge 'she'. M díi-go. B tií-če.
220 *giraa-ne 'big'. M gíráa-no. B čiya- (Mr čírʸaáne).
246 *kééme-ge 'old woman'. M kóómo-go. B kʰéémeče.
275 *geéne 'eat fruit'. M gééne-ʔi. B čeéne.
296 *gíí-()-ne 'yellow'. M gíí-giβa-no. B čí-xkʰʸá-ne-íβí (Mr čí-xkʰa-ne).
362 *xi̵gikk(o) 'smell'. M xígíkku-ʔi. B ičíxkʰʸï, íčiíkʰï (Mr ítsixkʰï, exception).
     Noncognate examples for Bora (ambiguous as to whether *g or *ǰ):
96   *(togií)-xi̵, *(toǰií)-xi̵ 'blowgun'. M gisí-xi̵. B tʰóčií-xʸï.
175 *meéme 'chonta palm'. M móomo. B meéme. Many more examples.

PBM   *g /__i > M g, B ts.
281   *gixí-βe 'die'. M gíxé-βe-ʔi. B tsixí-βe.
282   *gíxi-βé-tso 'kill'. M gíxé-βe-su-ʔi. B tsixí-βé-tsʰo.
287   *(tó)-g(i)íʹ-kkiníʹ 'lie down'. M 288 gíí-kkiní-ʔi. B 287 tʰó-tsííʹ-kʰïníʹ.
      Noncognate example:
357   (gikko) 'sew'. B tsixkʰo.
PBM   *g /__a > M g, B kʷ.
19   *(mé)-nékki-gai 'arm'. M nókki-gai. B (mé)-néxï-kʷa.
23   *(mé)-ʔóttsi-gai 'finger'. M úse-gai. B (mé)-ʔóxtsʰi-kʷa.
30   *(mé)-ttí-gaái 'toe'. M tí-gai. B (mé)-xtʰíʹ-kʷaá.
35   *βáaʔβága 'lungs'. M βáβáágano, βáaβaga. B βaʔβákʷa.
38 = 39   *gai-ppi 'man'. M gáí-ɸi. B kʷa-xpʰi.
40   *gai-ge 'woman'. M gáí-go. B kʷa-če.
45   *gaʔá-ro(bi) 'mother'. M gáʔá(rubi). B kʷaʔá-ro, kʷaʔá-ï.
56   *kííxï-gai 'fire'. M kíixi-gai. B kʰííxï-kʷa.
66   *míikïri-gai 'star'. M méékiri-gai. B míikʰíri-kʷa, míikʰïrï.
74   *(xíí)né-gai-yíʹ-ʔai 'sand'. M xíini-gai-yi-ʔai. B nékʷa-yíïʹ-ʔa, néékʷa-yï.
77   *gééʔo-ga 'doorway'. M gúʔú-ga. B čééʔo-kʷa.
78   *íkka-ga 'seat, stool'. M íkka-ga. B íxʸa-kʷa. Many more examples.

The environment *i__a does not produce palatalization; instead the labialization occurs as in the other examples before *a. (See also the discussion at the end of the rules for *g for more on this question.) Examples follow:

4   *ííʔ-gái-neé, *(mé)-ííʔgá(xii) 'tooth'. M íí-gai, íí-ga-ñe. B íʔkʷáxií, mé-ʔkʷáxií, íʔ-kʷá-nʸeé.
8   *nígaï 'head'. M nígai. B níikʷaï.
10   *nígaï-xiine, *nígaï-(ko) 'hair'. M nígai-xeene. B níikʷa-kʰo, íʔxine, níikʷákʰo-xí(ʔi).
196   *níxïi-ga(-ko) 'ear ornament'. M níxi-ga-ku. B níxïi-kʷa.
234   *() (mé)-ííʔgai-neé 'front teeth, incisors'. M di-xéxé-ba íí-ga-ño. B pʰiineéné mé-ʔkʷa-nʸeé.
273   *(mé)-ííʔgá-neé 'liver'. M íga-no, iigá. B íʔkʷá-neé, mé-ʔkʷá-neé.

The situation as regards the reflexes of *g before *ï is somewhat confusing. There appeared to be no good cognates in the wordlist for this environment. There were, however, a number of cases in Bora of the sequence /kʷï/, all of which appear to be a particular suffix, which in most of the cases seems to clearly mean (diminutive). Based only on this data the reflex of *g before *ï would appear to be /kʷ/.

The Bora dictionary, however, yields a large number of cases of the sequence /kï/, one at least of which has a good cognate with Muinane. In addition, the Muinane diminutive suffix is found to be /-gayi/. Based on this, I conclude that the Bora reflex for *g before *ï is actually /k/, but that the PBM suffix *-gayï (diminutive), which should have become -kʷayï in Bora, has been reduced to *-kʷï.

Examples of the PBM suffix *-gayï (diminutive):
89 *n(ɨɨ)ts(í)ga-(gayï) 'knife' (machete-small). M níísúga. B nɨɨtsʰíkʷa-(kʷï).
221 *()-ne-gayï 'small'. M áxášu-no-gayɨ. B áyá-né-kʷï.
224 *imí-ne, *imí-(gayï) 'good'. M ími-(no). B imí-kʷï.
250 *tée-ʔi-(gayï), *téé-(gai-ʔo) 'stream' (river-small). M tée-ʔi, téé-gai-ʔu. B tʰééʔi-kʷï.
331 *ɨɨxí-né-(gáyí) 'narrow'. M ííxe-ne. B ɨɨxí né-kʷí.
    Additional examples from the dictionaries:
    (koomíkó-gayï) 'little bird'. B kʰoomíkʰó-kʷï.
    (íkíínó-gayï) 'little pot'. M íkíñú-gayɨ.
PBM *g /__ï > M g, B k.
    Since there were almost no examples for this environment in the wordlist, these items are mostly from the dictionaries, and most are without cognates. (I found no Mr examples, but, taking the whole reflex system into account, it is logical to assume that the same reflex occurs before /ï/ as before /o/.)
    *káʔgíníko 'caguana'. M kááginɨku. B kʰáʔkínɨkʰo.
221 (ííɡíyiï) 'small'. B ííkíyiï.
276 (dɨɡíkkï) 'bite'. B tɨkíxkʰï.
    (gɨʔináro) 'write'. B kïʔnʸáro.
    (gíriríïβe) 'growl'. B kíriríïβe.
    (tsïɡíʔko) 'hiccup'. B tsʰïkíʔkʰo.
    (ígiríïβe) 'shrink'. B íkíríïβe.
    (βegíβégï) 'spongy'. B βekíβékï.
PBM *g /__o > M g, B k.
    Since there were almost no examples for this environment in the wordlist, these items are mostly from the dictionaries, and most are without cognates:
    *gókó(piʔéxï) 'dimple'. M gúgúkuʔi 'poke in'. B kókʰópʰiʔyéxï.
351 (gaagóo) 'throw'. B kʷaakóo.
    (kágoorínï) 'afflict'. B kʰákoorínï.
    (káʔgoxɨ) 'shell'. B kʰáʔkoxɨ.
    (dɨgoinóʔko) 'chew'. B tíkonʸóʔkʰo.
    (goʔgóxɨ) 'mushroom'. B koʔkóxɨ.
    (goróóxɨ) 'mushroom, mold'. B koróóxɨ.
    (góʔgómeébe) 'beloved'. B kóʔkómeépe.
    (góʔógaíkíníne) (meaning uncertain). B kóʔókʷaíkʰíníne.
    (gooko) 'laugh'. B koókʰo.
    (goorïï) 'gizzard'. B koorïï.
    (gooríβe) 'go without sleep'. B kooríβe.
    (ígókkaméi) 'rinse'. B íkóxkʰaméi.
    (tsógooróʔo) 'chameleon'. B tsʰókooróʔo.
    The only Mr example of /k/ is the following, which does not have a /k/ in Bora proper:
223 *áígookkó-né 'hot'. M áígúkku-no. B ačóókʰó, áčookʰó-né (Mr áikookʰó-ne).

The only examples for *ig are *aig or *(a)iga (see rules above). The labialization of *g to Bora /kʷ/ before *a must have occurred before the completion of the palatalization process, with the result that the labialization prevented the palatalization rule from applying.

It is unclear why examples of *ig before other vowels are lacking. I have one example from Thiesen and Thiesen (1975:1) with the environment *i__ï as follows:

*(ímíjeebe igíríʔkóne) 'he likes to growl'. B ímíčeepe ikʸíríʔkʰóne.

This is clearly a morphologically complex item, however, and rather than providing information about historical sound change it probably represents an example of a currently active morphophonemic rule. It seems likely that the historical reflex of *igï and *aigï would be Bora /iči/ and /ačï/, following the pattern for *aigo in the first rule above.

Bora /kʸ/ does not figure as a Bora reflex for *g in any of the above rules. Bora /kʸ/ is extremely rare. In addition to the Thiessen and Thiessen example above, there are two examples of /kʸ/ in the Bora dictionary, which are clearly innovations:

*(migééré) 'Miguel'. B mikʸééré. *(giʔrími). 'gringo'. B kʸiʔrími.

Of these three examples of /kʸ/, the first two show clear evidence of the palatalization process applying after *i. This suggests that the palatalization process is synchronically active and continues to apply even to new items (however, Bora /kʷ/ is apparently always resistant to palatalization, presumably because the labialization blocks it).

Even in the very recent past it is probable that [k], [kʷ] and [ts] were not contrastive in Bora (and Miraña, which differs only in the palatalized reflexes) but were all allophones of Bora /k/. Even now, they are in almost complete complementary distribution: /kʷ/ occurs only before /a/ except in the diminutive suffix /-kʷi/ (derived from *-gayï)—this suffix is extremely common; /k/ occurs only before /o/ and /i/ except for six examples in the dictionary, five before /a/ and one before /ɨ/; /ts/ occurs only before /ɨ/ except for ten examples in the dictionary, six before /a/, two before /o/ and one each before /e/ and /i/.

2.10. Glottal. This section presents the rules for the PBM glottal *ʔ.

PBM *ʔ /__C > M ∅, B ʔ.
       Before consonants PBM *ʔ is always lost in Muinane.
    1 *(mé)-ʔníxi-() 'tongue'. M néxe-ba. B nííxi-kʷa, mé-ʔníxi-kʷa.
    2 *ii̶ʔ-xɨ 'mouth'. M íi-xi. B íʔxʸíí.

4   *íí?-gái-neé, *(mé)-íí?gá(xɨɨ) 'tooth'. M íi-gai, íi-ga-ñe. B í?kʷáxɨɨ, mé-?kʷáxɨɨ,
     i?-kʷá-nʸeé.
16 = 244 = 245 = 272 *(mé)-íi?bá(ɨ) 'stomach'. M íiba. B í?páï, mé-?páïˋ.
31   *(iáábe) (mé)-?mɨɨ?e(é) 'skin'. M mée?e. B (mé)-?mɨɨ?eé, iáápe mɨɨ?e.
35   *βáa?βága 'lungs'. M βáβáágano, βáaβaga. B βa?βákʷa.
75   *ii?-xa 'his-house'. M íi-xa. B xaá, i?-xʸa.
105 *kɨ?jíba 'cebus monkey'. M kijíba. B kʰɨ?čípa.
109 *too?xɨ 'anteater'. M túuxe. B tʰo?xɨ.
111 *mee?dóba 'crocodile'. M méedúba. B me?tópa.
126 *xa?kó(kó)ga 'toad'. M xakúkúga. B a?kʰókʷa. Many more examples.

For purposes of the following rule, I am assuming that there were phonemically glottal-initial words in PBM; it is probable that phonetically all vowel-initial words began with a glottal. However, whether that glottal is to be considered phonemic depends on one's point of view, since it was probably not contrastive with its absence. (In all but one of the present-day Witotoan languages this same situation applies.) The question became significant, however, because word-initial /?/ did become contrastive with its absence in Bora, primarily through the frequent loss of word-initial *x in Bora (see *x, in §2.11).

On the other hand, as the list of apparent exceptions below shows, there are more "exceptions" to this rule than there are examples for it, i.e., there are more words listed in the Bora dictionary which begin with a vowel than there are words beginning with a glottal (written h in the practical orthography); if the vowel-initial words were derived in every case from loss of *x, we would expect that glottal-initial words would be more frequent. There are, however, at least four possible explanations for this situation which is why I have not treated these as exceptions: (1) Thiesen may have only written the glottal when it seemed practical to do so for orthographic purposes, e.g., when the word took prefixes. (2) There may be environments, either phonological or morphological, in which the glottal tended to be lost, or could not be distinguished from its absence in enough cases for new speakers to keep track of it, since glottal only contrasts with its absence in utterance-medial position. (3) Some of these words may have actually had an *x in them in PBM, which was subsequently lost in Muinane as well, in which case the *x could not be reconstructed. (I have proposed that at an earlier stage some Proto-Witotoan **x's were lost in PBM (see §4.6). It is also possible, however, that these were not lost until later.) (4) It is possible that PBM had phonemic glottal which contrasted with its absence in the same way that it does in present-day Bora, but that this contrast was later lost in Muinane (a very reasonable possibility). This situation could have come about in the same way that I proposed that it did in later Bora: through the loss of some word-initial *x's, which apparently did happen in some cases. Under this scenario, Bora vowel-initial words have two sources: *x and *∅, while Bora glottal-initial words come from *ʔ; in Muinane, on the other hand, while the *x-initial words retained the /x/, the merger was between *∅ and *ʔ.

PBM   *ʔ (or ∅?) /#__V > M ∅ (or ʔ), B ʔ.
  6   *(me)-ʔáájɨ̈ 'eye'. M ááji̋. B (me)-ʔáčɨ̈.
  9   *ɨ́miko 'forehead'. M ɨ́meku. B ʔɨ́mikʰo, ʔɨ́mɨ́kʰo-ɨ̈.
 22   *(mé)-ʔóttsɨ́ɨ 'hand'. M úse. B (mé)-ʔóxtsʰɨ́ɨ.
 23   *(mé)-ʔóttsɨ-gai 'finger'. M úse-gai. B (mé)-ʔóxtsʰɨ̈-kʷa.
 24   *(mé)-ʔóttsɨ́-gai-mɨ́ɨʔo 'fingernail'. M úse-gai-méeʔu. B (mé)-ʔóxtsʰɨ̈-kʷa-mɨ́ɨʔo.
153 = 154   *(ina)-ʔáami 'leaf'. M áame. B ɨ́na-ʔáámɨ, -ʔáámɨ́ɨ, ɨ́na-ʔáámɨ.
241   *(mé)-ʔótsɨ-(k)kéxɨ 'wrist'. M úse-kexe. B (mé)-ʔótsʰɨxkʰéxɨ.
323   *-ʔaččɨ́ɨxɨ̈ 'if'. M -aččɨxɨ. B -ʔaxčʰɨ́ɨxʸɨ̈.
      Items which may have had (unreconstructible) initial *x in PBM, based on comparison with Proto Huitoto-Ocaina:
16 = 244 = 245 = 272   *(mé)-ɨɨʔbá(ɨ̈) 'stomach'. M ɨ́iba. B ɨ́ʔpáɨ̈, mé-ʔpáɨ̈̃.
 75   *ɨɨʔ-xa 'his-house'. M ɨ́ɨ-xa. B xaá, ɨʔ-xʸa.
274   *ado 'drink'. M ádu-ʔi. B ato.
      Other apparent exceptions (see explanations above):
  2   *ɨ́iʔ-xɨ̈ 'mouth'. M ɨ̈ɨ-xɨ. B ɨ́ʔxʸɨ̈̃.
  4   *ɨ́ɨʔ-gái-neé, *(mé)-ɨ́ɨʔgá(xɨ̈) 'tooth'. M ɨ́ɨ-gai, ɨ́ɨ-ga-ñe. B ɨ́ʔkʷáxɨ́ɨ, mé-ʔkʷáxɨ́ɨ. ɨ́ʔ-kʷá-nʸeé.
 42   *taxɨ, *áɨ́-táxɨ́ɨ, *áɨ́xɨ́ɨ 'husband'. M átʸaxe, táxe, aixi. B tʰaxɨ, áxʸɨ̈̃, átʰʸáxɨ.
 43   *taába, *áɨ́-táabaá 'wife'. M táaba, átʸáaba. B tʰaápa, átʰʸáápaá.
 78   *ɨ́kka-ga 'seat, stool'. M ɨ́kka-ga. B ɨ́xʸa-kʷa.
 93   *aámɨ̈-(ba) 'spear'. M áámɨ-ga. B aamɨ́-pa.
129   *ɨ́n(a)ʔai 'macaw'. M ɨ́nóʔai. B ɨ́nʸaʔa.
133   *ainɨ̈ 'buzzard'. M áñɨ. B anʸɨ̈̃.
152   *ɨ́me-ʔe 'tree'. M ɨ́mo-ʔo. B ɨ́me-ʔe.
157   *ɨ́meʔé (tɨ́ɨ-xeʔe), *ɨ́meʔé-(ppáiko) 'sap'. M ɨ́moʔo tɨ́ɨ-xoʔo. B ɨ́meʔé-xpʰákʰʸo.
160   *ɨ́méʔe-i 'stick'. M ɨ́meeʔ-i. B ɨ́méʔe-i.
164   *ɨ́ttáko-gɨ́ɨxɨ̈ 'cassava flour'. M ɨ́ttáku. B ɨ́xtʰʸákʰo-čɨ̈xʸɨ̈. Many more examples.

There are very few reconstructed examples of PBM *ʔy. The example given here is the only clear case. The *y must be reconstructed in the protolanguage precisely because the glottal was lost in Muinane: glottal in Muinane was only lost before consonants. If it were not for this, I would not have reconstructed a *y in this word: the /y/s in both languages could have been generated by rules: for the Bora rule which could have applied, see the second rule below—most cases of Bora /ʔy/ are derived from palatalization of *ʔ; for the Muinane rule which could have applied see §2.15.

PBM   *ʔy > M y, B ʔy.
268   *ɨ́ɨʔyɨ́ɨ 'egg'. M ɨ́ɨyɨ. B ɨ́ɨʔyɨ́ɨ(́ɨ) (Mr ɨ́ɨʔɨ̈).

PBM *ʔ /(a)i__V > M ʔ, B ʔy.

92 *gáíʔooï(daaʔi) 'club'. M gáíʔuidaaʔe. B kʷáʔyoóï (Mr kʷáyïïʔo).

99 *tïpáíʔoó(ï) 'puma'. M tíɸaiʔui. B tʰ ïïpʰáʔyoóï (Mr tʰïïpʰáïyóóʔi).

143 *gáaniʔo 'louse'. M gáañiʔu. B kʷáániʔyo (Mr kʷáániʔo).

186 *()-ʔottsí-tï tsaane 'six'. M sa-ʔúse xúúga-ʔuse-tɨ sááno. B inʸexkʰïë-ʔoxtsʰɨ ..., í-ʔyoxtsʰɨ-tʰ ï tsʰa-ne (Mr í-ʔoxtsʰɨ-tʰ ï tsʰa-ne).

187 *()-ʔottsí-tï mííné(k)kïï 'seven'. M sa-ʔúse xúúga-ʔuse-tɨ míínokkí.
B inʸexkʰïë-ʔoxtsʰɨ ..., í-ʔyoxtsʰɨ-tʰ ï mínʸéékʰ ïï (Mr see 186).

188 *()-ʔottsí-tï () 'eight'. M sa-ʔúse xúúga-ʔuse-tɨ míínokkí sááno.
B inʸexkʰïë-ʔoxtsʰɨ ..., í-ʔyoxtsʰɨ-tʰ ï pʰápʰ iʔčʰ ïï (Mr see 186).

189 *()-ʔottsí-tï () 'nine'. M sa-ʔúse xúúga-ʔuse-tɨ igéénemeʔexé. B inʸexkʰïë-ʔoxtsʰɨ ...,
í-ʔyoxtsʰɨ-tʰ ï pʰ íínee-ʔóxtsʰ í (Mr see 186).

209 *díí-ʔóttsɨ 'thy hand'. M díí-ʔuse. B tí-ʔyóxtsʰi (Mr tí-ʔóxtsʰ ïi).

Noncognate examples:

130 *b(ai)rí(gai) 'toucan'. M bárʸígai. B perííʔyo (Mr lacking).

175 *meéme-(ʔegííʔo), *meéme-(ʔejííʔyo) 'chonta fruit'. M móomo.
B méémé-ʔečííʔyo (Mr lacking).

332 *(téʔe)tsi(-ne), ?* tsí(ʔïge) 'far'. M téʔesi-no. B tsʰ íʔyïče (Mr lacking).

PBM *ʔ /__V > M ʔ, B ʔ.

5 *tïxï-ʔo, *tïxï-ʔ(exï) 'nose'. M tíxi-ʔu. B tʰ ïxï-ʔo, tʰ íï-ʔexï.

7 *nïxï-mɨɨʔo 'ear'. M níxi-meeʔu. B nïïmiʔo.

12 *xïkk(e)ʔ(ai) 'beard'. M xíkkoʔai. B ïxkʰaʔe.

16 *(áá)-mɨɨʔo 'abdomen'. M 14 kɨidɨi mééʔu. B 16 (má)-áámiʔo.

29 *(mé)-ttí-ʔaáí 'foot'. M tí-ʔai. B (mé)-xtʰ íʔaá.

31 *(iáábe) (mé)-ʔmɨɨʔe(é) 'skin'. M mééʔe. B (mé)-ʔmíïʔeé, iáápe mɨɨʔe.

44 *giʔí-ro(bi) 'father'. M gíʔí(rubi). B čiʔí-yo, čiʔí-ï.

45 *gaʔá-ro(bi) 'mother'. M gáʔá(rubi). B kʷaʔá-ro, kʷaʔá-ï.

49 *teé-ʔi 'river'. M téé-ʔi. B tʰeé-ʔi.

64 *kóoxí-e(ppi) nïʔï-ba 'sun'. M (kúuxe-o) níʔi-ba. B nïʔ-pa (kʰóóxí-expʰi).

71 *tïï-ʔi 'rainbow'. M tɨi-ʔi. B tʰ ïï-ʔi.

74 *(xíí)né-gai-yï-ʔai 'sand'. M xííni-gai-yi-ʔai. B nékʷa-yïï-ʔa, néékʷa-yï. Many
more examples.

2.11. Fricatives.
This section presents the rules for the PBM fricatives
*x and *β.

PBM *x /#__ > M x, B ∅.

3 *(mé)-xï-niba 'lip'. M xí-niba. B (mé)-ïnipa.

12 *xïkk(e)ʔ(ai) 'beard'. M xíkkoʔai. B ïxkʰaʔe.

18 *(mé)-xíxɨ-ba(ï) 'shoulder'. M xíxe-bai. B mé-íxɨ-pa.

34 *(mé)-xɨɨbïï 'heart'. M xéebɨɨ. B (mé)-ïïpïï.

88 *xïgaá-xɨ 'axe'. M xígáá-xe. B íkʷaá-xi.

102 *xiíbai 'deer'. M xííbai. B iípa.

122 *xíinime 'snake'. M xíinimo. B íínʸimʸe.

126 *xaʔkó(kó)ga 'toad'. M xakúkúga. B aʔkʰókʷa.

129 *xɨɨβaá 'macaw'. M xéeβa. B ɨɨβaá.

142 *xïïko-gai 'flea'. M xííku-gai. B ïïkʰo-kʷa, ïïkʰo.

166 *xáʔadi 'cotton'. M xáʔadi. B aʔti.

172 *xííbií-(ʔe) 'coca'. M xííbi-(ʔo). B íípií.

85 = 253 *xïḯ-() 'path, trail'. M xíí-ʔai. B xïḯβa (x exception). Many more
examples.

PBM ***x /(a)i__ > M x, B x^y (Mr x^y /ai__, x /i__).**

2 *íiʔ-xï 'mouth'. M íi-xï. B íʔx^yïḯ (Mr íʔxíḯ).

42 *taxï, *áí-táxïí, *áíxïḯ 'husband'. M áttʸaxe, táxe, aixï. B tʰaxï, áxʸïḯ, átʰʸáxïí
(Mr áxʸïḯ).

57 *báí-gííxï 'ash'. M bai-gííxï. B pá-čiíxʸï (Mr pá-čiíxï).

62 *nííxa-ba 'rain'. M nííxa-ba. B nííxʸa-pa (Mr nííxa-pa).

75 *íiʔ-xa 'his-house'. M íí-xa. B xaá, iʔ-xʸa (Mr xaá).

103 *kíkiíxe 'bat'. M kíkíxe. B kʰíkʰiíxʸe (Mr kʰíkʰiíxe).

144 *gaáí-xï(-ba) 'mosquito'. M gáai-xï-ba. B kʷaá-xʸï (Mr kʷáá-xʸï).

164 *íttáko-gííxï 'cassava flour'. M íttáku. B íxtʰʸákʰo-číxʸï (Mr íxtʰʸakʰo).

289 ?*(í)xo(k)ííβe 'stand'. M xújééβe-ʔi. B íxʸokʰííβe (Mr íxokʰííβe).

323 *-ʔaččííxï 'if'. M -aččíxï. B -ʔaxčʰííxʸï (Mr -ʔaxčʰííxï).

372 *()-giixï 'dust'. M -gíixï. B pʰá-čixʸï, -číxʸïḯ, íínʸï-číxʸï (Mr pʰá-čiíxï, íínʸíxï číxï).
Noncognate examples:

350 *ká(βíiʔx)ááko, ?*ká(bóy)ááko 'push'. M kábúyaaku-ʔi. B kʰáβíiʔxʸákʰo
(Mr lacking).

PBM ***x /__ > M x, B x.**

1 *(mé)-ʔníxï-() 'tongue'. M néxe-ba. B nííxï-kʷa, mé-ʔníxï-kʷa.

5 *tíxï-ʔo, *tíxï-ʔ(exï) 'nose'. M tíxï-ʔu. B tʰíxï-ʔo, tʰíí-ʔexï.

10 *nígaï-xïine, *nígaï-(ko) 'hair'. M nígai-xeene. B nííkʷa-kʰo, íʔxine,
nííkʷákʰo-xí(ʔi).

14 *(mé)-ppíïï-xï 'chest'. M φéeyi-xe. B (mé)-xpʰíï-xï.

18 *(mé)-xíxï-ba(ï) 'shoulder'. M xíxe-bai. B mé-íxï-pa.

42 *taxï, *áí-táxïí, *áíxïḯ 'husband'. M áttʸaxe, táxe, aixï. B tʰaxï, áxʸïḯ, átʰʸáxïí.

52 *(ípá)-káa-xa-(neba), *káa-(mï) 'swamp'. M káa-me, íφá-káa-xa. B kʰááxánepa.

56 *kííxï-gai 'fire'. M kííxï-gai. B kʰííxï-kʷa.

61 *níkke-xï 'sky'. M níkke-xe. B níxkʰʸe-xï.

64 *kóoxí-e(ppi) niʔï-ba 'sun'. M (kúuxe-o) níʔi-ba. B niʔ-pa (kʰóóxí-expʰi).

67 *kóoxïí 'day'. M kúuxe. B kʰóóxïí.

72 *xííní-xï 'earth'. M xííni-(xe). B íínʸï-xï.

7 *níxï-miïʔo 'ear'. M níxi-meeʔu. B níími̊ʔo (∅ exception).

202 *á(x)áa-nï 'he'. M áxáa-nï. B áá-nïḯ (∅ exception).

5 *tíxï-ʔo, *tíxï-ʔ(exï) 'nose'. M tíxï-ʔu. B tʰíxï-ʔo, tʰíí-ʔexï (∅ exception only if
the second form, meaning 'nostril', is actually a cognate).

269 *(óka)-(x)ítto 'horn'. M íttu (∅ exception). B ókʰa-xíxtʰo.

Syllable-final /x/ in Bora normally occurs preceding aspirated stops and
is the reflex of PBM geminate voiceless stops. It is listed under each of
these individually. There are a few examples in the wordlist and in the
dictionary of word-final /x/. None of these examples appears to have a
Muinane cognate.

All available examples from Thiesen and Thiesen's phonology (1975:7)
and from the Bora dictionary of syllable-final /x/ followed by an unaspirated stop are as follows. The first two examples are from Thiesen and

Thiesen. It is unclear why they are not found in the dictionary (which was checked by computer).

> **B** *axtᵏʸúβaxa* 'blue cloth'.
> **B** *ó pʰatsʰárixkʸó* 'I bother'.

The next three examples are from the Bora dictionary. Note that the word for 'snail' has two forms, the first of which is quite normal phonologically and has a Muinane cognate, whereas the second, which is phonologically odd in several ways (note the initial /ts/ before /o/) appears to be some sort of deformation of the first form. In the last example there is a morpheme break between the /x/ and the /kʷ/. Thus we see that this type of combination is almost nonexistent in Bora, and shows no link with PBM.

> ***bó()*** 'owl'. **M** *búru.* **B** *póxpoó.*
> ***xíʰtts(ï)ko,*** *****?*** 'snail'. **M** *xísiku.* **B** *íxtsʰïkʰo, tsoxtsókʰo.*
> **B** *xíïxïx, xíïxïx-kʷa.* 'okay'.

In the dictionary /x/ also occurs once before /n/: /noxnópa/ 'casabe'; in Allin's data it occurs several more times. In all of these environments /x/ is very rare, and Thiesen and Thiesen (1975) found no examples of /x/ before /pʸ t ts k kʷ/, but only before /p tʸ kʸ č/ (they give no example for /č/). The dictionary does yield one example each before /ts, kʷ/, as shown above.

PBM **β /(a)i__* > M *β*, B *βʸ* (Mr *β*).
199 **aiβéxiï-be* 'chief'. **M** *aíβoxíí-bo.* **B** *aβʸéxiï-pe* (**Mr** *áiβéxiï-pe*).
288 **kaʔts(iï)βe, *(čai)ʔts(ii)βe* 'sit'. **M** *kásííβe-ʔi.* **B** *kʰárárixííβe, čʰaʔčʰííβʸe* (**Mr** lacking).
      Noncognate examples:
121 *(gagááíβe)* 'tail'. **B** *kʷakʷááβʸe* (**Mr** lacking).
279 *(piiβéte)* 'ability'. **B** *pʰiiβʸérʰe* (**Mr** lacking).
287 **kagááí-(βe)* 'lie down'. **M** *kágáí-kini-ʔi.* **B** *kʰakʷáá-βʸe* (**Mr** lacking).
292 *(áiiβétso)* 'burn'. **B** *áiiβʸétsʰo, aííβʸe* (**Mr** *aiiβe*).
312 *(mïrííβe), (maxááβe)* 'wet'. **B** *mïrííβʸe, maxááβe* (**Mr** lacking).
351 *(íččiβétso, íttsiβétso)* 'cause to leave'. **B** *íxčʰiβʸétsʰo* (**Mr** lacking).
PBM **β* > M *β*, B *β*.
 35 **βáaʔβága* 'lungs'. **M** *βáβáágano, βáaβaga.* **B** *βaʔβákʷa.*
102 **nííβï-gai* 'deer'. **M** *nííβï-gai.* **B** *nííβï-kʷa.*
129 **xíiβaá* 'macaw'. **M** *xéeβa.* **B** *ííβaá.*
227 **kíβe-ne.* 'black'. **M** *kíβo-no.* **B** *kʰííβe-ne.*
281 **gixí-βe* 'die'. **M** *gíxé-βe-ʔi.* **B** *tsixí-βe.*
282 **gíxi-βé-tso* 'kill'. **M** *gíxé-βe-su-ʔi.* **B** *tsíxi-βé-tsʰo.*
289 *?*(í)xo(k)ííβe* 'stand'. **M** *xúijééβe-ʔi.* **B** *íxʸokʰííβe.*
295 **aittíβá-ne* 'green'. **M** *attʸïβa-no.* **B** *axtʰʸïβa, axtʰʸïβá-ne.*
328 **kíβé-ne, *kíβéʔ-teé-né* 'dark'. **M** *kíβo-no, kíβó-to-no.* **B** *kʰííβe-ne, kʰííβé-ʔtʰeé-né.*

338 *tsíîʔxíβa-tí-ne 'dull'. M síixeβa-ti-no. B tsʰíʔxíβa-tʰí-ne.
339 *tsíîʔxíβá-ne 'sharp'. M síixéβa-no. B tsʰíʔxíβá-ne.
340 *xiin(í)-βá-ne 'dirty'. M xííni-βa-no. B iinⁿí-βá-ne.
342 *mééβa-ne 'smooth'. M móóβa-no. B mééβa-ne.
343 *tsa-tíkkeβe 'straight'. M sá-tíkkoβo. B tsʰatʰíxkʰe-βe.
361 *mattsí-βa 'sing'. M másíβa-ʔi. B maxtsʰí-βa.
126 *(β)íîríʔii 'toad'. M bíiriʔi (b exception). B βíîríʔii.

2.12. Nasals. This section presents the rules for the nasals *m and *n.

PBM *m /ai__ > M m, B mʸ.
The only cognate example for this rule in the wordlist appears to be a counterexample; the final morpheme, however, was probably added after the *ai was reduced to /a/, so this is not an adequate counterexample. There were a number of examples of /amʸ/ in the Bora dictionary, two of which yielded cognates:
*pikkí-gáimi 'type of ant'. M ɸíikkí-gaimi. B pʰixʸíkʷámʸiîpe (Mr lacking).
*()-gáimi 'mosquitos'. M éésú-gáimi. B kʷaámʸï (Mr lacking).
 24 *(mé)-ʔóttsí-gai-míiʔo 'fingernail'. M úse-gai-méeʔu. B (mé)-ʔóxtsʰí-kʷa-míîʔo (m exception).
271 *(mé)-ʔóttsí-gai-míiʔo 'claw'. M asi-ʔúsé-gai-méeʔu. B (mé)-ʔóxtsʰí-kʷa-míîʔo (m exception).
PBM *m /i__e > M m, B mʸ (Mr m).
122 *xíinime 'snake'. M xíinimo. B íinⁿimʸe (Mr íinime).
146 *píime(ba) 'ant'. M ɸiimo. B pʰíimʸepa (Mr lacking).
156 *(ébáxák)ím(ai)x(i), ??*im(áí)x(í) 'fruit'. M óbáxákímaxe. B imʸéxï (Mr iméxi).
PBM *m /i__i > M m, B m.
224 *imí-ne, *imí-(gayï), *(imiáá)-ne 'good'. M imi-(no). B imí-kʷï, imiáá-ne.
225 *imi-tí-ne 'bad'. M imi-ti-no. B imi-tʰyí-ne.
PBM *m > M m, B m.
 7 *níxï-miiʔo 'ear'. M níxi-meeʔu. B níîmiʔo.
 9 *ímiko 'forehead'. M ímeku. B ʔímɨkʰo, ʔímíkʰo-ï.
 14 *(kíîdïï) míi(kko)ʔo 'chest'. M kíidii méeʔu. B (mé)-míxkʰoʔo.
 15 *(mé)-míppaine 'breast'. M míɸaño. B (mé)-míxpʰanʸe.
 16 *(áá)-míiʔo 'abdomen'. 14 M kíidii méeʔu. 16 B (má)-áámiʔo.
 27 *(mé)-mímo-() 'knee'. M mému-ba. B (mé)-mímo-kʰo.
 31 *(iáábe) (mé)-ʔmíiʔe(é) 'skin'. M méeʔe. B (mé)-ʔmíîʔeé, iáápe míîʔe.
 41 *míamínaa 'people', M míyáminaa. B míamĭnaa, mĭnaa.
 46 *tsíimene 'baby, infant'. M séemene. B tsʰíimene.
 49 *moóai 'river'. M múúai. B moóa.
 66 *míikíri-gai 'star'. M méékiri-gai. B míikʰïrï-kʷa, míikʰïrï.
 75 *káamée-xa 'house'. M káamooxa. B kʰáámée-xa. Many more examples.
PBM *n /ai__i > M ñ, B ñ.
143 *gáainiʔo 'louse'. M gáañiʔu. B kʷáániʔyo.
335 *aini-(ne) 'thin'. M áñino. B ani.
PBM *n /ai__ > M ñ, B nʸ.
 4 *íîʔ-gáí-neé, *(mé)-íîʔgá(xii) 'tooth'. M íí-gai, íí-ga-ñe. B íʔkʷáxii, mé-ʔkʷáxii, íʔ-kʷá-nʸeé.

15 *(mé)-míppaine 'breast'. M mípaño. B (mé)-míxpʰanʸe.
95 *gáiníï-ga 'arrow'. M gañíí-ga. B kʷánʸíï-kʷa (Mr lacking).
112 *máaína?o 'iguana'. M mááñá?u. B máánʸa?o.
133 *ainï 'buzzard'. M áñi. B anʸï.
165 *baine 'tobacco'. M báño. B panʸe.
234 *() (mé)-íí?gai-neé 'front teeth, incisors'. M di-xéxé-ba íí-ga-ño. B pʰiineéné mé-?kʷa-nʸeé.
294 *tí-ppai-ne 'red'. M tíɸai-ño. B tʰíxpʰa-nʸe.
319 *míppáine-ppáiko 'milk'. M míɸaño-ɸái?u. B míxpʰánʸe-xpʰákʰʸo.
Doubtful item:
366 ?*(ai)n(ó)ïˀ(i)kko() 'fear'. M ñíˀikku-?i. B nóïˀkʰóče, nïˀnéβe.

PBM   *n /i__ > M n, B nʸ.
72 *xííní-xi 'earth'. M xííni-(xe). B íínʸï-xi.
122 *xíinime 'snake'. M xíinimo. B íínʸimʸe (Mr íinime).
129 *ín(a)?ai 'macaw'. M inó?ai. B ínʸa?a.
182 *míínéékkïï 'two'. M míínokki. B mínʸéékʰïï.
187 *()-?ottsi-tï mííné(k)kïï 'seven'. M sa-?úse xúúga-?use-ti míínokkí. B inʸexkʰïé-?oxtsʰí ..., í-?yoxtsʰi-tʰí mínʸéékʰïï.
192 *nii?née-né(-re) 'last'. M níínoono. B ni?nʸée-né-re.
256 *xíneé 'this'. M xíno. B ínʸeé.
305 *xíneé-ri 'here'. M xinééri. B ínʸeéri (Mr lacking).
336 *báá?rí-ne(-íβí) 'short'. M bááre-ne. B pá?rí-nʸeïβí.
340 *xiin(í)-βá-ne 'dirty'. M xííni-βa-no. B iinʸï-βá-ne.
369 *gii-ne 'down (below)'. M gíi-no. B číínʸe (Mr lacking). This rule applies even before *i, e.g., 122 (but not in Mr).

PBM   *n /__ > M n, B n.
1 *(mé)-?níxi-() 'tongue'. M néxe-ba. B nííxi-kʷa, mé-?níxi-kʷa.
3 *(mé)-xí-niba 'lip'. M xí-niba. B (mé)-ínipa.
7 *níxï-mii?o 'ear'. M níxi-mee?u. B níími?o.
8 *nígaï 'head'. M nígai. B nííkʷaï.
19 *(mé)-nékkï-gai 'arm'. M nókki-gai. B (mé)-néxï-kʷa.
41 *míamínaa 'people'. M míyáminaa. B míamínaa, mínaa.
46 *tsíimene 'baby, infant'. M séemene. B tsʰíímene.
48 *ní-ppaiko 'water'. M ɸai?u, ní-ɸáí?u. B ní-xpʰakʰʸo.
61 *níkke-xi 'sky'. M níkke-xe. B níxkʰʸe-xi.
62 *níixa-ba 'rain'. M níixa-ba. B níixʸa-pa.
64 *kóoxí-e(ppi) nïˀï-ba 'sun'. M (kúuxe-o) níˀi-ba. B nïˀ-pa (kʰóóxí-expʰi).
86 *ts(í)níkó?o 'fish net'. M síni-ku?u. B tsʰíníï, tsʰíní-kʰóó?o, tsʰíní-kʰóó?a.
221 *nomi-(ni-ni) 'small'. M núméné-ne. B nʸomi (nʸ exception).

2.13. Liquids. This section presents the rules for the PBM liquids *r and *y.

PBM   *r /ai__ > M rʸ, B y (Mr rʸ).
All three of the cognate examples for this rule in the wordlist have experienced some sort of modification of the preceding vowel, which in each case has prevented the rule from applying on one side or the other. It is unclear why this is so. One good cognate set was obtained from the

dictionaries; with this and by analogy with the following rule I consider this rule adequately established.

130 **b(ai)rí(gai)* 'toucan'. M *bár*ʸ*ígai*. B *períí*ʔ*yo*.
342 **(p)(ai)riïkí-ne* 'smooth'. M *pár*ʸ*ííki-no* B *p*ʰ*íriïk*ʰ*í-ne*.
350 **(k)átí(kkaáí)ro, ?*(g)átí(xi)ro* 'push'. M *gátíxeru-*ʔ*i*. B *k*ʰ*át*ʰ*íxk*ʰ*aáyo* (Mr same).

Noncognate example:

221 **()-ne-gayï* 'small'. M *áxášu-no-gayi*. B *áyá-né-k*ʷ*ï* (Mr *ár*ʸ*á-né-k*ʷ*ï*).

Example from the dictionaries:

**gáirii*ʔ*á(ro)* 'twist, squeeze'. M *gár*ʸ*íí*ʔ*áñi*ʔ*i*. B *k*ʷ*áyiï*ʔ*áro* (Mr lacking).

PBM **r /i__ > M r, B y* (Mr *r /i__i, r*ʸ */i__*).
44 **gi*ʔ*í-ro(bi)* 'father'. M *gí*ʔ*í(rubi)*. B *či*ʔ*í-yo, či*ʔ*í-ï* (Mr lacking).
82 **gíri-*ʔ*ijo* 'cooking pot'. M *girí-*ʔ*iju*. B *číyi-*ʔ*čo* (Mr *číri-*ʔ*čo*).
125 **čiráágai* 'coral snake'. M *číráágai*. B *č*ʰ*iiyák*ʷ*a* (Mr lacking).
220 **giraa-ne* 'big'. M *gíráa-no*. B *čiya-* (Mr *čír*ʸ*aáne*).

Noncognate example, origin ambiguous (**r* or **y*):

348 *(tákiyó*ʔ*kó, tákiró*ʔ*kó)* 'rub'. B *t*ʰ*ák*ʰ*iyó*ʔ*k*ʰ*ó* (Mr lacking).

PBM **r > M r, B r*.
45 **ga*ʔ*á-ro(bi)* 'mother'. M *gá*ʔ*á(rubi)*. B *k*ʷ*a*ʔ*á-ro, k*ʷ*a*ʔ*á-ï*.
66 **mííkïrï-gai* 'star'. M *méékiri-gai*. B *míík*ʰ*írï-k*ʷ*a, míik*ʰ*ïrï*.
126 **(β)íírí*ʔ*ií* 'toad'. M *bíírí*ʔ*i*. B *βíírí*ʔ*ii*.
130 **r(í)(?)oó(*ʔ*o)* 'toucan'. M *rí*ʔ*úú*ʔ*u*. B *ríioó*.
145 **má*ʔ*arí(miï-be)* 'termite'. M *má*ʔ*ari*. B *má*ʔ*arímiï-pe*.
261 **pamere, *pa-nee-(re)* 'all'. M *φámóro, φáá-no*. B *p*ʰ*ámeére, p*ʰ*áneére*.
267 **díïrïba* 'grease'. M *díïriba*. B *tíïrïpa*.
305 **xíneé-ri* 'here'. M *xinééri*. B *ín*ʸ*eéri*.
330 **k(a)rí(ko)-né* 'wide'. M *káréku-no*. B *k*ʰ*orii-né*.
336 **báá*ʔ*rí-ne(-íβí)* 'short'. M *bááre-ne*. B *pá*ʔ*rí-n*ʸ*eíβí*.
342 **rï(tí)rí(tï)-(ko-ne)* 'smooth'. M *ríri-ku-no*. B *rït*ʰ*írít*ʰ*ï*.
353 **gá(č)ére(á)ko* 'split'. M *gájéréku-*ʔ*i*. B *k*ʷ*áč*ʰ*éreák*ʰ*o*.
359 **xoorii-(ne)* 'swell'. M *xúúri-*ʔ*i*. B *oóri*.
369 **baári* 'down (on ground)'. M *báari*. B *paá(ri)*.

The PBM **r* was probably a voiced alveolar trill. The Bora reflex varies from a voiced alveolar trill to a voiced retroflexed alveolar fricative, whereas the Muinane reflex varies from a voiceless alveolar trill to a voiceless retroflexed alveolar affricate.

PBM **y > M y, B y*.
17 **y(óóβihi)* 'back'. M *yóobai*. B (Mr *yóóβihi*).
74 **(xíí)né-gai-yï-*ʔ*ai* 'sand'. M *xííni-gai-yi-*ʔ*ai*. B *nék*ʷ*a-yíí-*ʔ*a, néék*ʷ*a-yï*.
251 **(xíí)-négaiyï-*ʔ*áí* 'pebbles'. M *xíí-nigaiyi-*ʔ*ai*. B *nék*ʷ*ayíí-*ʔ*á*.
268 **íí*ʔ*yï* 'egg'. M *íyi*. B *íí*ʔ*yíï(í)* (Mr *íí*ʔ*ïï*).
352 **íjaáyo* 'hit'. M *íjáyu-*ʔ*i*. B *íčaáyo* (Mr lacking).

Noncognate examples (see also **r*, *ʔ and *∅ in §2.15):

58 **kííxï-gai-(yï)* 'charcoal'. M *kííxi-gai-kku*. B *k*ʰ*ííxí-k*ʷ*a-yï*.
147 **páaga-xï, *paagá-(yï)* 'spider'. M *φáaga-xe*. B *p*ʰ*aak*ʷ*á-yï, p*ʰ*áák*ʷ*a-xï*.
105 **(čuyíyi)* 'cebus monkey'. M *čuyíyi*.

15 *(mé)-mǐppaine 'breast'. M mɨ́ɸaño. B (mé)-mɨ́xpʰanʸe.
95 *gáinɨ́ɨ-ga 'arrow'. M gañɨ́ɨ-ga. B kʷánʸɨ́ɨ-kʷa (Mr lacking).
112 *mááɨna?o 'iguana'. M mááñá?u. B máánʸa?o.
133 *ainɨ̈ 'buzzard'. M áñɨ. B anʸɨ̈.
165 *baine 'tobacco'. M báño. B panʸe.
234 *() (mé)-íí?gai-neé 'front teeth, incisors'. M di-xéxé-ba íí-ga-ño. B pʰɨɨneéné
     mé-?kʷa-nʸeé.
294 *tɨ̌-ppai-ne 'red'. M tɨ́ɸai-ño. B tʰɨ́xpʰa-nʸe.
319 *mɨ̌ppáíne-ppáiko 'milk'. M mɨ́ɸaño-ɸái?u. B mɨ́xpʰánʸe-xpʰákʰʸo.
     Doubtful item:
366 ?*(ai)n(ó)ɨ̈?(i)kko() 'fear'. M ñɨ́?ikku-?i. B nóɨ̈?kʰóče, nɨ̈?néβe.
PBM   *n /i__ > M n, B nʸ.
72 *xɨ́ɨnɨ̈-xɨ 'earth'. M xɨ́ɨni-(xe). B íínʸɨ̈-xɨ.
122 *xɨ́inime 'snake'. M xɨ́inimo. B íínʸimʸe (Mr íínime).
129 *ɨ́n(a)?ai 'macaw'. M ɨ́nó?ai. B ɨ́nʸa?a.
182 *mɨ́ɨnéékkɨ̈ɨ̈ 'two'. M mɨ́ɨnokkɨ. B mɨ́nʸéékʰɨ̈ɨ̈.
187 *()-?ottsɨ́-tɨ̈ mɨ́ɨné(k)kɨ̈ɨ̈ 'seven'. M sa-?úse xúúga-?use-tɨ mɨ́ɨnokkɨ́.
     B ɨnʸexkʰɨ̈é-?oxtsʰɨ́ . . . , ɨ́-?yoxtsʰɨ̈-tʰɨ́ mɨ́nʸéékʰɨ̈ɨ̈.
192 *nii?née-né(-re) 'last'. M níínoono. B ni?nʸée-né-re.
256 *xineé 'this'. M xíno. B ɨ́nʸeé.
305 *xineé-ri 'here'. M xinééri. B ɨ́nʸeéri (Mr lacking).
336 *báá?rí-ne(-ɨ̈βɨ́) 'short'. M bááre-ne. B pá?rí-nʸeɨ̈βɨ́.
340 *xiin(ɨ̈)-βá-ne 'dirty'. M xɨ́ɨni-βa-no. B iinʸɨ̈-βá-ne.
369 *gíi-ne 'down (below)'. M gíi-no. B čiinʸe (Mr lacking). This rule applies even
     before *i, e.g., 122 (but not in Mr).
PBM   *n /__ > M n, B n.
1 *(mé)-?nɨ́xi-() 'tongue'. M néxe-ba. B nɨ́ɨ̈xi-kʷa, mé-?nɨ́xi-kʷa.
3 *(mé)-xɨ̌-niba 'lip'. M xɨ́-niba. B (mé)-ɨ́nipa.
7 *nɨ́xɨ̈-mɨɨ?o 'ear'. M nɨ́xi-mee?u. B nɨ́ɨ̈mɨ?o.
8 *nɨ́gai 'head'. M nɨ́gai. B nɨ́ɨ̈kʷaɨ̈.
19 *(mé)-nékkɨ̈-gai 'arm'. M nókki-gai. B (mé)-néxɨ̈-kʷa.
41 *mɨ́amɨ̌naa 'people'. M mɨ́yámɨnaa. B mɨ́amɨ̌naa, mɨ̌naa.
46 *tsɨ́ɨmene 'baby, infant'. M séemene. B tsʰɨ́ɨmene.
48 *nɨ̌-ppaiko 'water'. M ɸai?u, nɨ́-ɸáí?u. B nɨ̌-xpʰakʰʸo.
61 *níkke-xɨ 'sky'. M níkke-xe. B níxkʰʸe-xɨ.
62 *níixa-ba 'rain'. M níixa-ba. B níixʸa-pa.
64 *kóoxí-e(ppi) nɨ̈?ɨ̈-ba 'sun'. M (kúuxe-o) nɨ́?ɨ-ba. B nɨ̈?-pa (kʰóóxí-expʰi).
86 *ts(í)nɨ̈kó?o 'fish net'. M síni-ku?u. B tsʰɨ́nɨ̈ɨ̈, tsʰɨ́nɨ̈-kʰóó?o, tsʰɨ́nɨ̈-kʰóó?a.
221 *nomɨ-(nɨ-nɨ) 'small'. M núméné-ne. B nʸomɨ (nʸ exception).

2.13. Liquids. This section presents the rules for the PBM liquids *r and *y.

PBM   *r /ai__ > M rʸ, B y (Mr rʸ).
       All three of the cognate examples for this rule in the wordlist have
       experienced some sort of modification of the preceding vowel, which in each
       case has prevented the rule from applying on one side or the other. It is
       unclear why this is so. One good cognate set was obtained from the

dictionaries; with this and by analogy with the following rule I consider this
rule adequately established.

130 *b(ai)rí(gai) 'toucan'. M bár^yígai. B períí?yo.

342 *(p)(ai)riïkí-ne 'smooth'. M pár^yíiki-no B pʰíriïkʰí-ne.

350 *(k)átí(kkaáí)ro, ?*(g)átí(xi)ro 'push'. M gátíxeru-?i. B kʰátʰíxkʰaáyo
     (Mr same).
     Noncognate example:

221 *()-ne-gayï 'small'. M áxášu-no-gayi. B áyá-né-kʷï (Mr ár^yá-né-kʷï).
     Example from the dictionaries:
     *gáiriї?á(ro) 'twist, squeeze'. M gár^yíí?áñi?i. B kʷáyiï?áro (Mr lacking).

PBM *r /i__ > M r, B y (Mr r /i__i, r^y /i__).

44   *gi?í-ro(bi) 'father'. M gí?í(rubi). B či?í-yo, či?í-ï (Mr lacking).

82   *gíri-?ijo 'cooking pot'. M gírí-?iju. B číyi-?čo (Mr číri-?čo).

125 *čiráágai 'coral snake'. M čiráágai. B cʰiiyákʷa (Mr lacking).

220 *giraa-ne 'big'. M gíráa-no. B čiya- (Mr cír^yaáne).
     Noncognate example, origin ambiguous (*r or *y):

348 (tákiyó?kó, tákiró?kó) 'rub'. B tʰákʰiyó?kʰó (Mr lacking).

PBM *r > M r, B r.

45   *ga?á-ro(bi) 'mother'. M gá?á(rubi). B kʷa?á-ro, kʷa?á-ï.

66   *míïkíri-gai 'star'. M méékiri-gai. B míïkʰíri-kʷa, míïkʰíri.

126 *(β)ïïrí?ii 'toad'. M bíïri?i. B βïïrí?ii.

130 *r(í)(?)oó(?o) 'toucan'. M rí?úú?u. B ríioó.

145 *má?arí(miï-be) 'termite'. M má?ari. B má?arímiï-pe.

261 *pamere, *pa-nee-(re) 'all'. M ɸámóro, ɸáá-no. B pʰámeére, pʰáneére.

267 *díïrïba 'grease'. M díïriba. B tíïrïpa.

305 *xíneé-ri 'here'. M xinééri. B ín^yeéri.

330 *k(a)rí(ko)-né 'wide'. M káréku-no. B kʰorií-né.

336 *báá?ri-ne(-íβí) 'short'. M bááre-ne. B pá?rí-n^yeíβí.

342 *rï(tí)rí(tï)-(ko-ne) 'smooth'. M rírí-ku-no. B rïtʰírítʰï.

353 *gá(č)ére(á)ko 'split'. M gájéréku-?i. B kʷáčʰéreákʰo.

359 *xooríi-(ne) 'swell'. M xúúri-?i. B oóri.

369 *baári 'down (on ground)'. M báari. B paá(ri).

The PBM *r was probably a voiced alveolar trill. The Bora reflex varies
from a voiced alveolar trill to a voiced retroflexed alveolar fricative,
whereas the Muinane reflex varies from a voiceless alveolar trill to a
voiceless retroflexed alveolar affricate.

PBM *y > M y, B y.

17   *y(óóβihi) 'back'. M yóobai. B (Mr yóóβihi).

74   *(xíí)né-gai-yï-?ai 'sand'. M xííni-gai-yi-?ai. B nékʷa-yïï-?a, néékʷa-yï.

251 *(xíí)-négaiyï-?áí 'pebbles'. M xíí-nigaiyi-?ai. B nékʷayïï-?á.

268 *ííʔyïï 'egg'. M ííyi. B ííʔyïï(í) (Mr ií?ïï).

352 *íjaáyo 'hit'. M íjayu-?i. B íčaáyo (Mr lacking).
     Noncognate examples (see also *r, *? and *∅ in §2.15):

58   *kííxí-gai-(yï) 'charcoal'. M kííxi-gai-kku. B kʰííxí-kʷa-yï.

147 *páaga-xi, *paagá-(yï) 'spider'. M ɸáaga-xe. B pʰaakʷá-yï, pʰáákʷa-xi.

105 *(čuyíyi) 'cebus monkey'. M čuyíyi.

220 *(kóyɨno) 'big'. M kóyɨno.
368 *(gááyɨkkɨnɨ-ʔi) 'hold'. M gááyɨkkɨnɨ-ʔi.

The status of *y is somewhat unclear, since in many examples /y/ in both of the extant languages can also come from several other sources. However, because of examples such as 17 (with initial *y) and 268 (which could only have lost the glottal before a PBM consonant) and because, although Muinane generated epenthetic /y/s after front vowels, it appears that Bora did not (see §2.15), I conclude that I must posit a PBM *y phoneme. The items listed above would be hard to explain without positing a PBM *y phoneme.

2.14. Early vowel rules. These rules show the changes that occurred in the vowel system from the protolanguage into the two extant languages, notably the four-vowel rotation in Muinane and the loss of the offglide in *ai (in some cases in Muinane and in all cases in Bora). The vowel-harmony rules in Muinane (which apparently occurred after the separation of the two languages) are described in §2.15.

PBM   *a > M a, B a.
3   *(mé)-xɨ́-niba 'lip'. M xɨ́-niba. B (mé)-ɨ́nipa.
6   *(me)-ʔáájɨ̈̈ 'eye'. M áájɨ̈. B (me)-ʔáčɨ̈̈.
11   *niʔiba 'crocodile'. M níʔiba. B niʔpa.
32   *bákkɨ̈̈ 'bone'. M bákkɨ. B páxkʰɨ̈̈.
35   *βáaʔβága 'lungs'. M βáβáágano, βáaβaga. B βaʔβákʷa.
39   *tsaa-ppi 'one-male'. M sáa-ɸi. B tsʰaa-pʰi.
41   *mɨ́amɨ̈́naa 'people'. M mɨ́yámɨnaa. B mɨ́amɨ̈́naa, mɨ́naa.
42   *taxɨ, *áɨ́-táxɨ̈́, *áɨxɨ̈̈ 'husband'. M átⁿʸaxe, táxe, aixɨ. B tʰaxɨ, áxʸɨ̈̈, átʰʸáxɨ̈.
43   *taába, *áɨ́-táabaá 'wife'. M táaba, átⁿʸáaba. B tʰaápa, átʰʸáápaá.
45   *gaʔá-ro(bi) 'mother'. M gáʔá(rubi). B kʷaʔá-ro, kʷaʔá-ɨ.
52   *(ɨ́pá)-káa-xa-(neba), *káa-(mɨ) 'swamp'. M káa-me, ɨ́ɸá-káa-xa.
     B kʰááxánepa.
62   *nɨ́ɨxa-ba 'rain'. M nɨ́ɨxa-ba. B nɨ́ɨxʸa-pa. Many more examples.
PBM   *eCe > M eCe, B eCe.
275   *geéne 'eat fruit'. M gééne-ʔi, géénee-be. B čééne.
289   ?*(ɨ)xo(k)ɨ̈́ɨ̈́βe 'stand'. M xúJéééβe-ʔi, xúJééβee-be. B ɨ́xʸokʰɨ̈́ɨ̈́βe.
353   *gá(č)ére(á)ko 'split'. M gájéréku-ʔi. B kʷáčʰéreákʰo.
     This seems to be the only example of a rule which blocks the vowel rotation (i.e., prevents the next rule below from applying). This could not have been a later vowel-harmony rule in Muinane, because both *e's would have already become /o/. I found no clear counterexamples (though for 289 the change from *ɨ to *e is unexpected; see *ɨ below).
     The only apparent counterexample is the following item; the origin of the vowel following the *b, however, is doubtful:
291   *xɨ̈̈b(áɨ)ge 'tell'. M xɨ́ɨbege-ʔi, xɨ́ɨbogoo-bo. B ɨ̈́páče.

PBM *e /__ > M *o*, B *e*.

15 *(mé)-mḯppaine* 'breast'. M *míϕaño*. B *(mé)-mḯxp^{h}an^{y}e*.
19 *(mé)-nékkï-gai* 'arm'. M *nókkɨ-gai*. B *(mé)-néxï-k^{w}a*.
40 *gai-ge* 'woman'. M *gáí-go*. B *k^{w}a-če*.
75 *káamée-xa* 'house'. M *káamooxa*. B *k^{h}áámée-xa*.
100 *geéï* 'armadillo'. M *góóɨ*. B *čeéï*.
120 *giʔpe* 'mouse'. M *gíiϕo*. B *čiʔp^{hy}e*.
122 *xíinime* 'snake'. M *xíinimo*. B *íín^{y}im^{y}e*.
130 *nïge* 'toucan'. M *nígo*. B *nïče*.
146 *pɨime(ba)* 'ant'. M *ϕíimo*. B *p^{h}íim^{y}epa*.
152 *ïme-ʔe* 'tree'. M *ímo-ʔo*. B *íme-ʔe*.
165 *baine* 'tobacco'. M *báño*. B *pan^{y}e*.
170 *néebaba* 'annatto'. M *nóobaba*. B *néépapa*.
12 *xḯkk(e)ʔ(ai)* 'beard'. M *xíkkoʔai*. B *ïxk^{h}aʔe* (possible *a* exception). Many more examples.

PBM *ɨ > M *ɨ*, B *i*.

2 *ɨiʔ-xï* 'mouth'. M *íi-xɨ*. B *íʔx^yïi̇́*.
3 *(mé)-xḯ-niba* 'lip'. M *xɨ́-niba*. B *(mé)-ínipa*.
4 *ɨíʔ-gáí-neé*, *(mé)-ɨíʔgá(xɨɨ)* 'tooth'. M *íí-gai, íí-ga-ñe*. B *íʔk^{w}áxɨɨ, mé-ʔk^{w}áxɨɨ, íʔ-k^{w}á-n^{y}eé*.
8 *nígaï* 'head'. M *nígaɨ*. B *níík^{w}aï*.
11 *niʔiba* 'crocodile'. M *níʔiba*. B *niʔpa*.
16=244=245=272 *(mé)-ɨiʔbá(ï)* 'stomach'. M *íiba*. B *íʔpáï, mé-ʔpáɨ́ɨ̇*.
38=39 *gai-ppi* 'man'. M *gáí-ϕi*. B *k^{w}a-xp^{h}i*.
44 *giʔí-ro(bi)* 'father'. M *gíʔi(rubi)*. B *čiʔí-yo, čiʔí-ï*.
49 *teé-ʔi* 'river'. M *téé-ʔi*. B *t^{h}eé-ʔi*.
57 *báí-giíxï* 'ash'. M *bai-giíxɨ*. B *pá-čiíx^{y}ï*.
61 *níkke-xɨ* 'sky'. M *níkke-xe*. B *níxk^{hy}e-xɨ*.
62 *nííxa-ba* 'rain'. M *nííxa-ba*. B *nííx^{y}a-pa*. Many more examples.

PBM *o > M *u*, B *o*.

5 *tḯxï-ʔo*, *tḯxï-ʔ(exï)* 'nose'. M *tíxɨ-ʔu*. B *t^{h}íxï-ʔo, t^{h}íɨ́-ʔexï*.
7 *nḯxï-mɨɨʔo* 'ear'. M *níxɨ-meeʔu*. B *nɨ́ɨ́mɨʔo*.
9 *ïmiko* 'forehead'. M *ímeku*. B *ʔïmik^{h}o, ʔïmík^{h}o-ï*.
22 *(mé)-ʔóttsɨɨ* 'hand'. M *úse*. B *(mé)-ʔóxts^{h}ɨɨ*.
27 *(mé)-mímo-()* 'knee'. M *mému-ba*. B *(mé)-mímo-k^{h}o*.
44 *giʔí-ro(bi)* 'father'. M *gíʔi(rubi)*. B *čiʔí-yo, čiʔí-ï*.
45 *gaʔá-ro(bi)* 'mother'. M *gáʔá(rubi)*. B *k^{w}aʔá-ro, k^{w}aʔá-ï*.
49 *moóai* 'river'. M *múúai*. B *moóa*.
67 *kóoxɨɨ* 'day'. M *kúuxe*. B *k^{h}óóxɨɨ*.
68 *pekko* 'night'. M *ϕúkku*. B *p^{h}exk^{h}o*.
77 *gééʔo-ga* 'doorway'. M *gúʔú-ga*. B *čééʔo-k^{w}a*.
82 *gíri-ʔijo* 'cooking pot'. M *gírí-ʔiju*. B *číyi-ʔčo*. Many more examples.

PBM *ï > M *ɨ*, B *ï*.

2 *ɨiʔ-xï* 'mouth'. M *íi-xɨ*. B *íʔx^yïi̇́*.
3 *(mé)-xḯ-niba* 'lip'. M *xɨ́-niba*. B *(mé)-ínipa*.
5 *tḯxï-ʔo*, *tḯxï-ʔ(exï)* 'nose'. M *tíxɨ-ʔu*. B *t^{h}íxï-ʔo, t^{h}íɨ́-ʔexï*.
6 *(me)-ʔáájïɨ̇́* 'eye'. M *ááyɨɨ*. B *(me)-ʔáčïɨ̇́*.
7 *nḯxï-mɨɨʔo* 'ear'. M *níxɨ-meeʔu*. B *nɨ́ɨ́mɨʔo*.
9 *ïmiko* 'forehead'. M *ímeku*. B *ʔïmik^{h}o, ʔïmík^{h}o-ï*.

12 *xíkk(e)ʔ(ai) 'beard'. M xíkkoʔai. B íxkʰaʔe.
14 *(mé)-ppɨ́ɨ̈-xɨ 'chest'. M φéeyi-xe. B (mé)-xpʰɨ́ɨ̈-xɨ.
15 *(mé)-mɨ́ppaine 'breast'. M mɨ́φaño. B (mé)-mɨ́xpʰanʸe.
18 *(mé)-xɨ́xɨ-ba(ɨ̈) 'shoulder'. M xíxe-bai. B mé-ɨ́xɨ-pa.
19 *(mé)-nékkɨ̈-gai 'arm'. M nókki-gai. B (mé)-néxɨ̈-kʷa.
29 *(mé)-ttɨ̈-ʔaáí 'foot'. M tí-ʔai. B (mé)-xtʰɨ́ʔaá.
89 *n(ɨ̈)ts(ɨ́)ga-(gayɨ̈) 'knife'. M nɨ́ɨ́súga (u exception). B nɨ̈ɨtsʰɨ́kʷa-(kʷɨ̈).
365 *íbáts(ɨ̈)(ʔxáko) 'blow'. M ébásu-ʔi (u exception). B ɨpátsʰɨ̈ʔxákʰo.
99 *tɨ́páíʔoó(ɨ̈) 'puma'. M tɨ́φaiʔui (i exception). B tʰɨ́ɨ́pʰáʔyoóɨ̈
      (Mr tʰɨ́ɨ́pʰáiyóóʔi).
340 *xiin(ɨ́)-βá-ne 'dirty'. M xííni-βa-no (i exception). B iinʸɨ̈-βá-ne.
150 = 161 *tsókkómɨ̈xɨ 'grass'. M súkkumexe (e exception). B tsʰóxkʰómɨ̈xɨ.
156 *(ébáxák)ím(ai)x(ɨ), ??*im(áí)x(ɨ̈) 'fruit'. M óbáxákímaxe (e exception).
      B imʸéxɨ̈.
289 ?*(ɨ)xo(k)ɨ́ɨ́βe 'stand'. M xújééβe-ʔi, xújééβee-be (e exception). B íxʸokʰɨ́ɨ́βe.
356 *doʔxín(ɨ̈) 'tie'. M dúxéne-ʔi (e exception). B toʔxínɨ̈. Many more examples.

PBM *ɨ > M e, B ɨ.
  1 *(mé)-ʔníxɨ-() 'tongue'. M néxe-ba. B níɨ̈xɨ-kʷa, mé-ʔníxɨ-kʷa.
  7 *nɨ́xɨ̈-mɨ̈ɨ̈ʔo 'ear'. M níxɨ-meeʔu. B nɨ́ɨ̈mɨ̈ʔo.
  9 *ímɨko 'forehead'. M ímeku. B ʔɨ́mɨkʰo, ʔɨ́mɨ́kʰo-ɨ̈.
  10 *nígaɨ̈-xɨɨne, *nígaɨ̈-(ko) 'hair'. M nígai-xeene. B níɨ̈kʷa-kʰo, íʔxɨne,
       níɨ̈kʷákʰo-xɨ́(ʔi).
  14 *(mé)-ppɨ́ɨ̈-xɨ 'chest'. M φéeyi-xe. B (mé)-xpʰɨ́ɨ̈-xɨ.
  16 *(áá)-mɨ̈ɨ̈ʔo 'abdomen'. 14 M kɨ̈idɨ̈ méeʔu. 16 B (má)-áámɨ̈ʔo.
  18 *(mé)-xɨ́xɨ-ba(ɨ̈) 'shoulder'. M xíxe-bai. B mé-ɨ́xɨ-pa.
  22 *(mé)-ʔóttsɨ̈ 'hand'. M úse. B (mé)-ʔóxtsʰɨ̈.
  27 *(mé)-mímo-() 'knee'. M mému-ba. B (mé)-mímo-kʰo.
  31 *(iáábe) (mé)-ʔmɨ̈ɨ̈ʔe(é) 'skin'. M méeʔe. B (mé)-ʔmɨ́ɨ̈ʔeé, iáápe mɨ̈ɨ̈ʔe.
  34 *(mé)-xɨ̈ibɨ̈ɨ̈ 'heart'. M xéebɨ̈ɨ̈. B (mé)-ɨ́ɨ̈pɨ̈ɨ̈.
  42 *taxi, *áí-táxɨ̈, *áíxɨ̈ɨ̈ 'husband'. M átʸaxe, táxe, aixɨ. B tʰaxi, áxʸɨ̈ɨ̈, átʰʸáxɨ̈ɨ̈.
       Many more examples.

PBM *ai /__Pal.Con. (ɨ̈,dʸ,čj,šñ,rʸ) > M a, B a (all environments).
  4 *íɨ̈ʔ-gáí-neé, *(mé)-íɨ̈ʔgá(xɨ̈) 'tooth'. M íɨ̈-gai, íɨ̈-ga-ñe. B íʔkʷáxɨ̈ɨ̈, mé-ʔkʷáxɨ̈ɨ̈,
       íʔ-kʷá-nʸeé.
  15 *(mé)-mɨ́ppaine 'breast'. M mɨ́φaño. B (mé)-mɨ́xpʰanʸe.
  42 *taxi, *áí-táxɨ̈, *áíxɨ̈ɨ̈ 'husband'. M átʸaxe, táxe, aixɨ. B tʰaxi, áxʸɨ̈ɨ̈, átʰʸáxɨ̈ɨ̈.
  43 *taába, *áí-táabaá 'wife'. M táaba, átʸáaba. B tʰaápa, átʰʸáápaá.
  95 *gáínɨ̈ɨ̈-ga 'arrow'. M gañɨ̈ɨ̈-ga. B kʷánʸɨ̈ɨ̈-kʷa.
  112 *mááinaʔo 'iguana'. M mááñáʔu. B mááňʸaʔo.
  133 *ainɨ̈ 'buzzard'. M áñɨ. B anʸɨ̈.
  165 *baine 'tobacco'. M báño. B panʸe.
  214 *táí-tɨ́ɨ̈bo-ga 'my bow'. M ta-ɨ̈ɨ̈bu-ga. B tʰá-tʰʸɨ́poo-kʷa.
  234 *() (mé)-íɨ̈ʔgai-neé 'front teeth, incisors'. M di-xéxé-ba íɨ̈-ga-ño. B pʰɨ̈ineéné
       mé-ʔkʷa-nʸeé.
  277 *aittɨ́mɨ 'see'. M átʸíme-ʔi. B axtʰʸɨ́mɨ.
  294 *tɨ́-ppai-ne 'red'. M tɨ́φai-ño. B tʰɨ́xpʰa-nʸe.
  295 *aittɨ́βá-ne 'green'. M atɨ́ʸíβa-no. B axtʰʸíβa, axtʰʸɨ́βá-ne.
  308 *(áx)áittso-(ne), ?*(gaʔ)áittso-(ta) 'few, soon'. M áxášu-no. B kʷaʔáxčʰo-tʰa.
  319 *mɨ́ppáíne-ppáiko 'milk'. M mɨ́φaño-φáíʔu. B mɨ́xpʰánʸe-xpʰákʰʸo.

PBM *ai /__ > M *ai*, B *a*.

4   *íí?-gái-neé, *(mé)-íí?gá(xɨɨ) 'tooth'. M íí-gai, íí-ga-ñe. B í?kʷáxɨɨ, mé-?kʷáxɨɨ, í?-kʷá-nʸeé.

19 *(mé)-nékkɨ-gai 'arm'. M nókkɨ-gai. B (mé)-néxɨ-kʷa.

23 *(mé)-?óttsɨ-gai 'finger'. M úse-gai. B (mé)-?óxtsʰɨ-kʷa.

29 *(mé)-ttɨ̈-?aáí 'foot'. M tɨ̈-?ai. B (mé)-xtʰíí?aá.

30 *(mé)-ttɨ̈-gaái 'toe'. M tɨ-gai. B (mé)-xtʰɨ̈-kʷaá.

38 = 39 *gai-ppi 'man'. M gái-ɸi. B kʷa-xpʰi.

40 *gai-ge 'woman'. M gái-go. B kʷa-če.

42 *taxɨ, *ái-táxɨɨ, *áíxiɨ̈ 'husband'. M áttʸaxe, táxe, aixɨ. B tʰaxɨ, áxʸiɨ̈, átʰʸáxɨɨ.

48 *nɨ̈-ppaiko 'water'. M ɸaí?u, nɨ̈-ɸáí?u. B nɨ̈-xpʰakʰʸo.

49 *moóai 'river'. M múúai. B moóa.

56 *kɨ̈íxɨ-gai 'fire'. M kɨ̈íxɨ-gai. B kʰɨ̈íxɨ-kʷa.

57 *bái-giíxɨ̈ 'ash'. M bai-giíxɨ. B pá-čiíxʸɨ̈.

158 *ba(i)(k)ké-(?eke), *bá(i)(k)keé 'root'. M bakó-?oko (a exception). B páxkʰʸeé.

291 *xiɨ̈b(ái)ge 'tell'. M xɨ̈ɨbege-?i, xɨ̈ɨbogoo-bo (o exception). B iɨ̈páče.

156 *(ébáxák)ím(ai)x(ɨ), ??*im(ái)x(ɨ̈) 'fruit'. M óbáxákímaxe (a exception).
       B imʸéxɨ̈ (e exception).

130 *b(ai)rí(gai) 'toucan'. M bárʸígai. B periíʸyo (e exception).

360 *ɨttsam(áá)i, *ɨtts(o) 'think'. M ésámáái-?i. B ɨxtsʰaméí (ei exception), ɨxtsʰo.
       Exceptional item in which Bora lost the expected palatalization:

128 *páá(i)bɨ(?o) 'hummingbird'. M ɸááibe. B pʰáápɨ?o. Many more examples.

PBM *aɨ̈ > M *aɨ*, B *a, aɨ̈*.
       (The conditioning for the two Bora reflexes is unclear.)

8   *nígaɨ̈ 'head'. M nígaɨ. B niíkʷaɨ̈.

10 *nígaɨ̈-xɨɨne, *nígaɨ̈-(ko) 'hair'. M nígaɨ-xeene. B niíkʷa-kʰo, í?xɨne,
       niíkʷákʰo-xɨ̈(?i).

18 *(mé)-xɨ̈xɨ-ba(ɨ̈) 'shoulder'. M xɨ̈xe-bai. B mé-ɨ̈xɨ-pa.

16 = 244 = 245 = 272 *(mé)-iɨ̈?bá(ɨ̈) 'stomach'. M íiba (a exception). B í?páɨ̈,
       mé-?páiɨ̈.

235 *(mé)-?nɨ̈xɨ́-(gá)-nɨx(ɨ)k(áɨ̈) 'tip of tongue'. M néxe-ba-nixeke (e exception).
       B mé-?nɨ̈xɨ́-kʷá-nɨxkʰáɨ̈.

PBM *oɨ̈ > M *uɨ*, B *oɨ̈*.

92 *gáí?oóɨ̈(daa?i) 'club'. M gáí?uɨdaa?e. B kʷá?yoóɨ̈.

171 *díí-?oɨ̈ 'chili pepper'. M déé-?ui. B tɨ̈ɨ, tíí-?oɨ̈.

99 *tɨ̈páí?oó(ɨ̈) 'puma'. M tɨ̈ɸai?ui (ui exception). B tʰɨ̈ɨpʰá?yoóɨ̈
       (Mr tʰɨ̈ɨpʰáiyóó?i).

366 ?*(ai)n(ó)ɨ̈?(ɨ)kko() 'fear'. M nɨ̈?ikku-?i (i exception). B nóɨ̈?kʰóče, nɨ̈?néβe.

The three diphthongs (vowel sequences) which figure in the preceding rules did not all undergo offglide loss in Bora: *ai lost the offglide in all cases and *aɨ̈ in some cases, whereas *oɨ̈ always retained the offglide.

PBM *V?V > M *V?V*, B *V? /__stops, nasals*.
       Identical vowels:

64 *kóoxɨ́-e(ppi) nɨ̈?ɨ̈-ba 'sun'. M (kúuxe-o) ní?ɨ-ba. B nɨ̈?-pa (kʰóóxɨ́-expʰi).

65 *pékkó-e(ppi) nɨ̈?ɨ̈-ba 'moon'. M (ɸúkkuo) ní?ɨ-ba. B nɨ̈?-pa pʰéxkʰó-expʰi.

91 *bo?ódó-ga 'paddle'. M bú?údú-ga. B po?tó-kʷa, po?tó-xɨ.

11 *niʔiba 'crocodile'. M níʔiba. B niʔpa.
66 *xaʔadi 'cotton'. M xáʔadi. B aʔti.
284 *gaʔape 'fly'. M gáʔáɸe-ʔi. B kʷaʔpʰe.
297 *gaʔape-né, *gáʔap(é)(k)kïnï-né 'full'. M gáʔáɸo-no, gáʔáɸikkïnï-no.
     B kʷaʔpʰe, kʷáʔpʰé-kʰïnïné.
298 *béʔe-ne 'new'. M bóʔo-no. B péʔne.
     The following is the only possible example in which the vowels are not
     identical:
366 ?*(ai)n(ó)ïʔ(i)kko() 'fear'. M nïʔikku-ʔi. B nóïʔkʰóče, nïʔnéβe.
PBM *VʔV > M VʔV, B VʔV /__r,#.
     Identical vowels:
44 *giʔí-ro(bi) 'father'. M gíʔí(rubi). B čiʔí-yo, čiʔí-ï.
45 *gaʔá-ro(bi) 'mother'. M gáʔá(rubi). B kʷaʔá-ro, kʷaʔá-ï.
86 *ts(í)nïkóʔo 'fish net'. M síni-kuʔu. B tsʰínïï, tsʰínï-kʰóóʔo, tsʰínï-kʰóóʔa.
126 *(β)ïïríʔii 'toad'. M bííriʔi. B βííríʔii.
129 *ín(a)ʔai 'macaw'. M ínóʔai. B ínʸaʔa.
145 *máʔarí(mïï-be) 'termite'. M máʔarimáʔarímïï-pe.
152 *íme-ʔe 'tree'. M ímo-ʔo. B íme-ʔe.

2.15. Later vowel rules (Muinane). This section presents various rules,
mostly of vowel harmony, that functioned only in Muinane and apparently
applied after the completion of the vowel-rotation process detailed in
§2.14. Therefore, the rules are specified only in the second column, showing Early Muinane (EM) changes to Modern Muinane (M). The forms in
the first and third columns are given only for reference. Environments
given are all Muinane environments (i.e., subsequent to the vowel rotation), not protoenvironments.

Because of the fact that only the modern form is given of each Muinane
word, without the intermediate form which many of the rules imply, I
underline the Muinane vowel in question in each example. Also, in
Muinane verbs whose citation form ends in the /-ʔi/ suffix, I have also
included the form with the third person masculine singular suffix /-bo/
(which has a conditioned allomorph /-be/) to show synchronic alternation,
if any, between /e/ and /o/ in the stem.

There is one vowel, /o/ (from *e), for which a certain amount of
rule-ordering is necessary. This is clarified below.

PBM *e > (EM o /aiC__ > M o), B e.
15 *(mé)-míppaine 'breast'. M míɸañǫ. B (mé)-míxpʰanʸe.
40 *gai-ge 'woman'. M gái-gǫ. B kʷa-če.
165 *baine 'tobacco'. M báñǫ. B panʸe.
199 *aiβéxïï-be 'chief'. M aíβǫxíí-bo. B aβʸéxïï-pe.
294 *tí-ppai-ne 'red'. M tíɸai-ñǫ. B tʰíxpʰa-nʸe.
4 *ííʔ-gái-neé, *(mé)-ííʔgá(xïi) 'tooth'. M íí-gai, íí-ga-ñę (e exception). B íʔkʷáxïi,
     mé-ʔkʷáxïi, íʔ-kʷá-nʸeé.

PBM *e > (EM o /iC__ > M e), B e.
61 *níkke-xɨ 'sky'. M níkkę-xe. B nɨxkʰʸe-xɨ.
103 *kíkiíxe 'bat'. M kíkixę. B kʰɨkʰiíxʸe.
336 *báá?rí-ne(-íβí) 'short'. M bááre-nę. B pá?rí-nʸeíβí.
358 *aakí(t)te 'fall'. M áákéttę-?i. B aakʰitʰʸe.

PBM *e > (EM o /eC__ > M e), B e.
10 *nígaï-xɨine, *nígaï-(ko) 'hair'. M nígai-xeenę. B niíkʷa-kʰo, í?xine, niíkʷákʰo-xɨ(?i).
31 *(iáábe) (mé)-?mɨɨ?e(é) 'skin'. M mée?ę. B (mé)-?mɨɨ?eé, iáápe mɨɨ?e.
46 *tsɨimene 'baby, infant'. M séemęnę. B tsʰɨimene.
90 *mɨine-(ga) 'canoe'. M méénę-ga. B mɨine.
212 *amɨɨ?-áí-?óttsi-ne 'your hands'. M amɨɨ-?ai-?use-nę. B amɨ?á-?óxtsʰi-ne.
226 *tsítsɨɨ-ne 'white'. M séséé-nę. B tsʰitsʰɨɨ-ne, tsʰitsʰɨ.
241 *(mé)-?ótsɨ-(k)kéxɨ 'wrist'. M úse-kęxe. B (mé)-?ótsʰɨxkʰéxɨ.
243 í?xiine 'body hair'. M íxée-nę. B í?xi-ne.
281 *gíxɨ-βe 'die'. M gíxé-βę-?i. B ɨ ɨ̣xí-βe.
282 *gíxɨ-βé-tso 'kill'. M gíxé-βę-su-?i. B tsíxɨ-βé-tsʰo.
331 *ɨɨxɨ-né-(gáyɨ́) 'narrow'. M ɨ́ɨxe-nę. B ɨɨxɨ né-kʷɨ́.

As can be seen in item 46, the preceding rule applied recursively to succeeding syllables. This remains a synchronic phonological rule in Muinane, and is frequently seen to apply to certain suffixes such as /no/ (various meanings) and /ko/ (object marker). The second rule above, however, is not a synchronic rule in Muinane: the /-no/ suffix does not change to /-ne/ after stems ending in /i/ (Walton, Hensarling and Maxwell, in prep., §2.5.3). The present day application of the morphophonemic rules to /no/ follows (only one example of each allomorph is given, although there are numerous examples).

PBM *-ne > (EM -no > M -ne /e__), B -ne.
46 *tsɨimene 'baby, infant'. M séemene. B ɔ ɨimene.
PBM *-ne > (EM -no > M -no /i__), B -ne.
335 *íttsi-(ne) 'thin'. M ísi-no. B ɨxtsʰi.
PBM *-ne > (EM -no > M -no /__), B -ne.
225 *ími-tɨ́-ne 'bad'. M ími-ti-no. B ími-tʰʸɨ́-ne.

In Early Muinane, however, /no/ must have changed also after /i/, based on item 336 in the second rule above. This item provides evidence for rule layering: the Early Muinane /o/ must have changed before the /i/ did. Therefore, the two preceding rules, the only ones with a preenvironment, must have occurred before the rest of the vowel-harmony rules (with the exception of the /ai__ blocking rule below, also for /o/). Item 336 thus went through four stages:

Proto-Bora-Muinane: *báá?rí-ne*
Early Muinane A: *báári-no* (vowel rotation process)
Early Muinane B: *báári-ne* (see second rule for /e/ above)
Modern Muinane: *bááre-ne* (see rules for /i/ below)

The later rules for Early Muinane /o/ follow. These rules are both synchronic rules in Muinane today.

PBM **e* > (EM *o /__Ci* > M *e*), B *e*.
49 **teé-?i* 'river'. M *téé-?i*. B *tʰeé-?i*.
115 **meéni* 'collared peccary'. M *méeni*. B *meéni*.
160 **íméʔe-i* 'stick'. M *ímee̱ʔ-i*. B *íméʔe-i*.
250 **tée-?i-(gayï)*, **téé-(gai-?o)* 'stream'. M *te̱e̱-?i, téé-gai-?u*. B *tʰéé?í-kʷï*.
284 **ga?ape* 'fly'. M *gá?áɸe̱-?i, gá?áɸoo-bo*. B *kʷa?pʰe*.
285 **ïge* 'walk'. M *íge̱-?i, ígoo-bo*. B *ïče*.
288 **ka?ts(ïï)βe*, **(čai)?ts(ii)βe* 'sit'. M *kásííβe̱-?i, kásííβoo-bo, xújééβee-be*.
    B *kʰárárixííβe, čʰa?čʰííβʸe*.
291 *neé* 'say'. M *ne̱é-?i, no̱ó-bo*. B *neé*.
291 *xïïb(ái)ge* 'tell'. M *xííbege̱-?i, xííbogoo-bo*. B *ïïpáče*.
355 **tseeʔdi* 'dig'. M *sée̱di-?i*. B *tsʰeʔti*.

The following two items appear to follow the rule as well, in the infinitive form, but on inspection of their third person singular masculine form it is clear that they never had an /o/ vowel. For these items see **e* in §2.14.

275 **geéne* 'eat fruit'. M *géene̱-?i, géenee-be*. B *čeéne*.
289 *?*(í)xo(k)ííβe* 'stand'. M *xújééβe̱-?i, xújééβee-be*. B *ixʸokʰííβe*.

This rule applies to more than one preceding syllable, as can be seen in the second form of item 291.

PBM **e* > (EM *o /__Cu* > M *u*), B *e*.
68 **pekko* 'night'. M *ɸúkku*. B *pʰexkʰo*.
77 **géé?o-ga* 'doorway'. M *gú?ú-ga*. B *čéé?o-kʷa*.
211 **mé-?óttsi-ne* 'our hands'. M *mú-?use-ne (mo̱- + úse + -no)*. B *mé-?óxtsʰi-ne*.
265 **éékoó* 'flesh'. M *úúku*. B *?éékʰoó*.
278 **geébo* 'hear'. M *gúúbu-?i*. B *čeépo*.
111 *mee?dóba* 'crocodile'. M *mée̱dúba (e exception)*. B *me?tópa*.
PBM **e* > (EM *o /__* > M *o*), B *e*.
See examples in §2.14. The following exceptions may represent other unidentified vowel harmony rules.
233 *?*m(é)?n(í)-(kkaï)* 'crown of head'. M *míni-?ai (i exception)*. B *mé?ní-xkʰaï*.
74 **(xíí)né-gai-yḯ-?ai* 'sand'. M *xííni̱-gai-yi-?ai (i exception)*. B *nékʷa-yíí-?a, néékʷa-yï*.
251 **(xíí)-négaiyí́-?áí* 'pebbles'. M *xíí-ni̱gaiyi-?ai(i exception)*. B *nékʷayíí-?á*.
207 **dii-té-pi* 'they (f.d.)'. M *díítḭ-ɸe (i exception)*. B *tiitʰʸé-pʰi*.
207 **dii-té-tsi* 'they (m.d.)'. M *díítḭ-si (i exception)*. B *tiitʰʸé-tsʰi*.

Compare the dual forms of number 207 above with the plural form
below, which did not undergo any vowel harmony change:

207 *díi-te 'they (pl)'. M díi-tǫ. B tii-t^{hy}e.

PBM *i > (EM i /__Ce > M e), B i.

336 *báá?rí-ne(-í$\tilde{\beta}$í) 'short'. M báárę-ne. B pá?rí-n^{y}eí$\tilde{\beta}$í.

358 *aakí(t)te 'fall'. M áákę́tte-?i. B aak^{h}ít^{hy}e.

PBM *i > (EM i /__ > M i), B i.
(See examples in §2.14.)

130 *r(i)(?)oó(?o) 'toucan'. M rí?úú?u (i exception). B rííoó.

288 *ka?ts(íï)βe, *(čai)?ts(ii)βe 'sit'. M kásííβe-?i (i exception), kásííβoo-bo.
B k^{h}árárixííβe, č^{h}a?č^{h}íí$\tilde{\beta}^y$e.

PBM *i > (EM e /__xe > M i), B i.

81 *kïgá-íixi, *kïgá-(taxi), *kïgá-(í?kï) 'bed'. M kíga-iixe, kíga-taxe. B k^{h}ík^{w}a-íixí,
k^{h}ïk^{w}á-í?k^{hy}ï.

235 *(mé)-?níxí-(gá)-nix(i)k(áï) 'tip of tongue'. M néxe-ba-nixeke.
B mé-?níxí-k^{w}á-nixk^{h}áï.

243 *í?xiine 'body hair'. M íxée-ne. B í?xi-ne.

281 *gixí-βe 'die'. M gíxé-βe-?i. B tsixí-βe.

282 *gíxi-βé-tso 'kill'. M gíxé-βe-su-?i. B tsíxi-βé-ts^{h}o.

316 *í?xí-(?ono), *í?xi-(xi) 'fur'. M íxé-?ene. B í?xi-xi.

331 *íixí-né-(gáyï) 'narrow'. M íixe-ne. B íixí né-k^{w}í.

235 *(mé)-?níxí-(gá)-nix(i)k(áï) 'tip of tongue'. M néxe-ba-nixeke (e exception; the
Muinane rule applies here in two places—in the second instance it follows
the rule, and in the first it remains /e/). B mé-?níxí-k^{w}á-nixk^{h}áï.

PBM *i > (EM e /__(y)a > i), B i.

38 *míámínáa-ppi 'man'. M míyáminaa-ɸi. B míamínáa-xp^{h}i.

41 *míamínaa 'people'. M míyáminaa. B míamínaa, mínaa.

344 *(i)miáá-ne 'correct'. M 344 *míyáá-no. B 343 ímiáá-ne.

346 *(i)mía-() 'right'. M imíya-nago-no. B ímiá-néxk^{h}í.

PBM *i > (EM e /__(y) > M e), B i.

14 *(mé)-ppíiï-xi 'chest'. M ɸéęyi-xe. B (mé)-xp^{h}íï-xi.
Noncognate examples:

89 (míi(y)o?o) 'knife'. M méęyu?u.

132 (biriye) 'parakeet'. M bíręyo.

PBM *i > (EM e /__ > M e), B i.
See examples in §2.14. The following exceptions may represent other unidentified vowel harmony rules.

86 *ts(i)níkó?o 'fish net'. M síni-ku?u (i exception). B ts^{h}íníï, ts^{h}íní-k^{h}óó?o,
ts^{h}íní-k^{h}óó?a.

89 *n(ii)ts(í)ga-(gayï) 'knife'. M níísúga (i exception). B níits^{h}ík^{w}a-(k^{w}ï).

233 ?*m(é)?n(í)-(kkai) 'crown of head'. M míni-?ai (i exception). B mé?ní-xk^{h}aï.

PBM *ɸ > (EM /e,i__V > M y), B ɸ.

14 *(mé)-ppíiï-xi 'chest'. M ɸéęyi-xe. B (mé)-xp^{h}íï-xi.

41 *míamínaa 'people'. M míyáminaa. B míamínaa, mínaa.

349 *giiïkï 'pull'. M gíïyiki-?i, gíki-?i. B čiïk^{h}ï.

PBM *ïï > (EM ïï > M ï), B ïï.
This rule seems to have functioned in free variation with the previous one, as can be seen in the two variant Muinane forms for 349.

349 *giïïkï 'pull'. M gíïyïkɨ-ʔi, gíkɨ-ʔi. B čiïkʰï.

PBM *ïï > (EM ïï > M ï), B ïï.

196 *nïxíï-ga(-ko) 'ear ornament'. M níxɨ-ga-ku. B nïxíï-kʷa.

2.16. Features not considered. The following features have not been considered in detail in this reconstruction of PBM and merit further study:

(1) The tone system. The systems of Bora and Muinane are both two-tone systems, but there is a great deal of variation between the two.

(2) Vowel length. There is significant fluctuation in vowel length, both morphophonemically within the languages and between the two. I have followed the vowel length in Muinane for the most part in reconstructing the protolanguage words. One tendency I did notice was that glottal and preconsonantal /x/ both seem to shorten the preceding vowel in Bora.

(3) Syllable-final glottal. In the reconstruction I have assumed that all Bora glottals were inherited from the protolanguage. However, it is possible that some of them were generated spontaneously, based in some way on tone and vowel length.

3
Proto Huitoto-Ocaina

The table in (12) is a proposed phoneme chart for Proto Huitoto-Ocaina (PHO). It contains twelve consonants, five vowels and two suprasegmental phonemes (nasalization and accent). I am treating nasalization as a suprasegmental here rather than as five additional vowels as was done in Ocaina. The origin of the nasalization is uncertain, and the statistical analysis was simplified by treating nasalization as a suprasegmental. The reconstructed phoneme chart is much simpler than in any of the four daughter languages. As is always the case with reconstructed systems, it is impossible to know which features may have been totally lost from the protolanguage system and are now unreconstructible. The oral vowel system is the same as that of Nɨpode, except that there was apparently no *u* in the protolanguage (see *o* in §3.14).

Relative frequencies have been calculated for the protophonemes and are indicated as before. They were calculated based on the reconstructed words in the wordlist. The values match up well with the expected values from the sound-change rules in most cases. The frequencies are given with half a percentage point of precision for the consonants and a whole percentage point for the vowels. Of the words in the list, only between 42 percent and 50 percent (between 159 and 187 out of 375) are cognates between Huitoto and Ocaina. The relationships are, therefore, a bit more difficult to determine than for Bora and Muinane.

At this point, I should present an additional protophoneme chart, that of Early Huitoto, the mother language of the three Huitotos. It happens, however, that the Early Huitoto phoneme chart is identical to the Nɨpode phoneme chart (table (5)). Nɨpode seems to be structurally unchanged

57

from Early Huitoto.[33] In the rules that follow this fact should be carefully borne in mind.

(12)   Proto Huitoto-Ocaina phonemes

p	t		k	$ʔ$	i	$ï$
6	15		11.5	3 Init.	21	18
				11 Final		
b	d $[r]$	dz	g		e	a	o
3	9	2	5		13	25	23
			h			
			12.5			
$β$						
1.5						
m	n				oral vowels: 84.5	
6.5	12				nasalized vowels: 15.5	
		y			accent system	
		.5				

899 consonants, 978 oral vowels, 179 nasal vowels

3.1–5 Consonant reflexes

3.1. Fricativization and implosives. Three of the phonemes in the stop series—*p, *t and *k—became fricatives under certain circumstances in the extant languages, but not all in the same one. Early Huitoto *p and *t became fricatives /φ/ and /θ/ in Minica and Murui, whereas PHO *p and *k became fricatives /φ/ and /x/ in Ocaina. No fricativization occurred in Nipode. A similar process occurred in Muinane (§2.3), but I assume that the process occurred independently in the two halves of the Witotoan family.

As expected, since *p became /φ/ in Ocaina, there are very few examples of Ocaina /p/ in the data (22, 94, 115, 116, 126, 153, 154, 241), only one of which is a possible cognate (126). (241 appears to be a candidate for a cognate with Huitoto /b/, but on closer observation, the morpheme containing the /p/ proves to be unrelated to that with the /b/, since the vowels do not correspond.)

---

[33]The Nipode community is much smaller than the other two Huitoto language communities and its language has not been used as a trade language, as the other languages have. The Huitoto languages thus fit the generally recognized pattern that central, high-prestige dialects are more innovative and change more rapidly than marginal, low-prestige dialects.

/p/ and /t/ in Minica and Murui are reflexes of Early Huitoto *b and *d, which were retained in Nipode. These in turn are derived from PHO *ʔb and *ʔt (examples of the former are quite rare).[34]

3.2. Alveolar and alveopalatal stops and affricates. The PHO phonemes *t, *d, and *dz have had a complex history. *d had allophonic variation between [d] initially and a voiced alveolar flap [r] medially. This allophonic variation passed into Ocaina, with /dy/ initially and /r/ medially, then became phonemic as a few examples of /dy/ developed word medially.[35] A few cases of *d also became /ĵ/ in Ocaina. *t split in a very complicated way into /t, ts, ty, č/ in Ocaina.

In Huitoto *d became /r/ in all cases, leaving a hole in the system. This hole was filled when *t split into /t/ (before /i/) and /d/. Subsequently /d/ split into /d/ (after glottal, which was lost otherwise in Huitoto) and /d/. /t/ and /d/ also developed the reflexes /č/ and /ĵ/. Thus *t underwent a five-way split into /t, d, d, č, ĵ/ in Early Huitoto.

I have reluctantly proposed a protophoneme *dz. This proved necessary to account for the anomaly of Ocaina /dz/ corresponding to Huitoto /t, d, d/ (§3.9). It was not necessary to propose a corresponding voiceless phoneme *ts, since Ocaina /ts/ seems to derive fairly well from *t. Their distribution when compared with Proto Bora-Muinane is also very different.

The system became further complicated in Huitoto. Nipode retained the Early Huitoto system unchanged, but Minica and Murui went on to change Early Huitoto *t into /θ/ and *d into /t/, as mentioned in the previous section.

The Ocaina phonemes /s, š/ present problems, since they do not appear to have any relationship to Proto Huitoto-Ocaina and were presumably derived from borrowings. The items in which they occur are /s/: 91, 95, 18, 207, 221, 295, 308, 329, 355; /š/: 50, 374.

3.3. Nasal consonants. Ocaina has two series of nasals, fortis and lenis, that do not contrast word-initially (§1.6). Although they do contrast word medially, they are even there in near complementary distribution, determined mainly by the preceding vowel (§3.12). Thus *m split into /m/ and /m̥/ in Ocaina; and *n underwent a major split similar to the one that affected *t, becoming /n, ñ, n̥, ñ̥/ in Ocaina (and /n, ñ/ in Huitoto).

An additional nasal phoneme /ŋ/ apparently developed from *g in Huitoto, occurring in one morpheme only, the feminine suffix /ŋo/ (also

---

[34]See also §1.3.

[35]There is no word-initial /r/ in Ocaina, nor does the language have a nonpalatalized /d/ phoneme.

used as the singular marker for a number of animals).[36] In Murui this phoneme became /ñ/ in all cases and in Minica and Nipode it became /ñ/ after /i/ in some cases.

3.4. Geminate consonants. An alternate origin for the fortis-lenis contrast in Ocaina nasals could possibly be geminate nasals in Proto Huitoto-Ocaina. Unfortunately, Proto Bora-Muinane does not help us in this case, since it had no geminate nasals, only geminate stops; and the cognates reflect no difference. The possibility that these nasals were geminates is tantalizing, however, especially since one other Ocaina phoneme, /k/, is a possible reflex of a PHO geminate.

The reflexes of PHO *k in Ocaina appear to be /x/ in about 80% of the cases and /k/ in about 20%.[37] The latter percentage is too high to consider these cases of /k/ in Ocaina as simple exceptions to the rule *k > Ocaina /x/, but the environments which would condition such a split are, unfortunately, not apparent.[38] It is possible that these cases of /k/ could be a remnant of a PHO geminate *kk, which in turn would correspond to the PBM geminate *kk. One fact that would seem to support this idea is that half of the Ocaina reflexes of PBM *kk are /k/ (see 25, 126, and 240 in §§4.3 and 8), and half are /ʔx/ (items 66, 87 and 98). The latter is the expected reflex. None is either /ʔk/ or /x/. In fact, none of the cases of Ocaina /k/ derived from PHO *k is preglottalized,[39] which is unexpected considering the frequency of preglottalized stops in Ocaina, but which is precisely what would be expected if they came from geminates, since a consonant could be either geminate or preglottalized, but not both.

However, proposing that Proto Huitoto-Ocaina had a geminate *kk corresponding to PBM *kk would introduce a whole new level of complexity to the analysis of the protolanguage stops. It would mean that the

---

[36]In Ocaina this morpheme is /ko/, and in Proto Bora-Muinane it is *ge. I have reconstructed it as *-goï or *-gaï. The /ŋ/ does not appear to have been produced in the environment of Proto Huitoto-Ocaina nasalized vowels, as might be expected, but instead in the environment i̱_o (see §3.9).

[37]There are quite a few additional occurrences of /k/ in Ocaina, but these turn out to be reflexes of PHO *g in word-medial position. Specifically, about half of the occurrences of /k/ in Ocaina are derived from *k and half from *g.

[38]There does seem to be some restriction in the distribution of these cases of /k/ in Ocaina, as they seem to never be either preceded or followed by PHO *e or *i and are often preceded by /i/, /aï/, or /oï/. However, /x/ occurs in all of the same environments. Suggestively, PBM /kk/ seems to be subject to these same environmental restrictions.

[39]Ocaina does have a number of examples of /ʔk/, but in every case these are reflexes of PHO *ʔg.

voiceless geminate stops of Proto Bora-Muinane would have to be taken all the way back to Proto Witotoan, even though there is a fairly clear correspondence between them and preglottalized stops in Proto Huitoto-Ocaina. And it would mean that Early Huitoto /d̶/ would have to be suspected as the reflex of a PHO *tt, even though there are a number of cases in which /d̶/ corresponds to Ocaina /ʔt(y)/. No evidence for a distinct geminate *pp in Proto Huitoto-Ocaina exists.[40]

Another alternative which might resolve the difficulty would be to propose that these cases of /k/ are a reflex of PHO *ʔk. However, the very fact that the glottal never occurs with them would make the rule a very strange one. This must, therefore, simply be left as a problem which has not yet been fully resolved.[41]

3.5. Loss of glottal. Ocaina has glottals freely in both syllable-initial and syllable-final position, whereas Huitoto essentially has no glottals. I assume that this is a case of loss in Huitoto, rather than a generation of some sort in Ocaina. A similar loss of glottal occurred in Muinane, in syllable-final position only (§2.4), but I assume that it occurred independently.

3.6–7 Vowel reflexes

3.6. Vowel system changes. Proto Huitoto-Ocaina apparently only had five vowels /a, e, i, o, ï/, which were expanded to six in Huitoto by a split of *o into /o/ and /u/. I maintain this in spite of the fact that /o/ and /u/ in Huitoto currently have fairly good contrast (compare Nïpode 352 /bu-d̶á-de/ 'hit', 353 /bo-d̶á-de/ 'split', 351 /bï-d̶á-de/ 'throw'). Also, some of the factors conditioning the split are not completely clear.

There are several excellent overriding reasons for assuming that /o/ and /u/ were not distinguished in Proto Huitoto-Ocaina:

a. The /u/ phoneme in Huitoto is significantly less common (6–7%) than any of the other vowels (16–22%).
b. There is no evidence in Ocaina which would suggest that there was a contrast between PHO *u and *o, whereas there is residual evidence in Ocaina of a contrast between PHO *ï and *o: though these two vowels

---

[40]Early Huitoto /ɓ/ is not a possibility, since it is not a reflex of PBM *pp, but of PHO *ʔb, whose previous history is unclear; see §4.1.

[41]A similar possibility exists that Ocaina fortis nasals could be derived from preglottalized nasals in PHO or PW. However, this founders on the complete lack of evidence in Huitoto, PHO, or PBM. See §§3.10 and 4.5.

fell together in Ocaina, they had different roles in the split of *t into Ocaina /t^y/ and /ts/.

c. Going back another step, there is no trace of any **u in Proto Witotoan. Huitoto words with /u/ have the same correspondences as those with /o/ when compared with Proto Bora-Muinane.

d. Minor (1956:137) states that, in Nɨpode, "of the thirty-six possible clusters of two diverse vowels, thirty-two occur. The four nonoccurring sequences *eu, *ou, *uï, *uo have not been observed even in extended sequences of vowels." All of these sequences contain the vowel /u/. Restrictions of this sort are precisely what would be expected if /u/ had been derived from *o. The lack of these clusters is predicted by the rules I have set forth.[42]

The history of the vowels from Proto Huitoto-Ocaina to Ocaina had three stages:

a. In Ocaina the five protovowels were apparently at an early stage reduced to only three (a very unusual system for a language in this region),[43] by collapsing *$ï$ and *o into /o/, and *i and *e into /i/, with a resulting system of *i, *a, *o.

b. The collapsed *i then split again, moving back to /ï/ in most environments to fill the hole left by the lack of a high back vowel, and remaining /i/ in other environments.

c. Finally, some of the remaining cases of *i became *ai and finally /a/. *a remained essentially unchanged. This left Ocaina with a simple four-vowel system, as represented in (13). Since then Ocaina has added a few forms with /e/, perhaps mostly from borrowings. Only one of the Ocaina words with /e/ has a cognate with any other Witotoan language (item 87), in which the /e/ is apparently derived from *ai. There is no /ē/ in Ocaina.

Thus, Ocaina went from five vowels to three and back to five, so that it now has the exact same vowel inventory /a, e, i, o, ï/ that Proto Huitoto-Ocaina had, both systems even having an unrounded high back vowel /ï/

---

[42]Several other vowel sequences involving /o/ or /u/ occur which, according to the rules, should not occur; these are, presumably, accretions of various kinds.

[43]The only other nearby language with a three-vowel system that I know of is Quichua in Ecuador.

instead of the more usual /u/.[44] However, there is no one-to-one correspondence between the original five vowels and the current five vowels:
Ocaina /i/ almost never corresponds to PHO *ɨ, but instead corresponds
consistently to PHO *e or *i; PHO *ɨ corresponds to Ocaina /o/; PHO *e
never corresponds to Ocaina /e/, the latter being so rare as almost not to
count in the current vowel inventory; PHO *e and *i show up as Ocaina
/i, i, a/. This would seem a very unlikely scenario, if it were not for the
wealth of examples demonstrating that *o and *ɨ have identical Ocaina
reflexes and that *e and *i have identical Ocaina reflexes (somewhat
obscured by the complex phoneme split rules the resulting *i phoneme
later underwent).

For more discussion on the theoretical implications of Ocaina's vowel
system history, see §7.

(13)   PHO > O vowel shifts in three stages

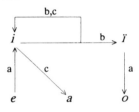

3.7. Nasalization. Ocaina is the only one of the six languages that has
a nasalized vowel series. The data suggest that the nasalization may have
been a Proto Witotoan feature and that it was subsequently lost in the
other five languages. It appears, however, to have left very little trace in
the other languages, and what evidence it has left is extremely indirect.

In the Tucanoan language family, geographically a near neighbor of the
Witotoan family, nasalization is a syllable-level feature[45] and produces a
series of nasal allophones of voiced oral consonants. In most of the
languages, nasal and oral consonants do not contrast, but are in complementary distribution. In Western Tucanoan this system has broken

---

[44]What pressures would have caused Ocaina to produce this particular system again
is an interesting question. Areal pressures would not seem likely to have done so, since
most of the neighboring languages have a six-vowel system containing both /u/ and /i/.
The sound-change rules reveal the cause and show that the similarity is purely
coincidental: Ocaina /i/ developed from earlier /i/, which, not being rounded, would
understandably have remained unrounded during the backing process.

[45]It actually seems to function on the phonological morpheme level, and can spread
from one morpheme to another; see Kaye 1971; Stolte 1980; Barnes 1984:255.

down to some degree. Even there, however, all nasal consonants are derived historically from the syllable-level nasalization system (Wheeler in preparation).

There are two Proto Huitoto-Ocaina phonemes which provide evidence that vowel nasalization was a Proto Huitoto-Ocaina feature which produced nasal allophones of oral consonants in some cases: the phonemes *y and *dz. For the former I have proposed the Ocaina reflexes /y, ñ, ñ/. For *dz the nasal reflex /n/ occurs in Huitoto and is the only evidence in Huitoto of the Proto Huitoto-Ocaina nasalization. Both of these cases are based on somewhat meager evidence. There is no clear evidence that the nasalization was originally a system affecting all voiced consonants, like that in the Tucanoan languages.

For more details on this, see *dz in §3.9 and *y and the examples that follow *y of nasalization in conjunction with other voiced consonants in §3.13.

The Huitoto nasal phoneme /ŋ ~ ŋ ~ ñ/ was apparently derived from *g, but nasalized vowels apparently played no part in its development (§3.3).

3.8–14 PHO sound changes

The following seven sections (3.8–14) present detailed discussion of and evidence for the sound changes proposed between PHO and the daughter language Huitoto and Ocaina, following the same organization and conventions used for the discussion of PBM in §§2.8–15. Unlike the PBM data, few rules yielded a surplus of examples. Therefore, for most rules all cognate examples are listed.

The forms in the three Huitoto languages and the reflexes in the rules are listed separated by the alternation sign (~). Since the three Huitoto languages are so closely related, particularly Minica and Murui, the examples are often the same. In these cases, the form for Minica or Murui, or both, is replaced with a double quote (") to indicate that it is identical to the previous form. In most cases, it is the Murui example that is the same as Minica and is marked with a double quote. If a cognate does not exist or is not known in one of the Huitoto languages, but is in the others, a dash (–) indicates that the cognate is missing.

Keep in mind that accent is phonemic in Nipode and in Minica, but not in Murui. Therefore, if the Murui word is marked with a double quote, the accent of the Minica word should be ignored for Murui. Occasionally the author was uncertain about the accenting of a Minica word, in which case no accent is marked.

In the Huitoto material, a period (.) between vowels indicates a syllable break, which is marked in Huitoto in all cases to distinguish this situation from a one-syllable diphthong. In many cases this distinction is significant in a rule.

For the consonant phonemes the rules are always given for the consonants with and without preglottalization, unless the consonant in question was never preglottalized in the protolanguage. Preglottalization was extremely common in Proto Huitoto-Ocaina, as it is in Ocaina, and in many cases preglottalization is significant for a sound change rule for the consonant in question.

3.8. Voiceless stops. This section presents the rules for the PHO voiceless stops *p, *?p, *t, *?t, *k, and *?k.

PHO   *p > O φ, H p~φ~φ.
PHO   *?p > O ?φ, H p~φ~φ.
  1 *(h)ïyï?pe 'tongue'. O hïñóó?ɸï. H i.ípe~i.íɸe~".
  2 *póe 'mouth'. O ɸooï. H pú.e~ɸú.e~".
  3 *p(óe i)?goï, ?*p(óe ini) 'lip'. O ɸa-?óó?ko. H pú.e ini~ɸú.e igoï~".
  5 *topo 'nose'. O ƥooɸo. H dópo~dóɸo~".
  8 *ï?po-(gï) 'head'. O oo?ɸo. H ípo~ïɸó-kï~ïɸo-gï.
 10 *ï?po-?tï() 'hair'. O oo?ɸo, o?ɸo-to?óóɸe. H ïpó-dï.i ~ïɸó-tïrai~ïɸo-tïraï.
 65 *pï() 'moon'. O ɸoƥoome. H píbï.i~ɸï.ui~ɸïβui.
 75 *(ho)po 'house'. O ɸoo(ho), -xo. H hópo~hóɸo~hoɸo, ɸo.
 87 *p(ai)?koa-ti 'fishhook'. O ɸe?xoo-ti. H pákua-ti~ɸákua-θi~ɸago-θi.
117 *p(íí)to 'agouti'. O ɸííƥo. H --ɸï.ïdo~ɸïdo.
128 *pi?tíí?to 'hummingbird'. O ɸa?tíí?ƥo. H pitído~ɸiθído~".
171 *hi?pí-dai 'chili plant'. O ha?ɸíí-ja. H --híɸi-rai~".
 85 ?*tï(do)(p)e(ta) 'path'. O tóβï?ƥa (β exception). H díro-pe~díro-ɸe~-.
151 ?*()pedï 'hill'. O ƥaβííro (β exception). H íperï~íɸerï~.
 63 *hai(dí)(p)oï 'wind'. O hïβóóƥo (β exception). H hairípoï~heríɸo~a.íɸï.
126 ??*(n)op(aï)goï 'toad'. O opépeko (p exception). H nopáïŋo~noɸáïŋo ~noɸaïño.

The rules for *t and *?t are quite complex. The rules for *t and *?t are separated in several cases, since glottal is quite essential to the distribution in this case. The correlation between Ocaina /?t, ?tʸ/ and Huitoto /ɗ~t~t/ is not as high as would be desirable and is only fully confirmed by going back one more step and looking at the correlation of these with PBM *tt and *tts. I have not determined why the glottal often seems to be lost in Ocaina and why occasionally what would be expected to be /ɗ~t~t/ in Huitoto shows up as /d/. However, I do not list these as exceptions.

PHO *t /__i > O t, H t~θ~θ.
PHO *ʔt /__i > O ʔt, H t~θ~θ.
 87 *p(ai)ʔkoa-ti 'fishhook'. O φeʔxoo-ti. H pákua-ti~φákua-θi~φago-θi.
168 *(h)aʔkáíʔ-ti(dai) 'yam'. O aʔxaaʔti. H -~hakái-θairai~-.
186–189 *ené(da) péti 'other hand?' O añíira φáti.
     H ené-pebamo~ené-φeθimo~ene-φebehimo.
190 *(ha)naʔg(á)-péti 'ten'. O hanāʔ φáti, hanaa-ʔφïφóroʔ.
     H nagá-peba~nagá-φeθi~naga-φebekuiro.
  4 *iʔtiʔ-to 'tooth'. O aʔtiiʔtʸo. H íti-do~íθi-do~".
128 *piʔtíʔto 'hummingbird'. O φaʔtííʔtʸo. H pitído~φiθído~".
163 *hōʔtí(ti) 'cassava plant'. O hōʔtááti. H húti~húθi~huθi.e.
222 *doti(-de-te) 'cold'. O dʸótï. H ročí-re-de~roθí-re-de~" (č~θ~θ exception).
PHO *t /__e > O t, H d.
PHO *ʔt /__e (no examples) > O ʔt, H (?).
313 *hokó-te 'wash'. O hoxoo-tï. H hokó-de~"~".

The Ocaina suffix on the preceding example is a doubtful cognate with the corresponding Huitoto suffix. The Huitoto suffix means third-person singular indicative, whereas now the Ocaina suffix is not apparently a separate morpheme at all. (Ocaina uses no suffix for this function today.) Since it is the only example for the environment */__e/, however, I have included it for what it is worth. Number 282 in the wordlist appears to be a possible candidate for a cognate with the same suffix (but a different Ocaina root); the Ocaina suffix in 282, however, means causative.

PHO *t /i__ae,aï > O tʸ, H j.
PHO *ʔt /i__ae,aï > O ʔtʸ, H ǰ.
 49 *(i)tae 'river'. O tʸaaï. H -~ïje~".
250 *(i)tae-() 'stream'. O tʸaβáága. H íje~ijé-tu.e~ije-kuera.
199 *(iʔt)iʔtáï-ma 'chief'. O aʔtiʔtʸó-ma, φarááʔφï-ma. H ijáï-ma~"~".
PHO *t /__a(i) > O tí, H d.
 93 *(toki) da-ta 'spear'. O oïdʸáátʸa. H -~dukí-ra-da~-.
 95 *(tïk)ói da-ta 'arrow'. O oïdʸáátʸa. H tïkúi-ra-da~-~-.
181 *ta() 'one'. O tʸa-. H da~da, dá.a~dahe, da.e.
185 *ta-()oido 'five'. O tʸaʔ-φïïφoroʔ. H hubéba~hu-bekuiro~da-bekuiro.
204 *tā(g)ē 'it'. O tʸā(hï̃), tʸa. H dáge~-~-.
210 *ta onōï̃ 'his hand'. O tʸáʔonōō. H da ónoï~-~-.
183 *(amani) tá(he) 'three'. O hanāā-maʔ-tʸáá-maʔ. H da.ámani~"~da(h)e
     amani.
160 *dáta 'stick'. O dʸáátʸa. H ráda~"~".
334 *hetákï 'thick'. O hïtʸááxo. H hédakï.e-de~"~".
149 ?*taï-(máïʔï) 'bush'. O tʸamáâʔï. H da.ḯ-re~táï-re~- (d~t exception).
192 *(i)táï-poe-dza(no) 'last'. O tʸáφoïïdzanó. H idái-pu.e-na,
     írai-pu.e-na~írai-pu.e-na~iraï.e (d, r~r~r exception).
155 ?*t(ã́) 'flower'. O tsï̃́ (ts exception). H tápi.a~θáφi.a~" (t~θ~θ exception).

PHO *ʔt /__a(i) > O (ʔ)tʸ, H d̃~t~t, d.
137 *áʔta-βa 'hen'. **Ou** átʸa-βa. **H** adá-βa ~ atá-βa ~ ". This is apparently a Quichua borrowing and so may not actually be cognate.
178 *(po)kaníʔta 'cane'. **O** ɸookaníʔ̃tʸa. **H** kani-da ~ kaní-kaï ~ –.
289 *naiʔtai 'stand'. **O** niïʔtʸa. **H** naidá.i-de ~ náidai-de ~ ".
367 ?*ta(ʔtai-te) 'squeeze'. **O** tsaaka (ts exception). **H** aidá-de, dádai-de ~ naïtá-de ~ –.
353 ?*(bo)-ʔtá-(de) 'split'. **O** taarï (t exception). **H** bo-dá-de ~ bo-tá-de ~ ".)
300 ?*(háʔ)ta(pé-dete) 'dry'. **O** háá̃ʔta (ʔt exception). **H** tapé-re-de ~ θaɸé-re-de ~ " (t ~ θ ~ θ exception).

Example 300 (above) has the expected reflexes in both Ocaina and Huitoto before *i, not before *a. It is tempting, therefore, to reconstruct the vowel as *i. Since /a/ clearly occurs in both cases, however, it must simply be treated as an exception.

PHO *t /oi__o > O č, H d.
PHO *ʔt /oi__o > O ʔč, H d.
233 ?*()oito 'crown of head'. **O** kõčo, **H** – ~ – ~ – ïɸogï muido.
144 *(oi)ʔtó() 'mosquito'. **O** ã̃ʔčooko. **H** uidódo ~ " ~ ".
PHO *t /__o otherwise > O tʸ, H d.
5 *topo 'nose'. **O** tʸooɸo. **H** dópo ~ dóɸo ~ ".
142 ?*(p)aïd(á)to 'flea'. **O** oróóβïtʸo. **H** païrádo ~ ɸaïrádo ~ ".
160 *dató() 'stick'. **O** dʸatʸooɸo. **H** radóti ~ radóθï ~ ".
117 *(íí)to 'agouti'. **O** ɸííʸo. **H** – ~ ɸí.ïdo ~ ɸïdo.
97 *tõ() 'tapir'. **O** tʸõõhã. **H** turúma ~ θurúma ~ " (t ~ θ ~ θ exception).
354 ?*tõ-ʔ(tá-te) 'pierce'. **O** tʸõõʔɸo. **H** ju-dá-de ~ ju-tá-de ~ " (j exception).
148 *odo-taï(no) 'chigger'. **O** orootʸo. **H** í.ojoɳo ~ í.ojoɳo, órokoɳo ~ i.ojaïño (j exception).
349 ?*tõ() 'pull'. **O** tsõõʔmï (ts exception). **H** tonó-de ~ θonó-de ~ " (t ~ θ ~ θ exception).
275 = 364 *()tõ() 'suck fruit'. **O** tsõõʔño (ts exception). **H** jijó-de ~ čičó-de ~ – (j ~ č exception).
PHO *ʔt /__o otherwise > O (ʔ)tʸ, H d̃~t~t, d.
4 *iʔtiʔ-to 'tooth'. **O** aʔtiiʔtʸo. **H** íti-do ~ íθi-do ~ ".
128 *piʔtíʔto 'hummingbird'. **O** ɸaʔtííʔtʸo. **H** pitído ~ ɸiθído ~ ".
66 *oʔkóʔto 'star'. **O** oʔxóóʔtʸo. **H** ukúdo ~ ukúdu ~ ".
102 *kïʔto 'deer'. **O** xooʔtʸo. **H** kí̃do ~ kí̃to ~ ".
351 *(ai)nãï̃-() 'throw'. **O** aнãã-tʸo. **H** – ~ ñáï-te ~ – (suffix not cognate).
PHO *t /__ï > O ts, H d.
33 = 266 *tïhé 'blood'. **O** tsihíĩ. **H** dí.e ~ " ~ ".
85 ?*tí(do)(p)e(ta) 'path'. **O** tóβïʔtʸa (t exception). **H** dï̃ro-pe ~ dí̃ro-ɸe ~ –.
165 *tïʔó() 'tobacco'. **O** tʸoʔooko (tʸ exception). **H** dï.ó-na ~ " ~ ".)
94 *tï() 'bow'. **O** tsipóxatʸa. **H** tïkúi-ña ~ θïkui-raï ~ θïkui-ra (t ~ θ ~ θ exception).
214 ?*k(oe)-tï() 'my bow'. **O** ki-tsipóxatʸa. **H** kue tïkúiña ~ kú.e θïkúiraï ~ ku.e θïkuirakuiɸo (t ~ θ ~ θ exception).
377 *(ho)pó-tïʔb(i) 'small house'. **O** ɸohoo-tsiβo. **H** hopó-čuβi ~ hoɸó-čupi ~ – (č exception).

PHO *ʔt /__ï > O (ʔ)t, H d̃ ~ t ~ t.
227 = 328 *hiʔtíʔ-() 'black'. **O** hïʔtóóʔ-ɸï. **H** hídï-re-de ~ hítï-re-de ~ ".
10 *ïʔpo-ʔtï() 'hair'. **O** ooʔɸo, oʔɸo-toʔóóɸe. **H** ïpó-dï.i ~ ïɸó-tïrai ~ ïɸo-tïraï.
161 *(dai)ʔtïháĩ́(hā) 'grass'. **O** tʸoháá́(hā) (tʸ exception). **H** ráidï.aï ~ ráitï.aï ~ raitïkïño.
371 *hee(), *(e)hiʔtï 'ripe'. **O** hïïʔto. **H** hé.e-de ~ " ~ e.iθï (θ exception).

The last rule above is the only one in which the preglottalization of *t determines the Ocaina reflex. However, the rule seems to hold quite well. *t and *ï produce mutual changes in each other in Ocaina: *ï converts *t into /ts/, after which /ts/ converts *ï into /i/ (instead of the expected Ocaina /o/); see *ï below.

Ocaina /ts/ only occurs before PHO *ï as predicted by the preceding rule in three out of nine cases (33 = 266, 94 = 214 and 377); it occurs in the other four cases before *a (155 and 367) or *o (349 and 275 = 364), two of these (155 and 349) with Huitoto reflexes of /t ~ θ ~ θ/, which are also exceptions. It is unclear what happened in these cases. Comparison with Proto Bora-Muinane only confirms the rule set forth above: two of the examples that follow the above rule have Proto Bora-Muinane cognates (33 = 266 and 94; see §4.3), whereas none of the exceptions do.

There are no examples of word-initial /d/ in Nïpode as a reflex of PHO *t, although there are quite a few words in Nïpode that do begin with /d/. These turn out to be reflexes of *dz (see *dz in §3.9).

PHO *k /ï__ï > O h, H k.
131 ʔ*(k)(oi)yïkï 'parrot'. **O** káyooho. **H** ui.íkï ~ ui.íkï ~ θarokï.
78 *()i-dá-bïkï 'seat'. **O** biiñi-ráá-βoho, biiñiráá-ko. **H** rá.ï.i-ra-bï-kï ~ " ~ raï-ra-ko.
196 ʔ*ko(máʔ-tï)-kï 'earring'. **O** xoñōō-tʸaβóko (k exception). **H** kumá-dï-kï ~ héɸo í-hï ~ heɸo itïkï.
PHO *k /sometimes (env. unclear) > O k, H k.
25 ʔ*ïdzá-k(aido) 'leg'. **O** odzá-kona. **H** ïdá-kairo ~ ", rï.aï-kairo ~ ".
126 *goaïkí(ho) 'toad'. **O** gokóóho. **H** gúku ~ gúaïkï ~ –.
140 *(do)ʔ-hidakï(ŋo) 'bee'. **O** dʸoʔíírako. **H** hiráŋo ~ " ~ hirakïño.
178 *(po)kaníʔta 'cane'. **O** ɸookaníïʔtʸa. **H** kaní-da ~ kaní-kaï ~ –.
196 ʔ*ko(máʔ-tï)-kï 'earring'. **O** xoñōō-tʸaβóko. **H** kumá-dï-kï ~ héɸo í-hï ~ heɸo itïkï.
208 *k(oe) onōĩ 'my hand'. **O** k-oʜōō. **H** kue ónoï ~ kú.e ónoï ~ ku.e ono-jï.
214 ʔ*k(oe)-tï() 'my bow'. **O** ki-tsipóxatʸa. **H** kue tïkúiña ~ kú.e θïkúiraï ~ ku.e θïkuirakuiɸo.
269 ʔ*(mó)kaï(to) 'horn'. **O** mókaatʸo. **H** tíkaï ~ θíkaï ~ ".
314 *(a)(ï)kï 'worm'. **O** ïïko. **H** áïkï ~ " ~ ".
131 ʔ*(k)(oi)yïkï 'parrot'. **O** káyooho. **H** ui.íkï ~ ui.íkï ~ θarokï (Ø exception).
PHO *k /usually (env. unclear) > O x, H k.
34 *kome(kï) 'heart'. **O** xomïí-ʜōti. **H** komékï ~ " ~ ".
52 *kïné-b() 'swamp'. **O** xonííβaga. **H** kïné-re ~ kïné-bï ~ kïne-re.
58 *kó() 'charcoal'. **O** xóñaa(tʸo). **H** kó.okï ~ " ~ ".

 80 *kïnahī 'hammock'. O xonaahī. H kínai ~ " ~ ".
102 *kïʔto 'deer'. O xooʔt̬ʼo. H kído ~ kíto ~ ".
130 *nokáiʔto 'toucan'. O ñoxaaʔčo. H nokáido ~ " ~ ".
196 ?*ko(máʔ-tï)-kï 'earring'. O xoñōō-t̬ʼaβóko. H kumá-dï-kï ~ héφo í-hï ~ heφo
      itïkï.
197 *(p)ōïʔéko(da) 'mask'. O φōʔïïxora, orïïʔka. H hígape ~ hígaφe ~ u.i.eko iko.
200 *kōē 'I'. O xō, xōï̃. H kúe ~ " ~ kue, ku.e.
205 *kaï-gaï 'we (f.d.)'. O xak(a). H – ~ káïŋaï ~ kaiñaï.
211 *kaï onōï̃ 'our hands'. O xa-ʔoнōō. H kaï óno-ge ~ kaï ónoï ~ kaï ono-jï.
230 *óko 'eat!'. O óóxo. H óko ~ gú.i ~ guiño.
134 ?*(k)oodz(a) 'curassow'. O xóódzoho. H jó.oda ~ jó.oda, hó.oda ~ – (j ~ j,h ~ –
      exception). Many more examples.
PHO *ʔk > O ʔx, H k.
168 *(h)aʔkáíʔ-ti(dai) 'yam'. O aʔxaaʔti. H – ~ hakái-θairai ~ –.
 17 *he(dáï)ʔkï(mo) 'back'. O hïïʔxo(mó). H heráïkï ~ emódo bora ~ emodo.
 87 *p(ai)ʔkoa-ti 'fishhook'. O φeʔxoo-ti. H pákua-ti ~ φákua-θi ~ φago-θi (k ~ k ~ g
      exception).

3.9 Voiced stops. This section presents the rules for the PHO voiced
stops *b, *ʔb, *d, *ʔd, *dz, *ʔdz, *g, and *ʔg.

PHO *b /#__ > O b, H b.
 14 *(he)bae-goï() 'chest'. O 14 bagóóʔya. H 244 hébe-goï ~ " ~ hebe-gï.
258 *bő 'who'. O bő. H bu ~ " ~ ".
296 *boda 'yellow'. O bóóra. H borá-re-de ~ " ~ ".
305 *bē() 'here'. O bá, bï̃. H benó ~ bené ~ benomo.
256 *bi-hē, *bi-ʔe 'this'. O bïï, bïhā, baʔi-, bï-. H bedá ~ bí.e ~ ".
PHO *b /__ > O β, H b.
 52 *kïné-b() 'swamp'. O xoníïβaga. H kïné-re ~ kïné-bï ~ kïne-re.
 92 *()-bïi(g)ï 'club'. O biija-βóóho. H bïgï ~ bï.igï ~ bïgï.
 78 *()i-dá-bïkï 'seat'. O biiñi-ráá-βoho, biiñiráá-ko. H rá.ï.i-ra-bï-kï ~ " ~ raï-ra-ko.
172 *híibí(ʔe) 'coca'. O hiibiro (b exception). H hibí.e ~ hí.ibi.e ~ hi.ibe.
PHO *ʔb > O β, H б ~ p ~ p.
377 *(ho)pó-tïʔb(i) 'small house'. O φohoo-tsiβo. H hopó-čuбi ~ hoφó-čupi ~ –.

Because of the rarity of this phoneme, I include below the only other
examples of Nïpode /б/ in the wordlist:

376 (tiʔbekai-te) 'dent'. O (no cognate). H číбekai-de ~ čípekai-de ~ ".
359 (píiʔboko-te) 'swell'. O (no cognate). H pí.iбuku-de ~ φí.ipuku-de ~ –.

*d generally became /r/ in Huitoto and split into /dʸ/ initially and /r/
medially in Ocaina. This indicates that in Proto Huitoto-Ocaina there
already existed the two allophones [d] initially and [r] medially, and this
was probably the case also in Proto Witotoan. There is only one example
in Leach (1971) of word-initial /r/; /dʸ/ only occurs medially in noncognates.

PHO *d /#__ > O *d^y* H *r.*
156 *dīā(hī)* 'fruit'. O *d^yāāhī̃, hixāā.* H *rí.a* ~ " ~ *ri.ara.*
160 *dáta* 'stick'. O *d^yááť^ya.* H *ráda* ~ " ~ ".
160 *dató()* 'stick'. O *d^yaťoop̌o.* H *radóti* ~ *radóθi* ~ ".
222 *doti(-de-te)* 'cold'. O *d^yótï.* H *roč̌i-re-de* ~ *roθi-re-de* ~ ".
275 *dï?* 'eat meat'. O *d^yaa, d^yoo.* H *rí̃-de* ~ *rï̃-te* ~ *rï-te.*
264 *(igó)daï(kā)* 'bark'. O *d^yaká̃.* H *igóraï* ~ " ~ ".
 93 *(tokï) da-ta* 'spear'. O *oïd^yááť^ya.* H – ~ *dukï̃-ra-da* ~ –.
 95 *(tïk)ói da-ta* 'arrow'. O *oïd^yááť^ya.* H *tïkúi-ra-da* ~ – ~ –. (93 and 95 were originally separate words; see *oi*).
 71 *?*(d)ódzi-(goe)?do* 'rainbow'. O *ójii?o* (∅ exception; perhaps originally /?__?/). H *róti-gue.o* ~ *róθi-gue.o* ~ *roθi-guero.*
PHO *d /i__(a)i > O *ǰ,* H *r.*
171 *hi?pí-dai* 'chili plant'. O *ha?p̌íí-ǰa.* H – ~ *hip̌i-rai* ~ ".
132 *?*()di()* 'parakeet'. O *ǰíïyi.* H *gáirikoŋo* ~ " ~ *gairiθï.*
PHO *d /__ > O *r,* H *r.*
126 *(h)edaï* 'toad'. O *ïïra.* H *héro* ~ " ~ *heroki.*
140 *(do)?-hidakï(ŋo)* 'bee'. O *d^yo?íïrako.* H *hiráŋo* ~ " ~ *hirakïño.*
142 *?*(p)aïd(á)to* 'flea'. O *oróóβiť^yo.* H *païrádo* ~ *p̌aïrádo* ~ ".
148 *odo-taï(no)* 'chigger'. O *orooť^yo.* H *í.oǰoŋo* ~ *i.oǰoŋo, órokoŋo* ~ *i.oǰaïño.*
151 *?*()pedï* 'hill'. O *ť^yaβïïro.* H *ïperï* ~ *ip̌erï* ~ .
198 *-dáïma* 'medicine man'. O *hï?xap̌oráá̃ma.* H *manó-ri-raïma* ~ *áima,*
     hï̃.ido-raïma ~ *aima.*
270 *()pódo* 'feather'. O *ť^yap̌óóro.* H *ipóro* ~ *ip̌óro* ~ ".
296 *boda* 'yellow'. O *bóóra.* H *borá-re-de* ~ " ~ ".
330 *iháídaï* 'wide'. O *aháára.* H *áiju.e, i.airo-re-de* ~ *éijoï.o, i.airo-re-de* ~ *dï.aro-θe.*
353 *?*(bo)-?tá-(de)* 'split'. O *taarï* (probably not cognate suffix). H *bo-dá-de* ~ *bo-tá-de* ~ "(possible *d* exception).
263 *?*á(d)e* 'long'. O *áá̃ñi* (*ñ* exception). H *áre* ~ " ~ ".
332 *?*a(d)e* 'far'. O *aanï* (*n* exception). H *are* ~ " ~ ".
 63 [no reconstruction] 'wind'. O *hïβóód^yo* (*d^y* exception). H (no cognate).
 65 [no reconstruction] 'moon'. O *p̌od^yoome* (*d^y* exception). H (no cognate).
 91 [no reconstruction] 'paddle'. O *mō?sod^yááβoho* (*d^y* exception). H (no cognate).
287 [no reconstruction] 'lay'. O *tïïd^ya* (*d^y* exception). H (no cognate).
321 [no reconstruction] 'in'. O *had^ya* (*d^y* exception). H (no cognate).

The Ocaina exceptions above have no cognates in Huitoto. It is unclear where they came from. They could not apparently have been derived from *dz*, except the last one, since *dz* only became /d^y/ after *ai*.

PHO *?d > O *?,* H *r~r~r* or .~.~r.
 72 *aenï̃?-ē, aenï̃?-dōē* 'earth'. O *añōō?ï̃.* H *énï.e* ~ " ~ *enïru.e.*
 71 *?*(d)ódzi-(goe)?do* 'rainbow'. O *ójii?o.* H *róti-gue.o* ~ *róθi-gue.o* ~ *roθi-guero.*
 51 *hō?dáhī* 'lake'. O *hō?á̃áhī.* H *hórai* ~ " ~ ".

The Huitoto reflexes of *dz* are the same as those of *t,* but the Ocaina reflexes are totally different, for which reason it was necessary to propose a separate protophoneme. It appears that *dz* fell together with *t* very early in the history of Early Huitoto and then split along with *t into other phonemes. The slight differences in the Huitoto rules below as compared with those for *t are probably not significant (e.g., /t ~ θ ~ θ/ after /ai/ is actually common among the *t examples, but since these cases also occurred before /i/ it was not necessary to propose a separate rule).

Two of the reflexes of /dz/, however, are different from those of *t. The Huitoto /n/ reflex must have been produced before *dz fell together with *t. Four of its five occurrences are in one morpheme, *dzĩʔ-, which appears to mean interrogative. This rule is uncertain, in that nasalization of the vowel is only apparent in one of the cases (304), but it is sufficiently likely that I have proposed it.

The Huitoto reflex of /d/ for *dz occurs in one case word-medially (item 306) and I have analyzed it in this case as deriving from *ʔdz, parallel to the derivation of /d/ from *ʔt discussed in §3.8. The remaining cases occur word-initially, however, which is never the case for *t; /d/ appears to be the general word-initial reflex for *dz (when not nasalized). It is unclear what the intermediate form was that was retained after the word-medial cases fell together with *t.

I have included all of the examples reconstructed of *dz, even those which have no cognate.

PHO   *dz /__V̆ > O dz, H n.
259   *dzĩʔ 'what'. O dzoʔ. H nï-póde ~ – ~ –.
302   *dzĩʔ-() 'how'. O dzoʔ-xáʔmï, dzoʔ-ɸīīráʔ. H naitó ~ nĩ́.eθe ~ ".
303   *dzĩʔ-() 'when'. O dzoʔ-kã, dzoʔ-aa. H nï-rúi-do ~ " ~ ".
304   *dzĩʔ-() 'where'. O dzõõ(ʔ). H nï-nó, nï-né ~ " ~ ".
192   *(ï)tái-poe-dza(no) 'last'. O ťáɸoïïdzanó. H idái-pu.e-na, írai-pu.e-na ~ íraï.e.
PHO   *dz /ai__ > O ďˀ, H t ~ θ ~ θ.
179   *(ï)háidzaï 'salt'. O hááidʸa. H í.aitaï ~ í.aiθaï ~ ".
PHO   *dz /o__i > O ǰ, H t ~ θ ~ θ.
71   ?*(d)ódzi-(goe)ʔdo 'rainbow'. O ójiiʔo. H róti-gue.o ~ róθi-gue.o ~ roθi-guero.
PHO   *dz /i__i > O ǰ, H ǰ.
74   ??*(koni)dzĩĩʔ(ï) 'sand'. O jíõõʔï. H kónijï.e ~ – ~ konijï.e.
PHO   *dz /#__ > O dz, H d ~ t ~ t.
53   *dzod(o)-p(o) 'spring of water'. O dzóóroʔɸi. H do() ~ to-rá-no ~ to-ra-ɸo.
310   *dzo- 'flow'. O dzooro, dzooï. H dó-de ~ tó-te ~ ".
54 = 55 *(nopïko dzoa) 'rapids'. O (no cognate). H nopïko dú.a ~ noɸíko tú.a ~ –.
281   *(dzĩï) 'die'. O (no cognate). H dï.í-de ~ tï.í-de ~ –.
114   *(dzoʔdzo) 'river turtle'. O dzooʔdzo. H (no cognate).
PHO   *dz /__ > O dz, H d.
134   ?*(k)oodz(a) 'curassow'. O xóódzoho. H jó.oda ~ jó.oda, hó.oda ~ –.
25   ?*ïdzá-k(aido) 'leg'. O odzá-kona. H ïdá-kairo ~ ", rḯ.aï-kairo ~ ".
352   *(adzï) 'hit'. O aadzi. H (no cognate).

PHO *?dz > O ?dz, H d̯~t~t̯.
306   ?*()?dzï() 'there'. O dziráhï̃?. H badï̃~batíne~ ". It is unclear whether
reflexes in 306 were historically word initial or word medial; in the former
case it would go under the /#__ rule above. However, by analogy with *t
the Huitoto reflex of *?dz should be Nɨpode /d/, so this rule is probable in
any case.
114   (dzo?dzo) 'river turtle'. O dzoo?dzo. H (no cognate).
PHO *g /#__ > O g, H g.
126   *goaïkï̃(ho) 'toad'. O gokóóho. H gúku~gúaïkï̃~–.
364   ?*()gō 'suck'. O gōō. H mugú-de~–~–~–.
275   *gōï 'eat fruit' O gōō. H –~guí-te~gui-te.
PHO *g /(a)ï__o > O k, H ŋ~ŋ~ñ.
PHO *?g /(a)ï__o > O ?k, H ŋ~ŋ~ñ.
205   *kaï-gaï 'we (f.d.)'. O xak(a). H –~káïŋaï~kaïñaï.
207   *i(aï)-gaï-haï. H –~í.aï-ŋu.aï~i.aï-ñu.aï.
126   ??*(n)op(aï)goï 'toad'. O opépeko. H nopáïŋo~noɸáïŋo~ noɸaïño.
206   *(o)maï̃?-gaï 'ye (f.d.)'. O mō?k(a). H –~ómï-ŋo~omi-ñoï.
246   *ha?ï̃(do)-goï 'old woman'. O ha?ū-ko. H e.íro-gï~e.íro-gi, e.íri-ŋo.
      Noncognate examples (some Ocaina examples are listed if part of the word is
      cognate or if the suffix is suspicious):
100   *n(ē)nï̃(goï) 'armadillo'. O ñōōnō (no suffix). H ñeníŋo~ "~ñeniño.
139   (ïmï̃-goï) 'piranha'. O d̯o?yoo?xo (no cognate). H térobeño~ïmï̃ŋo~ïmiño.
140   *(do)?-hidakï̃(goï) 'bee'. O d̯o?ï̃ïrako (no suffix). H hiráŋo~ "~hirakiño.
145   (kadákï̃-goï) 'termite'. O ohïx̃o? (no cognate). H karáŋo~karákïŋo~karakiño.
145   (igïdakï̃-goï) 'termite'. O ohïx̃o? (no cognate). H ígïdaŋo~ígïdakïŋo~igïdiño.
146   (dakï̃-goï) 'ant'. O amōōxo (no cognate). H rakíŋo~rakïŋo~rakiño.
147   (hebekï̃-goï) 'spider'. O (no cognate). H hébekïŋo~ "~hebekiño.
148   *-taï-(goï), -(kaï-goï), odó-, (i?o)- 'chigger'. O oroob̯'o (no suffix). H í.ojoŋo,
      orókoŋo~í.ojoŋo, órokoŋo~i.ojaïño, orokoño.
132   ?*(gai)di(kaï-goï) 'parakeet'. O jíïyi (no suffix). H gáirikoŋo~ "~gairiθï.
161   *(dai)?tï(kï-goï) 'grass'. O b̯'oháā́(hā) (no suffix). H ráidï.aï~ráitï.aï~raitïkiño.

The following are examples in which the Huitoto suffix -ŋo was added
to a stem ending in *i; in these cases it became -ño. Because these are the
only examples in which this suffix does not follow *ï, it may have been
added to these forms in the recent past, after it became well established
with its nasal consonant. Neither example has a cognate for the suffix.

45   *éʔï-(goï) 'mother'. O áʔï? (no suffix). H á-ño~éi-(ño)~e.i.
113 *mainí-(goï) 'tortoise'. O mañii?xo (no suffix). H meníño~ "~".

PHO *g /i__ (no examples) > O k, H g.
PHO *?g /i__ > O ?k, H g.
31   ?*()ni?gaï 'skin'. O xonï̃ï̃?ka. H íni~igóï-raï~igoï.
3   *p(óe i)?goï, ?*p(óe ini) 'lip'. O ɸa-?óó?ko. H pú.e ini~ɸú.e igoï~".
PHO *g /o__ > O k, H g.
PHO *?g /o__ (no examples) > O ?k, H g.
246 *ha?ï̃(do)-goï 'old woman'. O ha?ū-ko. H e.íro-gï~e.íro-gi, e.íri-ŋo~u.aikï-ño.

early in the history of Early Huitoto and then split along with *t into other phonemes. The slight differences in the Huitoto rules below as compared with those for *t are probably not significant (e.g., /t ~ θ ~ θ/ after /ai/ is actually common among the *t examples, but since these cases also occurred before /i/ it was not necessary to propose a separate rule).

Two of the reflexes of /dz/, however, are different from those of *t. The Huitoto /n/ reflex must have been produced before *dz fell together with *t. Four of its five occurrences are in one morpheme, *dzĩʔ-, which appears to mean interrogative. This rule is uncertain, in that nasalization of the vowel is only apparent in one of the cases (304), but it is sufficiently likely that I have proposed it.

The Huitoto reflex of /d/ for *dz occurs in one case word-medially (item 306) and I have analyzed it in this case as deriving from *ʔdz, parallel to the derivation of /d/ from *ʔt discussed in §3.8. The remaining cases occur word-initially, however, which is never the case for *t; /d/ appears to be the general word-initial reflex for *dz (when not nasalized). It is unclear what the intermediate form was that was retained after the word-medial cases fell together with *t.

I have included all of the examples reconstructed of *dz, even those which have no cognate.

PHO　*dz /__V̄ > O dz, H n.
259　*dzĩʔ 'what'. O dzoʔ. H nï-póde ~ – ~ –.
302　*dzĩʔ-() 'how'. O dzoʔ-xáʔmï, dzoʔ-ɸïïráʔ. H naitó ~ nï.eθe ~ ".
303　*dzĩʔ-() 'when'. O dzoʔ-kã, dzoʔ-aa. H nï-rúi-do ~ " ~ ".
304　*dzĩʔ-() 'where'. O dzõõ(ʔ), dzoo. H nï-nó, nï-né ~ " ~ ".
192　*(i)tái-poe-dza(no) 'last'. O tʸáɸoïïdzanó. H idái-pu.e-na, írai-pu.e-na ~ írai-pu.e-na ~ iraï.e.
PHO　*dz /ai__ > O dʸ, H t ~ θ ~ θ.
179　*(ï)háidzaï 'salt'. O hááidʸa. H ï.aitaï ~ ï.aiθaï ~ ".
PHO　*dz /o__i > O ǰ, H t ~ θ ~ θ.
71　ʔ*(d)ódzi-(goe)ʔdo 'rainbow'. O ójiiʔo. H róti-gue.o ~ róθi-gue.o ~ roθi-guero.
PHO　*dz /i__i > O ǰ, H ǰ.
74　ʔʔ*(koni)dziĩʔ(ï) 'sand'. O ǰíõõʔï. H kónïǰï.e ~ – ~ konïǰï.e.
PHO　*dz /#__ > O dz, H d ~ t ~ t.
53　*dzod(o)-p(o) 'spring of water'. O dzóóroʔɸi. H do() ~ to-rá-no ~ to-ra-ɸo.
310　*dzo- 'flow'. O dzooro, dzooï. H dó-de ~ tó-te ~ ".
54 = 55　*(nopíko dzoa) 'rapids'. O (no cognate). H nopíko dú.a ~ noɸíko tú.a ~ –.
281　*(dzïï) 'die'. O (no cognate). H dï.í-de ~ tï.í-de ~ –.
114　*(dzoʔdzo) 'river turtle'. O dzooʔdzo. H (no cognate).
PHO　*dz /__ > O dz, H d.
134　ʔ*(k)oodz(a) 'curassow'. O xóódzoho. H ǰó.oda ~ ǰó.oda, hó.oda ~ –.
25　ʔ*ïdzá-k(aido) 'leg'. O odzá-kona. H ïdá-kairo ~ ", rï.aï-kairo ~ ".
352　*(adzï) 'hit'. O aadzi. H (no cognate).

PHO *?dz > O ?dz, H d̯~t~t.

306 ?*()?dzï() 'there'. O dziráhï̃?. H badï̃~batíne~". It is unclear whether reflexes in 306 were historically word initial or word medial; in the former case it would go under the /#__ rule above. However, by analogy with *t the Huitoto reflex of *?dz should be Nɨpode /d/, so this rule is probable in any case.

114 (dzo?dzo) 'river turtle'. O dzoo?dzo. H (no cognate).

PHO *g /#__ > O g, H g.

126 *goaïkï̃(ho) 'toad'. O gokóóho. H gúku~gúaïkï̃~–.

364 ?*()gō 'suck'. O gōō. H mugú-de~–~–~–.

275 *gōï 'eat fruit' O gōō. H –~guí-te~gui-te.

PHO *g /(a)ï__o > O k, H ŋ~ŋ~ñ.

PHO *?g /(a)ï__o > O ?k, H ŋ~ŋ~ñ.

205 *kaï-gaï 'we (f.d.)'. O xak(a). H –~káïŋaï~kaïñaï.

207 *i(aï)-gaï-haï. O ï̈-ká(ha). H –~í.aï-ŋu.aï~i.aï-ñu.aï.

126 ??*(n)op(aï)goï 'toad'. O opépeko. H nopáïŋo~noɸáïŋo~ noɸaïño.

206 *(o)maï̃?-gaï 'ye (f.d.)'. O mō?k(a). H –~ómï-ŋo~omi-ñoï.

246 *ha?í(do)-goï 'old woman'. O ha?ū-ko. H e.íro-gï~e.íro-gi, e.írï-ŋo.

Noncognate examples (some Ocaina examples are listed if part of the word is cognate or if the suffix is suspicious):

100 *n(ē)nï̃(goï) 'armadillo'. O ñōōnō (no suffix). H ñenï̃ŋo~"~ñeniño.

139 (imï̃-goï) 'piranha'. O d̯'o?yoo?xo (no cognate). H térobeño~ïmï̃ŋo~ïmiño.

140 *(do)?-hidakï̃(goï) 'bee'. O d̯'o?íïrako (no suffix). H hiráŋo~"~hirakiño.

145 (kadákï-goï) 'termite'. O ohï̈xo? (no cognate). H karáŋo~karákï̃ŋo~karakiño.

145 (igïdakï-goï) 'termite'. O ohï̈xo? (no cognate). H igïdaŋo~ígïdakiŋo~igïdiño.

146 (dakï̃-goï) 'ant'. O amōōxo (no cognate). H rakíŋo~rakï̃ŋo~rakiño.

147 (hebekï-goï) 'spider'. O (no cognate). H hébekiŋo~"~hebekiño.

148 *-taï-(goï), -(kaï-goï), odó-, (i?o)- 'chigger'. O oroot̯'o (no suffix). H í.ojoŋo, orókoŋo~í.ojoŋo, órokoŋo~i.ojaïño, orokoño.

132 ?*(gai)di(kaï-goï) 'parakeet'. O jíïyi (no cognate). H gáirikoŋo~"~gairiθï.

161 *(dai)?tï(kï-goï) 'grass'. O t̯'oháá̃(hā) (no suffix). H ráidï.aï~ráitï.aï~raitïkiño.

The following are examples in which the Huitoto suffix -ŋo was added to a stem ending in *i; in these cases it became -ño. Because these are the only examples in which this suffix does not follow *ï, it may have been added to these forms in the recent past, after it became well established with its nasal consonant. Neither example has a cognate for the suffix.

45 *é?ï-(goï) 'mother'. O á?ï? (no suffix). H á-ño~éi-(ño)~e.i.

113 *mainí-(goï) 'tortoise'. O mañii?xo (no suffix). H meníño~"~".

PHO *g /i__ (no examples) > O k, H g.

PHO *?g /i__ > O ?k, H g.

31 ?*()ni?gaï 'skin'. O xonï̃í?ka. H íni~igóï-raï~igoï.

3 *p(óe i)?goï, ?*p(óe ini) 'lip'. O ɸa-?óó?ko. H pú.e ini~ɸú.e igoï~".

PHO *g /o__ > O k, H g.

PHO *?g /o__ (no examples) > O ?k, H g.

246 *ha?í(do)-goï 'old woman'. O ha?ū-ko. H e.íro-gï~e.íro-gi, e.írï-ŋo~u.aikï-ño.

82 *no(g)o() 'cooking pot'. O ñoxooťo (x exception). H nógo ~ " ~ ".
PHO *g /ï__ï > O h, H g.
PHO *ʔg /ï__ï (no examples) > O ʔ, H g.
92 *()-bḯ(g)ï 'club'. O biija-βóóho. H bí́gï ~ " ~ ".
PHO *g /a__ > O h, H g.
204 *tāgē 'it'. O ťā(hï̃), ťa. H dáge ~ - ~ -.
PHO *ʔg /a__ > O ʔ (see *ʔh), H g.
190 *(ha)naʔg(á)-péti 'ten'. O hanāʔ ɸáti, hanaa-ʔɸïɸóroʔ.
      H nagá-peba ~ nagá-ɸeθi ~ naga-ɸebekuiro.

The preceding three rules are proposed by analogy with rules which applied to *k and to *h. *k became *h in the environment *ï__ï, following which *ʔh became /ʔ/.

PHO *g /ai__iʔ > O g, H g.
PHO *ʔg /ai__iʔ (no examples) > O gʔ, H g.
314 *()āïg(i) 'worm'. O agiïma. H igïroï ~ (a)igïroï ~ aïgiro.
PHO *g /ae__ > O g, H g.
PHO *ʔg /ae__ (no examples) > O ʔ, H g.
14 *(he)bae-goï() 'chest'. O 14 bagóóʔya. H 244 hébe-goï, ", hebe-gï.

The Huitoto reflex /ŋ ~ ŋ ~ ñ/ of *g set forth above occurs in only one morpheme, meaning (feminine) when applied to people and (singular) when applied to many animals, which I have reconstructed as PHO *goï or (in the feminine dual pronouns) *gaï; in Ocaina it is realized as /ko/ or /ka/ and in Huitoto as /ŋo ~ ŋo ~ ño/ or /ŋaï ~ ŋaï ~ ñaï/ (contracted in 207 to /ŋu ~ ŋu ~ ñu/ because followed by a vowel). The Proto Bora-Muinane cognates, only having the meaning (feminine), have *ge and the Proto Witotoan form I have reconstructed as **gaï. The vast majority of the occurrences of this morpheme in Huitoto are after *ï or *aï, and I am assuming that this is the environment which produced it.[46]

An example showing the historical alternation in this morpheme is 246, 'old woman' in which there are competing forms with the morpheme preceded by either /o/ or /i/; the /g/ occurs after /o/ and /ŋ/ after /ï/. The competing forms of this word may have come into existence because of confusion of this word's protolanguage form **haʔí(do)-goï with 40 *dï-goï 'woman'. *haʔí(do)-goï matches 47 *haʔí(do)-ma 'old man', which has an unambiguous *o.

---

[46]At first this may seem like an unlikely conditioning environment for nasality. However, [ï] is the homorganic vocoid for [g] and [ŋ]. It would thus create greater constriction of the oral air flow than any other combination, making a tendency toward nasal release more plausible. There is no evidence that vowel nasalization was involved in any way.

However, being a separate morpheme, and a very common and impor-
tant one at that, the -ŋo suffix was later added to a few words whose stems
do not end in /aï/ or /ï/, such as 203 apé-ŋo 'she' (which also has masculine
and plural forms). The vast majority of the cases in which this morpheme
does not currently occur after /ï/ are cases of contraction, most of which
are easily reconstructible as such, as can be seen from the examples. Thus
the suffix now occurs in a few cases after /a/, /o/, and /e/ (though never
after /u/); in those few (presumably recently generated) cases in which it
ended up after /i/, the /ŋ ~ ŋ ~ ñ/ seems to have changed to /ñ ~ ñ ~ ñ/,
following the lead of Murui, in which all cases of /ŋ/ changed to /ñ/.

There are a very few words in Huitoto which currently have the sequence /igo/ (184, 189, 212, 237, 344), none of which have cognates with
Ocaina. Therefore, these do not really contradict my proposed origin for
the ŋo morpheme.

The remaining reflexes of *g are somewhat rare, but are reasonable and
so are set forth as shown.

3.10. Glottal. Proto Huitoto-Ocaina glottal is always lost in Huitoto.
Between vowels, however, in nearly every case it leaves behind a phonemic
syllable break as distinguished from a one-syllable vowel cluster (diphthong; see §1.3).

PHO   *ʔ /a__e,ï > O ʔ, H ∅.
  90   *()áʔe 'canoe'. **O** hōɸááʔï. **H** nókae ~ nokáe ~ noka.e.
 111   *(na)ʔïma 'crocodile'. **O** hōʔóóma. **H** tïkïnaïma ~ θïkïnaïma ~ ".
PHO   *ʔ /a__ > O ʔ, H .~.~..
 173   *ōnáʔō 'Banisterium'. **O** ōnáāʔō. **H** úna.o ~ " ~ ".
PHO   *ʔ /e__í > O ʔ, H .~.~..
PHO   *ʔ /é__i# > O ʔ, H ∅ ~ ∅ ~..
PHO   *ʔ /é__i > O ʔ, H ∅ ~ ∅ ~ ∅.
 246   *heʔï(do)-goï 'old woman'. **O** haʔïï-ko. **H** e.íro-gï ~ e.íro-gï, e.írï-ŋo ~ u.aikï-ño.
  47   *heʔï-(do)-ma 'old man'. **O** haʔïï-ma. **H** e.íro-ma ~ éiro-ma, éi-kome ~ eiro-ma,
    u.aikï-ma.
  45   *éʔï-(goï) 'mother'. **O** áʔïʔ (no suffix). **H** á-ño ~ éi-(ño) ~ e.i.
 333   *iaïn(oi)deʔi 'near'. **O** áánïraʔ. **H** a.íno-mo ~ áïno-ri ~ i.aïrei.

I combined the preceding four examples above into one rule because
their conditioning environments only differed by stress, and the stress is
not consistent among the three Huitoto languages. Apparently the loss of
syllable break occurred after the stress placement was established.[47]

---

[47]This does not represent a synchronic rule, as is demonstrated by Minica má.ika(hï)
in 163.

PHO *ʔ /V_V > O ʔ, H ..
38–39 *íʔí 'man'. O ooʔí. H í.í- ~ " ~ ".
72 *aeníʔ-ē, *aeníʔ-dōē 'earth'. O añōōʔí. H éní.e ~ " ~ eníru.e.
74 ??*(koni)dziíʔē 'sand'. O jíōōʔí. H kónijí.e ~ – ~ konijí.e.
165 *tiʔó() 'tobacco'. O ťoʔooko. H dï.ó-na ~ " ~ ".
197 *(p)ōíʔéko(da) 'mask'. O ɸōʔííxora, orííʔka. H hígape ~ hígaɸe ~ u.i.eko iko.
256 *bí-hāē, *bi-ʔe 'this'. O bíí, bíhā, baʔi-, bï-.H bedá ~ bí.e ~ ".
265 *ōʔá-(tï), *ōʔá-(īhī) 'flesh'. O ōʔāāhī. H ú.a-tï ~ í.e-θï ~ ".
283 *íʔí 'swim'. O ōōʔō. H í.í-de ~ " ~ ".
PHO *ʔ /#_V > O ʔ, H [ʔ].
210 *ta onōí 'his hand'. O ťáʔonōō. H da ónoï ~ – ~ –.
211 *kaï onōí 'our hands'. O xa-ʔonōō. H kaï óno-ge ~ kaï ónoï ~ kaï ono-jï.
212 *(o)māíʔ-(to) onōí 'your hands'. O mō-ʔonōō. H dáïgo óno-ge ~ ómoï
ónoï ~ omoï ono-jï.

The last rule above really only has meaning when prefixes are added to vowel-initial words. Huitoto, however, has few if any prefixes (or to state it another way, those items which might be treated as prefixes have been analyzed as separate words by the linguists involved). Therefore, the effects of this rule can only be clearly seen in Ocaina.

/ʔ/ occurs in Ocaina between vowels, word-finally and before /ɸ t tʸ č ts k x s š dz y m ñ/; it never occurs in the Ocaina data before /b ɟ dʸ g h β n ñ ɱ ʀ r/ (i.e., its occurrence is limited before voiced consonants, especially voiced stops).

As reconstructed, *ʔ does not have the restriction before voiced stops that is apparent in Ocaina. In three out of four cases of /ʔ/ plus voiced stop, however, the sequence was eliminated. *ʔb lost the glottal, becoming /β/, *ʔd (allophonically [ʔr]) lost the stop, becoming /ʔ/, and *ʔg became *ʔk. Only the sequence *ʔdz was retained unchanged. The consonant after *ʔ was also lost in one other sequence, *ʔh becoming *ʔ.

As reconstructed, *ʔ occurs in Proto Huitoto-Ocaina before the consonants *p, *t, *k, *b, *d, *dz, *g, *h, and *y, but not before *β, *m, or *n, thus being restricted only before voiced fricatives and nasals (§4.5). It is occasionally reconstructed in stem-final position, but whether it occurred word-finally in Proto Huitoto-Ocaina is unclear, since if the Proto Huitoto-Ocaina grammatical system had the Huitoto suffixes, these glottals would always be followed by a consonant.

As can be seen below, glottal stop was apparently lost in Ocaina before certain consonants (notably *t) in some cases for no explainable reason and before *b (which in Ocaina became /β/) in every case. It could easily have been lost in other cases also (after *β, *m, and *n), leaving no trace. Therefore, it must be assumed that the frequency in Proto Huitoto-Ocaina of *ʔC must have been even higher than its already high frequency in Ocaina.

This is surprising, since /ʔ/ is already the most common consonant phoneme in Ocaina, comprising 17% of all consonants, 5% syllable-initial and 12% syllable-final. It is possible that some of its occurrences in Ocaina, especially before consonants, are the result of generation, perhaps caused by tone change or vowel quality (possibilities include 4, 14, 27, 29, 31, 32, 50, 57, 59, 66). This is suggested also by the fact that the correspondence of preconsonantal glottal stop between Ocaina and Proto Bora-Muinane is not very good. No solution is apparent, however, so I have reconstructed all Ocaina glottal stops in the protolanguage.

Here follows a summary of the rules for preconsonantal *ʔ; examples are not given, since these have already been listed under the individual consonants and are often listed in separate rules there.

PHO *ʔp	>	**O** ʔϕ	>	**H** p~ϕ~ϕ	
PHO *ʔk	>	**O** ʔx	>	**H** k	
PHO *ʔt /_i	>	**O** ʔt	>	**H** t~θ~θ	
PHO *ʔt /_e (no examples)	>	**O** (ʔt)	>	**H** (ʔ)	
PHO *ʔt /i_ae,aï	>	**O** ʔtʸ	>	**H** ǰ	
PHO *ʔt /oi_o	>	**O** ʔč	>	**H** d	
PHO *ʔt /_a,o otherwise	>	**O** (ʔ)tʸ	>	**H** d~t~t, d	
PHO *ʔt /_ï	>	**O** (ʔ)t	>	**H** d~t~t	
PHO *ʔb	>	**O** β	>	**H** ƀ~p~p	
PHO *ʔd	>	**O** ʔ	>	**H** r~r~r or .~.~r	
PHO *ʔdz	>	**O** ʔdz	>	**H** d~t~t	
PHO *ʔg /a_	>	**O** ʔ (see *ʔh)	>	**H** g	
PHO *ʔg /(a)ï_o	>	**O** ʔk	>	**H** ŋ~ŋ~ñ	
PHO *ʔg /_	>	**O** ʔk	>	**H** g	
PHO *ʔh /i_i#,ï#	>	**O** ʔ	>	**H** h	
PHO *ʔh /#_	>	**O** ʔ	>	**H** h	
PHO *ʔh /_	>	**O** ʔ	>	**H** ɸ	
PHO *ʔy /ï,ē_	>	**O** ʔn	>	**H** .	
PHO *ʔy /á,õ,ï̃_ (no cognates)	>	**O** ʔn	>	**H** (.i)	
PHO *ʔy /i,e_	>	**O** ʔy	>	**H** .	
PHO *ʔy /a,o,ï_	>	**O** ʔy	>	**H** ǰ	

The following four examples involve cases of reconstructed syllable-final *ʔ. It is uncertain what followed *ʔ in these cases, since this portion of the word does not match in the cognates. In 290 Ocaina was left with a word-final /ʔ/, but in 275 it lost the glottal.

227 = 328 *hiʔtíʔ-() 'black'. **O** hiʔtóóʔ-ϕï. **H** hídï-re-de ~ hitï-re-de ~ ".
275 *dïʔ-(te) 'eat meat'. **O** dʸaa, dʸoo. **H** rí-de ~ rí̄-te ~ rï-te.

290 *hi?-(te) 'give'. O híĩʔ. H í-de ~ ɸeká-de ~ ".
354 ?*tō-ʔ(tá-te) 'pierce'. O tʸōōʔɸo. H ju-dá-de ~ ju-tá-de ~ ".

3.11. Fricatives. This section presents the rules for the PHO fricatives *h, *ʔh, and *β.

PHO *h /#__a,ai > O h, H, h.
228 *hái 'go!'. O háái̧. H mai hái ~ mai hai ~ ".
63 *hai(dí)(p)oï 'wind'. O hïβóódʸo. H hairípoï ~ hairíɸo ~ ".
345 *(h)(ai)dî?-p(aití) 'left'. O ïrooʔ-ɸatí(∅ exception).
H harí-pene ~ harí-ɸene ~ harï-ɸebehï.
168 *(h)aʔkáí?-ti(dai) 'yam'. O aʔxaaʔti (∅ exception). H -~ hakái-θairai ~-.

The preceding rule has as many exceptions as examples that follow the rule; there is probably some conditioning factor, but it is not apparent.

PHO *h /#__eʔ,iʔ,iy > O h, H ∅.
47 *heʔí-(do)-ma 'old man'. O haʔíĩ-ma. H e.íro-ma ~ éiro-ma, éi-kome ~ eiro-ma, u.aïkï-ma.
246 *heʔí(do)-goï 'old woman'. O haʔíĩ-ko. H e.iro-gï ~ e.íro-gï, e.írï-ŋo ~ u.aikï-ño.
1 *(h)ïyíʔpe 'tongue'. O hïñóóʔɸï. H i.ípe ~ i.íɸe ~ ".
290 *hi?-(te) 'give'. O híĩʔ. H í-de ~ ɸeká-de ~ ".
PHO *h /#__e,i > O h, H h.
17 *he(dáï)ʔkï(mo) 'back'. O híĩʔxo(mó). H heráïkï ~ " ~-.
334 *hetákï 'thick'. O hïtʸááxo. H hédakï.e-de ~ " ~ ".
371 *hee(), *(e)hiʔtï 'ripe'. O híĩʔto. H hé.e-de ~ " ~ e.iθï.
171 *hiʔpí-dai 'chili plant'. O haʔɸíí-ja. H -~ híɸi-rai ~ ".
171 *hiʔpí?-hï(βe) 'chili'. O haʔɸíí-ʔoβï. H hípi-hï ~ híɸi-hï ~ ".
227 = 328 *hiʔtí?-() 'black'. O híʔtóó?-ɸï. H hídï-re-de ~ híti-re-de ~ ".
294 = 371 *hīáï(hī) 'red'. O tsíí?o, hããhī. H hí.aï-re-de ~ " ~ ".
172 *híibí(ʔe) 'coca'. O hiibiro. H hibi.e ~ hí.ibi.e ~ hi.ibe.
126 *(h)edaï 'toad'. O ïïra (∅ exception). H héro ~ " ~ herokï.
PHO *h /#__o,ï > O h, H h.
75 *(ho)po 'house'. O ɸoo(ho), -xo. H hópo ~ hóɸo ~ hoɸo, ɸo.
255 *(ho)po-() 'shelter'. O ɸohóóβonï. H hïpo-ko ~ hoɸó-ka.iɸe ~ bïθaini.
313 *hokó-te 'wash'. O hoxoo-tï. H hokó-de ~ " ~ ".
321 ??*ho() 'in'. O haa, hadʸa. H hópo ~ ".
377 *(ho)pó-tïʔb(i) 'small house'. O ɸohoo-tsiβo. H hopó-čuɓi ~ hoɸó-čupi ~-.
51 *hōʔdáhī 'lake'. O hōʔááhī. H hórai ~ " ~ ".
163 *hōʔtí(ti) 'cassava'. O hōʔtááti. H húti ~ húθi ~ huθi.e.
98–101 *hïʔko 'jaguar'. O hōʔxo. H híko ~ " ~ ".
268 *hï̃() 'egg'. O hóóʔto. H hígï ~ " ~ ".
PHO *h /nonhigh V or diph.__i#,ï# > O h, H ∅.
80 *kïnahī 'hammock'. O xonaahī. H kínai ~ " ~ ".
51 *hōʔdáhī 'lake'. O hōʔááhī. H hórai ~ " ~ ".
205 *kaï-hï 'we (pl.)'. O xa(ho). H kaï ~ kaï ~ kaï.
48 *(haï-)nō-hï 'water'. O ñōō(-hï̃). H háïnoi ~ " ~ hïnui.

PHO   *h /i__i#,ï# > O h, H h.
PHO   *ʔh /i__i#,ï# > O ʔ, H h.
319 *mōnoï ihī 'milk'. O mōnoo-hǐ̃. H mónoï-hi ~ mónoï ihi ~ monoï ihi.
157 *(a)m(éna) ihī 'sap'. O ahīī, mááhī̃. H ihi ~ aména ero ihi ~ (amena) i.
171 *hiʔpíʔ-hï(βe) 'chili'. O haʔɸíí-ʔoβï. H hípi-hï ~ híɸi-hï ~ ".
PHO   *ʔh /__ > O ʔ, H . (see next paragraph).
140 *(do)ʔ-hidakï(goï) 'bee'. O ďoʔíírako. H hiráŋo ~ " ~ hirakïño.
372 *aenǐ̃ʔ-hiβóda 'dust'. O ahooʔïβóra, añōōʔǐ̃βóra. H enǐ́-čoma ~ " ~ hi.ora.

After a *ʔ, *h is lost (other than in the next to last rule above) in both
languages. It seems likely, therefore, that most of the cases of *ʔh are
unreconstructible, since they are now indistinguishable from simple cases
of *ʔ (see §3.10). *h is reconstructible in 140 and 372 only because a prefix
ending in *ʔ was added to the Ocaina word but not to the Huitoto word.

PHO   *h /__ > O h, H ..
163 *máhī(kahï) 'sweet cassava'. O maahī. H ma.íka(hï) ~ má.ika(hï) ~ ma.íka.
 85 = 253 *nahǐ̃(to) 'path, trail'. O naahō, tóβïʔℓ̌ʷa. H í.o ~ " ~ na.ǐ̃θo.
207 *i(aï)-gaï-haï 'they (f.d.)'. O ī̃-ká(ha). H – ~ í.aï-ŋu.aï ~ i.aï-ñu.aï.
207 *i(aï)-maï-haï 'they (m.d.)'. O ī̃-má(ha). H apé-maï-jïnoï
     ~ í.ai-jïnoï ~ i.aï-ma.i.aï.
371 *hee(), *(e)hiʔtï 'ripe'. O hïïʔto. H hé.e-de ~ " ~ e.iθï.
330 *iháidaï 'wide'. O aháára. H í.airo-re-de ~ " ~ dï.aro-θe.
256 *bí-hē, *bi-ʔe 'this'. O bǐ̃ï, bíhā, baʔi-, bï-. H bedá ~ bí.e ~ ".
  6 *ohí(tï) 'eye'. O ohíí. H u.í-hï ~ u.í-hï ~ u.i-θï.
 44 *mōhō 'father'. O mōō(hō). H mó.o ~ " ~ ".
179 *(ï)háidzaï 'salt'. O hááiďℓ̌a. H í.aitaï ~ í.aiθaï ~ ".
161 *(dai)ʔtïhǎ́ǐ̃(hā) 'grass'. O ℓ̌ohǎ́ǎ́(hā). H ráidï.aï ~ raïtï.aï ~ raitïkïño.
 33 = 266 *tïhé 'blood'. O tsihíí. H dḯ.e ~ " ~ ".
336 *ïhǎ́() 'short'. O īháhǐ̃. H i.ánori-de ~ íanori ~ i.anori-de (. ~ ∅ ~. exception).
PHO   *β /__a > O β, H β.
137 *áʔta-βa 'hen'. O áℓ̌ℓ̌a-βa. H adá-βa ~ atá-βa ~ ". This stem is probably a
    Quichua borrowing, but the suffix is probably native.
122 (iβána) 'snake'. O (no cognate). H iβána ~ – ~ –.
193 (kaβáje) 'snake'. O (no cognate). H kaβáje ~ – ~ –.
129 *(ae)(β)a(do) 'macaw'. O ɸaaro (ɸ exception). H áβa ~ éɸa ~ " (β ~ ɸ ~ ɸ
    exception).
PHO   *β /__ > O β, H ..
372 *aenǐ̃ʔ-hiβóda 'dust'. O ahooʔïβóra, añōōʔǐ̃βóra. H enǐ́-čoma ~ " ~ hi.ora.
171 *hiʔpíʔ-hï(βe) 'chili'. O haʔɸíí-ʔoβï H hípi-hï ~ híɸi-hï ~ " (the syllable *hï is
    doubtful).
 89 (čoβéʔtïdaï). O (no cognate). H čoβédïrï ~ jo.étïrï ~ jo.etïraï (β ~. ~. exception).

This protophoneme is relatively rare, and all of the cognates are word-
medial. (129 is word-initial in Ocaina but word-medial in Huitoto and in
Proto Bora-Muinane.) About half of the cases of Ocaina /β/ were derived
from *b, in this same word-medial environment. The Huitoto reflexes

PHO *n /ai__ > O n, H ñ.
351 *(ai)nāǐ-() 'throw'. O anãāʋ'o. H – ~ ñáï-te ~ –. This is a bit of a shot in the dark.
PHO *n /ae,e__ > O ñ, H n.
372 *aenǐʔ-hiβóda 'dust'. O ahooʔïβóra, añōōʔïβóra. H enǐ-čoma ~ " ~ hi.ora.
72 *aenǐʔ-ē, *aenǐʔ-dōē 'earth'. O añōōʔǐ. H énï.e ~ " ~ enïru.e.
152–160 *aména 'tree'. O amǐïña. H aména ~ " ~ ".
186–189 *ené(da) péti 'other hand?'. O añíira φáti. H ené-pebamo ~ ené-φeθimo ~ ene-φebehimo.
113 *mení-(goï) 'tortoise'. O mañiiʔxo. H meníño ~ " ~ ".
PHO *n /o__ > O n, H n.
170 *nonǒ() 'annatto'. O ñonǒǒya. H nonó-kï ~ " ~ ".
15 *mōnoï 'woman's breast'. O mōno. H mónoï ~ " ~ ".
22–23 *onǒǐ 'hand'. O onōō(po). H ónoï ~ " ~ ".
240 *onǒǐ-(kona) 'lower arm'. O onǒ-kona. H onó-paiko ~ onó-φaiko ~ ono-φai.
241 *onǒǐ-() 'wrist'. O onǒ-poka. H onó-bekï ~ onói-koiño ~ ono-jïkï.
319 *mōnoï ihī 'milk'. O mōnoo-hǐ. H mónoï-hi ~ mónoï ihi ~ monoï ihi.
311 *m(o)nái-(tahi) 'sea'. O maanǐ. H monái-ja.i ~ monái-jahi ~ monai-ja.i.
31 ʔ*()niʔgaï 'skin'. O xonǐǐʔka. H íni ~ igói-raï ~ igoï.
100 *n(ē)nǐ(goï) 'armadillo'. O ñǒǒnō. H neníŋo ~ " ~ ñeniño.
173 *ōnáʔō 'Banisterium'. O ōnãāʔō. H úna.o ~ " ~ ".
67 *móna 'day'. O mooña, moñamó (ñ exception). H móna ~ " ~ aremona.
61 *móna 'sky'. O bïmōñá, xïʋ'amóóña (ñ exception). H móna ~ " ~ ".

3.13. Semivowel. This section presents the rules for the PHO semivowel *y.

PHO *y /ǐ,ē__ > O ñ, H ..
1 *(h)ïyǐʔpe 'tongue'. O hïñǒǒʔφï. H i.ípe ~ i.íφe ~ ".
PHO *ʔy /ǐ,ē__ > O ʔñ, H ..
70 *amēʔyo 'lightning'. O 69 amǐʔño. H amé.o ~ " ~ ".
PHO *y /ā,ō,ǐ__ (no cognates) > O ñ, H (.i).
PHO *ʔy /ā,ō,ǐ__ (no cognates) > O ʔñ, H (.i).
PHO *ʔy /i,e__ > O ʔy, H ..
29 *eʔyǐ-() 'foot'. O ïʔyóó(ga). H e.ǐ-ba ~ é.ï-ba ~ e.ï-jǐ.
PHO *y /a,o,ï__ > O y, H .i.
PHO *ʔy /a,o,ï__ > O ʔy, H .i.
123 ʔ*()óʔyo 'anaconda'. O toxóóʔyo. H nú.io ~ " ~ ".
131 ʔ*(k)(oi)yïkï 'parrot'. O káyooho. H ui.íkï ~ ui.ǐkï ~ θarokï.

Nasalization of vowels is very common in Ocaina. Because of the case of *y above and a few other suggestive items, such as the suspiciously similar forms of 69 amǐʔño 'thunder' and 70 ïïβáʔyo 'lightning', both of whose consonants differ only in their nasalization, it is possible that the vowel nasalization found in Ocaina was closely linked to the generation of nasal consonants at some point in the past, since vowel nasalization in Ocaina generally occurs next to nasals. Items 69 and 70, however, are the only good examples I could find to suggest this, and their relationship is somewhat questionable, since the first two vowels do not match. Also, there are good near-minimal pairs for nasal versus oral vowels, such as 307 *añii-* 'other' and 367 *āāñi* 'squeeze', and nasalized vowels may occur next to voiceless consonants and (rarely) next to voiced oral consonants in Ocaina, as shown in the following sets. In conclusion, there is not enough information available to make any certain hypothesis (see also §3.7).

In the following sets, a nasalized vowel appears in Ocaina following a voiced consonant.

256 **PHO** **bí-hē, *bi-ʔe* 'this'. **O** *b: bíí, bíhā, baʔi-, bï-.* **H** *bedá ~ bí.e ~* ".
258 **PHO** **bố* 'who'. **O** *b: bố* **H** *bu ~* " *~* ".
305 **PHO** **bē()* 'here'. **O** *b: bá, bíˀ* **H** *benó ~ bené ~ benomo.*
156 **PHO** **dīā(hī)* 'fruit'. **O** *dˀ: dˀāāhīˀ, hïxāā.* **H** *rí.a ~* " *~ri.ara.*
304 **PHO** **dzíˀ?-()* 'where'. **O** *dz: dzōō(?), dzoo.* **H** *nï-nó, nï-né ~* " *~* ".
 74 **PHO** *??*(koni)dziíˀʔē* 'sand'. **O** *jˇ: jíōōʔï.* **H** *kónijï.e ~ ~ ~ konijï.e.*
122 [no reconstruction] 'snake'. **O** *g: gōhốốʔïʔtsi.* **H** (no cognate).
356 [no reconstruction] 'tie'. **O** *g: gāā.* **H** ".
364 **PHO** *?*()gō* 'suck'. **O** *g: gōō.* **H** *mugú-de ~ – ~ –.*

In the following sets, a nasalized vowel appears in Ocaina preceding a voiced consonant.

141 [no reconstruction] 'a fly'. **O** *b: áábeko.* **H** (no cognate).
 52 **PHO** **kïné-b()* 'swamp'. **O** *β: xonííβaga, ñihííβaga.* **H** *kïné-re ~ kïné-bï ~ kïne-re.*
315 [no reconstruction] 'wing'. **O** *β: ɸōнốốβïka.* **H** (no cognate).
372 **PHO** **aenīˀ-hiβóda* 'dust'. **O** *β: ahooʔïβóra, añōōʔïβóra.*
      H *enīˀ-čoma ~* " *~ hi.ora.*
170 **PHO** **nonố()* 'annatto'. **O** *y: ñoнốốya.* **H** *nonó-kï ~* " *~* ".

3.14. Vowels.
For the most part, vowel length in Ocaina is not taken into account in these rules, since this feature is assumed to have been generated in Ocaina (see §3.15). For **a* I list Ocaina /a/ and /aa/ separately just to show the distinction (but without proposing any rules). For the remaining vowels, I have left the long and short forms mixed together, since the rules are already complicated. Vowel nasalization in Ocaina is likewise not taken into account, since this is assumed to be a protolanguage feature that was completely lost in Huitoto.

PHO **a /__ > **O** *a,* **H** *a.*
      Examples with Ocaina /a/:
 25 *?*ïdzá-k(aido)* 'leg'. **O** *odzá-kona.* **H** *ïdá-kairo ~* ", *rí.aï-kairo ~* ".
 47 **heʔíí-(do)-ma* 'old man'. **O** *haʔíí-мa.* **H** *e.íro-ma ~ éiro-ma, éi-kome ~ eiro-ma,*
      u.aïkï-ma.
 61 **móna* 'sky'. **O** *bïмōñá, xïtˀamóóña.* **H** *móna ~* " *~* ".
 67 **móna* 'day'. **O** *mooña, moñamó.* **H** *móna ~* " *~ aremona.*

70 *amḗʔyo 'lightning'. O 69 *amḯʔño. H amé.o ~ " ~ ".
111 *(na)ʔḯma 'crocodile'. O hōʔóóma. H tḯkḯnaïma ~ θḯkḯnaïma ~ ".
137 *áʔta-βa 'hen'. Ou áṱa-βa. H adá-βa ~ atá-βa ~ ". This item is apparently a
      Quichua borrowing, so it may not actually be a cognate.
140 *(do)ʔ-hidakï(goï) 'bee'. O ḓoʔḯḯrako. H hiráŋo ~ " ~ hirakïño. Many more
      examples.
      Examples with Ocaina /aa/ (usually penultimate or stressed or both):
49 *(i)máni 'river'. O maanḯ. H imáni ~ " ~ ".
51 *hōʔdā́hī 'lake'. O hōʔā́ā́hī. H hórai ~ " ~ ".
78 *()i-dá-bïkï 'seat'. O biiñi-ráá-βoho, biiñiráá-ko. H rá.ï.i-ra-bï-kï ~ " ~ raï-ra-ko.
80 *kïnahī 'hammock'. O xonaahī. H kḯnai ~ " ~ ".
85 = 253 *nahḯ(to) 'path, trail'. O naahō, tóβïʔṱa. H í.o ~ " ~ na.ïθo.
90 *()ā́ʔe 'canoe'. O hōɸā́ā́ʔï. H nókae ~ nokáe ~ noka.e.
129 *(ae)(β)a(do) 'macaw'. O ɸaaro. H áβa ~ éɸa ~ ".
156 *dīā(hī) 'fruit'. O ḓā́āhḯ, hïxāā. H rí.a ~ " ~ ri.ara. Many more examples.
155 ʔ*t(ā́) 'flower'. O tsī́ī (ii exception). H tápi.a ~ θáɸi.a ~ ". This may have been
      conditioned by the /ts/; see rules for *t in §3.8.
134 *(k)oodz(a) 'curassow'. O xóódzoho (o exception). H jó.oda ~ jó.oda, hó.oda ~ –.
142 ??*(p)aïd(á)to 'flea'. O oróóβïṱo (o exception). H païrádo ~ ɸaïrádo ~ ".
317 *m(ó)ʔt(a) 'navel'. O mááʔṱo (o exception). H móda ~ mútida ~ ".

PHO *e and *i apparently went through four stages of sound change in
Ocaina. First, they fell together at a very early stage, apparently as *i;
second, this *i split into /i/ and *i, most becoming the former; third, the
remaining cases of *i split into /i/ and *ai; finally, all cases of *ai were
reduced to /a/. In Huitoto, on the other hand, *e and *i apparently
remained unchanged. Therefore, the following rules combine *e and *i.
The stages are not clearly distinguished in the rules, since the environments allow the rules to be treated simultaneously; actually, for clarity of
presentation the major rules are listed in essentially reverse chronological
order. For each rule, I list examples with *e first, then with *i.

Number 256 is fascinating, because it is a microcosm of all of the main
rules affecting *e and *i and shows all three Ocaina reflexes: /i, i, a/. It is
also unclear which of two two-morpheme Ocaina forms corresponds to
Huitoto /bí.e/, since the rules would allow this to be derived from either
*bí-hāé or *bi-ʔe (Ocaina /bíhā/ or /baʔi-/). Numbers 202 and 203 also
contain all three reflexes, though not all of the same vowel.

PHO *e,i /__Ce,i,ai > O a, H e,i.
47 *heʔḯ-(do)-ma 'old man'. O haʔḯ-ma. H e.íro-ma ~ éiro-ma, éi-kome ~ eiro-ma,
      u.aïkï-ma.
113 *mení-(goï) 'tortoise'. O mañiiʔxo. H meníño ~ " ~ ".
186–189 *ené(da) péti 'other hand?'. O añííra ɸáti. H ené-pebamo
      ~ ené-ɸeθimo ~ ene-ɸebehimo.
190 *(ha)naʔg(á)-péti 'ten'. O hanāʔ ɸáti, hanaa-ʔɸïɸóroʔ. H nagá-peba ~
      nagá-ɸeθi ~ naga-ɸebekuiro.

246 *heʔí(do)-goï 'old woman'. O haʔū-ko. H e.íro-gï ~ e.íro-gï, e.írï-ŋo ~ u.aikï-ño.
  4 *iʔtiʔ-to 'tooth'. O aʔtiiʔ^vo. H íti-do ~ íθi-do ~ ".
128 *piʔtíʔto 'hummingbird'. O ɸaʔtííʔ^vo. H pitído ~ ɸiθído ~ ".
157 *(a)m(éna) ihī 'sap'. O ahīī, m ̃áhī. H ihi ~ aména ero ihi ~ (amena) i.
163 *hōʔtí(ti) 'cassava plant'. O hōʔtááti. H húti ~ húθi ~ huθi.e.
171 *hiʔpí-dai 'chili plant'. O haʔɸíí-ja. H – – híɸi-rai ~ ".
171 *hiʔpíʔ-hï(βe) 'chili'. O haʔɸíí-ʔoβï. H hípi-hï ~ híɸi-hï ~ ".
256 *bí-hāē, *bi-ʔe 'this'. O bíí, bíhā, baʔi-, bï-. H bedá ~ bí.e ~ ".
330 *iháídaï 'wide'. O aháára. H i.airo-re-de ~ " ~ dï.aro-θe.
PHO *ii /__Ce,i > O ii, H i.i or i.
172 *híibí(ʔe) 'coca'. O hiibiro. H hibí.e ~ hí.ibi.e ~ hi.ibe.
132 ?*()di() 'parakeet'. O jííyi. H gáirikoŋo ~ " ~ gairiθï.
     Noncognate examples:
 76 [no reconstruction] 'roof (woven)'. O ayííβi. H (no cognate).
 78 [no reconstruction] 'stool'. O biiñi-ráá-βoho. H (no cognate).
131 [no reconstruction] 'parrot'. O čōīɸi. H (no cognate).
221 [no reconstruction] 'small'. O síítiʔ. H (no cognate).
288 [no reconstruction] 'sit'. O biiñiʔi. H (no cognate).
331 [no reconstruction] 'narrow'. O iibi. H (no cognate).

The last rule has only one good cognate (which however has good cognates in Bora and Muinane as well). It has no exceptions in Ocaina, however, even for noncognate items, as the additional examples show.

PHO *e,i /__ha(e) > O i, H e,i.
336 *īh ̃á() 'short'. O īh ̃áhī. H i.ánori-de ~ íanori ~ i.anori-de.
256 *bí-hāē, *bi-ʔe 'this'. O bíí, bíhā, baʔi-, bï-. H bedá ~ bí.e ~ ".
PHO *(e),i /__a > O ∅, H (e),i.
333 *iaïn(oi)deʔi 'near'. O áánïraʔ. H a.ïno-mo ~ áïno-ri ~ i.aïrei.
156 *dīā(hī) 'fruit'. O d^vāāhī, hïxāā. H rí.a ~ " ~ ri.ara.
294=371 *hīāï(hī) 'red'. O tsííʔo, hāāhī. H hí.aï-re-de ~ " ~ ".
PHO *e,i /e,iC__ > O i, H e,i.
256 *bí-hāē, *bi-ʔe 'this'. O bíí, bíhā, baʔi-, bï-. H bedá ~ bí.e ~ ".
186–189 *ené(da) péti 'other hand?'. O añííra ɸáti. H ené-pebamo
         ~ ené-ɸeθimo ~ ene-ɸebehimo.
  4 *iʔtiʔ-to 'tooth'. O aʔtiiʔ^vo. H íti-do ~ íθi-do ~ ".
 45 *éʔī-(goï) 'mother'. O ā́ʔīʔ. H á-ño ~ éi-(ño) ~ e.i.
 47 *heʔī-(do)-ma 'old man'. O haʔīī-ma. H e.íro-ma ~ éiro-ma, éi-kome ~ eiro-ma,
     u.aïkï-ma.
 74 ?*(koni)dziï ̈ʔē 'sand'. O jiōōʔī. H kónijï.e ~ ~ ~ konijï.e.
113 *mení-(goï) 'tortoise'. O mañiiʔxo. H meníño ~ " ~ ".
128 *piʔtíʔto 'hummingbird'. O ɸaʔtííʔ^vo. H pitído ~ ɸiθído ~ ".
157 *(a)m(éna) ihī 'sap'. O ahīī, m ̃áhī. H ihi ~ aména ero ihi ~ (amena) i.
171 *hiʔpí-dai 'chili plant'. O haʔɸíí-ja. H – – híɸi-rai ~ ".
171 *hiʔpíʔ-hï(βe) 'chili'. O haʔɸíí-ʔoβï. H hípi-hï ~ híɸi-hï ~ ".
172 *híibí(ʔe) 'coca'. O hiibiro. H hibí.e ~ hí.ibi.e ~ hi.ibe.
186–189 *ené(da) péti 'other hand?' O añííra ɸáti. H ené-pebamo ~
         ené-ɸeθimo ~ ene-ɸebehimo.

199 *(iʔt)iʔtáï-ma 'chief'. O aʔtiʔťʸó-ma, ɸarááʔɸï-ma. H ijáï-ma ~ " ~ ". Many
     more examples.

The following is not really an exception. The rule ï > i /ts__ applied first.

33 = 266 *tïhé 'blood'. O tsihíí. H dí̈.e ~ " ~ ".
PHO *e,i /aiC__ > O i, H e,i.
260 *-ne, *(āī)-ne 'not'. O -ñi, -ñi, ãá, ããñi. H -ñe ~ " ~ ".

The last environment is extremely rare, and the only example has no
Huitoto evidence for the environment. I have included it because it is
analogous to the previous rule, and is the only way to explain the retention
of the Ocaina /i/.

PHO *e,i /ah__ > O i, H e,i.
 80 *kïnahī 'hammock'. O xonaahī. H kínai ~ " ~ ".
 51 *hōʔdáhī 'lake'. O hōʔááhī. H hórai ~ " ~ ".
163 *máhī(kahï) 'sweet cassava'. O maahī. H ma.ika(hï) ~má.ika(hï) ~ma.ika.
PHO *e,i /__ > O ï, H e,i.
  1 *(h)īyīʔpe 'tongue'. O hīñóóʔɸï. H i.ípe ~i.íɸe ~ ".
  2 *póe 'mouth'. O ɸooï. H pú.e ~ɸú.e ~ ".
 17 *he(dáï)ʔkï(mo) 'back'. O hïïʔxo(mó). H heráïkï ~ " ~-.
 29 *eʔyï-() 'foot'. O ïʔyóó(ga). H e.ï-ba ~é.ï-ba ~e.ï-jï̈.
 34 *kome(kï) 'heart'. O xomïï-mōti. H komékï ~ " ~ ".
 52 *kïné-b() 'swamp'. O xonïïßaga. H kïné-re ~kïné-bï ~kïne-re.
 70 * amēʔyo 'lightning'. O 69 amïʔño. H amé.o ~ " ~ ".
 72 *aenïʔ-ē, *aenïʔ-dōē 'earth'. O añōōʔï̈. H énï̈.e ~ " ~enïru.e.
 90 *()áʔe 'canoe'. O hōɸááʔï. H nókae ~nokáe ~noka.e.
126 *(h)edaï 'toad'. O ïïra. H héro ~ " ~herokï.
151 *()pedï 'hill'. O ťʸaßíïro. H íperï ~íɸerï ~-.
152–160 *aména 'tree'. O amïïña. H aména ~ " ~ ".
  6 *ohí(tï) 'eye'. O ohíí. H u.í-hï ~u.í-hï ~u.i-θï̈.
 31 ʔ*()niʔgaï 'skin'. O xonïïʔka. H íni ~igóï-raï ~igoï.
38–39 *ïʔí 'man'. O ooʔï. H ï̈.í- ~ " ~ ".
 48 *(haï-)nō-hī 'water'. O ñōō(-hï̈). H háïnoi ~ " ~hïnui.
 49 *(i)máni 'river'. O maanï. H imáni ~ " ~ ".
103 *(tï)nōī 'bat'. O nōōï, nōááʔɸïʔťʸa. H jï̈ni ~ " ~ ".
118 *minï̈() 'rat'. O mïñōóko. H mïñï̈.e ~ " ~ ".
133 *īno() 'buzzard'. O ï̈ïnóóčo. H íno ~ " ~ ".
140 *(do)ʔ-hidakï(goï) 'bee'. O ɗʸoʔíírako. H hiráŋo ~ " ~hirakiño.
178 *(po)kaníʔta 'cane'. O ɸookanïïʔťʸa. H kaní-da ~kaní-kaï ~-.
202 *i-ma, *(iʔ)i-ma 'he'. O aʔii-ma, ïï-ma. H apé-ma ~aɸé-mï̈.e ~imï̈.e.
203 *i-goï, *(iʔ)i-goï 'she'. O aʔiiko, ïïko, ña. H apéŋo ~aɸéŋo ~(ma)iñaiño.
 42 *ïni 'husband'. O ōōna (a exception). H íni ~ " ~ ".
263 ʔ*á(d)e 'long'. O ááñi (i exception). H áre ~ " ~ ".
  1 *(h)īyīʔpe 'tongue'. O hīñóóʔɸï. (i exception) H i.ípe ~i.íɸe ~ ".
 87 *p(ai)ʔkoa-ti 'fishhook'. O ɸeʔxoo-ti (i exception). H pákua-ti ~ɸákua-θi
     ~ɸago-θi.

74 ??*(koni)dziḯʔē 'sand'. O jíôôʔï (i exception). H kónijï.e ~- ~ konijï.e.
71 ?*(d)ódzi-(goe)ʔdo 'rainbow'. O ójïiʔo (i exception). H róti-gue.o ~ róθi-gue.o
     ~roθi-guero.
377 *(ho)pó-tïʔb(i) 'small house'. O ɸohoo-tsiβo (o exception). H hopó-čuɓi
     ~ hoɸó-čupi ~–.
100 *n(ē)nḯ(goï) 'armadillo'. O ñóóнō (o exception). H neníŋo ~ "~ñenïño. Many
     more examples.

The following six items are also exceptions to the preceding rule. In
these items it would be unclear whether the original vowel was *ï or *i
and whether the exceptional forms were in Ocaina or Huitoto. In looking
at Proto Bora-Muinane, however, the only cognate (117) has the Proto
Bora-Muinane form *páttï, and must have been derived from PW *píʔto
'agouti' (see §4.10). It is probable that these cases of *i changed to /ï/ in
Huitoto as a result of vowel harmony, but there is insufficient information
to posit a rule.

117 *p(íi)to 'agouti'. O ɸíḯɓ'o. H –~ɸï.ido ~ ɸïdo (ï exception).
232 *(i)nḯ 'sleep!'. O ḯïnō. H mai ínï ~ ínï ~ " (ï exception).
280; (81) *(i)nḯ 'sleep. O ïïnō. H ïnï-de ~ "~ " (ï exception).
81 *(i)nḯ- 'bed'. O ïnōʔxatsííβo. H –~–~ïnï-ra (ï exception).
314 *()āïg(i) 'worm'. O agïïma. H igïroï ~ (a)igïroï ~ aïgiro (ï exception).
314 *(a)(ï)kï 'worm'. O ïïko. H áïkï ~ "~ " (ï exception).

*o and *ï fell together as /o/ in Ocaina, just as *e and *i fell together as
/ï/. Since in both Ocaina and Huitoto other factors caused splits, however,
it is impractical to treat them together.
    The first two rules below which produce Huitoto /u/ are apparently quite
late rules, occurring after the rules producing loss of *h and *ʔ. For this
reason I have simplified the rules by using an Early Huitoto environment,
rather than a Proto Huitoto-Ocaina environment.

PHO *o > O o, H u /__a,e,i (Early Huitoto rule).
265 *ōʔá-(tï), *ōʔá-(ïhï) 'flesh'. O ôʔāāhï. H ú.a-tï ~ í.e-θï ~ ".
  6 *ohí(tï) 'eye'. O ohḯḯ. H u.i-hï ~ u.i-hï ~ u.i-θï.
 87 *p(ai)ʔkoa-ti 'fishhook'. O ɸeʔxoo-ti. H pákua-ti ~ ɸákua-θi ~ ɸago-θi.
200 *kōē 'I'. O xō, xôḯ. H kúe ~ "~ kue, ku.e.
192 *(i)tái-poe-dza(no) 'last'. O ɓ'áɸoïïdzanó. H idái-pu.e-na,
     írai-pu.e-na ~ írai-pu.e-na ~ iraï.e.
  2 *póe 'mouth'. O ɸooï. H pú.e ~ ɸú.e ~ ".
123 ?*()óʔyo 'anaconda'. O toxóóʔyo. H nú.io ~ "~ ".
 48 *(haï-)nō-hï 'water'. O ñōō(-hï). H háïnoi ~ "~ hïnui (o ~ o ~ u exception).
     (See also diphthongs below whose first constituent is *o.)
PHO *o > O o, H o /__ï (Early Huitoto rule).
  3 *p(óe i)ʔgoï, ?*p(óe ini) 'lip'. O ɸa-ʔóóʔko. H pú.e ini ~ ɸú.e igoï ~ ".

PHO *o > O o, H u /environment unclear (probably vowel harmony).
66 *oʔkóʔto 'star'. O oʔxóóʔtᵛo. H ukúdo ~ ukúdu ~ ".
97 *tõ() 'tapir'. O tᵛõõhã. H turúma ~ θurúma ~ ".
126 *goaïkí(ho) 'toad'. O gokóóho. H gúku ~ gúaïkï ~ –.
163 *hõʔtí(ti) 'cassava plant'. O hõʔtááti. H húti ~ húθi ~ huθi.e.
173 *õnãʔõ 'Banisterium'. O õnããʔõ. H úna.o ~ " ~ ".
196 ?*ko(máʔ-tï)-kï 'earring'. O xoñõõ-tᵛaβóko. H kumá-dï-kï ~ héɸo í-hï ~ heɸo itïkï.
258 *bṍ 'who'. O bṍ. H bu ~ " ~ ".
354 ?*tõ-ʔ(tá-te) 'pierce'. O tᵛõõʔɸo. H ǰu-dá-de ~ ǰu-tá-de ~ ".
364 ?*()gõ 'suck'. O gõõ. H mugú-de ~ ~ ~ –.
365 *poo(no-ʔte) 'blow'. O ɸooɸo. H pú.úno-de ~ ɸú.ú-de ~ ɸuri-de.
PHO *o > O o, H o /__.
4 *iʔtiʔ-to 'tooth'. O aʔtiiʔtᵛo. H íti-do ~ íθi-do ~ ".
5 *topo 'nose'. O tᵛooɸo. H dópo ~ dóɸo ~ ".
8 *ïʔpo-(gï) 'head'. O ooʔɸo. H ïpo ~ ïɸó-kï ~ ïɸo-gï.
10 *ïʔpo-ʔtï() 'hair'. O ooʔɸo, oʔɸo-toʔóóɸe. H ïpó-dï.i ~ ïɸó-tïrai ~ ïɸo-tïraï.
15 *mõnoï 'woman's breast'. O mõno. H mónoï ~ " ~ ".
22–23 *onõĩ́ 'hand'. O onõõ(po). H ónoï ~ " ~ ".
34 *kome(kï) 'heart'. O xomïí-moti. H komékï ~ " ~ ".
44 *mõhõ 'father'. O mõõ(hõ). H mó.o ~ " ~ ".
51 *hõʔdãhī 'lake'. O hõʔããhī. H hórai ~ " ~ ".
53 *dzod(o)-p(o) 'spring of water'. O dzóóroʔɸi. H do() ~ to-rá-no ~ to-ra-ɸo.
58 *kó() 'charcoal'. O xóñaa(tᵛo). H kó.okï ~ " ~ ".
61 *móna 'sky'. O bïmõñá, xïtᵛamóóña. H móna ~ " ~ ".
321 ??*ho() 'in'. O haa, hadᵛa (a exception). H hópo ~ " ~ ".
311 *m(o)nái-(tahi) 'sea'. O maanï (a exception). H monái-ǰa.i ~ monái-ǰahi ~ monai-ǰa.i.
317 *m(ó)ʔt(a) 'navel'. O mááʔtᵛo (a exception). H móda ~ mútida ~ ".
53 *dzod(o)-p(o) 'spring of water'. O dzóóroʔɸi. H do() ~ to-rá-no ~ to-ra-ɸo (a exception).
318 ??*pó(e)- 'saliva'. O ɸóñoohī. H páʔa.ie ~ ɸé.ikï ~ ɸa.ikï (a exception).
255 *(ho)po-() 'shelter'. O ɸohóóβonï. H hïpo-ko ~ hoɸó-ka.iɸe ~ bïθaini (ï exception).
PHO *ï > O i /ts,dz__, H ï. (Ocaina rule occurring after rules that applied to *t.)
33 = 266 *tïhé 'blood'. O tsihīí. H dí.e ~ " ~ ".
94 *tï() 'bow'. O tsipóxatᵛa. H tïkúi-ña ~ θïkui-raï ~ θïkui-ra.
214 ?*k(oe)-tï() 'my bow'. O ki-tsipóxatᵛa. H kue tïkúiña ~ kú.e θïkúiraï ~ ku.e θïkuirakuiɸo.
306 ?*()ʔdzï() 'there'. O dziráhīʔ. H badḯ ~ batïne ~ ".
377 *(ho)pó-tïʔb(i) 'small house'. O ɸohoo-tsiβo. H hopó-čuβi ~ hoɸó-čupi ~ – (u exception).
PHO *ï > O o /__, H ï.
1 *(h)ïyïʔpe 'tongue'. O hīñṍóʔɸi. H i.ípe ~ i.íɸe ~ ".
8 *ïʔpo-(gï) 'head'. O ooʔɸo. H ïpo ~ ïɸó-kï ~ ïɸo-gï.
10 *ïʔpo-ʔtï() 'hair'. O ooʔɸo, oʔɸo-toʔóóɸe. H ïpó-dï.i ~ ïɸó-tïrai ~ ïɸo-tïraï.
17 *he(dáï)ʔkï(mo) 'back'. O hïïʔxo(mó). H heráïkï ~ " ~ –.
25 ?*ïdzá-k(aido) 'leg'. O odzá-kona. H ïdá-kairo ~ ", rí.aï-kairo ~ ".
29 *eʔyí́-() 'foot'. O ïʔyóó(ga). H e.í-ba ~ é.ï-ba ~ e.ï-ǰï.

38–39 *ɨʔí 'man'. O ooʔɨ̈. H ɨ̈.í- ~ " ~ ".
42 *ɨ̈ni 'husband'. O ōōna. H ɨ́ni ~ " ~ ".
52 *kɨné-b() 'swamp'. O xonɨ̈́ɨ̈βaga. H kɨné-re ~ kɨné-bɨ̈ ~ kɨ̈ne-re.
65 *pɨ̈() 'moon'. O ɸodʲoome. H píbɨ̈.i ~ ɸɨ́.ui ~ ɸɨ̈βui.
72 *aenɨ̈ʔ-ē, *aenɨ̈ʔ-dōē 'earth'. O añōōʔɨ̈. H énɨ̈.e ~ " ~ enɨ̈ru.e.
74 ??*(koni)dzɨɨ̈ʔē 'sand'. O jíōōʔɨ̈. H kóniȷ̈ɨ̈.e ~ – ~ konɨȷ̈ɨ̈.e.
126 *goaɨ̈kɨ́(ho) 'toad'. O gokóóho. H gúku ~ gúaɨ̈kɨ̈ ~ – (u ~ ɨ̈ ~ – exception). Many more examples.

The diphthongs are included separately here because they have various unusual features. *ai, *aɨ̈ and *oɨ̈ were quite common, a heritage they derive from Proto Witotoan (see §4). Huitoto vowel sequences derived from loss of *h or *ʔ are not listed here, since they can be found under *h or *ʔ (§§3.10, 3.11).

The rules for *ai that follow are admittedly somewhat ad hoc, although several things are clear: (a) in the environment /#h__ the diphthong does not lose its second element; (b) the /ɨ/ reflexes in Ocaina are too common to be simple exceptions, and the ad hoc rule given does cover them all.

PHO   *ai /#h__dz̧ > O ai, H ai.
179   *(ɨ̈)háidzaɨ̈ 'salt'. O hááidʲa. H ɨ́.aitai ~ ɨ́.aiθaɨ̈ ~ ".
PHO   *ai /#h__ > O aɨ̈, H ai.
228   *háɨ̈ 'go!'. O hááɨ̈. H mai hái ~ mai hai ~ ".
PHO   *ai /n,#h__t,d > O ɨ̈, H ai.
311   *m(o)nái-(tahi) 'sea'. O maanɨ̈. H monái-ja.i ~ monái-jahi ~ monai-ja.i.
289   *naiʔtai 'stand'. O nɨ̈ɨ̈ʔtʲa. H naidá.i-de ~ náidai-de ~ ".
63   *hai(dí)(p)oɨ̈ 'wind'. O hɨ̈βóódʲo. H hairípoɨ̈ ~ hairíɸo ~ ".
345   *(h)(ai)dɨ̈́ʔ-p(aití) 'left'. O ɨ̈rooʔ-ɸatí. H harɨ̈́-pene ~ harɨ̈́-ɸene ~ harɨ̈-ɸebehɨ̈ (a exception).
PHO   *ai /aiC__# > O i, H ai.
168   *(h)aʔkáɨ̈ʔ-ti(dai) 'yam'. O aʔxaaʔti. H – ~ hakái-θairai ~ –.
PHO   *ai /__ > O a, H ai.
171   *hiʔpí-dai 'chili plant'. O haʔɸíí-ja. H – ~ híɸi-rai ~ ".
203   *(mai)nai-goɨ̈ 'she'. O aʔiiko, ɨ̈ɨ̈ko, ña. H apéŋo ~ aɸéŋo ~ (ma)iñaiño.
289   *naiʔtai 'stand'. O nɨ̈ɨ̈ʔtʲa. H naidá.i-de ~ náidai-de ~ ".
192   *(ɨ̈)tái-poe-dza(no) 'last'. O ɨ̈́áɸoɨ̈ɨ̈dzanó. H idái-pu.e-na, ɨrai-pu.e-na ~ ɨrai-pu.e-na ~ iraɨ̈.e.
130   *nokáiʔto 'toucan'. O ñoxaaʔčo. H nokáido ~ " ~ ".
168   *(h)aʔkáɨ̈ʔ-ti(dai) 'yam'. O aʔxaaʔti. H – ~ hakái-θairai ~ –.
314   *()āɨ̈g(i) 'worm'. O agɨ̈ɨ̈ma. H igɨ́roɨ̈ ~ (a)igɨ́roɨ̈ ~ aɨ̈gɨro.
330   *iháidaɨ̈ 'wide'. O aháára. H ɨ̈.airo-re-de ~ " ~ dɨ̈.aro-θe.
314   *(a)(ɨ̈)kɨ̈ 'worm'. O ɨ̈ɨ̈ko (ɨ̈ exception). H áɨ̈kɨ̈ ~ " ~ " (aɨ̈ exception). See the last set of exceptions for *e to see why I reconstructed this as *ai. Also compare the other 314 example above.
87   *p(ai)ʔkoa-ti 'fishhook'. O ɸeʔxoo-ti (e exception). H pákua-ti ~ ɸákua-θi ~ ɸago-θi (a exception).

The last item above is the only example of Ocaina /e/ which has a cognate in Huitoto. /e/ is a very rare vowel in Ocaina: there were only nine words containing it in the wordlist (10, 65, 87, 126, 131, 141, 158, 243, 374). Ocaina /e/ does not ever derive from PHO *e, and it is unclear what its source is. Number 87 is exceptional in both Ocaina and Huitoto, and the Proto Witotoan reconstruction is also exceptional and problematical since Proto Bora-Muinane *i is always the result of umlaut, and is derivable from various Proto Witotoan vowels. The fact that Huitoto (which seems to have the least modified vowel system in the entire family) has /a/ in this word, however, and Proto Bora-Muinane has *i, makes *ai the only logical choice.

It seems likely that most if not all cases of *oï were originally derived from *aï. What is not clear is whether this split had already occurred in Proto Huitoto-Ocaina or not. I have assumed that it had and thus have posited both *aï and *oï. I have not reconstructed Huitoto /oï/ as *aï unless either Ocaina or one of the Huitoto languages shows /a(ï)/ for the form.

Nevertheless, it is possible that *aï and *oï did not yet contrast phonemically in Proto Huitoto-Ocaina. Most of the examples of *oï that I have reconstructed occur after an *o in the previous syllable, or else in the suffixes *goï (feminine, singular), which clearly alternates with *gaï in some cases, or *koï (masculine). (*koï does not seem to have an alternate form with *aï.) Since the correspondence between Ocaina /o/ and Huitoto /oï/, on the one hand, and Ocaina /a/ and Huitoto /aï/, on the other, is largely consistent, however, I assume that the split had already occurred in Proto Huitoto-Ocaina and reconstruct both diphthongs.

PHO *aï /oC__ > O o, H various combinations. of aï,oï,o,ï.
148 *-taï-(goï), *-(kaï-goï), *odó-, *(i?o)- 'chigger'. O orooƥo (no suffix). H i.ojoŋo, orókoŋo ~ i.ojoŋo, órokoŋo ~ i.ojaïño, orokoño.
206 *(o)mãï?-gaï 'ye (f.d.)'. O mõ?k(a). H - ~ómï-ŋo ~ omï-ñoï.
206 *(o)mãï?-(to) 'ye (pl)'. O mõ(?to). H ómaï ~ ómoï ~ omoï.
206 *(o)mãï?-koï 'ye (m.d.)'. O mõ?(xo). H ómaï-ko ~ ómï-koï ~ omï-ko.
212 *(o)mãï?-(to) onõï 'your hands'. O mõ-?onõõ. H dáïgo óno-ge ~ ómoï ónoï ~ omoï ono-ïï.

Of the five examples for the preceding rule, four are forms of the second-person dual or plural pronoun. No detailed rule has been stated for the Huitoto forms, since there is considerable variation among the Huitoto languages in the reflexes of *aï in this environment.

PHO *aï /__ > O a, H aï.
68 *naï() 'night'. O naƥó. H náï.ïo ~ náï.(ï)o ~ naï.o(na).
161 *(dai)?tïhãï̃(hã) 'grass'. O ƥoháǽ(hã). H ráidï.aï ~ ráitï.aï ~ raitïkïño.

179 *(ï)háidzaï 'salt'. O hááidᵛa. H í.aitaï ~ í.aiθaï ~ ".
198 *-dáïma 'medicine man'. O hïʔxaɸorááᴍa. H manó-ri-raïma ~ áima,
     hí.ïdo-raïma ~ aima.
205 *kaï-hï 'we (pl.)'. O xa(ho). H kaï ~ kaï ~ kaï.
207 *i(aï)-maï-haï 'they (m.d.)'. O ïï-ᴍá(ha). H apé-maï-jïnoï
     ~ í.ai-jïnoï ~ i.aï-ma.i.aï.
207 *i(aï)-gaï-haï 'they (f.d.)'. O ïï-ká(ha). H ~ ~ í.aï-ŋu.aï ~ i.aï-ñu.aï.
211 *kaï onõï 'our hands'. O xa-ʔoᴎõõ. H kaï óno-ge ~ kaï ónoï ~ kaï ono-jï.
264 *(igó)daï(kã) 'bark'. O dᵛaká. H igóraï ~ " ~ ".
269 ?*(mó)kaï(to) 'horn'. O mókaaᵗᵛo. H tíkaï ~ θíkaï ~ ".
276 *aïnï 'bite'. O aanï. H aïní-de ~ " ~ ".
294 = 371 *hïãï(hï) 'red'. O tsííʔo, hããhï. H hí.aï-re-de ~ " ~ ".
351 *(ai)nãï-() 'throw'. O aᴎããᵗᵛo. H ~ ~ ñáï-te ~ ~.
     The next four forms have *-gaï, three of them exceptional, having /o/, /oï/, or /u/:
206 *(o)mãïʔ-gaï 'ye (f.d.)'. O mõʔk(a). H ~ ~ ómï-ŋo ~ omï-ñoï (~ ~ o ~ oï
     exception).
 31 ?*()niʔgaï 'skin'. H íni ~ igóï-raï ~ igoï (oï exception).
205 *kaï-gaï 'we (f.d.)'. O xak(a). H ~ ~ káïŋaï ~ kaiñaï.
207 *i(aï)-gaï-haï 'they (f.d.)'. O ïï-ká(ha). H ~ ~ í.aï-ŋu.aï ~ i.aï-ñu.aï (u exception).
149 ?*taï-(mãïʔï) 'bush'. O tᵛaᴍááʔï. H da.ï-re ~ táï-re ~ ~ (a.ï ~ aï ~ exception).
333 *iaïn(oi)deʔi 'near'. O ááᴎïraʔ. H a.íno-mo ~ áïno-ri ~ i.aïrei (a.ï ~ aï ~ aï
     exception).
205 *kaï-gaï 'we (f.d.)'. O xak(a). H ~ ~ káïŋaï ~ kaiñaï (~ aï ~ ai exception).
207 *i(aï)-maï-haï 'they (m.d.)'. O ïï-ᴍá(ha). H apé-maï-jïnoï
     ~ í.ai-jïnoï ~ i.aï-ma.i.aï (~ ~ ai ~ aï exception and aï ~ ~ ~ a.i exception).
330 *ihaídaï 'wide'. O aháára. H i.airo-re-de ~ " ~ dï.aro-θe (o exception).
126 *(h)edaï 'toad'. O ïïra. H héro ~ " ~ herokï (o exception).
142 ??*(p)aïd(á)to 'flea'. O oróóβiᵗᵛo(o exception). H païrádo ~ ɸaïrádo ~ ".
199 *(iʔt)iʔtáï-ma 'chief'. O aʔtiʔtᵛó-ma, ɸaráážɸï-ᴍa (o exception).
     H ijáï-ma ~ " ~ ".
126 ??*(n)op(aï)goï 'toad'. O opépeko (e exception). H nopáïŋo ~ noɸáïŋo ~
     noɸaïño .

The following rule is rather imprecise, because the factors determining
whether /o/ or /oï/ occur in Huitoto are unclear. Also, there is often
variation in the Huitoto examples in even a single morpheme. *oï only
occurs in a few morphemes, but those morphemes are extremely common
ones. Therefore, I have arranged the list according to morphemes, rather
than in numerical order, so that the variation can be more easily seen.

PHO   *oï > O o, H o or oï.
          Suffix *-goï, various meanings:
126 ??*(n)op(aï)goï 'toad'. O opépeko. H nopáïŋo ~ noɸáïŋo ~ noɸaïño.
203 *i-goï, *(iʔ)i-goï 'she'. O aʔiiko, ïïko, ña. H apéŋo ~ aɸéŋo ~ (ma)iñaiño.
  3 *p(óe i)ʔgoï, ?*p(óe ini) 'lip'. O ɸa-ʔóóʔko. H pú.e ini ~ ɸú.e igoï ~ ".
 14 *(he)bae-goï() 'chest'. O 14 bagóóʔya. H 244 hébe-goï ~ " ~ hebe-gï (ï
     exception).

246 *he?í(do)-goï 'old woman'. O ha?ū̃-ko. H e.íro-gï ~ e.íro-gï, e.írï-ŋo ~ u.aikï-ño (ï exception).
  Suffix *-koï (masculine dual):
205 *ko-koï 'we (m.d.)' O xo(xo). H kóko ~ " ~ ".
206 *(o)māī̃?-koï 'ye (m.d.)'. O mõ?(xo). H ómaï-ko ~ ómï-koï ~ omï-ko.
  Morpheme *onõī̃ 'hand':
208 *k(oe) onõī̃ 'my hand'. O k-oнõõ. H kue ónoï ~ kú.e ónoï ~ ku.e ono-jï.
22–23 *onõī̃ 'hand'. O oнõõ(po). H ónoï ~ " ~ ".
240 *onõī̃-(kona) 'lower arm'. O oнó-kona. H onó-paiko ~ onó-ɸaiko ~ ono-ɸai.
212 *(o)māī̃?-(to) onõī̃ 'your hands'. O mõ-?oнõõ. H dáïgo óno-ge ~ ómoï ónoï ~ omoï ono-jï.
211 *kaï onõī̃ 'our hands'. O xa-?oнõõ. H kaï óno-ge ~ kaï ónoï ~ kaï ono-jï.
210 *ta onõī̃ 'his hand'. O ťá?oнõõ. H da ónoï ~ - ~ -.
241 *onõī̃-() 'wrist'. O oнó-poka. H onó-bekï ~ onói-koiño ~ ono-jïkï (oi exception).
  Morpheme *mõnoï 'woman's breast':
15 *mõnoï 'woman's breast'. O mõнo. H mónoï ~ " ~ ".
319 *mõnoï ihī̃ 'milk'. O mõнoo-hī̃. H mónoï-hi ~ mónoï ihi ~ monoï ihi.
  Uncertain morpheme:
63 *hai(dí)(p)oï 'wind'. O hiβóóďo. H hairípoï ~ hairíɸo ~ ".

The diphthong proposed in the following rule is somewhat doubtful. That diphthongs (vowel sequences) without a high vowel existed is shown by *oe below, which is quite certain. The only clue that the diphthong *ae existed, however, is the exceptional item, 49, which has /aaï/ in Ocaina, showing that the diphthong must have been either *ai or *ae in 49 (and therefore probably also in 250; the forms in 250 are probably suffixed derivatives of 49). The other examples below are assumed to derive from *ae by analogy with 49 and because they lack any other explanation.[48] Proto Bora-Muinane gives little help, since although there are several cognates, they all seem to have different reflexes. However, the analysis is not unreasonable.

PHO *ae > O a, H e.
14 *(he)bae-goï() 'chest'. O 14 bagóó?ya. H 244 hébe-goï ~ " ~ hebe-gï.
250 *(i)tae-() 'stream'. O ťaβáága. H íje ~ ijé-tu.e ~ ije-kuera.
256 *bí-hāē, *bi-?e 'this'. O bíī̃, bíhã, ba?i-, bï-. H bedá ~ bí.e ~ ".
372 *aenī̃?-hiβóda 'dust'. O ahoo?iβóra, añõõ?ī̃βóra. H enï-čoma ~ " ~ hi.ora.
72 *aenī̃?-ē, *aenī̃?-dõē 'earth'. O añõõ?ī̃. H énï.e ~ " ~ enïru.e.
49 *(i)tae 'river'. O ťaaï (aï exception). H - ~ íje ~ ".

The following diphthong is unusual in that it is the only diphthong whose second (nonsyllabic) element is never lost in Ocaina (several others keep the second element in a minority of cases). More exceptionally, in final

---

[48]Other cases of Ocaina /a/ matching Huitoto /e/ can be analyzed as a simple *e, but only before *e or *i in the next syllable.

position it is the first element which is lost, not the second. Another unusual fact is that it is the only case where a two-syllable diphthong in Huitoto does not result from loss of a consonant between the two vowels. However, in spite of all of these unusual features, I see no reason to posit any other source for this diphthong than the one I have proposed.

PHO   **oe > O ï /_ #* **(late rule), H** *u.e* **or** *ue.*
363   **kïʔkóe* 'vomit'. O *xooʔxï.* H *kïkúe-de ~ " ~ ".*
72   **aenîʔ-ḝ, *aenîʔ-dóē* 'earth'. O *añôôʔî.* H *énï.e ~ " ~ enïru.e.*
PHO   **oe > O oï /_ ,* **H** *u.e* **or** *ue.*
2   **póe* 'mouth'. O *ɸooï.* H *pú.e ~ ɸú.e ~ ".*
192   **(i)tái-poe-dza(no)* 'last'. O *ʋ̃áɸoïïdzanó.* H *idái-pu.e-na, írai-pu.e-na ~ írai-pu.e-na ~ iraï.e.*
200   **kōē* 'I'. O *xō, xōî.* H *kúe ~ " ~ kue, ku.e.*
PHO   **oi /_ #* **(stressed)** *> O oï,* **H** *uï.*
95   **(tïk)ói da-ta* 'arrow'. O *oïd̯ʸáát̯ʸa.* H *tïkúi-ra-da ~ ~ ~ –* (originally separate words, as evidenced by the /dʸ/ in Ocaina).
PHO   **oi /_ #* **(unstressed)** *> O oï,* **H** *i.*
103   **(tï)nōî* 'bat'. O *nōōî, nōáá́ʔɸiʔʋ̃a.* H *jĩni ~ " ~ ".*
PHO   **oi /_Ci > O oa,* **H** *i.*
103   **(tï)nōî* 'bat'. O *nōōî, nōáá́ʔɸiʔʋ̃a.* H *jĩni ~ " ~ ".* (See **e,i* for the logic behind this rule.)
PHO   **oi /_ > O o,* **H** *uï.*
197   **(p)ōïʔéko(da)* 'mask'. O *ɸōʔîîxora, orîîʔka.* H *hĩgape ~ hĩgaɸe ~ u.i.eko iko.*
233   *?*()oito* 'crown of head'. O *kōčo.* H *– ~ ~ – ïɸogï muido.*
275   **gōï* 'eat fruit'. O *gōō.* H *– – ~ guí-te ~ gui-te.*
144   **(oi)ʔtó()* 'mosquito'. O *âʔčooko* (a exception). H *uidódo ~ " ~ ".*
131   *?*(k)(oi)yïkï* 'parrot'. O *káyooho* (a exception). H *ui.íkï ~ ui.íkï ~ θarokï.*
333   **iaïn(oi)deʔi* 'near'. O *áánïraʔ* (ï exception). H *a.íno-mo ~ áïno-ri ~ i.aïrei* (o exception).
PHO   **ia > O a,* **H** *i.a.*
PHO   **iaï > O a,* **H** *i.aï.*
156   **dīa(hī)* 'fruit'. O *d̯ʸāāhî, hïxāā.* H *rí.a ~ " ~ ri.ara.*
333   **iaïn(oi)deʔi* 'near'. O *áánïraʔ.* H *a.íno-mo ~ áïno-ri ~ i.aïrei.*
294 = 371   **hīaî(hī)* 'red'. O *tsííʔo, hāāhī.* H *hí.aï-re-de ~ " ~ ".*
PHO   **oa > O o,* **H** *ua.*
PHO   **oaï > O o,* **H** *uaï.*
87   **p(ai)ʔkoa-ti* 'fishhook'. O *ɸeʔxoo-ti.* H *pákua-ti ~ ɸákua-θi ~ ɸago-θi* (*ua ~ ua ~ o* exception).
126   **goaïkí(ho)* 'toad'. O *gokóóho.* H *gúku ~ gúaïkï ~ –* (*u ~ uaï ~ –* exception).

3.15. Features not considered. The following features have not been considered in detail in this reconstruction of Proto Huitoto-Ocaina and merit further study.

1. The pitch-accent system. The Huitoto languages have a simple accent system (with a possible tendency towards a pitch-accent system only on geminate vowels, and only in Nɨpode), whereas Ocaina has a full pitch-accent system. As stated in §1.7, a preliminary inspection of the data suggests that Proto Huitoto-Ocaina had an ordinary accent system, which has become somewhat complicated in Ocaina. In some of the words, accent has been marked on the reconstructed form, but the Proto Huitoto-Ocaina accent system has not been analyzed in detail.

2. Vowel length. Long (geminate) vowels are much more common in Ocaina than in Huitoto. It seems probable that most of these were generated in Ocaina rather than having existed in the protolanguage.

There is good evidence, both external and internal, that most of the long vowels in Ocaina were not derived from the protolanguage: (a) Huitoto DOES have some geminate vowels (these are two syllables according to Minor's 1956 analysis). At least one of these (172) has a cognate with Bora and Muinane as well as Ocaina. In this case all of the languages have the geminate vowel, indicating that geminate vowels from Proto Witotoan were not lost in these languages, though they were not very common. (b) The high frequency of the long vowels in Ocaina is greater than in any of the other languages, although Bora and Muinane do have a significant number. (c) Ocaina vowel length seems to be strongly correlated to either penultimate syllable position or stress or both. It may be that at some stage there was a tendency for stress to occur normally in penultimate position and that this in turn lengthened the vowel. The stress then shifted in many cases, causing the vowel length to become phonemicized. For an example of a rule that may depend on the existence of a doubled *i in the protolanguage, however, see *ii above.

4

Proto Witotoan

Table (˙) is a proposed phoneme chart for Proto Witotoan (PW), the reconstructed parent language of all six of the languages represented in this study. It was reconstructed from the two intermediate proto languages reconstructed above, Proto Bora-Muinane (PBM) and Proto Huitoto-Ocaina (PHO). It contains twelve consonants, five vowels and three suprasegmental phonemes (nasalization and two tones). I have listed the two diphthongs (vowel sequences) **ai and **aï in parentheses because they are so common. I have also given the percentage they would have if they were to be treated as separate phonemes, although I have not treated them as such; Their counts are included in those for **a, **i and **ï.

Relative frequencies have been calculated for the proto phonemes, and these are indicated as before. They were calculated based on the reconstructed words in the wordlist. The values match up well with the expected values from the sound-change rules in most cases. The frequencies are given with a percentage point of precision.

Of the words in the wordlist, only between 25% and 35% (between 92 and 131 out of 375) are cognates between Proto Huitoto-Ocaina and Proto Bora-Muinane. In spite of this rather low cognate count, the relationships were no more difficult to establish than were those between Huitoto and Ocaina, since the sound changes were not nearly so complex. The vowel systems of modern Huitoto and modern Bora retain a high level of correspondence.

Table (14) is almost identical to table (12), the phoneme chart for Proto Huitoto-Ocaina; the only differences are that PHO *y is not represented and that the tone system of Proto Bora-Muinane is assumed to be derived from Proto Witotoan. The phoneme inventory for Proto Bora-Muinane is quite different (table (9)). Proto Bora-Muinane experienced a significant number of consonant splits, increasing the consonant inventory accordingly. The Proto Bora-Muinane vowel system also added another vowel through the split of PW **e into PBM *e and *i. Considering the complex system of splits and mergers that occurred in the Proto Bora-Muinane vowels, it is surprising that this is the only systematic difference in the vowels.

(14)   Proto Witotoan phonemes

p	t		k	ʔ	i		ï
7	13		10	6 Init. 13 Final	18		16
b	d [r]	dz	g		e	a	o
5	5	1	9		18	27	22
				x	(ai)		(aï)
				11	(5)		(7)
β					oral vowels: 87		
1					nasalized vowels: 13		
m	n				two tones		
8	12						

334 consonants, 361 oral vowels, 54 nasal vowels

4.1 Consonant reflexes

The consonant changes from Proto Witotoan to Proto Bora-Muinane and to Proto Huitoto-Ocaina were apparently not nearly as complex as the later changes in the two subfamilies. The changes of interest occurred in the stop phonemes and almost entirely in Proto Bora-Muinane, not Proto Huitoto-Ocaina.

**p split into *p and *x in Proto Bora-Muinane, the former occurring word-initially, the latter word-medially. This may seem like an unlikely occurrence, until it is considered that the likely intermediate form was *ɸ, which would then make sense.[49] The environment would make sense, too, since sounds are more likely to be fricativized in word-medial position than in word-initial position.

**k similarly split into *k and *x in Proto Bora-Muinane, but not in the same environment as for the **p split. Here the primary condition factor was the following vowel, *x occurring primarily before high vowels and *k elsewhere.

---

[49]A similar sound change occurred in Spanish, in which *f became /x/ in certain word-initial situations.

**t split into **t* and **ts* in Proto Bora-Muinane, based primarily on the following vowel. Interestingly, the same split occurred in Ocaina. There is no correspondence whatsoever between the two sound changes, however, and there is no single cognate which has /ts/ in both Ocaina and in Proto Bora-Muinane. The reason for this is simple: **t* became /ts/ in Ocaina only after **ɨ*, whereas ***t* became **ts* in Proto Bora-Muinane primarily after Proto Bora-Muinane **i* and **i* and never after **ɨ*. The phonetic motivation may have been similar in both cases, however. There are cases in natural language in which a high central vowel produces an alveolar sibilant reflex (see discussion in §2.5); in Ocaina, **ɨ* may have been sufficiently central at some stage to have the same effect.

Another minor reflex of ***t* was Proto Bora-Muinane **č*, producing an additional phoneme.

**d split into **d* and **r* in Proto Bora-Muinane; these were allophones in Proto-Witotoan and remained allophones in Proto Huitoto-Ocaina. The same split occurred later in Ocaina. In this case, the two correspond well. This Proto Bora-Muinane **r* presumably started out as a voiced alveolar flap, since it derived from ***d*, but later apparently developed into a trill, since both Bora and Muinane now have a trill, fricative, or affricate as its reflex.

One of the most interesting features is the addition of the voiceless geminate stop series **pp*, **tt*, **tts*, **čč*, and **kk* to Proto Bora-Muinane. These were produced from Proto Witotoan preglottalized voiceless stops and retain reflexes in both Bora and Muinane (the former are now preaspirated). This probably was a fairly late rule. It is even possible that Proto Bora-Muinane retained the preglottalized forms and that these preglottalized forms passed directly to geminate and preaspirated forms in Muinane and Bora respectively. It seems more natural to me, however, for preaspirated forms to come from voiceless geminates than from preglottalized forms, so I am positing the geminates in Proto Bora-Muinane. Thráinsson (1978) has proposed a similar scenario in Icelandic, in which underlying geminated aspirated stops (e.g. /pʰpʰ/) surface as preaspirated (e.g., as the sequence [hp]).

As is seen in §3, Proto Witotoan **ʔt* also produced a new phoneme in Early Huitoto (retained in Nɨpode), the phoneme /d/; thus there are several cognate sets which have **tt* in Proto Bora-Muinane (realized as /tt/ in Muinane and /xtʰ/ in Bora), /d/ in Nɨpode and /ʔt/ in Ocaina (see 137, 227, 317 in §6).

In contrast to the voiceless stops, the question of the existence of preglottalized voiced stops in Proto Witotoan is quite confusing. In spite of the fact that these can be fairly well reconstructed in both Proto Bora-Muinane and in Proto Huitoto-Ocaina, no forms can be confidently reconstructed for Proto Witotoan (§4.4), and the rules I have proposed are somewhat ad hoc.

4.2 Vowel reflexes

As was true for the consonants, the changes to the vowel systems were apparently not as complex as those occurring later.

Two simple splits occurred in Proto Bora-Muinane, **e* splitting into *e and *i and **o* splitting into *o and *ɨ (the conditioning environments were quite different). The former increased the vowel inventory by one;[50] the latter did not, since there already was an *ɨ.

A number of vowels (notably **o*, **ɨ*, **ai*, and **e)* changed to *i in Proto Bora-Muinane under certain circumstances when contiguous to high or front vowels (a process very similar to the umlaut process occurring in a number of Germanic languages).[51] This apparently is the ONLY source of PBM *i, since all cases of PW **i* were lost (see next paragraph). It may seem rather unlikely for a major vowel to be derived exclusively from a process like umlaut (although in the Germanic languages this is certainly the case), but the motivation in this case is clear: to fill the hole left by the loss of **i*. An inspection of all cognate sets with PBM *i shows quite a high adherence to the rules.[52]

**i* apparently became *ai in all cases in Proto Bora-Muinane (which means that the only evidence for the Proto Witotoan contrast between **i* and **ai* comes from Proto Huitoto-Ocaina, primarily from Huitoto). Some cases of *ai then reverted to *i by the umlaut rule mentioned above. The diphthong *ai was already fairly common, thus becoming even more common. In addition, the diphthong **aï* became *ai, making *ai even more common. Subsequent to this, various sound changes occurred to *ai (among other things producing *a), reducing its frequency to some extent. This is the Proto Bora-Muinane diphthong which later produced most of the palatalization in the daughter languages, especially Bora.

**aï* also apparently underwent a split in Proto Huitoto-Ocaina into *aï and *oï. It is possible, however, that this split occurred later and that *oï did not exist in Proto Huitoto-Ocaina (§3.14).

Both **ai* and **aï* were apparently common in Proto Witotoan. They show a fair amount of variation with **i* and **ɨ* respectively, throughout the history of the languages. There is also a possibility that they themselves

---

[50]This split later triggered the Muinane vowel rotation. See §§1.1 and 2.6 for details.

[51]Except that the result is not rounded; only one of the vowels affected is rounded, however, so this is not surprising. Also, it has been pointed out that front rounded vowels apparently never occur in any language in the New World, but are common in Eurasia, a fascinating areal restriction (see §5.3). There would, therefore, be no areal tendency to retain rounding on an umlauted vowel.

[52]Details are given in §4.8.

could have been originally produced by a split from *i and *ï, respectively. Lacking evidence to show the nature of such a split, however, I am reconstructing them separately.

4.3–10 PW sound changes

PW sound-change rules follow, with examples of each and commentary, using the same conventions as in previous sections. Because of the relatively low cognate count, all examples of each rule are given.

Double asterisks mark the Proto Witotoan phonemes, and single asterisks intermediate phonemes.

As was the case in both of the first-stage reconstructions presented, Proto Bora-Muinane and Proto Huitoto-Ocaina material in parentheses is only attested in one or the other of their respective daughter languages, and Proto Witotoan material in parentheses is only attested in one or the other of the subfamilies. Parentheses with nothing inside, (), indicate that the reconstruction is in some way incomplete.

4.3 Voiceless stops. This section presents the rules for PW voiceless stops **p, **ʔp, **t, **ʔt, **k, and **ʔk.

PW **p /#__ > PBM *p, PHO *p.
87 **paiʔko 'fishhook'. PBM *pííkkï-gai. PHO **p(ai)ʔkoa-ti*.
117 **píʔto 'agouti'. PBM (*pátti*). PHO **p(íí)to*.
128 ***pi(ʔti)ʔto* 'hummingbird'. PBM **páá(i)bi(ʔo)*. PHO *piʔtíʔto.
284 ?***(gaʔa)pe* 'fly'. PBM *gaʔape. PHO (*pee*).
299 ?***(i)paï* 'round'. PBM *paï, ?**pá(tté)ï*. PHO (*ikoïpoï*).
354 ?***(ka)pai()* 'pierce'. PBM *kápáítiïkkï-nï. PHO (*paiʔ*).
365 **poonoʔ 'blow'. PBM (*pooni*). PHO **poo(noʔ-te)*.
375 ***pï(e)* 'year'. PBM **pí(k)kaba*. PHO (*pïemóna*).
PW **p /__ > PBM *x, PHO *p.
5 ***topo-(ʔo)* 'nose'. PBM *tïxï-ʔo. PHO *topo.
7 ??***()po* 'ear'. PBM *níxï-miiʔo. PHO (*hepo*).
255 ?***()po-(ga)* 'shelter'. PBM *niïxï-ga. PHO **(ho)po-()*.
255; (75) ?***xopo-(ga)* 'shelter'. PBM **(iixó)-ga*. PHO **(ho)po-()*.
1; (235) ??***()pe* 'tongue'. PBM **(mé)-ʔníxï-()*. PHM **(h)ïyïʔpe*.
235; (1) ?***()pe (ï)kaï* 'tongue tip'. PBM **(mé)-ʔnïxï-(ga)-*, *nïx(ï)k(aï)*.
PHO (*ïyïʔpe ïkoï*).

The next two examples were probably both derived from item 2 ***(-)po(e)* 'mouth' (see **ʔp below), which apparently occurred only in word-medial position at the time of this sound change. Subsequently the first syllable (which may have been a prefix) was lost in Proto Huitoto-

Ocaina and in these examples in Proto Bora-Muinane. These are, therefore, not really exceptions to this sound-change rule.

   3   **po(e)-(i)ni(ba) 'lip'. **PBM** *(mé)-xǐ-niba. **PHO** ?*p(oe ini).
   318 **po(e)-no-() 'saliva'. **PBM** *xīī-(ní-ba). **PHO** ??*pó(e)-(no-hī).
   PW **ʔp /__ > **PBM** *pp, **PHO** *ʔp.
   59; 247 **xi(moo)ʔ-piʔo 'smoke,cloud'. **PBM** (aimóo-ppai(ʔ)o). **PHO** (hiʔpííʔo).

The next two examples appear to be exceptions to the previous rule. As
the Proto Bora-Muinane forms suggest, however, if they were originally
suffixes, then they would have been added to various stems, most of which
would not end in *ʔ. They would thus have the usual word-medial reflex.

   2   **(-)po(e) 'mouth'. **PBM** *iiʔ-xī. **PHO** *poe.
   75; (255) ??**xop(o) 'house'. **PBM** *iiʔ-xa, *káamóó-xa. **PHO** *(ho)po.

The following is a late rule that specifies a split of PW **t into PBM *t
and *ts. This split apparently occurred in Proto Bora-Muinane after most
of the vowel changes, since it depends on the split of **e into *e and **i
already having occurred. The *ts reflex occurs primarily before *i and *i.[53]
This produced a significantly limited distribution of *t and *ts in Proto
Bora-Muinane (see §2.8).

PW **t > **PBM** *č /ai__e, **PHO** *t.
   353 ?**(gai)taide(ako) 'split'. **PBM** *gá(č)ére(á)ko. **PHO** ?*(boʔ)tá-(de).
PW **t > **PW** *ts /#__a,o, **PHO** *t.
   181; 183; 186; 188 **ta() 'one'. **PBM** *tsaane. **PHO** *ta(he).
   185 **ta-() 'five'. **PBM** *tsá-ʔottsí. **PHO** *ta-()oido.
   150 ?**to() 'grassland'. **PBM** *tsókkómïxi. **PHO** (toháʔaβo).
   343 ?**(t)a(t)íʔkï() 'straight'. **PBM** *tsa-tíkkeβe. **PHO** (ha(h)íkïna) (h exception).
   344 ?**(t)a(t)íʔkï()-be 'correct'. **PBM** (tíkkeβe-be). **PHO** (ha(h)íkïgobe) (h
         exception).
   306 ?**tā(ʔï) 'there'. **PBM** (taʔï) (t exception). **PHO** (tā).
   131 **tooda 'parrot'. **PBM** (jóóra) (j exception). **PHO** (tóóda).
PW **t > **PBM** *t /__a,o, **PHO** *t.
PW **ʔt > **PBM** *tt /__a,o, **PHO** *(ʔ)t.
   242 **(ï)ta() 'lower leg'. **PBM** *(mé)-tákki-(ï). **PHO** *(ïtátoï).
   137 **(k)aʔta-βa 'hen'. **PBM** *ka(ttá-βa). **PHO** *áʔta-βa. This item is probably a
         borrowing, so it may not actually be a cognate; see wordlist.
   317 **móʔta(ba) 'navel'. **PBM** (móttaba). **PHO** *m(ó)ʔt(a).
   269 **(m)oka(x)íʔto 'horn'. **PBM** *(óka)-(x)ítto. **PHO** ?*(mó)kaï(to).
PW **t > **PBM** *ts /__i,i, **PHO** *t.
PW **ʔt > **PBM** *tts /__i,i. **PHO** *(ʔ)t
   73; (55) **goti- 'stone'. **PBM** (gíitsi-ba). **PHO** (gotíʔ-kï).

---

[53]See (3) for more on the phonetic nature of Proto Bora-Muinane *i.

55; (73) **goti-() 'rapids'. PBM (gíitsi-ga). PHO (gotí?-i).
69 ?**(gï)díte 'thunder'. PBM *()tsittsi. PHO (gïdí-te).
226 ?**(o)te(te) 'white'. PBM *tsítsii-ne. PHO (ote-de-te).
283 **íʔtï̈ 'swim'. PBM *ittsi. PHO *íʔí̈ (? exception).
PW **t > PBM *t /__e,ï, PHO *t.
PW **ʔt > PBM *tt /__e,ï, PHO *(ʔ)t.
250; (49) **tae(ʔi)-() 'stream'. PBM *tée-ʔi-(gayï). PHO *(i)tae-().
49; (250) **tae(ʔi) 'river'. PBM *teé-ʔi. PHO *(i)tae.
5 **topo-(ʔo) 'nose'. PBM *tíxï-ʔo. PHO *topo.
33; 266 **tï̈-xē(ʔe) 'blood'. PBM *tíï̈-(xéʔe). PHO *tïhé.
94; 95 **tï() 'bow'. PBM *tïïbó-ga. PHO *tï().
97 **tō() 'tapir'. PBM (tíïʔi). PHO *tō().
117 **píʔto 'agouti'. PBM (pátti). PHO *p(íi)to.
227 ?**(xi)ʔtï-() 'black'. PBM (báttïne). PHO *hiʔtíʔ-().
342 **dï(t)ï() 'smooth'. PBM *rï(tí)rí(tï)-(ko-ne). PHO (díhï-de-te) (h exception).
343 ?**(t)a(t)íʔkï() 'straight'. PBM *tsa-tíkkeβe. PHO (ha(h)íkïna) (h exception).
344 ?**(t)a(t)íʔkï()-be 'correct'. PBM (tíkkeβe-be), ?*(tsaí)mi(yé).
     PHO (ha(h)íkïgobe) (h exception).
355 ?**(t)aïʔde 'dig'. PBM *tseeʔdi (ts exception). PHO (dáïʔ-te) (d exception).
PW **k /a,i__a,ai,aï > PBM *x, PHO *k.
279 **gaka 'know'. PBM *gaaxá(-kï). PHO (áka).
141 **gïnikaï 'fly'. PBM (gíinixa). PHO *(ïní)kï.
PW **k /__a,ai,aï > PBM *k, PHO *k.
84 **koom(ï) 'village'. PBM *kóomií. PHO (komíní).
137 **káda-βa 'hen'. PBM *ká(ra-ka). PHO (káda-βa). This form is probably a
     Tucano or Spanish borrowing, so it may not actually be a cognate; see §6.
370 **kai(), **(k)aime 'up'. PBM *kaame. PHO (kaipo), (aime).
269 **(m)oka(x)íʔto 'horn'. PBM *(óka)-(x)ítto. PHO ?*(mó)kaï(to).
235 ?**()pe (ï)kaï 'tongue tip'. PBM *(mé)-ʔnixi-(ga)-nix(i)k(aí). PHO (ïyíʔpe ïkoï).
23; 24; 30; 271 **-(k)aï 'finger'. PBM *-gai (g exception). PHO -(kai).
130 **no(k)ai(ʔto) 'toucan'. PBM *nïge (g exception). PHO *nokáiʔto.
PW **k /__o > PBM *k, PHO *k.
315 ?**x(ï)xaiko 'wing'. PBM (xíxiko). PHO (iáiko).
34 ?**ko() 'heart'. PBM (kíïdiï). PHO *kome(kï).
58 **koxo 'charcoal'. PBM *kííxí-gai-(kko). PHO *kó(o-kï).
134 **koga 'curassow'. PBM (kígáʔe). PHO *(k)oodz(a).
200 **(k)ōō-xe(ʔe) 'I'. PBM *oó(-xéʔe) (∅ exception). PHO *kōē.
74 ?**(k)onigiïʔï 'sand'. PBM *(xíí)né-gai-yí-ʔai (x exception).
     PHO ??*(koni)dziïʔ(ï). This last exception has *ï after the *x in Proto
     Bora-Muinane. It is therefore possible that this rule applied after a few of
     the vowel-change rules, although it clearly applied before most of them.
PW **k /__ï,i,oi > PBM *x, PHO *k.
102 ??**()kï() 'deer'. PBM *xiíbai. PHO ?*(e)kï(to).
109 **xé(ā)kï 'anteater'. PBM *xííxï. PHO (héākï).
221 ?**()ki() 'small'. PBM (áxáitso-ne). PHO (kiβi-).
257 **kiʔi-() 'that'. PBM *xe(ʔ)é-ne. PHO (kiʔima).
PW **ʔk > PBM *kk, PHO *(ʔ)k.
240; (19) ??**(o)nōíʔk() 'lower arm'. PBM *(mé)-nékkí-(gatsítto).
     PHO *onōí-(kona).

19; (240) *??**(o)nõ̃ĩ̃ʔk()* 'arm'. **PBM** **(mé)-nékkï-gai.* **PHO** **onõ̃ĩ̃-(kaido).*
343 *?**(t)a(t)í̃ʔkï()* 'straight'. **PBM** **tsa-tï̃kkeβe.* **PHO** *(ha(h)í̃kï̃na).*
344 *?**(t)a(t)í̃ʔkï()-be* 'correct'. **PBM** *(tï̃kkeβe-be), ?*(tsaí)mi(yé).*
      PHO *(ha(h)í̃kï̃gobe).*
25 ***(ï)dzaʔkai(do)* 'leg'. **PBM** *(mé-tákki).* **PHO** *?*ï̃dzá-k(aido).*
126 ***(go)xaï̃ʔkï()* 'toad'. **PBM** *(xáákkïba), *xaʔkó(kó)ga.* **PHO** **goaïkí̃(ho).*
98; 99; 101 ***xí̃ʔko* 'jaguar'. **PBM** *(xï̃kko).* **PHO** **hí̃ʔko.*
87 ***paiʔko* 'fishhook'. **PBM** **pí̃ikkï-gai.* **PHO** **p(ai)ʔkoa-ti.*
66 *?**()ʔkoʔdo()* 'star'. **PBM** **mí̃ïkí̃rï̃-gai (k* exception). **PHO** **oʔkóʔto.*

4.4. Voiced stops. This section presents the rules for the PW voiced
stops ****b**, ****ʔb**, ****d**, ****ʔd**,****dz**, ****g**, and ****ʔg**. The first two rules for PW
b below, indicating that some instances of PW ****b became **m* in one or
the other of the subfamilies, are somewhat uncertain. In both cases the
conditioning environment is claimed to be nasalization of a contiguous
vowel, but in each rule the nasalization was retained in only one example
in Ocaina (the only language in the whole family which currently has
phonemically nasalized vowels). In addition, the rule for PW ****d** becoming
*n is the reverse of the one for ****b**. This analysis must therefore be
considered highly tentative. If correct, these rules would be the only ones
which corroborate the existence of the nasalized vowels in Proto Witotoan.

PW **b /V̄__ > PBM *b, PHO *m.
202 *?**i-(b)ai* 'he'. **PBM** *(aáí-be).* **PHO** **i-ma, *(iʔ)i-ma.*
111 *?**naiʔĩ(b)a* 'crocodile'. **PBM** **niʔiba.* **PHO** **(na)ʔĩma.*
PW **b /__ V̄ > PBM *m, PHO *b.
271; (24) ***()-(k)aï-(be)* 'claw'. **PBM** **(mé)-ʔóttsï-gai-mí̃iʔo.* **PHO** *(onõ̃ĩ̃-k(aï)-be).*
24; (271) ***()-(k)aï-(b)e(ʔo)* 'fingernail'. **PBM** **(mé)-ʔóttsï-gai-mí̃iʔo.*
      PHO *(onõ̃ĩ̃-k(aï)-be).*
258 *??**(b)õ()* 'who'. **PBM** **mí̃-(ʔa)-xa.* **PHO** **bõ̃.*
PW **b /__ > PBM *b, PHO *b.
344 *?**(t)a(t)í̃ʔkï()-be* 'correct'. **PBM** *(tï̃kkeβe-be), ?*(tsaí)mi(yé).*
      PHO *(ha(h)í̃kï̃gobe).*
272; (14; 244) ***xebae* 'belly'. **PBM** *(xï̃ibï̃ï).* **PHO** *(hebae).*
14; (244; 272) ***xebae-gaï* 'chest'. **PBM** *(xï̃ibï̃ïga).* **PHO** **(he)bae-goï().*
172 ***xïibí-ʔe* 'coca'. **PBM** **xï̃ibii-(ʔe).* **PHO** **hïibí(ʔe).*
PW **ʔb > PBM *ʔb, PHO *b.
16; 244; 245; 272 *xeʔbae-()* 'abdomen'. **PBM** **(mé)-iiʔba(ï).* **PHO** **(he)bae-().*

The rule above for ****ʔb** is doubtful, since this item (meaning 'chest' or
'abdomen') also occurs in Proto Bora-Muinane in another form which lacks
the glottal (see items 14 and 272 in the previous rule). As mentioned in §4,
the status of glottals before voiced stops is quite unclear in Proto Witotoan.
      The next rule is also extremely doubtful. Number 275 follows it, but the
vowels do not match, making the cognate doubtful. Furthermore, there is very

little evidence in Bora or Muinane to indicate that this is what happened. In Proto Huitoto-Ocaina, however, this rule is unquestionably correct. The other two items, while apparently showing good cognates, do not follow the rule, since they are word medial in both subfamilies. One could posit that a prefix was added later in both subfamilies, but this would be begging the question. This rule must therefore be considered highly tentative.

PW **_d_ _/#__? (very unclear) > PBM *d, PHO *d.
  275 ***d(o)?* 'eat meat'. PBM *doó-(?i). PHO *dï?-(te).
  231; (274) **xidoo 'drink!'. PBM *d-ádoó. PHO (hido).
  274; (231) **xido 'drink'. PBM *ado. PHO (hidó).
    The following rule is also doubtful, since the presumed nasalization does not appear on either Ocaina example.
PW **_d_ _/ṽ__ > PBM *n, PHO *d (allophone [r]).
  115 ***me(d)o* 'collared peccary'. PBM *meéni. PHO (medo).
  224 ?***(e)meá(d)e* 'good'. PBM (ímiáá-ne). PHO (made).
PW **_d_ _/__ > PBM *r, PHO *d (allophone [r]).
  137 **káda-βa 'hen'. PBM *ká(ra-ka). PHO (káda-βa). This is probably a Tucano or Spanish borrowing, so it may not actually be a cognate; see §6.
  180 ***(báa)xïdi(ba)* 'cassava drink'. PBM (báaxïribá). PHO (-hïdi).
  353 ?***(gai)taide(ako)* 'split'. PBM *gá(č)ére(á)ko. PHO ?*(bo?)tá-(de).
  342 ***dï(t)ï()* 'smooth'. PBM *rï(tḯ)rḯ(tï)-(ko-ne). PHO (dïhï-de-te).
   53 ***dzoodo()* 'spring of water'. PBM (čooróga), (píítsíri-gai). PHO *dzod(o)-p(o).
  131 **tooda 'parrot'. PBM (joóra). PHO (tóóda).
  132 ?***()di()* 'parakeet'. PBM (tïrii?o). PHO ?*()di().
   69 ?***(gï)dïte* 'thunder'. PBM *()tsittsi (ts exception). PHO (gïdḯ-te).

The following rule is somewhat doubtful; but it is probably more reliable than the ***?b* rule, if for no other reason than that two examples occur, both of which have *?t in Proto Huitoto-Ocaina. The Proto Bora-Muinane exception is simply a case of loss of ***?.

PW **_?d_ > PBM *?d, PHO *?t.
  355 ?***(t)aï?de* 'dig'. PBM *tsee?di. PHO (dáï?-te).
   66 ?***()?ko?do()* 'star'. PBM *mïkírï-gai (r exception). PHO *o?kó?to.
PW **_dz_ > PBM *ts /__ ị,i, PHO *dz.
   53 ***dzoodo()* 'spring of water'. PBM (čooróga), (píítsíri-gai). PHO *dzod(o)-p(o).
PW **_dz_ > PBM *t /__ (see **t), PHO *dz.
  114 ?***dzo()* 'river turtle'. PBM (tïrííxi). PHO (dzo?dzo).
   25 ***(ï)dza?kai(do)* 'leg'. PBM (mé-tákki). PHO ?*ïdzá-k(aido).
  179 ***(ï)xaidzaï(ga)* 'salt'. PBM (áit(t)ega). PHO *(í)háidzaï.
   53 ***dzoodo()* 'spring of water'. PBM (čooróga) (č exception), (píítsíri-gai). PHO *dzod(o)-p(o).

In spite of the asymmetry that proposing the existence of PW **dz entails, the above rule is quite straightforward and has adequate examples,

so I am proposing it without disclaimer. On the Proto Bora-Muinane side
it functions in every way like PW **t (with the exception noted).

PW **g /#__o > PBM *g, PHO *g.
   73; (55) **goti- 'stone'. PBM (giitsi-ba). PHO (gotí?-kï).
   55; (73) **goti-() 'rapids'. PBM (gíítsi-ga). PHO (gotí?-i).
   275 **gōī(ne) 'eat fruit'. PBM *geéne. PHO *gōī.
PW **g /#__ > PBM *g, PHO *ɸ.
   45 **gā?ī 'mother'. PBM *ga?á-ro(bi). PHO *é?ī.
   141 **gïnikaï 'fly'. PBM (giinixa). PHO *(ïní)kï.
   279 **gaka 'know'. PBM *gaaxá(-kï). PHO (áka).
   351 ?**gain(āĩ) 'throw'. PBM (gáino). PHO *(ai)nāĩ-().
PW **g /i__i > PBM *g, PHO *dz.
   74 ?**(k)onigiĩ?ī 'sand'. PBM *(xíí)né-gai-yĩ-?ai. PHO ??*(koni)dziĩ?(ī).
PW **g /__ > PBM *g, PHO *g.
   14; (244; 272) **xebae-gaï 'chest'. PBM (xïibïïga). PHO *(he)bae-goï().
   374 **(i)gaï(baï) 'rope'. PBM *gáaibaï. PHO (igaï).
   246; (40) **-gaï (feminine). PBM *kééme-ge. PHO *ha?í(do)-goï.
   203; (40) ?**i-gaï 'she'. PBM *(aáí-)ge. PHO *(i?)i-goï, *(apé)-goï.
   40; (246; 203) **-gaï (feminine). PBM *gai-ge. PHO (dï-goï).
   134 **koga 'curassow'. PBM (kĩgá?e). PHO *(k)oodz(a) (dz exception).
PW **?g > PBM *?g, PHO *b?, ?t?
   273 ??**(?g)an(oxi) 'liver'. PBM *(mé)-í?gá-neé. PHO (banóhi).
   4 ??**iï?-gi-() 'tooth'. PBM *íí?-gái-neé. PHO *i?ti?-to.

The last rule above, for **?g, is almost not worth stating, since it shows
only that the status of PW **?g is uncertain. I state it simply to show that
there is a problem with all three of the preglottalized voiced stops.

4.5. Glottal. The next rule only applies to intervocalic PW **?, not to
syllable final position. Glottal was often lost in the latter environment.
Because this depended heavily on what the following consonant was,
however, and because the interrelationship is often complex, I have simply
included them under the individual consonants.[54]

PW **?/__V > PBM *?, PHO *?.
   45 **gā?ī 'mother'. PBM *ga?á-ro(bi). PHO *é?ī.
   59; 247 **xi(moo)?-pi?o 'smoke, cloud'. PBM (aimóo-ppai(?)o). PHO (hi?píí?o).
   74 ?**(k)onigiĩ?ī 'sand'. PBM *(xíí)né-gai-yĩ-?ai. PHO ??*(koni)dziĩ?(ī).

---

[54]I was only able to reconstruct glottals before **p, **t, **k, **x and doubtfully
before **b, **d, **g. dz, and **β are sufficiently rare that the lack of examples is
not surprising. I, therefore, conclude that they were never preglottalized. A few
examples of /?m/ and /?n/ do occur in both Bora and Ocaina, but I assume these are
later developments. The Bora examples occur mostly at morpheme breaks or because
of vowel loss, though I did carry a few over into the PBM reconstruction. No examples
of *m, *n, or *β were reconstructed in PHO (see §3.10).

111 *?**nai?ï̃(b)a* 'crocodile'. **PBM** *ni?iba*. **PHO** *(na)?ï̃ma*.
121 *?**(ib)o?oo* 'tail'. **PBM** *(ííbo?o)*. **PHO** *(o?oo)*.
166 ***xá?i()* 'cotton'. **PBM** *xá?adi*. **PHO** *(há?ikï)*.
172 ***xíibí-?e* 'coca'. **PBM** *xíibíí-(?e)*. **PHO** *híibí(?e)*.
206; 212 ***aïmäï̃?-()* 'ye'. **PBM** *ámïï̃?-()*. **PHO** *(o)mäï̃?-()*.
257 ***ki?i-()* 'that'. **PBM** *xe(?)é-ne*. **PHO** *(ki?ima)*.

As can be seen, the status of intervocalic **? is quite solid, even though its reconstructed count is only about half of that for preconsonantal **?.

4.6. Fricatives. This section presents the rules for the PW fricatives **x, ***?x*, and **β.

PW **x /#__*i,ai,o* > **PBM** **∅*, **PHO** *h.
179 ***(ï)xaidzaï(ga)* 'salt'. **PBM** *(áit(t)ega)*. **PHO** *(ï)háidzaï*.
231; (274) ***xidoo* 'drink!'. **PBM** *d-ádóó*. **PHO** *(hido)*.
274; (231) ***xido* 'drink'. **PBM** *ado*. **PHO** *(hidó)*.
59; 247 ***xi(moo)?-pi?o* 'smoke, cloud'. **PBM** *(aimóo-ppai(?)o)*. **PHO** *(hi?píí?o)*.
75; (255) *??**xop(o)* 'house'. **PBM** *ii?-xa, *káamóó-xa*. **PHO** *(ho)po*.
255; (75) *?**xopo-(ga)* 'shelter'. **PBM** *(iixó)-ga*. **PHO** *(ho)po-()*.
172 ***xíibí-?e* 'coca'. **PBM** *xíibíí-(?e)* (*x* exception). **PHO** *híibí(?e)*.
PW **x /#__*ae* > **PBM** *x, **PHO** **∅*.
72 ***xáéní?-xē* 'earth'. **PBM** *xíínï-xi*. **PHO** *aenï̃?-ē*.
372 ***xáéní?-()* 'dust'. **PBM** *(xíínï)-giixï*. **PHO** *aenï̃?-hiβóda*.
129 ***xaeβa(do)* 'macaw'. **PBM** *xíiβaá*. **PHO** *(ae)(β)a(do)*.
PW **x /#__ *a,e,ï*, **PBM** *x, **PHO** *h.
166 ***xá?i()* 'cotton'. **PBM** *xá?adi*. **PHO** *(há?ikï)*.
109 ***xé(ā)kï* 'anteater'. **PBM** *xííxï*. **PHO** *(hēākï)*.
272; (14; 244) ***xebae* 'belly'. **PBM** *(xíibïï)*. **PHO** *(hebae)*.
14; (244; 272) ***xebae-gaï* 'chest'. **PBM** *(xíibïïga)*. **PHO** *(he)bae-goï()*.
85; 253 ***(na)xï()* 'path'. **PBM** *xïï̃-()*. **PHO** *nahï̃(to)*.
98; 99; 101 ***xï̃?ko* 'jaguar'. **PBM** *(xïkko)*. **PHO** *hï̃?ko*.
315 *?**x(ï)xaiko* 'wing'. **PBM** *(xíxiko)*. **PHO** *(iáiko)* (*∅* exception).

The following three examples are not word initial, but they are initial in morphemes which very probably functioned as separate words at some stage. Therefore, I am not treating them as exceptions.

33; 266 ***tï-xē(?e)* 'blood'. **PBM** *tïï̃-(xé?e)*. **PHO** *tïhē*.
62 ***nō-xï* 'rain'. **PBM** *nííxa-ba*. **PHO** *nō-(kï), *nō-(hï)*.
180 ***(báa)xïdi(ba)* 'cassava drink'. **PBM** *(báaxïribá)*. **PHO** *(-hïdi)*.
PW **x /e,(i?)__ > **PBM** **∅*, **PHO** **?*.
16; 244; 245; 272 ***xe?bae-()* 'abdomen'. **PBM** *(mé)-ii?ba(ï)*. **PHO** *(he)bae-()*.

The previous example is unusual in that: (a) it is the only one which loses **x in PBM in word-medial position (the other PBM cognate for this word, listed above, is clearly word initial and does not lose the **x); (b) on the PHO side the example is clearly word initial and therefore has *h; if it did not, there would have been no way to reconstruct the **x, except by comparison with the other PBM cognate. This second point explains why there are no other examples of **x after **e or i. If this rule is correct, all trace of **x was lost in this environment. For this reason and since it is the only noninitial example which is preceded by a front vowel, I consider this rule probable.

PW **x /a,o,e__ > PBM *x, PHO *∅.
58   **koxo 'charcoal'. **PBM** *kíîxî-gai-(kko). **PHO** *kó(o-kï).
269 **(m)óka(x)ïʔto 'horn'. **PBM** *(óka)-(x)ítto. **PHO** ?*(mó)kaï(to).
315 ?**x(ï)xaiko 'wing'. **PBM** (xîxɨko). **PHO** (iáiko).
126 **(go)xaïʔkï() 'toad'. **PBM** (xáákkïba), *xaʔkó(kó)ga. **PHO** *goaïkí(ho).
200 **(k)ōō-xe(ʔe) 'I'. **PBM** *oó(-xéʔe). **PHO** *kōē.
201 **ō-xe(ʔe) 'thou'. **PBM** *ïï(-xéʔe). **PHO** *ō(ē).

PW **ʔx > PBM *x, PHO *ʔ.
72   **xáénïʔ-xē 'earth'. **PBM** *xíínï-xɨ. **PHO** *aenïʔ-ē.

PW **β > PBM *β, PHO *β.
129 **xaeβa(do) 'macaw'. **PBM** *xíiβaá. **PHO** *(ae)(β)a(do).
137 **(k)aʔta-βa 'hen'. **PBM** *ka(ttá-βa). **PHO** *áʔta-βa. The stem of this is probably a borrowing, but the suffix is probably native; see §6.

4.7. Nasals.

Of all the Proto Witotoan phonemes, **m and **n offer by far the best evidence, having both a large number of cognates and a completely transparent correspondence, with no allophonic splits. These correspondences alone would almost prove a genetic relationship between the two subfamilies.

PW **m > PBM *m, PHO *m.
15; (319) **mō(ʔpai)naï 'breast'. **PBM** *(mé)-mïppaine. **PHO** *mōnoï.
41   **()mïnaï 'people'. **PBM** *míamínaa. **PHO** (komïnï).
311; (49) **moo(n)ai 'sea'. **PBM** *moóai. **PHO** *m(o)nái-(tahi).
49; (311) **m(oon)ai 'river'. **PBM** *moóai. **PHO** *(i)máni.
70   ??**(n)ame() 'lightning'. **PBM** (námɨ-ba). **PHO** *améʔyo.
84   **koom(i) 'village'. **PBM** *kóomií. **PHO** (komïnï).
115 **me(d)o 'collared peccary'. **PBM** *meéni. **PHO** (medo).
117 ?**()mï() 'agouti'. **PBM** (bɨrímïxɨ). **PHO** *mï(goi).
152 ?**(aï)me() 'tree'. **PBM** *íme-ʔe. **PHO** *aména.
160 **(aï)me-nai-() 'stick'. **PBM** *ímé-(ne-ba). **PHO** *aména.
182; 187 **menai() 'two'. **PBM** *míínéékkïï. **PHO** (mena).
183; 188 **()m(e)n(ai)() ta() 'three'. **PBM** (míínéékkïïtsaane). **PHO** *(amani) tá(he).
206; 212 **aïmāïʔ-() 'ye'. **PBM** *ámïïʔ-(). **PHO** *(o)māïʔ-().
224 ?**(e)meá(d)e 'good'. **PBM** (imɨáá-ne). **PHO** (made).
301 **maime 'name'. **PBM** *meme. **PHO** *mame.
317 **móʔta(ba) 'navel'. **PBM** (móttaba). **PHO** *m(ó)ʔt(a).
320 ?**mï() 'with'. **PBM** *-ma. **PHO** (mïʔto).
370 **kai(), **(k)aime 'up'. **PBM** *kaame. **PHO** (kaipo), (aime).

PW **_n_ > PBM *_n_, PHO *_n_.

3   **_po(e)-(i)ni(ba)_ 'lip'. **PBM** *_(mé)-xí-niba_. **PHO** _?*p(oe ini)_.

15; (319) **_mō(ʔpai)naï_ 'breast'. **PBM** *_(mé)-mĭppaine_. **PHO** *_mōnoï_.

319; (15) **_mō(ʔpai)naï-()_ 'milk'. **PBM** *_mĭppáíne-ppái(k)o_. **PHO** *_mōnoï ehī_.

19; (240) _??**(o)nāĩʔk()_ 'arm'. **PBM** *_(mé)-nékkï-gai_. **PHO** *_onóĩ-(kaido)_.

240; (19) _??**(o)nāĩʔk()_ 'lower arm'. **PBM** *_(mé)-nékkĭ-(gatsítto)_.
   PHO *_onóĩ-(kona)_.

41 **_()mĭnaï_ 'people'. **PBM** *_mĭamĭnaa_. **PHO** _(komĭnï)_.

48 **_nō-()_ 'water'. **PBM** *_nĭ-ppaiko_. **PHO** *_(haï-)nō-hī_.

62 **_nō-xī_ 'rain'. **PBM** *_nííxa-ba_. **PHO** *_nō-(kï)_, *_nō-(hī)_.

72 **_xáénĩʔ-xē_ 'earth'. **PBM** *_xíínï-xi_. **PHO** *_aenĩʔ-ē_.

74 _?**(k)onigiĩʔĩ_ 'sand'. **PBM** *_(xíí)né-gai-yĭ-ʔai_. **PHO** _??*(koni)dziĩʔ(ī)_.

111 _?**naiʔĩ(b)a_ 'crocodile'. **PBM** *_niʔiba_. **PHO** *_(na)ʔĩma_.

130 **_no(k)ai(ʔto)_ 'toucan'. **PBM** *_nïge_. **PHO** *_nokáiʔto_.

133 **_īno_ 'buzzard'. **PBM** *_ainï_. **PHO** *_īno()_.

141 **_gïnikaï_ 'fly'. **PBM** _(gíinixa)_. **PHO** *_(ïnï)kï_.

160 **_(aï)me-nai-()_ 'stick'. **PBM** *_ímé-(ne-ba)_. **PHO** *_aména_.

170 **_naï()_ 'annatto'. **PBM** *_néebaba_. **PHO** *_nonó()_.

182; 187 **_menai()_ 'two'. **PBM** *_míínéékkiĩ_. **PHO** _(mena)_.

183; 188 _?**()m(e)n(ai)() ta()_ 'three'. **PBM** _(míínéékkiĩtsaane)_. **PHO** *_(amani)
   tá(he)_.

186–189 **_ene() ()_ 'other?'. **PBM** _(inekkïé)-_. **PHO** *_ené(da)_.

260 **_(ta)ʔāĩ-ne_ 'not'. **PBM** *_tsáʔaá-(ne)_. **PHO** *_(āī)-ne_.

273 _??**(ʔg)an(oxi)_ 'liver'. **PBM** *_(mé)-íʔgá-neé_. **PHO** _(banóhi)_.

318 **_po(e)-no-()_ 'saliva'. **PBM** *_xiĩ-(ní-ba)_. **PHO** _??*pó(e)-(no-hī)_.

351 _?**gain(āĩ)_ 'throw'. **PBM** _(gáino)_. **PHO** *_(ai)nāĩ-()_.

365 **_poonoʔ_ 'blow'. **PBM** _(pooni)_. **PHO** *_poo(noʔ-te)_.

367 **_īni(neko)_ 'squeeze'. **PBM** _((ai)n(ai)nïko)_. **PHO** _?*ī(ni)_.

372 **_xáénĩʔ-()_ 'dust'. **PBM** *_(xíínï)-giixï_. **PHO** *_aenĩʔ-hiβóda_.

311; (49) **_moo(n)ai_ 'sea'. **PBM** *_moóai_ (∅ exception). **PHO** *_m(o)nái-(tahi)_.

49; (311) **_m(oon)ai_ 'river'. **PBM** *_moóai_ (∅ exception). **PHO** *_(i)máni_.

70 _??**(n)ame()_ 'lightning'. **PBM** _(námi-ba)_. **PHO** *_amếʔyo_ (∅ exception).

4.8 Vowel umlaut process summary. Before proceeding with individual vowel rules, I need to discuss the umlaut process (movement of vowels to *_i_ or *_e_ through the influence of a neighboring vowel) which occurred in Proto Bora-Muinane (§4.2). This process affected Proto Witotoan **_i_, **_ï_, **_o_, **_e_, **_ai_, and **_ae_; it apparently had no effect on **_a_.

The only items which might show umlaut for **_a_, numbers 111 and 183 (which matches 188 with *_e_), have been analyzed otherwise as **_ai_ and **_e_, respectively. The only direct proof I have that the umlaut process did not affect **_a_ are numbers 45 and 166, both of which have a glottal (45 also has an irregular PHO reflex, but the PBM reflex is regular). Other cases of **_a_ either before or after **_i_ seem to be lacking.

Since the details of the umlaut process are likely to get lost for the reader in the rules for the individual vowels, I summarize the umlaut rules here. The first three rules below were early rules and have Proto Witotoan environments, whereas the last three apparently applied later and have Proto Bora-Muinane environments. The third and sixth rules, involving an *e environment, are somewhat doubtful, since they only apply to **e and are restricted to certain environments. See **e below for details; consonantal environments (not included in the summary given in (15) below) play a significant part in the rules both for **e and for **i and **ai. The fourth rule below is also restricted to a particular consonantal environment for **e.

(15)   Three early and four late PW > PBM umlaut rules

    a.   **PW** *ai(i),ɨ,o/#(C)__Ci(ai)* > **PBM** *i*, **PHO** unchanged.
           PW *ɨ,ai(i),ae/#(C)__Cɨ* > **PBM** *i*, **PHO** unchanged.
           PW *e/#(C)__Ce,Cai (Bora Ce)* > **PBM** *i*, **PHO** unchanged.
    b.   **PW** *e,ɨ,o* > **PBM** *i /iC__*, **PHO** unchanged.
           PW *ai(i)* > **PBM** *i /ɨC__*, **PHO** unchanged.
           PW *e* > **PBM** *i /eC__*, **PHO** unchanged.
           PW *ai(i),aɨ(ae)* > **PBM** *e /ai,eC__*, **PHO** unchanged.

4.9. Pure vowels. This section presents the rules for PW vowels **a, **e, **o, and **ɨ.

PW **a > PBM *a, PHO *a.
  70 *??**(n)ame()* 'lightning'. **PBM** *(námi-ba)*. **PHO** *améʔyo*.
 111 *?**naiʔi(b)a* 'crocodile'. **PBM** *ni?iba*. **PHO** *(na)ʔima*.
 129 ***xaeβa(do)* 'macaw'. **PBM** *xíiβaá*. **PHO** *(ae)(β)a(do)*.
 131 ***tooda* 'parrot'. **PBM** *(joóra)*. **PHO** *(tóóda)*.
 137 ***(k)aʔta-βa* 'hen'. **PBM** *ka(ttá-βa)*. **PHO** *áʔta-βa*.
 137 ***káda-βa* 'hen'. **PBM** *ká(ra-ka)*. **PHO** *(káda-βa)*.
 166 ***xáʔi()* 'cotton'. **PBM** *xáʔadi*. **PHO** *(háʔikɨ)*.
 181; 183; 186; 188 ***ta()* 'one'. **PBM** *tsaane*. **PHO** *ta(he)*.
 185 ***ta-()* 'five'. **PBM** *tsá-ʔottsí*. **PHO** *ta-()oido*.
 242 ***(ɨ)ta()* 'lower leg'. **PBM** *(mé)-tákki-(ɨ)*. **PHO** *(ɨtátoɨ)*.
 269 ***(m)oka(x)ɨʔto* 'horn'. **PBM** *(óka)-(x)itto*. **PHO** *?*(mó)kaɨ(to)*.
 273 *??**(ʔg)an(oxi)* 'liver'. **PBM** *(mé)-iʔgá-neé*. **PHO** *(banóhi)*.
 279 ***gaka* 'know'. **PBM** *gaaxá(-kɨ)*. **PHO** *(áka)*.
 306 *?**tã(ʔɨ)* 'there'. **PBM** *(taʔɨ)*. **PHO** *(tã)*.
 317 ***móʔta(ba)* 'navel'. **PBM** *(móttaba)*. **PHO** *m(ó)ʔt(a)*.
 343 *?**(t)a(t)íʔkɨ()* 'straight'. **PBM** *tsa-tíkkeβe*. **PHO** *(ha(h)íkɨna)*.
 344 *?**(t)a(t)íʔkɨ()-be* 'correct'. **PBM** *(tíkkeβe-be)*. **PHO** *(ha(h)íkɨgobe)*.
  45 ***gãʔɨ* 'mother'. **PBM** *gaʔá-ro(bi)*. **PHO** *éʔɨ (e* exception).

The first rule for **e below is one of the early umlaut rules mentioned in §§4.2 and 4.8 and has a Proto Witotoan environment. The remainder of the rules are later, having environments involving combinations of con-

sonants and vowels; these environments are Proto Bora-Muinane. The
PBM reflex *i̵ is produced only following the consonants **m, **x, and
**t̵.

PW **e /#(C)__Ce,ai > PBM *i̵, PHO *e.
    186–189 **ene() () 'other?'. PBM (inekkḯe)-. PHO *ené(da).
    182; 187 **menai() 'two'. PBM *míínéékkḯ. PHO (mena).
    183; 188 ?**()m(e)n(ai)() ta() 'three'. PBM (míínéékkḯ tsaane). PHO *(amani)
    tá(he).

The last two examples above both contain a morpheme meaning 'two',
which is identical in the PBM example, but has two markedly different
forms in Proto Huitoto-Ocaina.

PW **e > PBM *e /m__(C)e,i̵,#, PHO *e.
    160   **(ai̵)me-nai-() 'stick'. PBM *íme-(ne-ba). PHO *aména.
    152   ?**(ai̵)me() 'tree'. PBM *íme-ʔe. PHO *aména.
    115   **me(d)o 'collared peccary'. PBM *meéni. PHO (medo).
    370   **kai(), **(k)aime 'up'. PBM *kaame. PHO (kaipo), (aime).
    301   **maime 'name'. PBM *meme. PHO *mame.
PW **e > PBM *i̵ /m__(C)o,a, PHO *e.
    271; (24) **()-(k)ai̵-(be) 'claw'. PBM *(mé)-ʔóttsí-gai-mïíʔo. PHO (onóï̵-k(ai̵)-be).
    24; (271) **()-(k)ai̵-(b)e(ʔo) 'fingernail'. PBM *(mé)-ʔóttsí-gai-mïíʔo.
          PHO (onóï̵-k(ai̵)-be).
    70   ??**(n)ame() 'lightning'. PBM (námi̵-ba). PHO *améʔyo.
    224   ?**(e)meá(d)e 'good'. PBM (ími̵áá-ne). PHO (made).
PW **e > PBM *i̵ /#x__, PHO *e.
PW **e > PBM *i̵ /ʔx__, PHO *e.
    272; (14; 244) **xebae 'belly'. PBM (xi̵ibïḯ). PHO (hebae).
    14; (244; 272) **xebae-gai̵ 'chest'. PBM (xi̵ibïí̵ga). PHO *(he)bae-goï().
    109   **xé(ā)kḯ 'anteater'. PBM *xi̵i̵xḯ. PHO (héākï).
    72   **xáénï̃ʔ-xē 'earth'. PBM *xíínï̵-xi̵. PHO *aenï̃ʔ-ē.

In the following two related items, it is unclear what preceded the PBM
*x (derived from **p). The PHO form would suggest *ʔ, but there is no
trace of this in the PBM form.

    1; (235) ??**()pe 'tongue'. PBM *(mé)-ʔníxi̵-(). PHO *(h)ïyï̃ʔpe.
    235; (1) ?**()pe (ï)kaï 'tongue tip'. PBM *(mé)-ʔníxi̵-(ga)-nix(i̵)k(aḯ).
          PHO (ïyï̃ʔpe ïkoï).
PW **e > PBM *i̵ /ex__, PHO *e. This is a late umlaut rule.
    16; 244; 245; 272 **xeʔbae-() 'abdomen'. PBM *(mé)-ii̵ʔba(ï). PHO *(he)bae-().
          This assumes that this rule precedes the **x loss rule.
PW **e > PBM *e /ox,i̵x__, PHO *e.
    200   **(k)ōō-xe(ʔe) 'I'. PBM *oó(-xéʔe). PHO *kōē.
    201   **ō-xe(ʔe) 'thou'. PBM *ïḯ(-xéʔe). PHO *ō(ē).
    33; 266 **tī̵-xē(ʔe) 'blood'. PBM *ti̵ḯ-(xéʔe). PHO*tī̵hē.

PW ****e*** > PBM ***i** /it__, PHO ***e**. This is a late umlaut rule.
  69 *?**(gï)dïte* 'thunder'. PBM **()tsittsi*. PHO *(gïdḯ-te)*.
PW ****e*** > PBM ***i** /t__, PHO ***e**.
  226 *?**(o)te(te)* 'white'. PBM **tsítsi̵-ne*. PHO *(ote-de-te)*. This rule applied twice
    in this example.
PW ****e*** > PBM ***e** /__, PHO ***e**.
  344 *?**(t)a(t)í́ʔkí̵()-be* 'correct'. PBM *(tǐkkeβe-be)*, *?*(tsaí)mi(yé)*.
    PHO *(ha(h)íkïgobe)*.
  224 *?**(e)meá(d)e* 'good'. PBM *(imi̵áá-ne)*. PHO *(made)*.
  353 *?**(gai)taide(ako)* 'split'. PBM **gá(č)ére(á)ko*. PHO *?*(boʔ)tá-(de)*.
  186–189 ***ene()* *()* 'other?'. PBM *(inekkïë)-*. PHO **ené(da)*.
  284 *?**(gaʔa)pe* 'fly'. PBM **gaʔape*. PHO *(pee)*.
  260 ***(ta)ʔáĩ-ne* 'not'. PBM **tsáʔaá-(ne)*. PHO **(ãĩ)-ne*.
  172 ***xíibí-ʔe* 'coca'. PBM **xíibii-(ʔe)*. PHO **híibí(ʔe)*.
  355 *?**(t)aïʔde* 'dig'. PBM **tseeʔdi*. PHO *(dáïʔ-te)*.

The rules for ****o** are also quite complex, but are not heavily stratified chronologically (as are the rules below for ****i** and ****ai**). The ****o** > ***ï** rule apparently occurred after the early umlaut rule, since the rule affected PW ****o** and ****ï** somewhat differently.

Most cases of ****o** went to ***ï** in Proto Bora-Muinane. There are apparently three main situations in which they did not: (a) when doubled; (b) when word final; (c) when word initial and accented in the protolanguage (this third group is uncertain, since I have not analyzed the Proto Witotoan accent system). It is probable that the motivation for these three groups resisting the change to ***ï** is the same: vowel length, which in the second and third groups was probably conditioned by the other factor and then lost. However, I am presenting the three groups separately.

PW ****o** /#(C)__Ci > PBM ***i**, PHO ***o**. This is an early umlaut rule.
  73; (55) ***goti-* 'stone'. PBM *(gíitsi-ba)*. PHO *(gotíʔ-ki̵)*.
  55; (73) ***goti-()* 'rapids'. PBM *(gíitsi-ga)*. PHO *(gotíʔ-i)*.
  62 ***nõ-xī* 'rain'. PBM **níixa-ba*. PHO **nõ-(ki̵)*, **nõ-(hī)*.
  318 ***po(e)-no-()* 'saliva'. PBM **xiĩ-(ní-ba)*. PHO *??**pó(e)-(no-hī)*.
  74 *?**(k)onigiĩ́ʔĩ* 'sand'. PBM **(xíí)né-gai-yí́-ʔai*. PHO *??*(koni)dziĩ́ʔ(ī)*.
PW ****ó** /#C__ > PBM ***o**, PHO ***o**.
  150 *?**to()* 'grassland'. PBM **tsókkómi̵xi̵*. PHO *(tohá́ʔaβo)*.
  269 ***(m)óka(x)í̵ʔto* 'horn'. PBM **(óka)-(x)itto*. PHO *?*(mó)kaï(to)*.
  317 ***mó́ʔta(ba)* 'navel'. PBM *(móttaba)*. PHO **m(ó)ʔt(a)*.
PW ****oo** > PBM ***o**, PHO ***o**.
  311; (49) ***moo(n)ai* 'sea'. PBM **moóai*. PHO **m(o)nái-(tahi)*.
  84 ***koom(i)* 'village'. PBM **kóomií*. PHO *(komí̵ní)*.
  200 ***(k)õõ-xe(ʔe)* 'I'. PBM **oó(-xéʔe)*. PHO **kõë*.
  131 ***tooda* 'parrot'. PBM *(joóra)*. PHO *(tóóda)*.
  365 ***poonoʔ* 'blow'. PBM *(poonï)*. PHO **poo(noʔ-te)*.
  53 ***dzoodo()* 'spring of water'. PBM *(čooróga)*, *(píitsíri-gai)*. PHO **dzod(o)-p(o)*.
  275 ***d(o)ʔ* 'eat meat'. PBM **doó-(ʔi)*. PHO **dïʔ-(te)* (ï exception).

PW **o /__ʔoo > PBM *o, PHO *o.
121 ?**(ib)oʔoo 'tail'. PBM (íiboʔo). PHO (oʔoo).
PW **o > PBM *o /_ #, PHO *o.
274; (231) **xido 'drink'. PBM *ado. PHO (hidó).
315 ?**x(ï)xaiko 'wing'. PBM (xíxɨko). PHO (iáiko).
121 ?**(ib)oʔoo 'tail'. PBM (íiboʔo). PHO (oʔoo).
269 **(m)óka(x)ïʔto 'horn'. PBM *(óka)-(x)ítto. PHO ?*(mó)kaï(to).
98; 99; 101 **xïʔko 'jaguar'. PBM (xíkko). PHO *hïʔko.
59; 247 **xi(moo)ʔ-piʔo 'smoke, cloud'. PBM (aimóo-ppai(ʔ)o). PHO (hiʔpííʔo).
53 **dzoodo() 'spring of water'. PBM (čooróga), (píitsíri-gai). PHO *dzod(o)-p(o).
128 **pi(ʔti)ʔto 'hummingbird'. PBM *páá(i)bɨ(ʔo). PHO *piʔtíʔto.
115 **me(d)o 'collared peccary'. PBM *meéni (i exception). PHO (medo).
117 **píʔto 'agouti'. PBM (páttï) (ï exception). PHO *p(íí)to.
133 **īno 'buzzard'. PBM *ainï (ï exception). PHO *īno().
PW **o > PBM *o /i(C)_ #, PHO *o.
106 **io 'howler monkey'. PBM (ío, íyo). PHO (io, iyo).
231; (274) **xidoo 'drink!'. PBM *d-ádoó. PHO (hido).
255; (75) ?**xopo-(ga) 'shelter'. PBM *(iixó)-ga. PHO *(ho)po-().

The next rule is rather doubtful, since it only has one good example, has one clear exception, and has significant restrictions. In the one example in which it occurs, however, it acts twice in succession, and two different forms of the same word can be seen, one before and one after the rule applies. By analogy with the other vowels affected by this rule, therefore, I propose it as is.

PW **o > PBM *i /i(C)__, PHO *o. This is a late umlaut rule.
53 *dzoodo() 'spring of water'. PBM (čooróga), (píitsíri-gai). PHO *dzod(o)-p(o).
87 **paiʔko 'fishhook'. PBM *pííkki-gai (ï exception). PHO *p(ai)ʔkoa-ti.
2 **(-)po(e) 'mouth', PBM *íiʔ-xï. PHO *poe. This is not really an exception, since the preceding morpheme was almost certainly added later; see item 3 in the following rule for an example of the second morpheme in word-initial position.
PW **o > PBM *ɨ /__, PHO *o.
3 **po(e)-(i)ni(ba) 'lip'. PBM *(mé)-xï-niba. PHO ?*p(oe ini).
5 **topo-(ʔo) 'nose'. PBM *tíxï-ʔo. PHO *topo.
15; (319) **mō(ʔpai)naï 'breast'. PBM *(mé)-míppaine. PHO *mōnoï.
319; (15) **mō(ʔpai)naï-() 'milk'. PBM *míppáine-ppái(k)o. PHO *mōnoï ehī.
7 ??**()po 'ear'. PBM *níxï-mɨɨʔo. PHO (hepo).
34 ?**ko() 'heart'. PBM (kíïdïï). PHO *kome(kï).
48 **nō-() 'water'. PBM *nï-ppaiko. PHO *(haï-)nō-hī.
58 **koxo 'charcoal'. PBM *kíïxï-gai-(kko). PHO *kó(o-kï).
66 ?**()ʔkoʔdo() 'star'. PBM *míïkíri-gai. PHO *oʔkóʔto.
97 **tō() 'tapir'. PBM (tíïʔi). PHO *tō().
114 ?**dzo 'river turtle'. PBM (tírííxi). PHO (dzoʔdzo).
130 **no(k)ai(ʔto) 'toucan'. PBM *nïge. PHO *nokáiʔto.
134 **koga 'curassow'. PBM (kígáʔe). PHO *(k)oodz(a).
201 **ō-xe(ʔe) 'thou'. PBM *iï(-xéʔe). PHO *ō(ē).

255 ?**()po-(ga) 'shelter'. PBM *nǐ́ïxǐ-ga. PHO *(ho)po-().
258 ??**(b)ō() 'who'. PBM *mǐ-(ʔa)-xa. PHO *bǒ.
318 **po(e)-no-() 'saliva'. PBM *xïī-(ni-ba). PHO ??*pó(e)-(no-hī).
365 **poonoʔ 'blow'. PBM (poonï). PHO *poo(noʔ-te).
75; (255) ??**xop(o) 'house'. PBM *iiʔ-xa (i exception). PHO *(ho)po.
255; (75) ?**xopo-(ga) 'shelter'. PBM *(iixó)-ga (i exception). PHO *(ho)po-().
PW **ï /#(C)__Ci,ï > PBM *i, PHO *ï. This is an early umlaut rule.
141 **gïnikaï 'fly'. PBM (gíinixa). PHO *(ïní)kï.
283 **ï̃ʔtï̃ 'swim'. PBM *ittsi. PHO *ï̃ʔï̃.
375 **pï(e) 'year'. PBM *pí(k)kaba. PHO (pïemóna).
342 **dï(t)ï() 'smooth'. PBM *rï(tí)rḯ(tï)-(ko-ne) (ï exception). PHO *(díhï-de-te).
PW **ï > PBM *i /iC__, PHO *ï. This is a late umlaut rule.
283 **ï̃ʔtï̃ 'swim'. PBM *ittsi. PHO *ï̃ʔï̃.
69 ?**(gï)dïte 'thunder'. PBM *()tsittsi. PHO (gïdï-te).
111 ?**naiʔï̃(b)a 'crocodile'. PBM *niʔiba. PHO *(na)ʔïma.
72 **xáénï̃ʔ-xē 'earth'. PBM *xíínï-xɨ (ï exception). PHO *aenï̃ʔ-ē.
372 **xáénï̃ʔ-() 'dust'. PBM *(xíínï)-giixï (ï exception). PHO *aenï̃ʔ-hïβóda.
PW **ï > PBM ï /__, PHO ï.
33; 266 **tï-xē-(ʔe) 'blood'. PBM *tḯï̃-(xéʔe). PHO *tïhế.
94; 95 **tï() 'bow'. PBM *tïïbó-ga. PHO *tï().
98; 99; 101 **xï̃ʔko 'jaguar'. PBM (xḯkko). PHO *hï̃ʔko.
117 ?**()mï̃() 'agouti'. PBM (birímïxɨ). PHO *mï̃(goi).
85; 253 **(na)xï̃() 'path'. PBM *xïï̃-(). PHO *nahï̃(to).
109 **xế(ā)kï 'anteater'. PBM *xɨɨxï. PHO (hếākï).
102 ??**()kï() 'deer'. PBM *xiïbai. PHO ?*(e)kï(to).
227 ?**(xi)ʔtï-() 'black'. PBM (báttïne). PHO *hiʔtḯʔ-().
41 **()mḯnaï 'people'. PBM *mïamïnaa. PHO (komïnï).
180 **(báa)xïdi(ba) 'cassava drink'. PBM (báaxïribá). PHO (-hïdi).
343 ?**(t)a(t)ḯʔkï()'straight'. PBM *tsa-tḯkkeβe. PHO (ha(h)íkïna).
344 ?**(t)a(t)ḯʔkï()-be 'correct'. PBM (tḯkkeβe-be), ?*(tsaí)mi(yé).
PHO (ha(h)íkïgobe).
74 ?**(k)onigiï̃ʔï̃ 'sand'. PBM *(xíí)né-gai-yï̃-ʔai. PHO ??*(koni)dziï̃ʔ(ï̃).
126 **(go)xaïʔkï() 'toad'. PBM (xáákkïba). *xaʔkó(kó)ga. PHO *goaïkḯ(ho).
342 **dï(t)ï() 'smooth'. PBM *rï(tí)rḯ(tï)-(ko-ne). PHO (díhï-de-te).
315 ?**x(ï)xaiko 'wing'. PBM (xḯxiko). PHO (iáiko) (i exception).
84 **koom(ï) 'village'. PBM *kóomiï (i exception). PHO (komḯnï).
269 **(m)óka(x)ï̃ʔto 'horn'. PBM *(óka)-(x)ítto (i exception). PHO ?*(mó)kaï(to).
235 ?**()pe (ï)kaï 'tongue tip'. PBM *(mé)-ʔnixɨ-(ga)-nix(i)k(aï̃) (ɨ exception).
PHO (ïyï̃ʔpe ïkoï).
343 ?**(t)a(t)ḯʔkï() 'straight'. PBM *tsa-tḯkkeβe (e exception). PHO (ha(h)íkïna).
344 ?**(t)a(t)ḯʔkï()-be 'correct'. PBM (tḯkkeβe-be), ?*(tsaí)mi(yé) (e exception).
PHO (ha(h)íkïgobe).

4.10. Diphthongs and **ï.

PW **ï apparently became *ai in every case in Proto Bora-Muinane (except when already part of a diphthong; see first rule in stage one below), so I treat **ï and **ai together in most of the following rules. Many times a rule contains examples for only one or the other of these, but there seem to be no situations in which a distinction between PW **ï and

**ai* makes a significant difference in the application of a rule. As in most of the sound changes presented, I have proposed that the PHO vowels remained largely unchanged and that most of the changes occurred in Proto Bora-Muinane. The fact that PW ***i* and ***ai* as reconstructed are indistinguishable in Proto Bora-Muinane, however, makes it tempting to try to show that they were not distinguished in Proto Witotoan, but instead that their contrast in Proto Huitoto-Ocaina was the result of a split. Unfortunately, search as I may, I cannot see what the conditioning factors could have been for such a split. Since there appears to be no question that ***aï* and ***ï* were distinguished in Proto Witotoan, there seems to be no a priori reason to insist that the analogous pair ***ai* and ***i* were not.

There appear to be approximately four chronological stages in the rules applying to these two vowels on the PBM side, each stage of which depends on the output of the previous stages. Accordingly, I list them in chronological order, as far as this can be determined. The column in which the environment is specified (as always) indicates whether a PW or a PBM environment applied at each stage.

The rules are quite complex, and some may seem to be rather ad hoc. However, several things are quite clear. Firstly, although I have proposed that at one stage all instances of PW ***i* became *ai*, most of them did not remain *ai*, but were acted on by subsequent rules, becoming *a*, *e*, or *i* (and in one case *ï*). Specifically, of fifty-two instances of PW ***ai* and mutated ***i* which show cognates, nine became *a* in Proto Bora-Muinane, thirteen became *e*, thirteen became *i*, one became *ï*, and sixteen survived as *ai*. Secondly, in every case, in both subfamilies, the diphthong ***ai* lost its second element after nasal consonants; in Proto Bora-Muinane the first element usually became *e* in this case. There is a sizeable group of examples; this is therefore a significant early rule. Thirdly, the rules, though in some cases apparently ad hoc, cover the data fairly well, leaving few exceptions except in the default group (those which should have reflex *ai*; this shows that there are undoubtedly other factors which I have not been able to identify).

Stage one rules:

The first rule shows no change in a diphthong:

PW ***i* /__*o* > PBM ***i(y)*, PHO ***i(y)*.
   106   ***io* 'howler monkey'. **PBM** *(ío, íyo)*. **PHO** *(io, iyo)*.

No examples of the next rule are given here, since further rules changed most of them. See later stages for examples. The probable intermediate stages

of this vowel shift in Proto Bora-Muinane are given in the rule.[55] Since this
rule affected the input of all succeeding rules in Proto Bora-Muinane, but not
in Proto-Huitoto-Ocaina, I reiterate this rule in all succeeding rules.

PW **i /__ > **PBM** *ɨ>*ei*>*ɛi*>*æi*>*ai*, **PHO** *i.

Stage two rules:

The following rules must have applied after the preceding one, since they
would otherwise apply only to PW **ai, not **i. They must have applied
before the early umlaut rules (e.g., before the first rule for **ï as shown
by item 141 below), since they have a Proto Witotoan environment as far
as the vowels are concerned, e.g., item 141.

PW ***i,ai* /*ïx*__ > **PBM** **(ai*>*)* *i*, **PHO** **(i),ai*.
315   *?****x(ï)xaiko* 'wing'. **PBM** *(xíxɨko)*. **PHO** *(iáiko)*. The environment ***x*__
        produces PBM *i from **e as well, although not precisely in this same
        environment.
PW ***i,ai* /*ïd*__ > **PBM** **(ai*>*)* *i*, **PHO** **i,(ai)*.
132   *?****()di()* 'parakeet'. **PBM** *(tïrii?o)*. **PHO** *?***()di()*.
180   ***(báa)xïdi(ba)* 'chicha'. **PBM** *(báaxïribá)*. **PHO** *(-hïdi)*.
PW ***i,ai* /*ïn*__ > **PBM** **(ai*>*)* *i*, **PHO** **i,(a)*.
141   **gïnikaï 'fly'. **PBM** *(gíinixa)*. **PHO** **(ïní)kï*.
  3   ***po(e)-(i)ni(ba)* 'lip'. **PBM** **(mé)-xí-niba*. **PHO** *?***p(oe ini)*.
PW ***i,ai* /*m,n*__ > **PBM** **(ai*>*)* *e*, **PHO** **i,a*.
301   **maime 'name'. **PBM** *meme. **PHO** *mame.
202   *?****i-(b)ai* 'he'. **PBM** *(aáí-be)*. **PHO** *i-ma, **(i?)i-ma*.
367   ***ïni(neko)* 'squeeze'. **PBM** *((ai)n(ai)nɨko)*. **PHO** *?(ïni)*. The PBM
        reconstruction of this item is confusing. The Muinane form is *ñéñéku-?i*.
  74   *?****(k)onigiḯ?í* 'sand'. **PBM** **(xíí)né-gai-yí-?ai*. **PHO** *??***(koni)dziḯ?(ï)*.
160   ***(aï)me-nai-()* 'stick'. **PBM** **ímé-(ne-ba)*. **PHO** *aména.
182; 187 ***menai()* 'two'. **PBM** **míínéékkiḯ*. **PHO** *(mena)*.
183; 188 *?****()m(e)n(ai)()* *ta()* 'three'. **PBM** *(míínéékkiḯ tsaane)*. **PHO** **(amani)*
        tá(he).

---

[55] A more central route for this vowel shift is also possible; the question is not
significant since there was apparently no PW **ei. In several of the Germanic
languages (English, German, Dutch) a similar shift took place, although in these
languages it was part of a larger vowel rotation whose greatest complexity is seen in
English: **i:*>*ai*, *ai, **a:*, *ei>*ei*; **e:*>*i:*. In the English case the route of the **i:ai* shift
is significant, since contrast between it and the upward shift was maintained at all
times; it probably followed a more central route to do so. A detailed discussion of this
whole subject can be found in Labov, Yaeger, and Steiner 1972:200–8. In English the
**i:* did not merge with the *ai, the latter moving on to maintain contrast; in German,
on the other hand, it did, which is precisely what I am proposing happened in Proto
Bora-Muinane. In the Germanic languages a comparable vowel shift occurred with the
back vowels, but it appears that such a shift did not happen to PBM **ï.

320 ***mī̃()* 'with'. **PBM** *-ma (a* exception). **PHO** *(mī̃ʔto).*

PW ***i,ai /x,ʔ__* > **PBM** **(ai >) a,* **PHO** **i,ai.*
 231; (274) **xidoo 'drink!'. **PBM** **d-ádoó.* **PHO** *(hido).*
 274; (231) **xido 'drink'. **PBM** **ado.* **PHO** *(hidó).*
  62 ***nō-xī̃* 'rain'. **PBM** **nííxa-ba.* **PHO** **nō-(kï̃), *nō-(hī̃).*
 260 ***(ta)ʔāī́-ne* 'not'. **PBM** **tsáʔaá-(ne).* **PHO** **(āī̃)-ne.*
 166 ***xáʔi()* 'cotton'. **PBM** **xáʔadi.* **PHO** *(háʔikï̃).*
  45 ***gā̃ʔī̃* 'mother'. **PBM** **gaʔá-ro(bi).* **PHO** **éʔī̃.*
 179 ***(ī̃)xaidzaï̃(ga)* 'salt'. **PBM** *(áit(t)ega) (ai* exception). **PHO** **(ï̃)háidzaï̃.*
  59; 247 ***xi(moo)ʔ-piʔo* 'smoke, cloud'. **PBM** *(aim̃óo-ppai(ʔ)o) (ai* exception).
      PHO *(hiʔpííʔo).*
  74 *?**(k)onigiî̃ʔī̃* 'sand'. **PBM** **(xíí)né-gai-yï̃-ʔai (ai* exception).
      PHO *??*(koni)dziî̃ʔ(ī̃).*

The next rule must similarly have applied after the **i > *ai rule. It could
not have applied before that rule, since otherwise its output would be
converted back to **ai.* This same early umlaut rule applied to other vowels.
For those cases I have usually specified a Proto Witotoan environment with
following **i; however, for this rule a Proto Witotoan environment would be
meaningless, since all instances of **i were eliminated by the **i > **ai.* It is
very probable that the other cases of umlaut actually applied after the above
rule also and had a following PBM *ai rather than **i,* as a number of the
examples suggest (see **e and **o especially).

Stage three rule (early umlaut rule):

PW ***i,ai* > **PBM** *(ai >)* **i /#(C)__Cai,ï,* **PHO** **i,ai.*
 172 **xíibí-ʔe 'coca'. **PBM** **xííbiï̃-(ʔe).* **PHO** **híibí(ʔe).*
   4 *??**iï̃ʔ-gi-()* 'tooth'. **PBM** **íïʔ-gái-neé.* **PHO** **iʔtiʔ-to.*
 257 ***kiʔi-()* 'that'. **PBM** **xe(ʔ)é-ne.* **PHO** *(kiʔima).*
 367 ***īni(neko)* 'squeeze'. **PBM** *((ai)n(ai)niko).* **PHO** *?*(īni).*
 111 *?**naiʔī̃(b)a* 'crocodile'. **PBM** **niʔiba.* **PHO** **(na)ʔīma (a* exception).

The Bora form in the the following example is not really an exception,
since the last syllable is a separate morpheme. The first morpheme also
occurs in items 203 and 204, with other suffixes, and retained the same
form in 202 in Proto Bora-Muinane by analogy.

 202 *?**i-(b)ai* 'he'. **PBM** *(aáí-be).* **PHO** **i-ma, *(iʔ)i-ma.*

Stage four rules (Late umlaut rules):

PW ***i,ai* > **PBM** **(ai >) i /iC__,* **PHO** **i,(ai).*
 172 **xíibí-ʔe 'coca'. **PBM** **xííbiï̃-(ʔe).* **PHO** **híibí(ʔe).*
  73; (55) ***goti-* 'stone'. **PBM** *(gúitsi-ba).* **PHO** *(gotíʔ-kï̃).*

55; (73) **goti-() 'rapids'. PBM (gíítsi-ga). PHO (gotíʔ-i).
4 ??**iiʔ-gi-() 'tooth'. PBM *ííʔ-gái-neé (ai exception). PHO *iʔtiʔ-to.
74 ?**(k)onigiĩ̈ʔĩ 'sand'. PBM *(xíí)né-gai-yḯ-ʔai (ai exception). PHO ??*(koni)dziĩ̈ʔ(ĩ).

PW **i,ai > PBM *(i,ai>) e /ai,eC__, PHO *i,ai.

257 **kiʔi-() 'that'. PBM *xe(ʔ)é-ne. PHO (kiʔima).
353 ?**(gai)taide(ako) 'split'. PBM *gá(č)ére(á)ko. PHO ?*(boʔ)tá-(de) (a exception).

PW **i,ai > PBM *ai /__, PHO *i,ai.

311; (49) **moo(n)ai 'sea'. PBM *moóai. PHO *m(o)nái-(tahi).
351 ?**gain(ãĩ̈) 'throw'. PBM (gáino). PHO *(ai)nãĩ̈-().
354 ?**(ka)pai() 'pierce'. PBM *kápáitiĩ̈́kkï-nï. PHO (paiʔ).
49; (311) **m(oon)ai 'river'. PBM *moóai. PHO *(i)máni.
204 ?**i-() 'it'. PBM (aáí-be). PHO (i-e).
202 ?**i-(b)ai 'he'. PBM (aáí-be). PHO *i-ma, *(iʔ)i-ma.
133 **ĩno 'buzzard'. PBM *ainï. PHO *ĩno().
221 ?**()ki() 'small'. PBM (áxáitso-ne). PHO (kiβi-).
203; (40) ?**i-gaï 'she'. PBM *(aáí-)ge. PHO *(iʔ)i-goï (apé)-goï.
128 **pi(ʔti)ʔto 'hummingbird'. PBM *páá(i)bɨ(ʔo). PHO *piʔtíʔto.
59; 247 **xi(moo)ʔ-piʔo 'smoke, cloud'. PBM *(aimóo-ppai(ʔ)o). PHO (hiʔpííʔo).
370 **kai(), **(k)aime 'up'. PBM *kaame (a exception). PHO (kaipo), (aime).
130 **no(k)ai(ʔto) 'toucan'. PBM *nïge (e exception). PHO *nokáiʔto.
25 **(ï)dzaʔkai(do) 'leg'. PBM (mé-tákki) (i exception). PHO ?*ïdzá-k(aido).
87 **paiʔko 'fishhook'. PBM *píikkï-gai (i exception). PHO *p(ai)ʔkoa-ti.
117 **píʔto 'agouti'. PBM (páttï) (a exception). PHO *p(íí)to.

The Proto Witotoan diphthongs **aï and **ae underwent changes in Proto Bora-Muinane similar in many cases to those for **ai and **i. Since this is so and since they underwent many of the same rules, I intersperse the rules for both, so that the similarities and differences can be seen. Since **ae is so rare, it is often unclear whether it underwent a given rule or not. **ï was not involved in these changes, since it never merged with **aï.

It is likely that **ae merged completely with **aï at some stage in Proto Bora-Muinane, probably in stage three or four, since subsequent to this they are indistinguishable. The merger could not have happened earlier than this, because in stage two **ae and **aï undergo different changes after **x.

As with **ai, most of the instances of **aï and **ae were subsequently changed into something else, namely PBM *a, *e, *i, or *ï. Like **ai, **aï was usually changed to *e following nasals; but unlike **ai, it did not lose its second element in the remaining cases. Interestingly, one of the latest rules took all of the nonfinal instances of **aï and **ae that remained and converted them to *ï.

On the Proto Huitoto-Ocaina side, **aï split into *aï and *oï, based on the preceding vowel. These were in some cases further reduced to *a, *o or *ɨ̈. Because of the complexity, the rules for **aɨ̈ are given separately for Proto Bora-Muinane and for Proto Huitoto-Ocaina.

Proto Bora-Muinane rules

There are no stage one rules since **ae did not merge with **aɨ̈ until later.

Stage two rules:

PW **aɨ̈ /ĩm,ĩn__ > PBM *aɨ̈ (unlike **ai), PHO *aɨ̈/oɨ̈/o/ɨ̈/a.
206; 212 **aɨ̈māɨ̈ʔ-() 'ye'. PBM *ámiɨ̈ʔ-(). PHO *(o)māɨ̈ʔ-().
41 **()mɨ́naɨ̈ 'people'. PBM *mɨ́amɨ́naa. PHO (komɨ́ni). Neither one of these
examples appears to demonstrate this rule for Proto Bora-Muinane; in both
cases this is because a later stage worked changes.
PW **aɨ̈ /(m),n__ > PBM *e (like **ai), PHO *aɨ̈/oɨ̈/o/ɨ̈/a.
170 **naɨ̈() 'annatto'. PBM *néebaba. PHO *nonṍ().
240; (19) ??**(o)nāɨ̈ʔk() 'lower arm'. PBM *(mé)-nékkɨ̈-(gatsítto). PHO *onṍɨ̈-(kona).
19; (240) ??**(o)nāɨ̈ʔk() 'arm'. PBM *(mé)-nékkɨ̈-gai. PHO *onṍɨ̈-(kaido).
319; (15) **mō(ʔpai)naɨ̈-() 'milk'. PBM *mɨ́ppáine-ppái(k)o. PHO *mōnoɨ̈ ehī.
15; (319) **mō(ʔpai)naɨ̈ 'breast'. PBM *(mé)-mɨ́ppaine. PHO *mōnoɨ̈.
351 ?**gain(āɨ̈) 'throw'. PBM (gáino). PHO *(ai)nāɨ̈-().
PW **aɨ̈ /x__ > PBM *a (like **ai), PHO *aɨ̈.
126 **(go)xaɨ̈ʔkɨ() 'toad'. PBM (xáákkɨ̈ba), *xaʔkó(kó)ga. PHO *goaɨ̈kɨ́(ho).
PW **ae /x__ > PBM *ɨ̈ (like **e), PHO *ae.
129 **xaeβa(do) 'macaw'. PBM *xɨ́iβaá. PHO *(ae)(β)a(do).
PW **aɨ̈,ae > PBM *e /t__ (unlike **ai), PHO *aɨ̈,ae.
250; (49) **tae(ʔi)-() 'stream'. PBM *tée-ʔi-(gayi). PHO *(i)tae-().
49; (250) **tae(ʔi) 'river'. PBM *teé-ʔi. PHO *(i)tae.
179 **(ɨ̈)xaidzaɨ̈(ga) 'salt'. PBM (áit(t)ega). PHO *(ɨ̈)háidzaɨ̈.

Stage three rule (early umlaut rule):

PW **ae,(aɨ̈?) > PBM *i /#(C)__Cɨ̈ (like **ai), PHO *ae.
72 **xáénɨ̈ʔ-xē 'earth'. PBM *xííní-xi. PHO *aenɨ̈ʔ-ē.
372 **xáénɨ̈ʔ-() 'dust'. PBM *(xííní)-giixɨ̈. PHO *aenɨ̈ʔ-hiβóda.

Stage four rules (late umlaut rules and others):

PW **aɨ̈,(ae?) > PBM *e /ai,eC__ (like **ai), PHO *aɨ̈/oɨ̈/o/ɨ̈/a.
40; (246; 203) **-gaɨ̈ (feminine). PBM *gai-ge. PHO (dɨ̈-goɨ̈).
203; (40) ?**i-gaɨ̈ 'she'. PBM *(aáí-)ge. PHO *(iʔ)i-goɨ̈ (apé)-goɨ̈.
246; (40) **-gaɨ̈ (feminine). PBM *kééme-ge. PHO *haʔɨ́(do)-goɨ̈.

The actual gloss of 40 is 'woman', and of 246 is 'old woman', but the only part that is cognate is the suffix, meaning (feminine). The environment for the rule, however, depends on the full PBM form in both cases.

Unfortunately for purposes of providing a well-attested rule, the above rule only applies to one morpheme. However, all three examples have PBM environments which substantiate the rule, and by analogy with **ai* it seems a reasonable rule.

PW **aï̯,ae > PBM *a /i,ïC__ # (unlike **ai), PHO *aï/oï/o/ï/a,ae.
141 ****g̈inikaï 'fly'. PBM (g̈inixa). PHO *(ïni)kï.**
16; 244; 245; 272 ****xe?bae-(). PBM *(mé)-ïi?ba(ï). PHO *(he)bae-().**
41 ****()mínaï 'people, abdomen'. PBM *míamínaa. PHO (komíni).**
14; (244; 272) ****xebae-gaï 'chest'. PBM (xíibïïga). PHO *(he)bae-goï().**

Stage five rules are very late rules, almost entirely eliminating *aï* in PBM):

PW **aï̯,(ae?) > PBM *aï or *ai /__ # (conditioning uncertain), PHO *aï/oï/o/ï/a.
235 ?****()pe (ï)kaï 'tongue tip'. PBM *(mé)-?nixi-(ga)-nix(i)k(aï). PHO (ïyïʔpe ïkoï).**
299 ?****(i)paï 'round'. PBM *paï, ?*pá(tté)ï. PHO (ikoípoï).**
23; 24; 30; 271 ****-(k)aï 'finger'. PBM *-gai. PHO *-(kaï).**
374 ****(i)gaï(bai) 'rope'. PBM *gáaibaï. PHO (igaï).**
PW **aï̯,ae > PBM *ï /__, PHO *aï,ae.
152 ?****(aï)me() 'tree'. PBM *íme-?e. PHO *aména.**
160 ****(aï)me-nai-() 'stick'. PBM *ímé-(ne-ba). PHO *aména.**
206; 212 ****aïmãïʔ-() 'ye'. PBM *ámïïʔ-(). PHO *(o)mãïʔ-().**
272; (14; 244) ****xebae 'belly'. PBM (xíibïï). PHO (hebae).**
14; (244; 272) ****xebae-gaï 'chest'. PBM (xíibïïga). PHO *(he)bae-goï().**
206; 212 ****aïmãïʔ-() 'ye'. PBM *ámïïʔ-() (a exception). PHO *(o)mãïʔ-().**

Thus, in word-final position any *aï* that remained was realized as either *ai* or *aï* in Proto Bora-Muinane, with the conditioning environments unclear.

Any word-medial *aï* that remained (including those derived from **ae*) became *ï*. The existence of PW **aï* and **ae* is thus based almost entirely on the Proto Huitoto-Ocaina examples.

Proto Huitoto-Ocaina rules

The first two rules that follow are somewhat ad hoc; it is not unreasonable, however, that a diphthong would lose its second element in a nasal environment; there is also such a rule for **ai* (though with a different environment), as indicated above.

PW **aï > PBM *various, PHO *a /__me.
152 ?****(aï)me() 'tree'. PBM *íme-?e. PHO *aména.**
160 ****(aï)me-nai-() 'stick'. PBM *ímé-(ne-ba). PHO *aména.**
PW **aï > PBM *various, PHO *o /__maï.
206; 212 ****aïmãïʔ-() 'ye'. PBM *ámïïʔ-(). PHO *(o)mãïʔ-().**

PW **aï* > PBM *various, PHO *aï /o__.
126 **(go)xaï?kï() 'toad'. PBM (xáákkïba), *xa?kó(kó)ga. PHO *goaïkï(ho).
PW **aï* > PBM *various, PHO *oï /oC__.
240; (19) ??**(o)nãï?k() 'lower arm'. PBM *(mé)-nékkí- (gatsítto).
       PHO *onóï-(kona).
   19; (240) ??**(o)nãï?k() 'arm'. PBM *(mé)-nékkï-gai. PHO *onóï-(kaido).
319; (15) **mõ(?pai)naï-() 'milk'. PBM *míppáine-ppái(k)o. PHO *mõnoï ehï.
   15; (319) **mõ(?pai)naï 'breast'. PBM *(mé)-míppaine. PHO *mõnoï.
170 **naï() 'annatto'. PBM *néebaba. PHO *nonó() (o exception).

The following cases probably all involve suffixes which were fossilized after the above rule had applied and which are now freely added to other roots than those that have *o. In the first three examples, the suffix means (feminine). This assumption is somewhat conjectural; it is interesting that the above examples all are preceded by **n, whereas the examples that follow all are preceded by **g or **k. There are other examples, however, that begin with **g or **k that have PHO *aï, so no rule is apparent which could allow for consonantal conditioning.

    40; (246; 203) **-gaï (feminine). PBM *gai-ge. PHO (dï-goï).
   203; (40) ?**i-gaï 'she'. PBM *(aáí-)ge. PHO *(i?)i-goï (apé)-goï.
   246; (40) **-gaï (feminine). PBM *kéeme-ge. PHO *ha?í(do)-goï.
   235 ?**()pe (ï)kaï 'tongue tip'. PBM *(mé)-?nixi-(ga)-nix(i)k(aí). PHO (ïyï?pe ïkoï).
    14; (244; 272) **xebae-gaï 'chest'. PBM (xïïbïïga). PHO *(he)bae-goï().
PW **aï* > PBM *various, PHO *aï /__.
   355 ?**(t)aï?de 'dig'. PBM *tsee?di. PHO (dáï?-te).
    23; 24; 30; 271 **-(k)aï 'finger'. PBM *-gai. PHO *-(kaï).
   351 ?**gain(ãï) 'throw'. PBM (gáino). PHO *(ai)nãï-().
   374 **(i)gaï(baï) 'rope'. PBM *gáaibaï. PHO (igaï).
   179 **(ï)xaidzaï(ga) 'salt'. PBM (áit(t)ega). PHO *(í)háidzaï.
   206; 212 **aïmãï?-() 'ye'. PBM *ámïï?-(). PHO *(o)mãï?-().
   299 ?**(i)paï 'round'. PBM *pai, ?*pá(tté)ï. PHO (ikoípoi) (oï exception).
   141 **gïnikaï 'fly'. PBM (gíinixa). PHO *(ïní)kï (ï exception).
    41 **()mínaï 'people'. PBM *míaminaa. PHO (komíní) (ï exception).

The following vowel sequences are of very low frequency.

PW **éa > PBM *i, PHO *ea.
   109 **xé(ã)kï 'anteater'. PBM *xïíxï. PHO (héãkï).
PW **eá > PBM *ia, PHO *a.
   224 ?**(e)meá(d)e 'good'. PBM (ímiáá-ne). PHO (made).
PW **oe > PBM *ï, PHO *oe.
   318 **po(e)-no-() 'saliva'. PBM *xïï-(ní-ba). PHO ??*pó(e)-(no-hï).
     3 **po(e)-(i)ni(ba) 'lip'. PBM *(mé)-xí-niba. PHO ?*p(oe ini).
     2 **(-)po(e) 'mouth'. PBM *íi?-xï. PHO *poe.
PW **oi > PBM *ee, PHO *oi.
   275 **gõï(ne) 'eat fruit'. PBM *geéne. PHO *gõï.

5

In Summary

This final chapter brings together three things: (a) a summary of the sound changes that have taken place throughout the Witotoan family, presented in a single chart, (b) a projection of the time frame within which the Witotoan languages have developed from a single source, and (c) some considerations concerning comparative linguistic theory for which the Witotoan data have special relevance.

5.1 Witotoan sound changes

Table (16) is a summary of the sound changes taking place throughout the Witotoan family. Not all changes are indicated here, only those which affected the phonological structure of the languages, plus a few others which were particularly interesting. Items marked with a dagger (†) are not the primary source of the phoneme specified. These are not carried across the remainder of the table, since the same phoneme can also be found elsewhere in the column, and its later history can be seen there.

The Nɨpode phoneme system is apparently unchanged from the Early Huitoto system. Therefore, I have only given one column for both Early Huitoto and Nɨpode. Similarly, the Minica system is apparently unchanged from Proto Minica-Murui.

In three cases I have included items in the chart which cannot be clearly traced back to Proto Witotoan: the sequences *ʔb, *ʔd, and *ʔg in Proto Huitoto-Ocaina. I have included these because they all have unusual reflexes in Huitoto and Ocaina, one case (*ʔb) being the only source of an extant phoneme (Early Huitoto /б/). Why these are not reconstructible back to Proto Witotoan is unclear; the only cognates are confusing.

(16) Summary of Witotoan sound changes

PW	PBM	PHO	B	M	Hp	EH	Hn	PMM	Hr	O
a	a	a	a	a	a	a	a		a	a
e	e / i	e	e / i	o / e	e	e	e		i	ï / i / a†
i	a(i)†	i			i	i	i		i	
o	o / i†	o	o	u	o / u	o / u	o / u		o	o
ï	ï	ï	ï	i	ï	ï	ï		ï	
umlaut (various)	i		i	i						
ai	a(i)	ai	a†	ai	ai	ai	ai		ai	a†
aï	various†	aï / oï			aï / oï	aï / oï	aï / oï		aï / oï	o† / o†
p	p / x†	p	p^h / p^{hy}	φ	p		φ		φ	φ
ʔp	pp / x†	ʔp	xp^h / xp^{hy}	φ†	p†		φ†		φ†	ʔφ
t	t / ts / č	t	t^h / t^{hy} ; ts^h / $č^{h†}$; $č^h$	t / t^y ; s / š ; č	d / t		d / θ		d / θ	t^y / t / ts / č
ʔt	tt / tts / čč	(ʔ)t	xt^h / xt^{hy} ; xts^h / $xč^{h†}$; $xč^h$	tt / tt^y ; s† / š† ; čč	d / t†		t / θ†		t / θ†	ʔt^y / ʔt / ʔč
k	k / x†	k	k^h / k^{hy}	k	k		k		k	x / k
ʔk	kk	(ʔ)k	xk^h / xk^{hy}	kk	k†		k†		k†	ʔx

In Summary

PW	PBM	PHO	B	M	Hp	EH	Hn	PMM	Hr	O
b	b / m?†	b / m?†	p / pʸ	b	b		b		b	b / βᵗ
?		?b			ɓ		p		p	βᵗ
d[r]	d / r	d[r] / nᵗ	t / tʸ / r / y	d / r / rʸ	r		r		r	dʸ / r / ǰ
?d	?d	(?)tᵗ								
?		?d			r		r		r	?
dz	tᵗ	dz			dᵗ / dᵗ / tᵗ		dᵗ / tᵗ / θᵗ		dᵗ / tᵗ / θᵗ	dz / ǰᵗ / dʸᵗ
g	g	g / dzᵗ	kʷ / ts / č / k / kʸ	g	g / η		g / η		g / ñᵗ	g / kᵗ
?		?g			g		g		g	?k
?V	?	? / ?y		?	∅		∅		∅	?
x	x / ∅	h / ∅	x / xʸ / ∅	x	h / ∅		h / ∅		h / ∅	h
β	β	β	β / βʸ	β	β		β		β	β
m	m	m	m / mʸ	m	m		m		m	m / m̃
n	n	n	n / nʸ	n / ñ	n / ñ		n / ñ		n / ñ	n / ñ / n / ñ

Abbreviations used: PW Proto Witotoan, PBM Proto Bora Muinane, PHO Proto Huitoto Ocaina, B Bora, M Muinane, Hp Nipode Huitoto, EH Early Huitoto, Hn Minica Huitoto, PMM Proto Minica-Murui, Hr Murui Huitoto, O Ocaina.

5.2 The time frame

Taking into account the cognate percentages between the six extant languages, the intermediate protolanguages and the original proto language, and bearing in mind the sound change rules that the different languages underwent in common and the amount of linguistic change occurring at each stage, it is possible to produce a tree of relationships between the languages and even to develop a rough idea of the time depths involved.[56] Table (17) summarizes the genetic relationships between the languages and indicates the principal vowel system changes and a few of the more significant consonant system changes. No time estimates are intended for the sound changes; only the order is significant.

5.3 Some theoretical considerations

A number of tendencies can be seen in the Witotoan languages which are not seen in Eurasian comparative studies. One very prominent tendency is the following:

The Witotoan languages have an astonishing propensity for generating and retaining the high back unrounded vowel /ɨ/, both as a pure vowel and in diphthongs such as /aɨ/.

This is a strong areal tendency in Northwestern South America generally. Most of the languages in this area have the six vowel system /a, e, i, o, u, ɨ/ (a number have /ɨ/ or some other nonfront unrounded vowel instead of /ɨ/). Further, in the Witotoan family there are more cases of languages which have /ɨ/ but not its rounded counterpart /u/ than cases which have /u/ (if the protolanguage stages are included). Ocaina seems to have

---

[56]These time depths are based on the glottochronological method. As Terrence Kaufman (1990:27) has recently said, "There has been considerable controversy over the method and theory of glottochronology, leading to widespread doubt as to its validity over the past 20 years." Kaufman goes on to give a strong defense of the method, answering the most common objections. Without necessarily endorsing the method, I give the time depth estimates for what they are worth.

Based on this method, which states that 86% of basic vocabulary is retained per 1000 years, Proto Witotoan would have a time depth of over 7000 years. Not all of the words in the list used would be considered basic vocabulary, however, and it is likely that some cognates have been missed, since the vocabulary items were not always chosen with this in mind. I, therefore, tend to put the date at about 5500 years. Morris Swadesh arrived at an estimate of 5400 years in 1959 for the Witotoan family (see Kaufman 1990:43).

(17) Witotoan language family tree

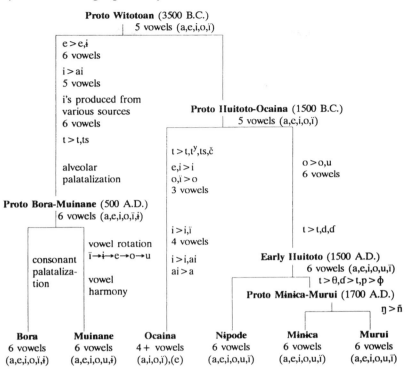

reproduced such a system from a completely different source, after having originally lost it. Resígaro, a nearby Arawakan language, also has /i/ but not /u/.

This whole tendency goes counter to the generally accepted tenets that back unrounded vowels are cross-linguistically marked (e.g., Hock 1986:20–21) and therefore rare, and that they do not normally occur in the absence of their rounded counterparts. Crothers (1987:115) states as his very first vowel-system universal that "All languages have /i a u/." In discussing possible exceptions, he seems to allow some leeway for three- and four-vowel systems having /o/ or /ɨ/ instead of /u/ (one of my early stages of Ocaina has /i, a, o/; see §3.6), but for five-vowel systems and larger he lists only three clear exceptions out of his corpus of 209 languages, all five-vowel systems with /o/ but not /u/, one of which is Ocaina (the other Witotoan languages were not part of the corpus). (Hopi seems to be a fourth exception, but he does not mention this, perhaps because there is doubt about the phonetic value of the phonemes described by Whorf.) Of the other two exceptions (Nez Perce and Seneca), one (Nez Perce) has essentially the same vowel system as Ocaina. It is this same exceptional system that I have reconstructed as the vowel system of both Proto Huitoto-Ocaina (with no direct relation to the current Ocaina vowel system) and Proto Witotoan.

As for Proto Bora-Muinane and Bora, for both of which I have proposed the vowel system /a, e, i, o, ï, ɨ/, Crothers (1987) does not even list a system having no /u/ but a contrast between /ï/ and /ɨ/ (but see discussion in §§1.1 and 2.6). Of his six-vowel systems (1987:141), not a single one lacks /u/ (except Hopi, see above); the vast majority have the six-vowel system of Huitoto or Muinane.

It is interesting to compare this regional preference for /ï/ with the fact that apparently not a single language in the Americas has front rounded vowels, the opposite extreme from back unrounded vowels (with the uncertain exception of Hopi), whereas front rounded vowels are found all across Eurasia. Crothers (1976) argues fairly convincingly that front rounded vowels are areally common in Eurasia due to spreading by language contact, but that they are extremely rare elsewhere and seldom arise spontaneously.

Another interesting point, which is related to the points above, is that I have proposed quite a number of cases of front vowels moving back to become back vowels. This may not seem surprising, except that Labov, Yaeger, and Steiner (1972:106) lay down the principle that 'in chain shifts, back vowels move to the front' and go so far as to say that this principle appears to have 'no exceptions in the data we have reviewed,' most of which is based on Indo-European languages, the remainder being apparently restricted to other Eurasian languages. Now, I certainly have a number of cases which do adhere to this principle, notable among them the PBM umlaut process. However, I have proposed the following cases which contradict the claim that the reverse never happens: PBM *e > M /o/ (§2.14); PHO *i > O /ï/ (§3.14); PW **ae > PBM *aï (§4.10). The first two of these occur as part of chain shifts, the former in a circular shift whose starting point is uncertain (see table 10) and the latter in the middle of a shift (see table 13). All of this can be summarized as follows:

> Whereas Eurasian languages favor vowel-fronting processes and because of areal influence tend to preserve the rounding on the resulting front vowels in spite of its marked nature, Northwestern South American languages favor vowel-backing processes and because of areal influence tend to preserve the unrounded quality of

the resulting back vowels, in spite of its marked nature, even to the exclusion of their rounded counterparts.

Both of these are thus areal tendencies which spread by language contact; the Northwestern South America tendency must be of early date and affected Proto Witotoan from antiquity.

6
Comparative Wordlist

This chapter presents the 377 cognate sets upon which this study is based. Each set includes up to twelve elements, the first of which is its number, ranging between 1 and 377.

An English gloss of the forms listed in the set appears immediately following the set number and is, in turn, followed by a corresponding Spanish gloss in parentheses. A Spanish gloss from the original word list compiled by Morris Swadish is marked by a dagger ([†]). (Item 377 was not part of the original list, but was added by the author.)

If it has been possible to reconstruct a proto Witotoan (PW) form for a given set, that reconstructed form immediately follows the Spanish gloss. If at least part of the reconstructed PW form is attested by both daughter languages—Proto Bora-Muinane (PBM) and Proto Huitoto-Ocaina (PHO)—it is precede by two asterisks (**). Any part of a reconstructed form that is not attested in both daughter languages is placed in parentheses. If no part of the reconstructed form is attested by both daughters, the entire form is placed in parentheses and asterisks are not used. Cognate counts are computed from asterisked forms only.

The next form(s) which may occur in a set is (are) reconstructed Proto Bora-Muinane (PBM) forms. They are preceded by a single asterisk unless completely lacking attestation by both daughter languages—Bora (B) and Muinane (M).

Next follow Proto Huitoto-Ocaina (PHO) forms, based on Huitoto (H) and Ocaina (O). These forms also bear one asterisk unless completely enclosed by parentheses.

Asterisked forms may be preceded by one or two question marks to indicate that a reconstruction is uncertain, (?*, ?**) or very uncertain (??*, ??**)

129

The final six elements of a set are forms from the various extant daughter languages—Bora (B), Muinane (M), Ocaina (O), Nipode Huitoto (Hp), Minica Huitoto (Hn), and Murui Huitoto (Hr). Upriver Ocaina (Ou) and Downriver Ocaina (Od) are occasionally distinguished. Bora forms not found in Thiesen (in preparation) but cited by Allin (1975) are marked by a double dagger (‡) and optional material in the daughter languages is placed in parentheses. Comments are enclosed in braces { }. Alternate forms in any daughter or protolanguage are separated by comma (,).

1 'tongue (lengua†)' PW *?‑?**()pe*
PBM *(mé)-ʔníxɨ-()* PHO *(h)ɨ̈yɨ̈ʔpe*
B *níïxɨ-kʷa, mé-ʔníxɨ-kʷa* M *néxe-ba*
O *hɨ̃ŏŏʔɸɨ̈* Hp *i.ïpe* Hn *i.ïɸe* Hr *i.ïɸe*

2 'mouth (boca†)' PW **(-)po(e)*
{3,318} PBM *íiʔ-xɨ̈ {ʔ-mouth}*
PHO *poe* B *íʔxʸiï, ámexɨ̈* M *íi-xɨ*
O *ɸooï* Hp *pú.e* Hn *ɸú.e* Hr *ɸu.e*

3 'lip (labio†)' PW **po(e)-(i)ni(ba)*
{2,318} PBM *(mé)-xɨ̈-niba {mouth-*
?} PHO *?*p(oe i)ʔgoï {see 31}, *p(oe*
ini) B *(mé)-ïnipa* M *xɨ́-niba {pl.}*
O *ɸa-ʔŏŏʔko* Hp *pú.e ini {mouth*
skin,2,31} Hn *ɸú.e igoï* Hr *ɸu.e igoï*
{mouth skin,2,31}

4 'tooth (diente†)' PW *?‑?**iiʔ-gi-() {23}*
PBM *íiʔ-gái-neé {tooth-finger-?,23},*
(mé)-íiʔgá(xɨ̈ɨ) PHO *iʔtiʔ-to*
B *íʔkʷáxɨ̈ɨ, mé-ʔkʷáxɨ̈ɨ, íʔ-kʷá-nʸeé*
M *íi-gai, íi-ga-ñe {pl}* O *aʔtiïʔtʸo*
Hp *íti-do* Hn *iθi-do* Hr *iθi-do*

5 'nose (nariz†)' PW **topo-(ʔo)*
PBM *tíxɨ̈-ʔo, *tíxɨ̈-ʔ(exɨ̈)* PHO *topo*
B *tʰíxɨ̈-ʔo, tʰɨ̈ɨ̈-ʔexɨ̈ {nose-hole}* M *tíxɨ-*
ʔu O *tʸooɸo* Hp *dópo* Hn *dóɸo*
Hr *doɸo*

6 'eye (ojo†)' PBM *(me)-ʔáájɨ̈ɨ̈*
PHO *ohɨ́-(tï)* B *(me)-ʔáčïï* M *áájɨ̈ɨ*
O *ohɨ̈ɨ̈* Hp *u.i-hï* Hn *u.i-hï* Hr *u.i-θï*

7 'ear {196} (oreja†)' PW *?‑?**()po*
PBM *níxɨ̈-mɨ̈ɨ̈ʔo* PHO *(hepo)*

B *nɨ̈ɨ̈mɨ̈ʔo* M *níxɨ-meeʔu* O *xoñŏŏ*
Hp *hépo* Hn *héɸo* Hr *heɸo*

8 'head {10} (cabeza†)' PBM *nígaï*
PHO *ɨ̈ʔpo-(gï)* B *niíkʷaï* M *nígai*
O *ooʔɸo* Hp *ïpo* Hn *ïɸó-kï* Hr *ïɸo-gï*

9 'forehead (frente†)' PBM *ɨ́mɨko*
PHO *(otó-kï)* B *ʔɨ́mɨkʰo, ʔɨ́mɨkʰo-ï*
M *ɨ́meku* O *dʸabóóho, dʸaʔɨ̈ɨ̈ʔxá*
Hp *otó-kï* Hn *oθó-kï* Hr *ui.eko muido*

10 'hair {8} (cabello†)' PBM *nígaï-*
*xɨ̈ɨne {head-hair,8,243}, *nígaï-(ko)*
PHO *ïʔpo-ʔtï() B *niíkʷa-kʰo,*
niíkʷákʰo-xɨ́(ʔi), íʔxɨne M *nígai-xeene*
O *ooʔɸo, oʔɸo-toʔóóɸe {head-hair?}*
Hp *ïpó-dï̈.i* Hn *ïɸó-tïrai* Hr *ïɸo-tïraï*
{head-hair,8,243}

11 'chin (mentón)' PBM *(xɨ́koxɨ),*
(méʔgáeé, méʔgáiï) PHO *(aïmáïko)*
B *méʔkʷáiï {cheek}* M *xɨ́kexe, xɨ́ko-*
O *hŏŏhɨ̈ ?* Hp *aïmáïko* Hn *aïmá-kï*
Hr *aïmako*

12 'beard (barba)' PBM *xɨ́kk(e)ʔ(ai)*
PHO *(aimákï)* B *ɨ̈xkʰaʔe* M *xɨ́kkoʔai*
O *hŏŏhɨ̈ ?* Hp *aimákï* Hn *aimákï*
Hr *aimakï*

13 'neck (cuello†)' PBM *(kédáäʔɨ), (mé-*
kéttïʔi) B *(mé)-kʰéxtʰïʔi* M *kódáäʔe*
O *ñŏmáä̈ʔŏ* Hp *kïmó-kairo*
Hn *kïmó-hï* Hr *kïmagoï*

14 'chest {16,244,245,272} (pecho†)'
PW **xebae-gaï PBM *(mé)-ppíïï-xɨ
{chest-flat,61}, *(xɨ́ɨbïïga, kïïdïï)
mɨ́ɨ(kko)ʔo, (...) PHO *(he)bae-
goï() {Huitoto 244} B (mé)-xpʰɨ́ï-xɨ,
(mé)-meʔčékʷa-xɨ, (mé)-mɨ́xkʰoʔo,
(mé)-kʷanána-xɨ, (mé)-kʷanóʔkʰo-xɨ,
(mé)-pʰɨ́tʰɨ́rïïkʰï-xɨ M ɸéeyi-xe {upper
chest}, xéebɨɨga méeʔu {heart
shell,34}, kɨ́ɨdɨɨ méeʔu O bagóóʔya
{equals Mɨnɨca in 16?} Hp hogóbe
Hn hogóbe Hr hogobe

15 'woman's breast {319} (teta, seno,
pechos)' PW **mõ(ʔpai)naï
PBM *(mé)-mɨ́ppaine PHO *mõnoï
B (mé)-mïxpʰánʸe, (mé)-mɨ́xpʰanʸe
M mɨ́ɸaño O mõno Hp mónoï
Hn mónoï Hr monoï

16 'abdomen {14,244,245,272} (vientre,
abdomen)' PW **xeʔbae-()
PBM *(áá)-mɨ́ɨʔo {14}, *(mé)-
ɨɨʔbá(ï) {244,245,272} PHO (hebae)
{Ocaina 14} B íʔpáï, mé-ʔpáïï, (má)-
áámɨʔo {ʔ-shell,14} M ííba O gáɸotʸo
Hp hébe, nemúigï Hn hébe, hébekï,
moi idu Hr hébe, ɸenaï hiʲakï

17 'back (espalda†)' PBM (yéebai), (má-
ʔaʲï, má-ʔaigï) {239}
PHO *he(dáï)ʔkï(mo) B má-ʔačï
M yóobai O hïïʔxo(mó) Hp heráïkï
Hn emódo, heráïkï {nape of neck},
ɸekániko {lower} Hr emodo

18 'shoulder (hombro)' PBM *(mé)-xɨ́xɨ-
ba(ï) PHO (peká-taitoï) B mé-íxɨ-pa
M xíxe-bai O dʸïxááβï Hp peká-
ʲaidoï Hn ɸeká-ʲaido Hr ɸeka-ʲaidu

19 'arm (brazo†)' PW ??**(o)nãïʔk()
PBM *(mé)-nékkɨ-gai PHO *onóï-
(kaido) {22,23,240,241}
B (mé)-néxï-kʷa {arm-finger?,23}
M nókkɨ-gai O dʸïxa Hp onó-bïkï
Hn onó-kairo Hr ono-kairo

20 'upper arm (brazo superior)'
PW (onãïk) PBM *(mé)-nékkɨ-(gai)-
(étsitto) B mé-néxï-kʷa-étsʰixtʰʸo
{19,240} M nókkɨ O dʸïxáá-βï
Hp dagɨ́-ʲo Hn tagɨ́-ʲo Hr narï-ʲo

21 'elbow (codo)' PBM (méniko), (me-
némiï) B (me)-némiï M méniku
O onó-kona Hp dagɨ́-čiru
Hn tagɨ́-kaiño Hr tagɨ́-ʲuru

22 'hand {208–213} (mano†)'
PBM *(mé)-ʔóttsɨ́ɨ PHO *onṍï
{19,23,240,241} B (mé)-ʔóxtsʰɨɨ
M úse O onṍõ(po) Hp ónoï Hn ónoï
Hr ono-ʲï, onoï

23 'finger (dedo de la mano)' PW **()-
(k)aï PBM *(mé)-ʔóttsɨ-gai
{hand-finger,4,(11?),19,24,30,50,87}
PHO *onṍï-(kaï), *onṍï-(βini)
{19,22,240,241} B (mé)-ʔóxtsʰɨ-kʷa
M úse-gai O onṍṍ-βiñi Hp onó-kaï
Hn onó-kaï Hr ono-kaï

24 'fingernail {271,23} (uña)' PW **()-
(k)aï-(b)e(ʔo)
PBM *(mé)-ʔóttsɨ-gai-mɨ́ɨʔo
PHO (onṍï-k(aï)-be) B (mé)-ʔóxtsʰɨ́-
kʷa-mɨ́ɨʔo M úse-gai-méeʔu
{hand-finger-shell,14} O xáátʸo
Hp onó-be-ko Hn onó-be-ko Hr ono-
ko-be

25 'leg (pierna†)' PW **(ï)dzaʔkai(do)
PBM (mé-tákki), (xóónoga, xéénoga)
PHO ?*ïdzá-k(aido) B (mé)-tʰáxkʰɨɨ
{242} M xúúnu-ga O odzá-kona,
odzáá-βïna, (odzáá-tsi) Hp ïdá-kairo
Hn ïdá-kairo, rɨ́.aï-kairo Hr ïda-kairo

26 'thigh (muslo)' PBM (mé-kkïbaá),
(ídï) B (mé)-xkʰɨ́paá M ídɨ O ɸoxoo
Hp rïáïti Hn moi iduraï, rɨ́aïθi
Hr mo.iʲï iduraï

27 'knee (rodilla†)' PBM *(mé)-mɨ́mo-()
PHO (kaïnï-kï) B (mé)-mɨ́mo-kʰo

M *mému-ba* O *hohóóʔxo* Hp *káiñï*
Hn *kaiñíkï* Hr *kañïkï* *ïɸo*

28 'shin (espinilla)' **PBM** *(xóónoga,
xéénoga)*, *(mé-(i)tooinóxi)*
B *-tʰ ʸóónʸoxi, mé-tʰ ʸoonʸóxi* {both
palatalizations anomalous} **M** *xúúnu-
ga* {lower leg} {242} **O** *ñañaβíroga*
Hp *ñeré-da* **Hn** *ñeré-gï* **Hr** *taiθï-bairo*

29 'foot (pie[†])' **PBM** **(mé)-ttḯ-ʔaái*
PHO **eʔγḯ-()* **B** *(mé)-xtʰ ïʔaá* **M** *tí-ʔai*
O *ïʔγóó(ga)* **Hp** *e.ḯ-ba* **Hn** *é.ï-ba*
Hr *e.ï-jï̈*

30 'toe (dedo del pie)' **PW** ***()-(k)aï*
{23} **PBM** **(mé)-ttḯ-gaái* {foot-
finger,23} **PHO** **eʔḯ-(kaï)*,
*eʔγḯ-(bini) **B** *(mé)-xtʰ ḯ-kʷaá* **M** *tí-gai*
O *ïʔγóó-biñi* **Hp** *e.ḯ-kaï* **Hn** *e.ḯ-kaï*
Hr *e.ï-kaï*

31 'skin (piel[†])' **PBM** **(iáábe) (mé)-
ʔmíïʔe(é)* **PHO** *ʔ*()niʔgaï*
B *(mé)-ʔmíïʔeé, iáápe míïʔe*
M *mée ʔe* **O** *xoñíïʔka* **Hp** *íni* {3}
Hn *igóï-raï* **Hr** *igoï* {3}

32 'bone (hueso[†])' **PBM** **bákkïï̈*
B *páxkʰ ïï̈* **M** *bákki* **O** *ñõʔóóʔkoβo*
Hp *íkuru* **Hn** *íkuru* **Hr** *ijaikï*

33 'blood {266} (sangre)' **PW** ***tï̈-
xē(ʔe)* **PBM** **tïï̈-(xéʔe)*, **tïï̈-(ppaiko)*
PHO **tïhé* **B** *tʰ ḯ-xpʰakʰ ʸo* {red-liquid,
294,(71),48} **M** *tíï-xóʔo* **O** *tsihïï̈* {294}
Hp *dḯ.e* **Hn** *dḯ.e* **Hr** *dï.e, dïru.e*

34 'heart (corazón[†])' **PW** *ʔ**ko()*
PBM **(kïïdïï)*, **(mé)-xïibïï̈*
PHO **kome(ki)* {360} **B** *(mé)-íípïï̈*
M *kïidii, xéebii* {14} **O** *xomïï̈-mõti*
Hp *komékï* **Hn** *komékï* **Hr** *komekï*

35 'lungs (pulmones)' **PBM** **βáaʔβága,
(xï̈-gitsï̈-ba), (maráʔ-ba), (maráá ʔ-o)*
B *βaʔβákʷa, βaxíʔkʰo, maráʔpa,
maráá ʔo* **M** *βáβáágano, βáaβaga*
{sing}, *xḯ-gisi-ba* {ʔ-blow-?,365}

O *ɸáβaaxo* {borrowed from
Muinane?} **Hp** *hágï-jï̈* **Hn** *ɸéko-jï̈,
háθai-jï̈* **Hr** *haθakï*

36 'penis (pene)' **PBM** *(náméʔo),
(xíïttïʔï)* **B** *náméʔo* **M** *xéettïʔï*
Hp *móda* **Hn** *hejína* **Hr** *hejïnaï*

37 'vulva (vulva)'
PBM *(iiʔógáʔnámáíʔxï)*
B *iiʔyókʷá ʔnámáʔxʸï* **Hp** *hiáni*
Hn *hiáni* **Hr** *hiani, moiɸo*

38 'man (hombre[†])' **PBM** **gai-ppi,
míámḯnáa-ppi {41} **PHO** **ḯʔí* **B** *kʷa-
xpʰi, míamḯnáa-xpʰi* {being-male}
M *gáí-ɸi* {being-male}, *míyáminaa-ɸi*
{human-male} **O** *ooʔï* **Hp** *ḯ.i-ma*
Hn *ḯ.i-ma* **Hr** *ḯ.i-ma*

39 'man (varón)' **PBM** **gai-ppi, *tsaa-
ppi* {one-male} **PHO** **ḯʔí* **B** *kʷa-xpʰi,
tsʰaa-pʰi* {one-male} **M** *gáí-ɸi* {being-
male}, *sáa-ɸi* {one-male} **O** *ooʔï*
Hp *ḯ.i-ta* {boy} **Hn** *ḯ.i-θa* **Hr** *ḯ.i-θa*
{boy}

40 'woman (mujer[†])' **PW** ***-gaï*
PBM **gai-ge, (míámḯná-ge)* {41}
PHO *(dï-goï), (mimi)* **B** *kʷa-če* **M** *gáí-
go* {being-female}, *míyámina-go*
{human-female} **O** *maami* **Hp** *rḯ-ŋo*
Hn *rḯ-ŋo* **Hr** *rï-ño*

41 'people (gente[†])' **PW** ***()mḯnaï*
PBM **míamïnaa* {38,40}
PHO *(komḯnï)* **B** *míamïnaa, mḯnaa*
M *míyáminaa* **O** *haróʔtiʔ* **Hp** *komïnï*
Hn *komḯnï* **Hr** *komïnï*

42 'husband (marido[†])' **PBM** **taxi, *áí-
táxií* {my-husband}, **áixïï̈* **PHO** **ï̈ni*
B *tʰaxi, áxʸïï̈, átʰ ʸáxií* **M** *áttʸaxe*
{my}, *táxe, aixi* **O** *õõna* **Hp** *ḯni*
Hn *ḯni* **Hr** *ïni*

43 'wife (esposa[†])' **PBM** **taába, *áí-
táabaá* {my-wife}, *(mega)* **B** *tʰaápa,*

mekʷa, *átʰʸáápaá* M *táaba*, *áttʸáaba*
O *mĩʔtõ* Hp *á.ï* Hn *á.ï* Hr *a.ï*

44 'father (papá†)' PBM **giʔí-ro(bi)*,
(kááni) PHO **mõhõ* B *čiʔí-yo*, *čiʔí-ï*
M *gíʔí(rubi)* *{vocative}*, *kááni*
O *mõõ(hõ)* Hp *mó.o* Hn *mó.o*
Hr *mo.o*

45 'mother (mamá)' PW ***gãʔĩ*
PBM **gaʔá-ro(bi)* PHO **éʔĩ-(goï)*
B *kʷaʔá-ro*, *kʷaʔá-ï* M *gáʔá(rubi)*
{vocative}, *sééxɨ* O *íídzaʔ*, *áʔĩʔ*
Hp *á-ño* Hn *éi*, *éi-ño* Hr *e.i*

46 'baby, infant {327} (criatura)'
PBM **tsíímene {327}* PHO *(kiβī)*
B *tsʰíímene* M *séemene* O *xaβīī*
{308,327,221} Hp *hí.ï-ta* Hn *úru.e*
Hr *uru.e*

47 'old man (viejo)' PBM *(ámia-te)*,
(kíjaʔote), *(keéme) {246,347}*
PHO **heʔí-(do)-ma {246; compare*
198} B *kʰeéme* M *ámiyaa-bo*, *ámiya-*
to {pl}, *kíjaʔuto* O *haʔíí-ma*
Hp *e.íro-ma* Hn *éiro-ma*, *éi-kome*
Hr *eiro-ma*, *u.aïkï-ma*

48 'water (agua†)' PW ***nõ-()*
PBM **nĩ́-ppaiko {water-liquid}*
PHO **(haï-)nõ-hī {ʔ-water-liquid,*
62,157} B *nĩ́-xpʰakʰʸo {33,157,266,*
319,324,325} M *φaiʔu*, *nĩ́-φáíʔu*
{water-liquid/gas,59,247,309}
O *ñõõ(-hĩ̄) {water-liquid,62,157}*
Hp *háïnoi* Hn *háïnoi* Hr *hïnui*

49 'river {250,311} (río†)'
PW ***m(oon)ai {see 311}*, ***tae(ʔi)*
PBM **moóai {311}*, **teé-ʔi {river-*
line,250,71} PHO **(i)máni {311}*,
*(i)tae {250} B *tʰeé-ʔi*, *moóa* M *téé-*
ʔi, *múúai {large}* O *maanï*, *tʲaaï*
Hp *imáni* Hn *imáni*, *íje* Hr *imani*, *ije*

50 'island (isla)' PBM *(-čó-gai)*,
(káméʔpaí) B *kʰaapʰáʔo*, *kʰaátsʰi*
M *-čú-gai {-island-finger,23}*

O *óóʔšona* Hp *ui.áti* Hn *ui.áθi*
Hr *ui.aθi*, *maïjokï*

51 'lake (lago†)' PBM *(káátsi)*,
(xïkkéeba), *(íneï)* PHO **hõʔdáhī*
B *íneï* M *káási*, *xikkóoba* O *hõʔááhī*
Hp *hórai* Hn *hórai* Hr *horai*

52 'swamp (pantano)' PBM **(ípá)-káa-*
xa-(neba), **káa-(mɨ)* PHO **kïné-bï*
B *kʰááxánepa* M *káa-me*, *íφá-káa-xa*
O *boʔiʔiʔtʲonó*, *xonííβaga*, *ñihííβaga*
Hp *kïné-re* Hn *kïné-bï*, *θakó-bï*
Hr *kïne-re*, *θoï-re-de*

53 'spring of water (fuente, ojo de
agua)' PW ***dzoodo()* PBM *(píítsíri-*
gai), *(gaapéga)*, *(čooróga)*
PHO **dzod(o)-p(o)* B *kʷaapʰékʷa*,
čʰoorókʷa M *píísírí-gai* O *dzóóroʔφi*
Hp *do() {310}* Hn *to-rá-no*
Hr *to-ra-φo*

54 'waterfall (caída de agua)'
PBM *(négai-gai)*, *(gíítsi-ga)*
PHO *(nopíko dzoa)* B *néékʷákʷá?*
{rock ?,73}ǂ M *gíísiga* Hp *nopí-ko*
dú.a {rock ?,55,73} Hn *noφí-ko tú.a*
Hr *čurua*

55 'rapids (catarata, raudal)' PW ***goti-*
() {73} PBM *(gíítsi-ga)*, *((ai)toʔka)*
PHO *(dzóʔ-te) {rock ?,54,73}*, *(gotíʔ-*
i) {73} B *tʰʸóʔkʰáǂ* M *gíísiga*
O *dʲahiiʔi*, *gotáʔ-i {rocky?,73}*
Hp *nopíko dú-a*, *jĩ̄.aï dó-de*
Hn *noφíko tú-a* Hr *to-ra-da*

56 'fire (candela, fuego†)' PBM **kííxï-*
gai, *(kotsííbai)* PHO *(idái-kï)*
B *kʰííxï-kʷa* M *kííxɨ-gai*, *kusííbai*
O *tʲaaro* Hp *irái-kï* Hn *irai* Hr *irai*

57 'ash (ceniza†)' PBM **bái-giíxï {?-*
powder, 372} B *pá-čiíxʲï* M *bai-giíxɨ*
O *oʔtiiʔi* Hp *hítu.egï* Hn *híθeφo*
Hr *huθeφo*

58 'charcoal (carbón)' **PW** **koxo
PBM **kííxí-gai-(kko)* *{56}*
PHO **kó(o-kï)*, **kó(na-)* **B** *k ʰíïxï-kʷa-yï* **M** *kíïxɨ-gai-kku* *(fire-?-piece,56)*
O *xóñaa(tʸo)* **Hp** *kó.o-kï* **Hn** *kó.o-kï*
Hr *ko.o-kï*

59 'smoke {247} (humo†)'
PW ***xi(moo)?-pi?o* **PBM** *(aimóo-ppai(?)o)*, *(ottsoï)* *{247,248,309}*
PHO *(hi?píí?o)* **B** *oxtsʰo* **M** *aimúu-ɸai(?u)* *{cloud-liquid/gas, 48,247,309}*
O *ha?ɸíí?o* **Hp** *úijï.e* **Hn** *úijï.e*
Hr *uijï.e*

60 'firewood (leña)' **PBM** **koó-* **B** *k ʰo?-pa*, *kʰoó-kʷa*, *kʰoó-i*, *kʰó-kʷaxkʰa*,
kʰó-βiïrï **M** *kúúxo-?o* *{firewood-wood,152}* **O** *dʸamōō(hï̃)* **Hp** *ré.ï-ïe*
Hn *ré.ï.e*, *ré.ï-ïe* **Hr** *re.ï-ai*

61 'sky (cielo†)' **PBM** *níkke-xɨ *{sky-flat,14}*, *(íéβe?óóga)* **PHO** *móna
{67} **B** *níxkʰʸe-xɨ*, *iéβe?óókʷa*
M *níkke-xe* **O** *bɨ̈mõ̃ñá*, *xïtʸamóóña*,
aamɨ(hõ) **Hp** *móna* **Hn** *móna*
Hr *mona*

62 'rain (lluvia†)' **PW** **nõ-xī *{48}*
PBM *nííxa-ba *{water-?,48}* **PHO** **nõ-(kï)*, **nõ-(hī)* *{48,157}* **B** *nííxʸa-pa*
M *nííxa-ba* **O** *ñõ̃õ(-hï̃)* *{water-liquid, 48,157}* **Hp** *nókï* **Hn** *nókï* **Hr** *nokï*

63 'wind (viento†)' **PBM** *(gíbó?o-ba, gíbé?o-ba)*, *(kííxe-ba)*, *(xiókko)*
PHO **hai(dí)(p)oï* **B** *k ʰíïxʸe-pa*,
(x)ioxkʰo **M** *gíbú?u-ba* **O** *hïβóód'o*,
hïβõ̃õ̃ **Hp** *hairípoï* **Hn** *hairíɸo*
Hr *hairiɸo, aïɸï*

64 'sun (sol†)' **PBM** **kóoxí-e(ppi) nï?ɨ-ba* *{day-? sun-?, 67,65}*
PHO *(hi?tóma)*, *(néena)* **B** *nï?-pa*
(kʰóóxí-expʰi) **M** *(kúuxe-o) ní?ɨ-ba*
O *nï̃ï̃na* *{borrowed from Bora?}*
Hp *hidóma* **Hn** *hitóma* **Hr** *hitoma*

65 'moon (luna†)' **PBM** **pékkó-e(ppi)*
nï?ɨ-ba *{night-? sun-?, 68,64}*
PHO **pï̈()* **B** *nï?-pa pʰéxkʰó-expʰi*
M *(ɸúkkuo) ní?ɨ-ba* **O** *ɸodʸoome*
Hp *pïbï.i* **Hn** *ɸï.ui* **Hr** *ɸïβui*

66 'star (estrella†)' **PW** *?**()?ko?do()*
PBM *míïkíri-gai **PHO** **o?kó?to*
B *mɨ̈ïkʰíri-kʷa*, *mɨ̈ïkʰïrï* **M** *méékɨri-gai* **O** *o?xóó?tʸo* **Hp** *ukúdo* **Hn** *ukúdu*
Hr *ukudu*

67 'day (día†)' **PBM** **kóoxɨ̈*
PHO *móna *{sky?,61}* **B** *k ʰóóxɨ̈*
M *kúuxe* **O** *mooña, moñamó*
Hp *móna* **Hn** *móna* **Hr** *aremona*

68 'night (noche†)' **PBM** *pekko
PHO **naï()* **B** *pʰexkʰo* **M** *ɸúkku*
O *natʸõ̃* **Hp** *náï.ïo* **Hn** *náï.(ï)o*
Hr *naï.o(na)*

69 'thunder (trueno)' **PW** ***(gï)dïte (U)*
PBM **()tsittsi, (da?ná?o)* **PHO** *(gïdï-te)* **B** *čʰixčʰi, ta?ná?o* **M** *sísi*
O *amï̃?ño* *{matches Huitoto 70}*
Hp *gïrí-de* **Hn** *gïrí-de* **Hr** *guru-de*

70 'lightning (relámpago)'
PW *??**(n)ame()* **PBM** *(námɨ-ba), (rorí?ko)* **PHO** **amé?yo* *{Ocaina 69}*
B *rorí?kʰʸo* **M** *náme-ba, námé-ba-no*
{verb} **O** *ïïβá?yo* **Hp** *amé.o* *{matches Ocaina 69}, borí-de* **Hn** *amé.o,*
borí-de **Hr** *ame.o* *{71}, bori-de*

71 'rainbow (arco iris)' **PW** *?* **PBM** **tïï-?i* *{red-line,294,49,250}*
PHO *?*(d)ódzi-(goe)?do* **B** *t ʰïï-?i*
M *tɨ̈ɨ-?i* **O** *ójïi?o* **Hp** *róti-gue.o*
Hn *róθi-gue.o* **Hr** *roθi-guero, ame.o*

72 'earth (tierra†)' **PW** ***xáénï̈?-xē*
PBM *xíínɨ-xɨ **PHO** **aenï̃?-ē*, **aenï̃?-dõē* **B** *íínʸï-xɨ* **M** *xíínɨ-(xe)* **O** *añõ̃õ̃?ï̃*
Hp *énï.e* **Hn** *énï.e* **Hr** *enïru.e*

73 'stone (piedra†)' **PW** ***goti-* *{55}*
PBM *(giitsi-ba)* *{252}, (négai-(ne)-ï)*

{54,74,251,252} PHO *(nopí-kï)* *{54,55}*, *(gotíʔ-kï)* *{55}* B *néékʷa-yï̈, néékʷá-nʸeï* M *gïisi-ba* O *gotíḯʔ-xo* Hp *nopí-kï* Hn *noɸí-kï* Hr *noɸï-kï*

74 'sand (arena†)' PW ?**(k)onigïḯʔî PBM *(xíí)né-gai-yï̈-ʔai {73,251,252}* PHO ?ʔ*(koni)dzïḯʔ(ï)* B *nékʷa-yïḯ-ʔa, néékʷa-yï {sing}* M *xíïnï-gai-yï-ʔai {earth-piece-ʔ-ʔ,72}* O *jíôôʔî* Hp *kónijï̈.e* Hn *gúama.e* Hr *konijï̈.e*

75 'house {377,255} (casa)' PW **xop(o) {but see 255; VU}* PBM *ïïʔ-xa, *káamée-xa, *(báae)-xa* PHO *(ho)po {255}* B *xaá, iʔ-xʸa {his-house}, páae-xa {communal without floor}, kʰáámée-xa {with floor}* M *íí-xa, káamooxa {with floor}* O *ɸoo(ho), -xo* Hp *hópo* Hn *hóɸo* Hr *hoɸo, ɸo {at home}*

76 'roof (techo)' PBM *(pá-gaáne), (tégaáne), (té-ʔoóba), (nibaʔo)* PHO *(edahi)* B *pʰá-kʷaáne, tʰékʷaáne, tʰé-ʔoópa* M *níbaʔu* O *moʔxóóʔɸi, ayííβi {of woven leaves}* Hp *érai* Hn *érei* Hr *erehi*

77 'doorway (puerta)' PBM *gééʔo-ga, (bágígaʔéxï)* B *čééʔo-kʷa, pátsíkʷaʔéxï* M *gúʔú-ga* O *tʸaaɸočá* Hp *náte, ïbáira* Hn *náθe, ïbái-ra* Hr *naθe, ibai-ro*

78 'seat, stool (banco)' PBM *ïkka-ga, (akííβe-ga)* PHO *()-dá-bïkï {seat-long+flat}* B *íxʸa-kʷa, akʰííβe-(kʷa)* M *ïkka-ga* O *biiñi-ráá-βoho, biiñi-rááko* Hp *rá.ï̈.i-ra-bï-kï* Hn *rá.ï̈.i-ra-bï-kï* Hr *raï-ra-ko*

79 'mat (estera)' PBM *kïgá-(taxi), *kïgá-(íʔkï), (inébaxi), (ííkaxi)* PHO *(da-níʔta)* B *inʸépaxi, ííkʰaxi, kʰïkʷá-íʔkʰyï {sleep-platform}* M *kígataxe {81}* Hp *ra-níďa* Hn *bïi-ra-nigï, ïnḯ-ra-nigï, ra-níta {sieve}* Hr *ioɸe*

80 'hammock (hamaca)' PBM *gaáí-ba* PHO *kïnahï* B *kʷaá-pʸa, kʷaá-pa* M *gáái-ba* O *xonaahï* Hp *kïnai* Hn *kïnai* Hr *kïnai*

81 'bed (catre, cama de barbacoa)' PBM *kïgá-ïïxï, *kïgá-(taxi), *kïgá-(íʔkï)* PHO *(i)nï̈() {280}* B *kʰïkʷá-íʔkʰyï {sleep-platform}, kʰïkʷa-ïïxï {sleep-barbacoa} ‡* M *kígaíixe, kíga-taxe {79}* O *ïnôʔxatsííβo, ɸohóóyo* Hp *bï̈.i-ra-ju* Hn *bï̈.i-ra-ju* Hr *ïnï-ra, bï-ira*

82 'cooking pot (olla)' PBM *gíri-ʔïjo* PHO *no(g)o()* B *číyi-ʔčo* M *gírí-ʔïju* O *ñoxooťʸo* Hp *nógo, kadéru {Spanish}* Hn *nógo* Hr *nogo*

83 'cultivated clearing {249} (roza, chagra)' PBM *gáíkko-ʔai* B *kʷáxkʰyoʔa {not planted}* M *gáíkku-ʔai {249}* O *hôʔtâáhï {163,249}* Hp *hakápoï* Hn *hakaïɸa.ï̈* Hr *ïjï*

84 'village (caserío)' PW **koom(ï)* PBM *kóomíí* PHO *(komïnï)* B *kʰóómíí* M *kúumi* O *óóxïma ɸohôô* Hp *ñú.eno* Hn *komïnï i-já-no* Hr *naïraï i-ja-no, komïnï i-ja-no*

85 'path, trail {253} (camino, sendero, trocha†)' PW **(na)xï̈() PBM *xï̈́-()* PHO ?*tí(do)(p)e(ta), *nahï̈(to)* B *xïïβa* M *xíí-ʔai* O *naahô, tóβïʔtʸa* Hp *í.o, díro-pe* Hn *í.o, díro-ɸe* Hr *na.ï̈θo*

86 'fish net (red)' PBM *ts(í)nïkóʔo {atarraya}, *(pó)-kóʔo* B *tsʰïnïḯ, tsʰïnï-kʰóóʔo, tsʰïnï-kʰóóʔa* M *sínïkuʔu, ɸú-kuʔu* O *boʔtááʔti, ïróxatï* Hp *jó.ihi* Hn *jó.ihi* Hr *jo.ihi*

87 'fish hook (anzuelo)' PW **p(ai)ʔko* PBM *pííkkï-gai* PHO *p(ai)ʔkoa-ti* B *pʰííxʸï-kʷa* M *ɸííkkí-gai {hook-finger?,23}* O *ɸeʔxoo-ti* Hp *pákua-ti* Hn *ɸáku.a-θi* Hr *ɸago-θi*

88 'axe (hacha)' PBM *xɨ́gaá-xɨ B ɨ́kʷaá-
xɨ M xɨgáá-xe {axe-flat,61,14} O φïɨ̈xo
Hp čo-βéma Hn háta Hr hata

89 'knife (cuchillo)' PBM *(mɨ́(y)oʔo),
*n(ɨɨ)ts(ɨ́)ga-(gayï) PHO (toβéʔtïdaï)
B nɨɨtsʰɨ́kʷa, nɨɨtsʰɨ́kʷa-kʷï {machete-
small} M mééyuʔu, nɨ́ɨsú-ga {machete;
vowels wrong; late borrowing from
Bora?} O mïrááboya Hp čoβédïrï
Hn jo.étïrï Hr jo.etïraï

90 'canoe (canoa)' PBM *mɨ́ɨne-(ga)
PHO *()áʔe B mɨɨne M mééne-ga
{canoe-long,93,94,160} O hōφáá́ʔï
Hp nókae Hn nokáe Hr noka.e

91 'paddle (remo)' PW ? PBM *boʔódó-
ga B poʔtó-kʷa, poʔtó-xɨ M búʔúdú-ga
O mōʔsodʸ́ááβoho Hp hɨ́.aï-be
Hn hɨ́.aï-be Hr haïra-be

92 'club (porra, macana)'
PBM *gáíʔoóï(daaʔɨ) PHO *()-bɨ́(g)ï
B páčoá-kʷa, kʷáʔyoóï M gáíʔuɨdaaʔe
O biija-βóóho Hp bɨ́gɨ Hn bɨ́gɨ Hr bɨ́gɨ

93 'spear (lanza)' PBM *aámï̈-(ba),
(káβaákko) PHO *(tokï) da-ta
B aamɨ́-pa, kʰáβaáxkʰo M áámɨ-ga
{spear-long,90} O oïdʸáátʸa Hp dukɨ́-
ra-joi-kï Hn dukɨ́-ra-θï, dukɨ́-ra-da
Hr dukï-ra-θï

94 'bow (arco)' PW **tï() PBM *tïïbó-
ga {214} PHO *tï() B tʰïpóó-kʷa
M tɨɨbú-ga {95} O tsipóxatʸa {borr.
fr. Bora?} Hp tïkúi-ña Hn θïkui-raï
Hr θïkui-ra

95 'arrow (flecha)' PW **tï()
PBM *gáínɨ́ï-ga, *tïïbó-(ga), (pígaï)
PHO *(kanɨ́ʔta) {178}, *(tïk)ói da-ta
B aamɨ́-kʷa, kʷánʸïḯ-kʷa, tʰïpóó-kʰo
M tɨɨbú-ga {arrow-long,94,90}, φégaɨ,
gañɨ́ɨ-ga {harpoon} O oïdʸátsaʔso,
oïdʸáátʸa Hp tïkúi-ra-da, kanïda
{178} Hn dukɨ́-ra-θï Hr dukï-ra-θï

96 'blowgun (cerbatana)' PBM *gittsɨ́-xï,
*(togïí)-xï, *(tojïí)-xï B tʰóčïí-xʸï,
čïxčʰḯ-xï M gisɨ́-xɨ {blow-tube,365}
O φahïíʔxatʸa {blow-?,365}
Hp obí-jakaï Hn obí-jakaï
Hr obi-jakaï

97 'tapir (danta)' PW **tō()
PBM (tïḯʔɨ), (ókáxïí) PHO *tō()
B ókʰáxïí, kʰáátʰïxé ɨʔtéexpʰi,
pɨ́íréenïíʔyo, kʰïïβépa M tɨ́ɨʔe
O tʸōōhā Hp turúma Hn θurúma
Hr θuruma, hïgadïma

98 'jaguar (tigre)' PW **xɨ̈ʔko
PBM (xɨ́kko), (ooʔïíbe), (tɨ́páíʔoóï)
PHO *hɨ̈ʔko {99,101} B ooʔïípʸe,
tʰïɨ́pʰáʔyoóï {99} M xɨkku {99,101}
O hōʔxo {101}, čiβaβááña
hïmáá́ʔxaxo Hp hánajari, hɨ́ko {119}
Hn hánajari, hɨ́ko {119} Hr hanajari,
hïko {ocelot}

99 'puma (león, puma)' PW **xɨ̈ʔko
PBM (xɨ́kko), *tɨ́páíʔoó(ï)
PHO (hɨ̈ʔko) {98,101} B tʰïɨ́pʰáʔyoóï
M xɨkku {98,101}, tɨ́φaiʔui O ?
Hp hɨ́ko {101} Hn hɨ́ko

100 'armadillo (armadillo, quinquincho,
carachupa)' PW ? PBM *geéï,
(dóótoɨ́ʔaamɨne), (káápínaï)
PHO *n(ē)nɨ́(goï) B čeéï,
tóótʰoɨ́ʔaamɨne, kʰáápʰínaï M góóɨ
O ñóóńō Hp ñenɨ́ŋo Hn ñenɨ́ŋo
Hr ñeniño

101 'dog {98,99} (perro[†])' PW **xɨ̈ʔko
PBM (xɨ́kko), (ooʔïíbe) PHO *hɨ̈ʔko
B ooʔïípʸe {98} M xɨkku {98,99}
O hōʔxo {98} Hp hɨ́ko Hn hɨ́ko
Hr hïko

102 'deer (venado)' PW ??**()kɨ́()
PBM *nɨ́íβï-gai, *xïíbai PHO *kɨ́ʔto
B nïíβï-kʷa, ïipa M nïíβï-gai {red},
xïíbái {white} O ïïxo, xooʔtʸo {small}
Hp kɨ́do Hn kɨ́to Hr kɨ́to

103 'bat (murciélago)' PBM *kíkiíxe
PHO *(tï)nōï B kʰíkʰiíxʸe M kíkíxe
O nōōï, nōááʔɸiʔtʸa Hp jïni Hn jïni
Hr jïni(θï), hïdokuiño

104 'otter (nutria)' PBM *tsokko
PHO (ïpóʔe) B tsʰoxkʰo M súkku
O hitóóro Hp ïpó.e Hn ïɸú.e Hr ïɸu.e

105 'cebus monkey (capuchín, machín)'
PBM *(čoyíyi), *kïʔjíba B kʰïʔčípa
M kïjíba, čuyíyi Hp hóma, díjï
Hn hóma Hr homa

106 'howler monkey (mono aullador)'
PW **ío PBM (ío, íyo), (name)
PHO (io, iyo) B name M íyu Hp í.u
Hn í.u Hr i.u

107 'spider monkey (marimonda, ma-
quisapa)' PBM (xïbííjaxi), *kïïmï
B kʰïïmï M xíbííjaxe, kíími {choyo}
O oorï Hp tíjo, mé.eku Hn néhoma
Hr guamï

108 'capybara (chigüiro, ronsoco)'
PBM (nimïtíïʔi), (oʔba)
PHO (-haino) B oʔpa M nimí-tííʔe
{guacurí-danta} O ñóóma
Hp meréhaiño Hn meréhaiño,
ɸeréhaiño Hr ɸerehaiño

109 'anteater (oso hormiguero)'
PW **xé(ã)kï PBM *xiíxï, *tooʔxi
PHO (héãkï) B iíxï, tʰoʔxi M xééxi,
túuxe O híããko, hōōʔã Hp eréño,
dobóji Hn eréño Hr ereño

110 'paca (paca, guagua, majas)'
PBM *takkï, (ainókkóʔega)
PHO (akaino) B tʰaxkʰï,
anʸóxkʰóʔekʷa M tákki O axaaño
Hp íme Hn íme Hr íme

111 'crocodile (caimán)'
PW ?**n(a)ʔï(b)a PBM *niʔiba,
*meeʔdóba PHO *(na)ʔïma B niʔpa,
meʔtópa M níʔiba {babilla}, méédúba
{black} O hōʔóóma Hp té.ema,

tïkínaïma Hn θé.ema, θïkínaïma
Hr naïma, θïkïnaïma

112 'iguana (iguana)' PBM *mááínaʔo,
(xóóčáíʔi) B máánʸaʔo M mááñáʔu,
xúúčáíʔi {chameleon} O mááñaʔo
{borr. from Bora?} Hp kúema
Hn kúema Hr kuema

113 'tortoise (tortuga)' PBM (xóʔópóko,
xéʔepéko), (iïβo) PHO *mainí-(goï)
B iïβo M xúʔúpúku O mañiiʔxo
{water} Hp uijóniño, meníño
Hn ɸúrikï, meníño Hr meniño

114 'river turtle (tortuga, motelo)'
PW ?**dzo() PBM (pááβaʔo),
(kïïmïxi), (tírííxi, tírééxi, tírííxe)
PHO (dzoʔdzo) B pʰááβaʔo, kʰïïmïxi
M tírééxe O dzooʔdzo Hp húri
Hn ɸurikï, húriniño Hr ɸurikï

115 'collared peccary (saíno)'
PW **me(d)o PBM *meéni
PHO (medo) B meéni M méeni
O nanóóβa, hááčoβa Hp méro
Hn méro Hr mero

116 'white-lipped peccary (jabalí
mayor)' PBM *páápaiba, (míneébe)
B pʰááphapʸa, míneépe M ɸááɸaiba
O hááčoβa, nanóóβa Hp e.ímo
Hn e.ímo Hr e.imo

117 'agouti (agutí)' PW ?**()mï(),
**píʔto PBM (páttï), (birímïxi)
PHO *p(íí)to, *mï(goi) B pirímïxi
{añuje} M ɸátti O ɸíítʸo, mōōno
Hp mïgui, okáina Hn mïgui, ɸí.ïdo,
okáina Hr mïgui, ɸïdo, okaina

118 'rat (rata)' PBM (gíʔipe), (nïïmíra),
(kïïβéba), (aatsárii) PHO *minï()
B nïïmíra, kʰïïβépa, aatsʰárii
M gíʔiɸo O miñóóko Hp miñí.e
Hn miñí.e Hr miñí.e

119 'cat (gato)' PBM *míítsii {Spanish}
PHO (hïʔko) B mííčʰii {Spanish}

M *míĩši* {*Spanish*} **Hp** *míči, híko* {*98,99,101*} **Hn** *míči, híko* {*98,99,101*} **Hr** *miči* {*Spanish*}

120 'mouse (ratón)' **PBM** **gi?pe,* *(kiïβéba),* *(bííččaï)* **B** *k^híïβépa,* *či?p^hye* **M** *giiɸo* {*field*}, *bííččai* {*house*} **O** *tsóraaxo* **Hp** *má.u* **Hn** *nonóči, nónoiči* **Hr** *okohï*

121 'tail (cola†)' **PW** *?**(ib)o?oo* **PBM** *(ííbo?o),* *(bógaá),* *(gagááíβe)* **PHO** *(o?oo)* **B** *pók^waá, k^wak^wáááβ^e* **M** *ííbu?u* **O** *o?oo* **Hp** *óda* **Hn** *óda* **Hr** *omakaï*

122 'snake (serpiente, culebra†)' **PBM** **xíinime, (íttï)* **PHO** *(iβána)* **B** *íín^yim^ye* **M** *xíinimo, ítti* {*small snake*} **O** *anï?ť^ʸóko, gōhǒ̒ó?ï?tsi,* *ť^yoroo?o* **Hp** *hái.o, iβána* **Hn** *hái.o* **Hr** *hai.o*

123 'anaconda, water boa (mapana)' **PBM** **bóóaá* {*Spanish?*}, **íígai(ko)* **PHO** *?*()ó?yo* **B** *póóaá, íík^wak^hʸo* **M** *búúa, ígáíβatï* **O** *toxóó?yo* **Hp** *nú.io* **Hn** *nú.io* **Hr** *nu.i.o*

124 'rattlesnake (cascabel)' **PBM** **táaka?e* **PHO** *(namaini)* **B** *t^háák^ha?e* **M** *táaka?o* {*sabanera*} **O** *namaañi* **Hp** *nonórai* **Hn** *nonórai* **Hr** *raïdï* {*matches Muinane Huitoto 125*}

125 'coral snake (coral)' **PBM** **čiráágai,* *(kábiïï)* **PHO** *(daïto)* **B** *č^híïyák^wa,* *k^hápiïï* **M** *čiráágai* **Hp** *ráïdu* {*matches Munui 124*} **Hn** *égïaïŋo* {*nonpoisonous*} **Hr** *egïaño*

126 'toad (sapo†)' **PW** ***(go)xaï?kï()* **PBM** **xa?kó(kó)ga, *(β)ïïríʔíi,* **mïï?míba, (xáákkïba), (...)* **PHO** **(n)op(aï)goï (VU),* **goaïkí(ho), *(h)edaï* **B** *a?k^hók^wa,* *βïïrí?íi, mï?mípa* **M** *xakúkúga, bííri?i,* *níxaga, míímeba, xáákkiba, βaúra*

O *gokóóho, ť^yooro, opépeko, ïïra* **Hp** *gúku, akáiño, nopáïŋo, héro* **Hn** *gúaïkï, noɸáïŋo, héro* **Hr** *noɸaïño, herokï*

127 'bird (pájaro)' **PBM** *(xééï),* *(koomíko), (če?réï)* **B** *k^hoomík^ho,* *č^he?réï* {*species*} **M** *xóóɨ* **O** *t^yaɸonōhï̂? ãã?tsi, aɸótsoyi,* *dʸá?ii?ta* **Hp** *íguijïkoï* **Hn** *óɸokuiño,* *jámaikuiño* **Hr** *θiǰi, oɸokuiño*

128 'hummingbird (picaflor, colibrí)' **PW** ***pi(?ti)?to* **PBM** **páá(i)bi(?o),* *(róóbíǰï)* **PHO** **pi?tí?to* **B** *p^háápi?o* **M** *ɸááibe, núúbéǰɨ* **O** *ɸa?tíí?ť^yo* **Hp** *pitído* **Hn** *ɸiθído* **Hr** *ɸiθido*

129 'macaw (guacamayo)' **PW** ***xaeβa(do)* **PBM** **xíɨβaá,* **ín(a)?ai, (íírída, ééréda, íiréda)* **PHO** **(ae)(β)a(do)* **B** *íiβaá, in^ya?a* **M** *xéeβa, inó?ai, ééréda* **O** *ɸaaro* {*blue*}, *kíírama* {*red*} **Hp** *áβa* **Hn** *éɸa* **Hr** *eɸa*

130 'toucan (tucán, pinsha)' **PW** ***no(k)ai(?to)* **PBM** **nïge,* *(xíïkkïgai), *r(í)(?)oó(?o),* **b(ai)rí(gai)* **PHO** **nokái?to* **B** *nïče,* *t^hó?rok^wa, ríioó, períí?yo* **M** *nígo,* *xíïkkigai, rí?úú?u, bár^yígai* **O** *ñoxaa?čo, jíooβï* **Hp** *nokáido* **Hn** *nokáido* **Hr** *nokaido*

131 'parrot (loro)' **PW** ***tooda* **PBM** *(kíïrába), (ǰoóra), (bíi?o),* *(pi?tói), (táráboï)* **PHO** *?*(tóóda),* *(manáini), *(k)(oi)yïkï* **B** *čoóra,* *pií?yo, p^hi?t^hʸói, t^hárápoï* **M** *kíïrába,* {*many more*} **O** *káyooho, čōīɸi, eere,* *ť^yóóra, manááñi, tsãïïko* **Hp** *ui.íkï,* *úi.ï* **Hn** *ui.íkï* **Hr** *θarokï*

132 'parakeet (perico, pihuicho)' **PW** *?**()di()* **PBM** *(biriye), (tïrii?o,* *tïriï?yo, tïrii?ro), *(pi?)tói(?o)* **PHO** *?*(gai)di(ko-goï)* **B** *míïx^ye?e,* *p^hi?t^hʸói, mooá?o, t^híriï?yo, t^hárápoï*

M bíreyo, tʸúiʔu O jííyi Hp gáirikoŋo
Hn gáirikoŋo Hr gairiθï̈

133 'buzzard (gallinazo)' PW **ïno
PBM *aini̇̈, (tsókkoga) PHO *ïno()
B anʸï M áñi̇̈, súkkuga O ïïnóóčo
Hp íno Hn íno Hr ino

134 'curassow (pavo)' PW **koga
PBM (kígáʔe) PHO ?*(k)oodz(a)
M kígáʔo O xóódzoho Hp jó.oda
Hn jó.oda, hó.oda, égui, múido
Hr muidokaï

135 'owl (lechuza)' PBM (βááó),
(máróóko, márééko), (bóro, béro),
(péétsoó), (peʔtsóko), (bóbboó),
(pïpíkkoba) PHO *mõnõ()
B pʰééts^hoó, pʰeʔts^hók^ho, póxpoó,
pʰïpʰí̇̈xk^hopa M βááú, mánúúku, búru
O mõõnõhõ Hp durída Hn turída,
búru {see Muinane} Hr monuiθï̈

136 'guan (pava de monte)'
PBM *pííkaxi̇̈ B p^híík^haxi̇̈, pʰaβa
{Spanish} M φéékaxe Hp múido
Hn múido Hr muidokaï̈

137 'hen (gallina)' PW **aʔta-βa
{Quichua}, **káda-(βa) {Tucano or
Spanish} PBM *ka(ttá-βa), *ká(ra-
ka) {Tucano}, (gájeráávʔe, gáigeráávʔe),
(kettíï) PHO *áʔta-βa {Quichua},
(káda-βa) B k^hára-k^ha, k^wáčeráávʔe,
k^hext^híï M kattá-βa O átʸa-βa {up},
kára-βa {down} Hp adá-βa
Hn atá-βa Hr ata-βa

138 'fish (pescado[†])' PBM (táaβa),
(amóóbe) B amóópe M táaβa
O ïhããma Hp čámu Hn jïkï.aï, čámu
Hr jïkï.aï

139 'piranha (caribe)' PBM *(nítta),
*gáíkkoxi̇̈ PHO (ïmí-goï)
B k^wáxk^hʸoxi̇̈ M gáíkku-xe, nítta
O dʸoʔyooʔxo Hp térobeño Hn ïmíŋo
Hr ïmïño

140 'bee (abeja)' PBM (níïbïri),
(míïbïriʔï), (íímíʔóeppi), (deʔtsiba)
PHO *(do)ʔ-hidakï(goï)
B íímíʔóexp^hi, téʔts^hipa M níïbïri,
míïbïriʔï O dʸoʔíïrako Hp hiráŋo
Hn hiráŋo Hr hirakïño

141 'fly (mosca)' PW **gïnikaï
PBM (gíinixa), (ééteba), (tsïïʔéï),
(naʔba) PHO *(ïnï)kï B éét^hepa,
ts^hïïʔéï, naʔpa M gíinixa O áábeko
Hp ïnïkï Hn ïníkï Hr ïnikï

142 'flea (pulga)' PBM *xíïko-gai
PHO ??*(p)aïd(á)to B íïk^ho-k^wa,
ïïk^ho {pl} M xíïku-gai O oróóβïtʸo
Hp païrádo Hn φaïrádo Hr φaïrada,
φaïrado

143 'louse (piojo[†])' PBM *gáainiʔo,
*gai(ʔtéxi̇̈) B k^wáániʔyo, k^waʔt^hʸéxi̇̈
M gáañiʔu O oʔφóóxako Hp ïbóma
Hn ïbóma Hr ïboma

144 'mosquito (zancudo)' PBM *gaáí-xï(-
ba), *gáí-(míï-taba), (opijï)
PHO *(oi)ʔtó() B k^waá-xʸï, k^wá-mʸíí-
t^hapa M gáai-xi-ba, upijï O áʔčooko
Hp uidódo Hn uidódo Hr uidodo

145 'termite (comején, hormiga blanca)'
PBM *(míjïgí(y)ï), *máʔarï(míï-be),
(táabane), (tákíʔki-ba), (mooá-ba)
PHO (kadákï-goï), (igïdakï-goï)
B t^hák^hïʔk^hi-pa, máʔarïmíï-pe, mooá-
pa M míjïgíyi, máʔari, táabano
O ohïï, ohïxoʔ Hp karáŋo, káraï
(pl.), ígïdaŋo Hn karákïŋo, igïdakïŋo
Hr karakïño, igïdïkïño

146 'ant (hormiga)' PBM *píime(ba)
PHO (dakí-goï) B p^híímʸepa
M φíimo O amõõxo Hp rakíŋo
Hn rakíŋo Hr rakiño

147 'spider (araña)' PBM *páaga-xi̇̈,
*paagá-(yï), (xíïmóʔai), (íïkkoxi̇̈),
(doʔgá-xi̇̈) PHO (hebekï-goï)
B p^haak^wá-yï, p^háák^wa-xi̇̈, toʔk^wá-xi̇̈

M φáaga-xe, xíímúʔai, ííkkuxe O oorï
Hp hébekïŋo, jútu Hn hébekïŋo
Hr hebekïño

148 'chigger (nigua, pigue)' PBM *níipa-
xɨ PHO *odó-taï-(goï), *odó-(kaï-goï),
*(iʔo)-taï-(goï) B níipʰa-xɨ M níiφa-xe
O orootʸo Hp í.ojoŋo Hn í.ojoŋo,
órokoŋo Hr i.ojaïño

149 'bush (monte)' PBM *báxïí
PHO ?*taï-(máíʔï) B páxïí M báxɨ
O tʸaɱáá́ʔï Hp da.ɨ́-re, hatíkï
Hn táï-re, haθíkï Hr haθikï

150 'open grassland (pajonal, sabana)'
PW ?**to() PBM *(námɨttïxɨ),
*tsókkómïxɨ PHO (tohá́ʔaβo)
B tsʰóxkʰómïxɨ {161} M námettixe,
námetexe, súkkumexe {weeds}
O tʸohá́áʔaβo Hp ñú.e-no Hn ñú.e-no

151 'hill (cerro, loma)' PBM *gáxïí,
*(káme)-gáxï, *(pá)-gaxï, *báaïí,
*(pá)-ʔbaï {293} PHO *()pedï
B kʰáme-kʷáxï, kʷáxïí, páïí, pʰá-
kʷaxï, pʰá-ʔpaï M (-)báaɨ, -gáxɨ
{gorge} O tʸaβííro Hp kaipó-ne-du,
íperï Hn kaiφó-ne-du, íφerï Hr a-ne-
du, i-du

152 'tree (árbol[†])' PW ?**(aï)me()
PBM *íme-ʔe {tree-wood,60}
PHO *aména B íme-ʔe M ímo-ʔo
O aɱïïña Hp aména Hn aména
Hr amena

153 'leaf (hoja[†])' PBM *(ína)-ʔáamɨ,
(-xïíʔoó), (míímï) B ína-ʔáámɨ,
-ʔáámɨí, ína-ʔáámɨ, -xïíʔoó, míímï,
xíʔoó M áame O opaaβi Hp rábe
Hn rábe Hr rabe

154 'tree leaf (hoja de árbol)'
PBM *(ína)-ʔáamɨ B ína-ʔáámɨ, -
ʔáámɨí, ína-ʔáámɨ M áame O opaaβi
Hp rábe Hn í.ibe Hr ibe

155 'flower (flor[†])' PW ? PBM (díika),
(gakko) PHO ?*ᵗt(á́) B kʷaxkʰo
M déeka, tá-dʸeeka-no {my flowers}
O tsíí Hp tápi.a, múji.ajeba
Hn θáφi.a Hr θaφi.a

156 'fruit (fruta[†])' PBM ??*(neeβá-ba),
(ǰeéne, geéne), *(ébáxák)ím(ai)x(ɨ),
*im(áɨ)x(ï) PHO *dīā(hī) B čeéne,
imʸéxï, neéβa, neeβá-pa
M óbáxákímaxe O dʸāāhï̃, hïxāā
Hp rí.a Hn rí.a Hr ri.ara

157 'sap (savia)' PBM *ímeʔé (tíí-xeʔe),
*ímeʔé-(ppáiko) PHO *(a)m(éna) ihī
{tree-liquid,152,48,62,319} B ímeʔé-
xpʰákʰʸo {tree-liquid,152,48} ‡
M ímoʔo tíí-xoʔo {tree blood,152,33}
O ahīī, má́áhī Hp ihi {liquid},
dahéme ? Hn aména ero ihi {tree inside liquid} Hr i {liquid}, amena i
{tree liquid}, igïe

158 'root (raíz[†])' PBM *ba(i)(k)ké-
(ʔeke), *bá(i)(k)keé, (-tane)
B páxkʰʸeé M bakó-ʔoko {yajé root},
-tano O tsiñíïʔōφe, tsiñíïʔȭʔko
Hp háinao Hn háina.o Hr haina.o

159 'seed (semilla[†])' PBM *battsó-(),
(néébaba), (painéβa-ï) PHO (naiβini)
B paxtsʰó-kʷa, paxtsʰó-ï, pʰanʸéβa-ï
M basúta, nóóbaba O naβiïñi Hp íhï
Hn íhï Hr ido

160 'stick (palo)' PW **(aï)me-nai-()
PBM *íméʔe-i, *ímé-(ne-ba), (ǰári-ga)
PHO *aména {152}, *dáta, *dató()
B íméʔe-i {tree-?,152}, íméʔe-kʰo,
ímé-ne-pa M ímeeʔ-i, ǰári-ga
O dʸáátʸa, dʸatʸooφo, aɱïïña
Hp ráda, radóti Hn ráda, radóθi,
aména Hr rada, radoθi, amena

161 'grass (hierba[†])' PBM *tsókkómïxɨ,
(páíxï), (pïíβa) PHO *(dai)ʔtïhá́í(hā)
B pïíβa, tsʰóxkʰómïxɨ {150}
M súkkumexe {weeds}, φáíxɨ

O *tʸohǎá̱(hā)* Hp *ráidǐ.aï* Hn *ráitǐ.aï* Hr *raitǐkǐño*

162 'corn, maize (maíz)' PBM *(béja),* *(ïxɨ)* B *ïxɨ, {kernel}* *íxɨ-ï, {ear}* *íxɨ-ʔo, {plant}* *íxɨ-ʔe* M *béja {borr. from Huitoto?}* O *xóɸiiro* Hp *béja* Hn *béja* Hr *beja*

163 'cassava (yuca)' PBM **(xáara), (páikoómï) {sweet}, *pɨikkaá, (baaxǐri-) {bitter}* PHO **hõʔtí() {bitter, plant}, *máhï(kahï)* B *paaxǐri-, pʰɨíkʰaá {bitter}, pʰákʰʸoómï {sweet}* M *ɸéekka, xáara {sweet}* O *oxóóma(tsíira) {tuber}, hõʔtááti {bitter, plant}, maahï {broth}* Hp *húhï {tuber}, húti {plant}, ma.ika(hï) {sweet}* Hn *húhï {tuber}, húθi {plant}, má.ika(hï) {sweet}* Hr *huhï {tuber}, huθi.e {plant}, ma.ika {sweet}*

164 'cassava flour (harina de yuca)' PBM **íttáko-gíïxï, *(máčo)-gíïxï* B *ɨxɨʰʸákʰo-číxʸï {cassava-powder}* M *íttáku, máču-giixɨ {eat-powder, 275,372}* Hp *haïjí-čoma {cassava-powder,372}* Hn *haïjí-čoma* Hr *kore*

165 'tobacco (tabaco)' PBM **baine* PHO **tïʔó()* B *panʸe* M *báño {pl.}* O *tʸoʔooko* Hp *dï.ó-na* Hn *dï.ó-na, jéra* Hr *dï.o-na*

166 'cotton (algodón)' PW ***xáʔi()* PBM **xáʔadi* PHO *(háʔikï)* B *aʔti* M *xáʔadi* O *ɸíãã, ɸíãã̱ha* Hp *há.ikï-na* Hn *há.ikï.e* Hr *haikï.e*

167 'gourd (calabazo poro)' PBM *(xáʔaxɨ), *dóoto-* B *tóótʰo, tóótʰo-ï* M *xááxe, xáʔaxe, dúutuʔu* Hp *hujéko* Hn *emókï, hujéko, jeθé-gï* Hr *emokï*

168 'yam (ñame)' PBM **kɨni(romi), *kɨnɨí-(ï)* PHO **(h)aʔkáíʔ-ti(dai)* B *kʰïni, kʰïnɨí-ï* M *kɨni-rumi* O *aʔxaaʔti* Hp *hakái-kï {plant},*

hakái-hï {tuber} Hn *hakái-θairai {plant}, hakái-hï {tuber}* Hr *hakai-hï*

169 'sweet potato (camote, batata)' PBM *(jíróómïba), (káátïï)* B *kʰáátʰïï* M *jínúúmɨba* O *bo𝑡ʸooɽʸo* Hp *repí-hï* Hn *reɸí-hï* Hr *reɸi-hï*

170 'annatto (achiote, bija)' PW ***naï()* PBM **néebaba* PHO **nonó̱()* B *néépapa* M *nóobaba* O *ñoñóóya* Hp *nonó-kï* Hn *nonó-kï* Hr *nono-kï*

171 'chili pepper (ají)' PBM **díí-ʔoï {fruit}* PHO **hiʔpíʔ-hï(βe) {fruit}, *hiʔpí-dai {plant}* B *tíí, tíí-ʔoï {fruit}* M *déé-ʔuɨ {fruit}, déé-giixɨ {chili-powder,372}, déé-xeʔe {plant}* O *haʔɸíí-ʔoβï {fruit}, haʔɸíí-ja {plant}* Hp *hípi-hï* Hn *hiɸi-hï {fruit}, hiɸi-rai {plant}* Hr *hiɸi-hï {fruit}, hiɸi-rai {plant}*

172 'coca (coca)' PW ***xíibí-ʔe* PBM **xíibií-(ʔe)* PHO **híibí(ʔe)* B *íípii* M *xíibi-(ʔo)* O *hiibiro* Hp *hibí.e* Hn *hí.ibi.e* Hr *hi.ibe*

173 'Banisterium (ayahuasca, yajé)' PBM **bá(k)ke(tamï), *(né)ba(k)ke* PHO **õnãʔõ* B *népaxkʰe* M *bákotamɨ* O *õnãã̱ʔõ* Hp *úna.o* Hn *úna.o* Hr *una.o*

174 'plantain (plátano)' PBM **íxɨ-()* PHO *(hikado)* B *ïxɨ, íxɨʔo* M *íxe-(ba)* O *hïxaaro* Hp *ó.ogodo* Hn *ó.ogodo* Hr *o.ogodo*

175 'chonta palm (chonta)' PBM **meéme, *meéme-(ʔegííʔo), *meéme-(ʔejííʔyo)* PHO *(haimina)* B *meéme, méémé-ʔečííʔyo {fruit}* M *móomo* O *hamiiña* Hp *né.egoï* Hn *óɸego-jï* Hr *oɸego-jï*

178 'cane (caña brava)' PBM *(bóiga), (néépáíxɨ-xɨ)* PHO **(po)kanïʔ-ta* B *néépʰáxʸï-xɨ* M *búi-ga*

O φookaníïʔtʸa Hp kaní-da {95}
Hn kaní-kaï Hr θïkï-kaï

179 'salt (salᵗ)' PW **(ï)xaidzaï(ga)
PBM (ïmoʔo), (áit(t)ega),
(kánáámaá), (kánaáma)
PHO *(ï)háidzaï B kʰánáámaá,
kʰánaáma M ímuʔu, áttʸoga {rock}
O hááidʸa Hp í.aitaï Hn ḯ.aiθaï
{rock} Hr ï̈.aiθaï

180 'chicha (chicha, masato)'
PW **(báa)xïdi(ba) PBM *méemeba,
(báaxíribá) PHO (-hïdi), (haïgábï)
B páaxíripáⁱ, méémepa {of pijuayo}
M móomoba {of chontaduro}
O hamííhorï {of pihuayo},
dʸaʔsóóhorï {of pineapple}, xoφííyahï
{of corn} Hp haïgá-bï Hn haïgá-bï
Hr haïga-bï

181 'one (unoᵗ)' PW **ta()
PBM *tsaane PHO *ta(he) B tsʰa-ne
M sáano O tʸa-, -maʔ Hp da Hn da,
dá.a Hr dahe, da.e

182 'two (dosᵗ)' PW **menai()
PBM *míínéékkïï̈ PHO (mena),
(hana) B mínʸéékʰïï̈ M míínokki
O hanaa-(maʔ) Hp ména Hn ména
Hr mena

183 'three (tresᵗ)' PW ?**()m(e)n(ai)()
ta() PBM (míínéékkïï̈ tsaane) {two
one}, (pápiʔtsíï̈, pápiʔčíï̈)
PHO *(amani) tá(he) B pʰápʰiʔčʰïï̈
M míínokkí sáano {two one}
O hanáá-maʔ-tʸáá-maʔ {two-one}
Hp da.áma-ni {one brotherless}
Hn da.áma-ni Hr da(h)e ama-ni

184 'four (cuatroᵗ)' PBM (igíínimiʔixí,
igéénemeʔexí, igíínimiʔixé),
(píinee-ʔóttsí) B pʰíinee-ʔóxtsʰí
{?-hand} M míínokkí míínokki {182},
igéénemeʔexé O nahïʔxanó
Hp pïgo-ména-ri.e {well-two-pl.}
Hn φïgo-ména-ri.e-(de) {well-two-pl.},
naga áma-de {each brother}, naga

áma-ri.e Hr naga ama-ga {each
brother}

185 'five (cincoᵗ)' PW **ta-()
PBM *tsá-ʔottsí {one-hand}
PHO *ta-()oido {one-?} B tsʰá-
ʔoxtsʰí M sa-ʔúse O tʸaʔ-φïï̈φoroʔ
{one-hand?} Hp hu-bé-ba Hn hu-bé-
kuiro, hu-bé-ba Hr da-be-kuiro
{one-limb}

186 'six (seis)' PW **ene() () ta()
PBM *(inekkïé)-ʔottsí . . . ,
*(í)-ʔottsí-tḯ tsaane PHO *ené(da)
péti (tahe) B inʸexkʰïé-ʔoxtsʰí . . . ⁱ,
í-ʔyoxtsʰí-tʰí tsʰa-ne M sa-ʔúse
xúúga-ʔuse-ti sááno {one-hand other?-
hand-? one} O añííra φáti {other
side} Hp ené-pebamo dá
Hn ené-φeθimo da Hr ene-φebehimo
dahe {other-hand? one}

187 'seven (siete)' PW **ene() () menai
PBM *(inekkïé)-ʔottsí . . . ,
*(í)-ʔottsí-tḯ míínéékkïï̈ PHO *ené(da)
peti (mena) B inʸexkʰïé-ʔoxtsʰí . . . ⁱ,
í-ʔyoxtsʰí-tʰí mínʸéékʰïï̈ M sa-ʔúse
xúúga-ʔuse-ti míínokki O añííra φati
hanááma? {other side two}
Hp ené-pebamo ména Hn ené-φeθimo
ména Hr ene-φebehimo mena {other-
hand two}

188 'eight (ocho)' PW **ene() ()
menai() ta() PBM *(inekkïé)-ʔottsí . . . ,
*(í)-ʔottsí-tï (míínéékkïï̈ tsaane)
PHO *ené(da) peti (tahe amani)
B inʸexkʰïé-ʔoxtsʰí . . . ⁱ, í-ʔyoxtsʰí-tʰí
pʰápʰiʔčʰïï̈ M sa-ʔúse xúúga-ʔuse-ti
míínokkí sáano O añííra φati
atʸora-biñïʔ {other side middle-finger}
Hp ené-pebamo da.ámani
Hn ené-φeθimo da ámani
Hr ene-φebehimo dahe amani

189 'nine (nueve)' PW ?**ene() ()
PBM *(inekkïé)-ʔottsí . . . ,
*(í)-ʔottsí-tï () PHO *ené(da) peti ()
B inʸexkʰïé-ʔoxtsʰí . . . ⁱ, í-ʔyoxtsʰí-tʰí

pʰíínee-ʔóxtsʰí M sa-ʔúse xúúga-ʔuse-
tɨ igééneme?exé O añííra ɸati
nahíʔxanó {other side four}
Hp enépebamo pïgoménari.e
Hn enéɸeθimo ɸígo amari.e
Hr eneɸebehimo naga amaga

190 'ten (diez)' PBM *pa-ʔottsɨɨ-kkï-
(neβa) {both?-hand-?}
PHO *(ha)na?g(á)-péti B pʰa-ʔóxtsʰí-
kʰí-neβa M ɸa-ʔúsee-kkɨ O hanã?
ɸáti {two sides}, hanaa-ʔɸïɸóro? {two-
hand?} Hp nagá-peba {both-sides}
Hn nagá-ɸeθi {both-sides}
Hr naga-ɸebekuiro {both-hand}

191 'first (primero)' PBM *(it)tï(k)kénï,
(ímígare), (tsáʔííxíttïre) PHO *na()
B tʰïxkʰénï M íttɨkonɨ, ímégaro,
sáʔííxíttɨro O na?a Hp náno
Hn náno ɸu.eri Hr nano

192 'last (último)' PBM *nii?née-né(-re),
(ájïba-) PHO *(i)tái-poe-dzã(no)
B ni?nʸé-re, ni?nʸée-né-re M níínoono,
ájïba-ri, -tɨ, -anɨno O tʸáɸoïïdzanó
Hp idái-pu.e-na, írai-pu.e-na
Hn íraï-ɸu.e-na Hr iraï.e

193 'rattle (sonajero, maraca)'
PBM (xáá-ko), (gáadai), (čeʔkéï)
B čʰeʔkʰéï M xáá-ku, gáadai
O tõõʔɸï Hp kaβáje, hó.ohi
Hn ɸiríθai Hr ɸiriθai

194 'drum (tambor)' PBM *kíímï-ba
PHO (hó.aïʔ-tido) B kʰíímïpa
M kíímɨ-ba Hp hú.aï-dïru Hn hú.aï
Hr hu.aï

195 'cushma (cushma)'

196 'ear ornament {7} (orejera, arete)'
PBM *níxíi-ga(-ko) PHO ?*ko(má?-
tï)-kï B níxíi-ï, níxíi-kʷa, níxíi-pa
M níxɨ-ga-ku O xoñõõ-tʸaβóko
Hp kumá-dï-kï Hn héɸo í-hï
Hr heɸo itïkï

197 'mask (máscara)'
PBM *máá?nii(ʔïmo)
PHO *(p)õïʔéko(da) B má?nii ‡
M maaníʔime O ɸõʔííxora, orííʔka
Hp híga-pe Hn híga-ɸe Hr u.i.eko iko

198 'medicine man (curandero)' PW ?
PBM (jííβáábeé), (táábómïnaaɸi)
PHO *-dáïma {compare 47}
B čííβáápeé M táábúmɨnaaɸi
O híʔxaɸoráááma Hp manó-ri-raïma
Hn áima, híído-raïma Hr aima

199 'chief (cacique, curaca, capitán)'
PBM *aiβéxíí-be PHO *(iʔt)iʔtáï-ma
B aβʸéxíí-pe M aíβoxíí-bo
O aʔtiʔtʸó-ma, ɸaráá?ɸï-ma
Hp ijáï-ma Hn ijáï-ma Hr ijaï-ma

200 'I (yo†)' PW **(k)õõ-xe(ʔe)
PBM *oó(-xéʔe) PHO *kõē B oó
M úú-xó?o O xõ, xõï Hp kúe Hn kúe
Hr kue, ku.e

201 'thou (tú†)' PW **õ-xe(ʔe)
PBM *ïï(-xéʔe) PHO *õ(ē) B ïï
M íí-xó?o O õ, õï, o Hp o Hn o Hr o

202 'he (él†)' PW **i-(b)ai PBM *díí-
be, (aáí-be), (aá-be), (áá-níí), (aá-di)
{204}, *á(x)áa-nï PHO *i-ma,
*(i?)i-ma, *(apé)-ma, (ïhã) B áá-níí,
aá-pʸe, aá-pe, aá-ti, tíí-pʸe M díí-bo,
áxáa-nɨ O aʔii-ma, ïï-ma, ïïhã,
ha(?)- Hp apé-ma, da Hn aɸé-mï.e
Hr imï.e

203 'she (ella)' PW **i-gaï {40}
PBM *díí-ge, *(aáí-)ge, *(ááí)-meé,
*(áxáa)-me PHO *i-goï {202}, *(i?)i-
goï, *(mai)nai-goï, *(apé)-goï {202},
(ïhã) B áá-mʸeé, aá-če, tíí-če M díí-
go, áxáa-mo O aʔiiko, ïïko, ïïhã, ña,
ha-, ha?- Hp apéŋo Hn aɸéŋo
Hr iñaiño, maiñaiño

204 'it (ello)' PW ?**i-() PBM (aáí-be)
{202,203,257}, (xáá-ne) PHO (i-e),

*tāgē B aá-pʸe M xáá-no O tʸã(hḭ̃),
ᵛʸa Hp dáge Hn í.e Hr i.e

205 'we (nosotros†)' PW (?) {pl}, (?)
{m.d.}, (?) {f.d.} PBM *mḭ́ḭ̃ʔ-ai {pl},
*mḭ̃ʔ-tsi {m.d.}, *mḭ̃ʔ-pḭ {f.d.}
PHO *kaï-hï {pl}, *ko-koï {m.d.},
*kaï-gaï {f.d.} B mḭ́ḭ̃ʔ-a {pl excl}, mḭ̃ʔ-
tsʰi {m.d.}, mḭ̃ʔ-pʰḭ {f.d.} M mḭ́ḭ-ʔai
{pl}, mḭ́-si {m.d.}, mḭ́-ɸe {f.d.}
O xa(ho) {pl}, xo(xo) {m.d.}, xak(a)
{f.d.} Hp kaï {pl}, kóko {m.d}
Hn kaï {pl}, kóko {m.d.}, káïŋaï
{f.d} Hr kaï {pl}, koko {m.d.},
kaiñaï {f.d.}

206 'ye {212,218} (vosotros†)'
PW **aïmãḭ́ḭ̃ʔ-() {pl}, **aïmãḭ̃ʔ-()
{m.d.}, **aïmãḭ̃ʔ-() {f.d.}
PBM *ámḭ́ḭ̃ʔ-ai, *ámḭ̃ḭ̃ʔ-tsi {m.d.},
*ámḭ̃ḭ̃ʔ-pḭ {f.d.} PHO *(o)mãḭ̃ʔ-(to)
{pl}, *(o)mãḭ̃ʔ-koï {m.d.}, *(o)mãḭ̃ʔ-
gaï {f.d.} B ámḭ́ḭ̃ʔ-a {pl}, ámḭ̃ʔ-tsʰi
{m.d.}, ámḭ̃ʔ-pʰḭ {f.d.} M amḭ́ḭ-ʔai
{pl}, amḭ́ḭ-si {m.d.}, amḭ́ḭ-ɸe {f.d.}
O mõ(ʔto) {pl}, mõʔ(xo) {m.d.},
mõʔk(a) {f.d.} Hp ómaï {pl},
ómaï-ko {m.d.} Hn ómoï {pl},
ómï-koï {m.d.}, ómï-ŋo {f.d.}
Hr omoï {pl}, omï-ko {m.d.},
omï-ñoï {f.d.}

207 'they (ellos†)' PW () {pl}, ()
{m.d.}, () {f.d.} PBM *díi-te, *(aáí)-
te {pl}, *dii-t(é)-tsi {m.d.}, *dii-t(é)-pḭ
{f.d.} PHO *i-() {pl}, *i(aï)-maï-haï
{m.d.}, *i(aï)-gaï-haï {f.d.} B aá-tʰʸe,
tii-tʰʸe {pl}, aatʰʸé-tsʰi, tiitʰʸé-tsʰi
{m.d.}, aatʰʸé-pʰḭ, tiitʰʸé-pʰḭ {f.d.}
M díi-to {pl}, díítḭ-si {m.d.}, díítḭ-ɸe
{f.d.} O ḭ̃ï-sa, áá {pl}, ḭ̃ï-má(ha)
{m.d.}, ḭ̃ï-ká(ha) {f.d.} Hp apé-makï
{pl}, apé-maï-jïnoï {m.d.}, dáï-jïnoï
{m.d.}, ? {f.d.} Hn aɸé-makï {pl},
í.ai-jïnoï {m.d.}, í.aï-ŋu.aï {f.d.}
Hr i-makï {pl}, i.aï-ma.i.aï {m.d.},
i.aï-ñu.aï {f.d.}

208 'my hand {22} (mi mano)'
PBM *táí-ʔóttsḭ {214} PHO *k(oe)
onõḭ̃ {Uncertain prefix} B tʰá-ʔóxtsʰḭ
M tá-ʔuse O k-onõõ Hp kue ónoï
Hn kú.e ónoï Hr ku.e ono-jï

209 'thy hand (tu mano)' PBM *díí-
ʔóttsḭ PHO (o) onõḭ̃ B tí-ʔyóxtsʰḭ
M díí-ʔuse O ónõõ {high tone on first
syllable} Hp oʔónoï Hn o ónoï
Hr o ono-jï

210 'his hand (su mano)' PBM *(díí)-be-
ʔóttsḭ, *(aáí)-be-ʔóttsḭ, *(áái-di)-ʔottsḭ
PHO *ta onõḭ̃ B aápʸe-ʔóxtsʰḭ, ááti-
ʔoxtsʰḭ‡ M díí-bo-ʔuse O tʸáʔonõõ
Hp apéma ónoï, da ónoï Hn aɸémï.e
ónoï Hr naimï.e ono-jï

211 'our hands (nuestras manos)'
PBM *mé-ʔóttsḭ-ne PHO *kaï onõḭ̃
B mé-ʔóxtsʰḭ-ne ‡ M mú-ʔuse-ne,
{mo- + úse + -no} O xa-ʔonõõ
Hp kaï óno-ge Hn kaï ónoï Hr kaï
ono-jï

212 'your hands {206} (vuestras
manos)' PW **aïmãḭ̃ʔ-() () {206}
PBM *amḭ́ḭ̃ʔ-áí-ʔóttsḭ-ne
PHO *(o)mãḭ̃ʔ-(to) onõḭ̃ B amḭ̃ʔá-
ʔóxtsʰḭ-ne‡ M amḭ́ḭ-ʔai-ʔuse-ne
O mõ-ʔonõõ Hp dáïgo óno-ge
Hn ómoï ónoï Hr omoï ono-jï

213 'their hands (sus manos de ellos)'
PBM *díí-te-ʔóttsḭ-ne, *(aáí)-te-ʔóttsḭ-
ne B aátʰʸe-ʔóxtsʰḭ-ne‡,
tíí-tʰʸe-ʔóxtsʰḭ-ne M díí-to-ʔuse-ne
O háá-ʔonõõ Hp apémakï óno-ge
Hn aɸémakï ónoï Hr na.imakï ono-jï

214 'my bow {94} (mi arco)'
PW **()-tï() PBM *táí-tḭ́ḭ̃bo-ga
PHO ?*k(oe)-tï() B tʰá-tʰʸḭ́poo-kʷa‡
M ta-tʸḭ́ḭbu-ga O ki-tsipóxatʸa {vowel
copying} Hp kue tïkúiña Hn kú.e
θïkúiraï Hr ku.e θïkuirakuiɸo

215 'thy bow (tu arco)' **PHO** *(o) tï()
M di-tííbu-ga **O** tsípóxatᵞa {high tone
on first syllable} **Hp** ó tïkúiña **Hn** ó
θïkúiraï **Hr** o θïkuirakuiφo

216 'his bow (su arco de él)' **M** dííbo
tííbu-ga **Hp** apéma tïkúiña, da
tïkúiña **Hn** aφémï.e θïkuiraï
Hr naimï.e θïkuirakuiφo

217 'our bow (nuestro arco)' **M** mo-
tííbu-ga **Hp** kaï tïkúiña **Hn** kaï
θïkuiraï **Hr** kaï θïkuirakuiφo

218 'your bow {206} (vuestro arco)'
M amíí?ai tííbu-ga **Hp** ómaï tïkúiña
Hn ómoï θïkuiraï **Hr** omoï
θïkuirakuiφo

219 'their bow (su arco de ellos)'
M dííto tííbu-ga **Hp** apémakï tïkúiña
Hn aφémakï θïkuiraï **Hr** na.imakï
θïkuirakuiφo

220 'big {262} (grande†)' **PBM** *mita-
ne, *giraa-ne, *kee-(pi)-ne, (bókkï-ne),
(...) **B** mitʰʸa-ne, mitʰʸa-, čiya-,
kʰemï- **M** mítʸa-no, gíráa-no, kééφi-
no, bókkï-no, kóyi-no, tᵞígaba **O** óóxï,
oxííha **Hp** áiju.e **Hn** áiju.e **Hr** aiju.e

221 'small {308} (pequeño†)'
PW ?**()ki() **PBM** *nomɨ-(nɨ-nɨ),
(áxáitso-ne-gayï), (áyá-né-gayï, áirá-né-
gayï), (ïʔxéné-gayï), (čoʔxï), (ïígíyiï)
PHO (kiβi-) **B** nᵞomɨ, aya, áyá-né-
kʷï, ïʔxéné-kʷï, čʰoʔxï, ïíkíyiï
M núméné-ne, áxášu-no, áxášu-no-gayɨ
O síítiʔ, sóógo, tóógo, xaβi-
{46,308,327} **Hp** hí.ï-re-de **Hn** dú.e-re-
de, hí.ï-re-de **Hr** hano-re-de

222 'cold (frío†)' **PBM** *tsïíko,
(dáíʔkoó) **PHO** *doti(-de-te)
B tsʰïíkʰo, táíʔkʰoó **M** sííku **O** dᵞótï
Hp ročí-re-de **Hn** roθí-re-de
Hr roθi-re-de

223 'hot (caliente†)' **PBM** *áígookkó-né,
(péémeβako-ne), (gánókóó-ne),
gánékóó-ne) **B** ačóókʰó, áčookʰó-né
M áígúkku-no, φóómoβaku-no
{warm}, gánúkúú-no {very} **O** dᵞóʔo
Hp utí-re-de **Hn** uθí-re-de **Hr** uθi-re-de

224 'good (bueno†)' **PW** ?**(e)meá(d)e
PBM *imí-ne, *imí-(gayï), *(ímɨáá)-
ne **PHO** (made) **B** imí-kʷï, ímɨáá-ne,
ímɨáá-pé **M** ími-(no) **O** φóhï̈
Hp ñú.era **Hn** ñú.era **Hr** mare

225 'bad (malo†)' **PBM** *ími-tí-ne **B** ími-
tʰʸí-ne, ími-tʰʸíí-pekʰe **M** ími-ti-no
O íïra **Hp** pu.éni-de **Hn** φï.éni-de
Hr maraiñe-de

226 'white (blanco†)' **PW** ?**(o)te(te)
PBM *tsítsɨɨ-ne **PHO** (ote-de-te)
B tsʰïtsʰïï-ne, tsʰïtsʰï **M** séséé-ne
O φïrááña **Hp** úte-re-de **Hn** úθe-re-de
Hr uθe-re-de

227 'black {328} (negro†)'
PW ?**(xi)ʔtï-() **PBM** *kíβe-ne,
(báttïne) **PHO** *hïʔtï?-() **B** kʰïíβe-ne,
kʰïíβé-mekʰe, páxtʰïne **M** kíβo-no
O hïʔtóóʔ-φï **Hp** hídï-re-de **Hn** hítï-re-
de **Hr** hitï-re-de

228 'go! (vaya, ve)' **PBM** *dí-pe
PHO *hái **B** tí-pʰʸe **M** di-φó **O** hááï
{high tone on first syllable} **Hp** mai
hái **Hn** mai hai **Hr** mai hai

229 'come! {286} (ven!)' **PBM** *dí-tsaa
PHO (ba? áihi) **B** tí-čʰa **M** di-sáá
O ba? ááhi {here come} {high tone
on first syllable} **Hp** mái bi **Hn** bi
Hr bi

230 'eat! {275} (come!)' **PBM** *maččoa
PHO *óko **B** maxčʰoó‡ **M** maččú
O óóxo {high tone on first syllable}
Hp óko **Hn** gú.i **Hr** guiño

231 'drink! {274} (bebe!)' **PW** **xidoo
PBM *d-ádoó **PHO** (hido) **B** t-átoó‡

M *d-adú* **O** *ñóóxo* {*high tone on first syllable*} **Hp** *híro* **Hn** *híro* **Hr** *hiro*

232 'sleep! {280} (duerme!)'
PBM *kígá* **PHO** *(í)nɨ̈* **B** *kʰïkʷááᵗ* **M** *kɨgá* **O** *ïïnõ* {*high tone on first syllable*} **Hp** *mai ínï* **Hn** *ínï* **Hr** *ïnï*

233 'crown of head (corona)'
PBM *?*m(é)?n(ɨ)-(kkaï̈), (čá?íímïgai)*
PHO *?*()oito* **B** *mé?nɨ̈-xkʰaïᵗ* **M** *míni-?ai, čá?íímigai* **O** *dʸoβáá?iⁱ̯a, kõčo* **Hp** *ípo harápo* **Hn** *haráɸo, íɸo iθéda, íɸo íɸo* **Hr** *ïɸogï muido*

234 'front teeth, incisors (dientes delanteros incisivos)'
PBM **(pɨ̈neéné) *(mé)-íí?gai-neé, (di-xéxé-ba) íí?gai-neé* **B** *pʰɨ̈neéné mé-?kʷa-nʸeé* {*see 4*}ᵗ **M** *di-xéxé-ba íí-ga-ño* **O** *matoobi* **Hp** *ha.ïkï̈.e* **Hn** *ha.ïkï̈.e* **Hr** *ato iku.aï, ato idu.aï*

235 'tip of tongue {1} (punta de la lengua)' **PW** *?**()pe (ï)kaï*
PBM **(mé)-?níxɨ-(gá)-nɨx(ɨ)k(áï)* **PHO** *(ïyï̈?pe ïkoï) {1}* **B** *mé-?níxɨ-kʷá-nɨxkʰáïᵗ* **M** *néxe-ba-nixeke* **Hp** *i.ípe íkoï* **Hn** *i.íɸe íkoï* **Hr** *i.ïɸe muido*

236 'long hair (pelo largo)'
PBM **(mííbaigi), *níiga()* **PHO** *(ïpó?-tï.i)* **B** *níikʷa-kʰo* **M** *méébaigi, nígai-xeene* **Hp** *ïpó-dï.i* **Hn** *ïɸó-tï.i*

237 'around the neck (toda la garganta y cuello)' **PW** *?* **PBM** *(kédáá?ɨ), (mé-kkeépaáxɨ)* **B** *mé-xkʰeépʰaáxɨᵗ* **M** *kódáá?e* **Hp** *kïmó-kairo* **Hn** *kïmó-kairo* **Hr** *kïmaïgo(ï)*

238 'Adam's apple (nuez de la garganta)' **PBM** *(íkke matsïï), (mé-mé?dóró)* **B** *mé-mé?tóróᵗ* **M** *íkko masí-yɨ* {*cord sing-round*} **O** *kãá**áxo* **Hp** *úri-ra-goï* **Hn** *aïguéjï* **Hr** *u.u-ra-kohï, ñaï-ra-kohï*

239 'upper back (espalda, parte superior)' **PBM** *(mará?ba), (má?ajï,*

má-?aigï), (yéebai) **B** *mará?pa, má-?ačï* **M** *yóobai* **O** *hïï?xo, hïï?xomó* **Hp** *emódo* **Hn** *emódo* **Hr** *emodo*

240 'lower arm (antebrazo)'
PW *??**(o)nãï̈?k()* **PBM** **(mé)-nékkí-(gatsítto) {20}* **PHO** **onõï̈-(kona) {19,22,23,241}* **B** *(mé)-néxï̈-kʷatsʰɨ̈xⁱ̯ᵒ* **M** *nókki* **O** *onṍ-kona* **Hp** *onó-paiko* **Hn** *onó-ɸaiko* **Hr** *ono-ɸai*

241 'wrist (muñeca)' **PBM** **(mé)-?ótsi-(k)kéxɨ, (tsɨ̈imé íïkï̈)* **PHO** **onõï̈-()* {*19,22,23,240*} **B** *(mé)-?ótsʰïxkʰéxɨ, tsʰɨ̈imé íïkʰï̈* **M** *úse-kexe* **O** *onṍ-poka* **Hp** *onó-bekï̈* **Hn** *onói-koiño* **Hr** *ono-jïkï*

242 'lower leg (la pierna inferior)'
PW ***(ï)ta() {25}* **PBM** **(mé)-tákki-(ï), (xóonoga, xéenoga)* **PHO** *(ïtá-toï)* **B** *(mé)-tʰáxkʰii {25}* **M** *tákkiyɨ* {*ankle*}, *xúunuga {28}* **Hp** *ïdá-jï̈* **Hn** *ïdá-joï* **Hr** *ïda-jo*

243 'body hair {10} (el pelo del cuerpo)' **PBM** **í?xɨ̈-ne {270}* **PHO** *(tapáíhï)* **B** *í?xɨ-ne* **M** *íxée-ne* **O** *tʸaɸáá**hï* {*of arm*} **Hp** *háinaï, áimaï* **Hn** *ábï itïraï* **Hr** *itïraï {10}*

244 'stomach {14,16,245,272} (estómago)' **PW** ***xe?bae-(g)aï, *xebae {14}* **PBM** **(mé)-íí?bá(ï) {272,245}, (xɨ̈bïï), *(mé-ke)-máččo-(ï), *maččo-(xota)* **PHO** **(he)bae-goï() {Ocaina 14}* **B** *í?páï, mé-?páï̈, mé-kʰe-máxčʰo-ï* **M** *íiba, maččxu-xuta {eat-?, 275}, xéebɨ̈* **O** *gáxoⁱ̯a* **Hp** *hébe-goï* **Hn** *hébe-goï, hébe-gï* **Hr** *hebe-gï*

245 'intestines {14,16,244,272} (intestinos†)' **PW** ***xe?bae-()*
PBM **(mé)-íí?bá(ï)* **PHO** *(hebae-o) {Ocaina 14}, (ma+níkï)* **B** *i?paï̈, mé?páï̈* **M** *íiba, íiba-no {pl}* **O** *mañíïko {intestin}* **Hp** *hébe.o* **Hn** *hébe.o* **Hr** *hebe.o, hebe-go*

246 'old woman (viejita)' PW *?**-gaï*
{40} PBM (ámia-tsa), *kééme-ge
{47,347} PHO *heʔí(do)-goï {47}
B kʰéémeče M ámiya-sa, kóómo-go
{old aunt} O haʔīï-ko Hp e.íro-gï
Hn e.íro-gï, e.írï-ŋo Hr u.aikï-ño,
uθuθairo, u.aïkïθairo

247 'clouds at rest {59} (nubes
quietasᵗ)' PW **xi(moo)ʔ-piʔo
PBM (áimóó-ppai(ʔ)o), (βaaímeitíne
ottso) {59,248,309} PHO (hiʔpíʔo)
B βaaímeitʰyíne oxtsʰoⁱ M áimúú-
φai(ʔu) {cloud-liquid/gas,48,59,309}
O haʔφííʔo, haʔφiʔoyíina, tsohóʔïʔxa
{cloud: borr. fr. Bora?} Hp úijï.e
Hn úijï.e Hr uijï.e

248 'storm clouds (nubes de tormenta)'
PBM (ïgene, ïjene ottso) {59,247,309},
(níxa aímóó-ppai) B ïčene oxtsʰoⁱ
M níxa aímúú-φai Hp pïdítiraï
Hn náïri.e Hr naïri.e

249 'corn field {83} (chagra)'
PBM *gáíkkoʔai, (pági), (ímiʔe) {83}
B kʷáxkʰyoʔa, ímiʔe M gáíkkuʔai
{burned off} {83}, φági {planted}
O hōʔtáắhī {83,163} Hp bejá-re
Hn bejá-re Hr beja-re

250 'stream {49} (quebrada)'
PW **tae(ʔi)-(-) PBM *tée-ʔi-(gayï)
{river-line-small,49,71}, *téé-(gai-ʔo),
(pákaáxa) PHO *(i)tae-() {49}
B tʰééʔi-kʷï, pʰákʰaáxa M tée-ʔi, téé-
gai-ʔu O tʸaβáága, ñōhïtsahííʔto,
ñōhïïʔxaнomó Hp íʃe Hn ijé-tu.e
Hr ije-kuera

251 'pebbles (piedrecillas, guijas)'
PBM *(xíí)-négaiyï-ʔáí, *négaiyí(-
gïíné) {73,74,252}, (giítsiï)
B nékʷayíí-ʔá, nékʷayí-kʷïíné̃ⁱ M xíí-
ниgaiyi-ʔai {sand?}, giísiyi Hp títi-hï,
guamá-hï Hn θíti-hï {pebble},
guamá-hï

252 'huge rocks (rocas)' PBM (negáíyí-
kobane) {73,74,251}, (giitsi-gaxï) {73}
B neekʷáyï-kʰopa-ne M giisi-gaxi
Hp nopí-kï {rock,73}, nopí-raï
Hn noφí-kï, iφí.e, noφí-raï Hr noφï-
kï, noφï-ko

253 'path {85} (trocha)' PW **(na)xī́()
PBM *xīí-() PHO *nahī́(to) B xīíβa
M xííʔai O naahō, tóβïʔtʸa Hp í.o,
díro-pe Hn í.o Hr na.ïθo

254 'venetian blinds (persianas)'
PBM (íʔbota) B íʔpotʰa M ? Hn bíí.i-
ra-nigï {79}

255 'shelter {75} (tambo)' PW ?**()po-
(ga), **xopo-(ga) {see 75}
PBM *nííxï-ga, *(iixó)-ga
PHO *(ho)po-() {75} B nííxï-kʷa
{house?-small?,250}, iixʸó-kʷa M níixe-
ga O φohóóβonï Hp hípo-ko
Hn hoφó-ka.iφe Hr bíθaini

256 'this (este)' PBM *xineé, *xi(xi),
(áánīí), (ááímeé), (eéne) PHO *bí-
hāē, *bi-ʔe B ínʸeé, áánīí, áámʸeé,
eéne M xíno, xííxe O bīí, bíhã, baʔi-,
bï- {m. sing., f. sing., m. pl., f. pl.},
báʔiiнa Hp bedá Hn bí.e Hr bi.e

257 'that (aquel)' PW **kiʔi-()
PBM *xe(ʔ)é-ne, (teé-), (diíbe) {204},
(áánīí) PHO (kiʔima) B (tʰ)-eé-ne,
(tʰ)-eé-xa, (tʰ)-eé-kʷa, tiípʸe, áánīí
M xóʔono O xaʔiiнa Hp badá
Hn bai.e Hr bai.e

258 'who (quien)' PW ?ʔ**(b)ō()
PBM ?*ka(aitéʔa)-xaa-, *mí-(ʔa)-xa
PHO *bố B míʔa, míʔa-xa,
kʰaatʰyéʔa, kʰaatʰyéʔa-xa M ká-xáá-
ni {m}, ká-xáá-mo {f}, míxí O bố
Hp bu Hn bu Hr bu

259 'what (que)' PBM (xínixi), (ïïná)
PHO *dzīí? B ïïná M xínéxe O dzoʔ
Hp nï-póde Hn mïníka Hr bu.e

260 'not (no)' PW **(ta)ʔáí-ne
PBM *(-tï), *tsáʔaá-(ne) PHO *-ne,
*(āī)-ne, (dama iʔte) B tsʰáʔaá
M čá(ʔano), -tɨ O -ñi, -ñi, āá, āāñi
Hp -ñe, damíďe Hn -ñe, dama ite
{only give} Hr -ñe, dama ite {only
give}

261 'all (todos)' PBM ((p)airïī-kï-ne),
*pamere, *pa-nee-(re) PHO (háíti?)
B pʰáneére, pʰámeére M ɸámóro {all
people}, ɸáá-no, párʸɨɨ-(kɨ-no) {every-
thing} {342} O číí, číɓa, háti?
Hp nána Hn nána Hr nana

262 'many {220} (muchos)' PBM *mita-
(ne), (gíráá-me), (tsiíti), (iʔnáʔo)
B mitʰʸane, iʔnáʔo M mitʸáá-bo
{powerful}, gíráá-mo, siíti O óóxï
Hp áijo Hn áijo (rá.a) Hr aiju.ena

263 'long (largo)' PBM *kááme(-ɓe)-ne
PHO *á(d)e B kʰááme-ne M káámo-
ɓo-no O ááñi Hp áre Hn áre Hr are

264 'bark (corteza)' PBM *(koo)-mííʔo,
(íméʔé) *(ʔajĩe)-mííʔo
PHO *(igó)daï(kā) B íméʔé ʔacíe-
mííʔo M (kuu)-mééʔu O dʸaká,
xonííʔka Hp igóraï Hn igóraï
Hr igora.ï

265 'flesh (carne)' PW ? PBM *éékoó,
*doó-(xeʔe), *(táí)-do, (atsími)
PHO *(daihíʔka), *ōʔá-(tï), *ōʔá-(īhī)
B ʔéékʰoó, toó, tʰá-tʸo {my flesh}
M úúku, dúú-xoʔo {edible}, asími
O dʸahííʔxa, ōʔāāhī Hp úa-tï, ríʃe
Hn jĩkï-θi, i.e-θï, ríʃe Hr jïkï-θi, i.e-θï

266 'blood {33} (sangre)' PW **tï-
xẽ(ʔe) PBM *tïí-(xéʔe), *tïí-(ppaiko)
PHO *tïhé B tʰíxpʰakʰʸo {red-liq-
uid,294,(71),48} M tíí-xoʔo O tsihíí
{294} Hp dí.e Hn dí.e Hr dï.e, dïru.e

267 'grease (grasa)' PW ? PBM *díïrïba
PHO *pa(de), *pa(ihī) B tíírïpa

M dɨ̈rɨba O ɸahī̈ Hp páre Hn ɸáre
Hr ɸare

268 'egg (huevo)' PW ? PBM *ííʸyíï
PHO *hĩ() B ííʸyíï(í) M ííyɨ
O hóóʔto Hp hígï Hn hígï Hr hīgï

269 'horn (cuerno)' PW **(m)óka(x)ïʔto
PBM *(óka)-(x)ítto, (iyáábetto)
PHO ?*(mó)kaï(to) B ókʰa-xíxtʰoᵗ,
iyáápextʰo M íttu O mókaatʸo {of
cow} Hp tíkaï Hn θíkaï Hr θikaï,
θigaï

270 'feather (pluma)' PW ? PBM *íʔxɨɨ-
ne {243} PHO *()pódo B íʔxi-xɨɨ,
íʔxi-xi, íʔxi-ne M íxée-ne O tʸaɸóóro
Hp ipóro Hn iɸóro Hr iɸoro

271 'claw {24,23} (uña)' PW **()-(k)aï-
(be) PBM *(mé)-ʔóttsí-gai-mííʔo,
*(atsi)-ʔóttsí-gai-mííʔo PHO (onó-
k(aï)-be) B (mé)-ʔóxtsʰí-kʷa-mííʔo
M asi-ʔúsé-gai-mééʔu {animal-hand-
finger-nail} O xáátʸo Hp onó-be-ko
Hn onó-be-ko Hr ono-ko-be

272 'belly {14,16,244,245} (barriga)'
PW **xeʔbae, **xebae {14}
PBM *(mé)-iiʔbá(ï), (xɨɨbīī) {244}
PHO (hebae) {Ocaina 14} B íʔpáï,
mé-ʔpáïʸ M íiba, xéebɨɨ O gááho
Hp hébe Hn hébe, hébe-kï, hébe-gï
Hr hebe, ɸenaï

273 'liver (hígado)' PW ??**(ʔg)an(oxi)
PBM *(mé)-íʔgá-neé PHO (banóhi)
B íʔkʷá-neé, mé-ʔkʷá-neé, -kʷá-neé,
-kʷá-ne-ne M íga-no, íigá {his}
O ɸaʔííxo Hp banó-hï Hn báno.i
{my} Hr bano.i

274 'drink (beber)' PW **xido
PBM *ado {231}, (ádíkíní)
PHO (hidó) B ato, atíkʰī, átïkʰíní
M ádu-ʔi O ñooxo Hp hiró-de
Hn hiró-de Hr hiro-de

275 'eat {230} (comer)' PW **d(o)ʔ
{meat}, **gōī(ne) {fruit} PBM *doó-
(ʔi) {meat}, *geéne {fruit}, *maččo
{164} PHO *dïʔ-(te) {meat}, *()tō(),
*gōī {fruit}, *okó B toó {meat}, čeéne
{fruit}, maxčʰo M dúú-ʔi {meat},
gééne-ʔi {fruit}, máčču-ʔi O dʸaa,
dʸoo {meat}, tsōōʔño, gōō {fruit},
ooxo Hp rí-de {meat},
rï.é-de, jïjó-de {fruit}, okó-de
Hn rí-te {meat}, rï.é-de, čičó-de,
jibá-de {fruit}, guí-te Hr rï-te {meat},
jï-te {fruit}, gui-te

276 'bite (morder)' PBM *ïïʔdo,
(digíkkï), (denókko), (dígeʔxíkï)
PHO *aïní B iʔto, tikíxkʰï, tenóxkʰo,
tíčeʔxíkʰï M éédu-ʔi O aanī
Hp aïní-de Hn aïní-de Hr aïni-de

277 'see (ver)' PBM *aittími(ïïté),
(míikkï), (díxïï), (ïïxe) B axiʰʸími,
tíxïï-kʰïnï, ïïxe M áttʸíme-ʔi, méekki-
ʔi O xaa Hp erói-de, kï.ó-de
Hn erói-de, kï.ó-de Hr kï.o-de

278 'hear (oír)' PBM *geébo, (. . .)
PHO *kaká B čeépo, čínʸémïï-kʰïnï,
níʔéxïï-kʰïnï, čeepí-kʰïnï, βïááβe
M gúúbu-ʔi O xaaxa Hp kaká-de
Hn kaká-de Hr kaka-de

279 'know (saber)' PW **gaka
PBM *gaaxá(-kï), (piiβéte)
PHO (áka) B kʷaaxákʰï, pʰiiβʸétʰe
{ability} M gááxa-ʔi O ááxa, ooroha
Hp onó-de Hn onó-de Hr u.iño-te

280 'sleep {232} (dormir)' PBM *kïga
PHO *(i)nī B kʰïkʷa M kíga-ʔi
O ïïnō Hp ïní-de Hn ïní-de Hr ïnï-de

281 'die {282} (morir)' PBM *gixí-βe,
(čééme), (. . .) PHO (dzïï) B tsixí-βe,
ápʰayééβe, aapátʰe, kʰánʸáyáïïβeínʸï,
ímoxíïβe, kʷáyeééβe, ámotʰʸááβe
M gíxé-βe-ʔi, čééme-ʔi, čóómo-bo {he
dies} O ïrá nïï {up}, ñomōōbi

{down} Hp dï.í-de Hn tï.í-de
Hr φi.odai-te

282 'kill {281} (matar)' PW ?
PBM *gíxi-βé-tso, *gíxi-(nï),
(gáikkáao), (gáiïïʔáro), (. . .)
PHO *()ne(ʔ)-() B tsíxi-βé-tsʰo,
čiiʔyání, ápʰaxʸïnï, kʷápʰíxïʔxákʰo,
kʷátsʰïʔkʰáo, tótsʰoʔkʰáo, kʷáyïïʔáro
M gíxé-βe-su-ʔi, gíxé-ni-ʔi, gáikkáau-ʔi
O ïrá ña ha-nïï-ta {ʔ-die-cause}
Hp méine-de Hn méine-te Hr meine-te

283 'swim (nadar)' PW **īʔtī
PBM *ittsi PHO *īʔī B ixčʰi M ísi-ʔi
O ōōʔō Hp í.ï-de Hn í.ï-de Hr ï.ï-de

284 'fly (volar)' PW ?**(gaʔa)pe
PBM *gaʔape, (gaaméne) PHO (pee),
(daiʔi) B kʷaaméne, kʷaʔpʰe
M gáʔáφe-ʔi O dʸaaʔi Hp pé.e-de
Hn φé.e-de Hr φe.e-de

285 'walk (andar)' PBM *ïge, (tadíʔkï),
(rixákko), (peé) PHO *maká(di)
B íče, tʰatïʔkʰï, rixʸáxkʰo, pʰeé
M íge-ʔi O maaxa Hp maká-de
Hn maká-de Hr makari-te

286 'come (venir)' PBM *tsaá-(pé),
(náʔxiʔe) PHO (bíʔ-te), (a, e, i, aihi)
B tsʰaá, náʔxiʔe M sáá-ʔi O aa-, ïï-,
aahi Hp bí-de Hn bí-te Hr bi-te

287 'lie down (acostado)' PBM *(tsïo)-
kïnï, (ááka-ne), *(tó)-g(í)ï-kkïnï
{288}, *kagááí-(βe), (. . .) B tʰó-tsïí-
kʰïnïᵗ {see Muinane 288},
tʰótsikʰáro, pʰárïxkʰáro, téʔexkʰáro,
kʷáčaxkʰáro, pótsʰexkʰáro,
kʰákʷayákʰo, ókʷáïxkʰáro,
βikʰʸoxkʰáro {trans.}, tʰotsíí-βe, pʰaríí-
βe, kʰakʷáá-βʸe, teʔéé-βe, kʷačááβe,
potsʰéé-βe, ókʷaíí-βe, βikʰʸóó-βe
{refl.} M síu-kiniï-bo {late borrowing
from Bora?}, ááka-no, kágáí-kini-ʔi
O ïïá, tïïdʸa {infinitive form} Hp bí.i-
de Hn bí.i-de Hr bï.i-de

288 'sit (sentarse, sentado)' PW *?*
PBM *(ak)iï-kkïnï, *kaʔts(iï)βe,*
(čai)ʔts(ii)βe, (...) B akʰïïβe,
kʰárárixííβe, tsʰonááβe, tsʰoʔnááβe,
čʰaʔčʰiíβʸe {sit down}, ákʰïï-kʰïnï,
kʰáráríxiï-kʰïnï, tsʰoʔná-kʰïnï, tsʰónaḯ-
kʰïnï, tʰéákʰïï-kʰïnï, tʰékʰáráríxiḯ-
kʰïnï, tʰétsʰónaḯ-kʰïnï {seated} M gíí-
kkíní-ʔi {see Bora 287},
kásííβe-ʔi O biiñiʔi Hp ráḯ.i-de
Hn ána ráḯ.i-de Hr ana raḯ-de

289 'stand (ponerse en pie, de pie)'
PBM *?**(gaaméne), *(i)xo(k)ïíβe*
PHO *naiʔtai B ïxʸokʰïíβe,
kʷaaméne, kʷámenéʔkʰï, kʷámenééβe
M xújééβe-ʔi O nïïʔtʸa Hp náida.i-de
Hn náida.i-de Hr naidai-de

290 'give (dar)' PBM *akkï, (éxekkájo,
éxekkáigo) PHO *hiʔ-(te) B axkʰï,
éxexkʰáčo M ákkɨ-ʔi O hïïʔ Hp í-de
Hn ɸeká-de Hr ɸeka-de

291 'say (decir)' PBM *xïïb(ái)ge, *neé,
(iʔxíβa) B ïïpáče {tell}, neé, iʔxʸíβa
M xííbege-ʔi, néé-ʔi O ïï, ãã
Hp dáḯ-de Hn dá.ḯ-de Hr rai-te

292 'burn (arder, quemar)'
PBM (xïgatso), (mɨrai-βe), (áiiβétso),
(kátsïʔxáko, (...) B áiiβʸétsʰo,
kʰátsʰïʔxákʰo, pʰeetʰétsʰo, áiïkʰï,
kʰáríʔxákʰo, anʸï, tsʰóiïkʰï,
rïʔʰïïβétsʰo, kʰáréreeβétsʰo {burn},
rïʔʰïíβe, pʰeétʰe, aiíβʸe, kʰárerééβe,
kʰárïʔʰïíβe, rïʔʰípa {pl} {sting}
M xígasu-ʔi, méraí-βe-ʔi O bii?
Hp bó.o-de Hn bó.o-de Hr bo.o-de

293 'mountain (montaña)' PBM *gáxiḯ,
*káme-(βo)-gáxï, *báaïḯ, *káme-(βo)-
ʔbáaï {515} B kʷáxiḯ, páiḯ,
kʰámekʷáxï, kʰáme-ʔpáï M -gáxɨ,
báai, káamo-βo baaí, káamo-βo-gaxɨ
Hp kaipó-ne-du, íperï
Hn kaiɸó-ne-du, íɸerï Hr a-ne-du

294 'red {371} (rojo)' PBM *tí-ppai-ne
{33,266} PHO *hīāï̃(hī) B tʰíxpʰa-
nʸe M tíɸai-ño O tsííʔo {33,266},
hāāhī {ripe,371} Hp hí.aï-re-de
Hn hí.aï-re-de Hr hi.aï-re-de

295 'green (verde)' PBM *aittíβá-ne
PHO *mokó-() B axtʰʸïβa, axtʰʸíβá-
ne M attʸíβa-no O moxóó-so, hiááʔo
Hp móko-re-de Hn móko-re-de
Hr moko-re-de

296 'yellow (amarillo)' PBM *gíí(-gíβa)-
ne, *gí(-kká)-ne-(íβí) PHO *boda
B čí-xkʰʸá-ne-íβí M gíí-giβa-no
O bóóra Hp borá-re-de Hn borá-re-de
Hr bora-re-de

297 'full (lleno)' PBM *gaʔape-né,
*(tsane) gáʔap(é)(k)kïní-né,
(gáittóokï) B kʷaʔpʰe, kʷáʔpʰé-
kʰïníné M gáʔáɸo-no,
gáʔáɸikkini-no, gáttʸúuki Hp orúi-de
Hn orúi-de Hr orui-de

298 'new (nuevo)' PBM *béʔe-ne
B péʔne M bóʔo-no, bo-, bu- O hïʔto-
Hp kómu.e Hn kómu.e Hr komu.e

299 'round (redondo)' PW *?**(i)paï
PBM *?*(ékíi), (-tɨɨrɨ, -teerɨ, -tiɨre),
*(pá(i)geβéʔroï), *pá(tté)ï
PHO (ikoípoï) B pʰáčeβéʔroï, pʰaï
M ɸáttíyi, ókéi, -teere Hp edóči-de,
rí.ídobi-de Hn íbogï, irúṇo, ikuíɸoï
Hr ibogï {sphere}, iruño {disk}

300 'dry (seco)' PW *?* PBM (píígai-ne),
(áraaβéne), (dááɾi-ne)
PHO *?*(háʔ)ta(pé-dete) B áraaβéne,
táárɨne M ɸííga-ño O hááʔta Hp tapé-
re-de Hn θaɸé-re-de Hr θaɸe-re-de

301 'name (nombre)' PW **maime
PBM *meme PHO *mame B meme
M mómo O maamï Hp mámekï
Hn mámekï Hr mamekï

302 'how (como)' PBM *mï?(j)ï,
*mï?(d)ï, (kébádï) PHO *dzȋ?-()
B mï?tï M míjï, kóbádi O dzo?-
xá?mï, dzo?-ɸïïrá? Hp naitó
Hn nȋ.eθe, nedi Hr nï.eθe

303 'when (cuando)' PBM *-kooka
{304}, (kótsómi), (mȋixȋ?xáa)
PHO *dzȋ?-() B -kʰookʰa {see
Muinane 304}, mȋixʸȋ?xáa
M (kú)súmi O dzo?-kā, dzo?-aa
Hp nï-rúi-do Hn nï-rúi-do Hr nï-rui-do

304 'where (donde)' PBM (kía),
(mȋtsií), (tsátsii), (kétsií) PHO *dzȋ?-()
B kʰía, mȋtsʰïí, tsʰátsʰii, kʰétsʰïí
M kúúka {see Bora 303} O dzoo,
dzōō, dzōō? Hp nï-nó, nï-né
Hn nï-nó, nï-né Hr nï-no, nï-ne

305 'here (aquí)' PBM *(xóó-ga-βï),
(ximáine), (íígeé), (ïtsii, ȋčii), *xíneé-ri,
*xíneé-(βï) PHO *bē() B íȋčeé, ȋčʰii,
ínʸeéri M xúú-(ga-βɨ), ximáño, xinééri,
xinóóβɨ O bá, bȋ Hp benó Hn bené,
benó Hr benomo

306 'there (allí, allá)' PW ?**tā(?ï)
PBM (xa?ï), (ta?ï), (eene), (omaina),
(e?-gee), (é?-tsiíí), (té-tsii), (té?ïge)
PHO ?*(tā), *()?dzï() B é?čeé, eče,
é?tsʰïíí, tʰétsʰii, tʰé?ïče M xa?í, ta?í,
óóno, omáña O tʸāā, dziráhȋ?
Hp badȋ, hadȋ Hn batïne, hadï
Hr batïne, hadï

307 'other (otro)' PBM *tsi-ppi {masc},
*tsí-(ppi-ge), *tsií-(ne), *tsi- PHO (ini-)
B tsʰi-xpʰi {man or animal}, tsʰií-nʸe
{thing}, tsʰií-kʷa {board}, tsʰií-?ye
{tree}, tsʰí-xpʰiče {woman} M si-,
sí-ɸi {masc} O añii- Hp hȋ.áï(.ïe)
Hn hȋ.áï(.e) Hr hȋ.aï.e

308 'few {221} (pocos)'
PBM ?*(tsánéedï-me), (mídï-ne),
(ï?xénére), (čó?xȋné-re), (áyáné-re),
*(áx)áittso-(ne), *(ga?)áittso-(ta)
PHO (kaiβȋ?) B ï?xéné-re, čʰó?xȋné-re,

áyáné-re, kʷa?áxčʰo-tʰa {soon, short
time} M áxášu-no, sánóodɨ-mo,
mídɨ-no O síítï?, sóógo, tóógo, xaβï?
{46,327,221} Hp hí.ïre Hn dú.era
Hr hanore

309 'fog (neblina)' PBM *(o)ttso-(ï),
(áimóo-ppaiko) {59,247,248}
B oxtsʰó-tȋ M áimúu-ɸai(?u) {cloud-
liquid/gas,48,59,247}, súɨ Hp úijȋ.e
Hn úijȋ.e, rójí, roθi Hr uijȋ.e, hȋjeru.e

310 'flow (fluir)' PBM (gaápe), (niiβa),
(koo) PHO *dzo- {53} B kʷaápe
M niiβa-?i (tone not known), kuu-?i
O dzooro, dzooï Hp dó-de Hn tó-te
Hr to-te

311 'sea {49} (mar)' PW **moo(n)ai
{see 49} PBM *moóai, (ȋȋβámȋ dokó-
ppáiko) PHO *m(o)nái-(tahi)
B moóa, ȋȋβámȋ tokʰó-xpʰákʰʸo
M múúai {49} O maanȋ {49}
Hp monái-jai Hn monái-jahi
Hr monai-ja.i

312 'wet (mojado)' PBM (pȋȋ-ppai-ne),
(máái-ne), (mïrííβe), (maxááβe),
(re?re), (ïȋrï), (ïȋrïβe), (rerékkï)
PHO (híhi) B mïrííβʸe, maxááβe,
re?re, ïȋrï, ïȋrïβe, reréxkʰï
M ɸéé-ɸa-ño, máá-ño O hááhi
Hp ïnó-re-de Hn rï.ái-de Hr ïno-re-de

313 'wash (lavar)' PBM *nittȋ-(kï),
(gáitsáitsa?xȋkï), gáčáča?xȋkï), (íjoáko),
(íbȋnïáko) PHO *hokó-te
B nixtʰʸí-kʰʸ, kʷáčʰáčʰa?xȋkʰʸ,
íčoákʰo, ípïnȋákʰo M nittɨ-?i
O hoxoo-tȋ Hp hokó-de Hn hokó-de
Hr hoko-de

314 'worm (gusano)' PBM *xï(?)íba,
(čé?ói, čó?ói), (áppaiko), (. . .)
PHO *()āīg(i), *(a)(ī)kï, (hidzako)
B ïȋpa, áxpʰakʰʸo, ámitʰʸópa,
íxtsʰȋ?o, tʰȋ?nïȋ, tʰʸiȋ?ȋmɨ,
íxtsʰȋȋmïkʰo M xȋ?iba, čú?úi

O *agïïma, ïïko, hïdzaako* Hp *igïroï,*
áïkï Hn *(a)igïroï, áïkï* Hr *aïgiro, aïkï*

315 'wing (ala)' PW *?**x(ï)xaiko*
PBM *(xïxiko), (nïgaá)* PHO *(iáiko)*
B *nïkʷaá* M *xíxeku* O *φōnŏŏβïka*
Hp *i.áiko* Hn *i.áiko* Hr *i.aiko*

316 'fur (piel peluda)' PBM **íʔxí-(ʔono),*
*íʔxi-(xi) PHO *(iʔtïdaï)* B *íʔxi-xi*
M *íxé-ʔene* Hp *idïraï* Hn *hé-tïraï-ri.e*

317 'navel (ombligo)' PW ***móʔta(ba)*
PBM *(móttaba), (íïxïba)*
PHO **m(ó)ʔt(a)* B *íïxʸïpa, íxïpa*
M *múttaba* O *mááʔtʸo* Hp *móda*
Hn *mútida* Hr *mutida*

318 'saliva {2,3} (saliva)' PW ***po(e)-*
no-() *{mouth-}* PBM **xïï-(ri),*
*xïï-(ní-ba) PHO *?ʔ*pó(e)-(no-hï)*
{mouth-liquid; see 2,3,48} B *ïïnípa,*
ïïni M *xïire* O *φóñoohï* Hp *páʔa.ie*
Hn *φé.ikï* Hr *φa.ikï*

319 'milk {15} (leche)'
PW ***mō(ʔpai)naï-()*
PBM **míppáine-ppáiko* *{breast-liq-*
uid,15,48} PHO **mōnoï ihï* *{breast*
liquid,15,157} B *mïxpʰánʸe-xpʰákʰʸo*
M *míφaño-φáiʔu* O *mōnoo-hï̃*
Hp *mónoï-hi* Hn *mónoï ihi*
Hr *monoï ihi*

320 'with (con)' PW *?**mï()*
PBM **-ma, (-ri)* PHO *(mïʔto)* B *-ma, -*
ri M *-ma* O *mïïʔto, -hï̃, -ʔ* Hp *dïga*
Hn *dïga* Hr *dïga*

321 'in (en)' PBM *(-βï), (paine)*
PHO *?ʔ*ho()* B *?* M *-βi, φaño*
O *haa, hadʸa* Hp *-mo, éro, hópo*
{house,75} Hn *-mo, éro, hóφo*
Hr *-mo, ero, hoφo*

322 'at (en, lugar definido)'
PBM *(tsatsíi), (-βï)* B *tsʰatsʰíi* M *-βi*
Hp *-mo* Hn *-mo* Hr *-mo*

323 'if (si)' PBM **-ʔaččííxï, (-ka)*
B *-ʔaxčʰíïxʸï, -kʰa* M *-aččo, -aččíxi*
Hp *-i.a* Hn *í.adï, ní.adï* Hr *-dena, -na*

324 'ice (hielo)' PBM *(ní-ppáikó aráábe-*
ga), (ní-ppaiko-ga) B *ní-xpʰákʰʸó*
aráábe-kʷa *{water ?,48},*
ní-xpʰákʰʸo-kʷa M *?* Hp *háïnoihï*
{water,62}

325 'snow (nieve)' PBM *(ní-ppáikó*
aráábega tsítsiine) B *ní-xpʰákʰʸó*
aráábe-kʷa tsʰítsʰiine

326 'freeze (helarse)' PBM *(tsiïkórí ní-*
ppaiko kóʔpeníne) B *tsʰïïkʰórí*
nïxpʰakʰʸo kʰóʔpʰeníne M *?*

327 'child {46} (niño)' PW *?* PBM **tsíí-*
me-ne, *(gaí-píí)-tsíí PHO *(kiβï)*
B *tsʰíí-me-ne, tsʰíí-me* *{pl}*
M *séémene, gaí-φíí-séé* *{being-male-*
child,38} O *xaβïï* *{46,308,221}*
Hp *kïní-ma* /hítaru Hn *úru.e* Hr *uru.e*

328 'dark {227} (oscuro)' PBM **kíβé-*
ne, *kíβeʔteé-né, *kíβe-(tsíí)
PHO **hiʔtïʔ-()* B *kʰíïβe-ne, kʰíβé-*
ʔtʰeé-néⁱ, kʰíïβe-tsʰíí M *kíβo-no,*
kíβó-to-no O *hïʔtóóʔ-φï* Hp *hídï-re-de*
Hn *hítï-re-de* Hr *hitï-re-de*

329 'cut (cortar)' PBM *?*gá-(βíríïko),*
*gá-(ʔdaʔíni), *kí-(tti), *kí-(ʔdaʔíni),
*kí-(βiïxkʰï), (dó-iʔáinï), (dó-ʔdaʔíni),
(dó-βiïkki), (tótóko, tétéko) B *kʷá-*
ʔtaʔíni, tó-iʔánʸï, tó-ʔtaʔíni,
tó-βiïxkʰï, kʰí-ʔtʸaʔíni, kʰí-βiïxkʰï, tʰá-
βiïxkʰï M *gáβíríïku-ʔi, kíttï-ʔi,*
tútúku-ʔi O *baaʔ, saβo, hïïbo, xaayo*
Hp *haidá-de* Hn *haitá-de, kotá-de*
Hr *haita-de, kota-de*

330 'wide (ancho)' PW *?*
PBM **k(a)rí(ko)-né, (mítane)*
PHO **iháidaï* B *kʰoríí-néⁱ, mítʰʸane*
M *káréku-no* O *aháára* Hp *áiju.e,*
í.airo-re-de Hn *áiju.e, í.airo-re-de*

{stretched out} Hr *aiju.e {big},
dï.aro-θe, heri.e*

331 'narrow (estrecho)' **PW ?**
PBM **ïïxí-né-(gáyḯ), (ḯttsíne), (áyane),
(páyokke)* **B** *ïïxí né-kʷḯꞓ, ḯxtsʰínʸe,
áyane, pʰáyoxkʰe* **M** *ïíxe-ne* **O** *iibi*
Hp *rïjḯ-re-de* **Hn** *rïjḯ-re-de*
Hr *hano-re-de*

332 'far (lejos)' **PBM ?*(kémïége),
*(téꞓe)tsi(-ne), *tsí(ꞓïge)* **PHO ?*a(d)e**
B *tsʰíꞓyïče, kʰémïéče* **M** *téꞓesi-no*
O *aanḯ* **Hp** *are, hḯka* **Hn** *are, hḯka*
Hr *are*

333 'near (cerca)' **PW ?** **PBM** *(pííti-ne),
(téꞓitsitï-ne), téꞓetsitï-ne), (pïïꞓíre-),
(íniíne)* **PHO** **iaïn(oi)deꞓi {see 336}*
B *pʰïïꞓíre, ínʸiínʸe* **M** *ɸíіti-no,
téꞓesi-ti-no* **O** *áánïraꞓ* **Hp** *a.íno-mo,
i.áno-ri* **Hn** *áïno-ri, íano-ri* **Hr** *i.aïrei,
i.ano-ri*

334 'thick (grueso)' **PBM** **pïími-(ne)*
PHO **hetákï* **B** *pʰïími* **M** *ɸééme-ne*
O *hïꞓʸááxo* **Hp** *hédakï.e-de*
Hn *hédakï.e-de* **Hr** *hedakï.e-de*

335 'thin (delgado)' **PBM** **ïttsi-(ne),
aini-(ne)* **B** *ani, ïxtsʰi* **M** *ísi-no, áñino*
O *bóho, xaβïïꞓꞓʸóɸoꞓ*
Hp *jḯ.aï-de* **Hn** *jḯ.aï-de* **Hr** *jḯ.aï-de*

336 'short (corto)' **PBM** **bááꞓrí-ne(-ïꞓβḯ)*
PHO **ïhã́() {see 333}* **B** *páꞓrí-nʸeïβḯ*
M *bááre-ne* **O** *ïhã́hḯ* **Hp** *i.ánori-de*
Hn *íanori* **Hr** *i.anori-de*

337 'heavy (pesado)' **PBM** *(békkï-ne),
(pátiïkḯ-ne)* **B** *pʰátiïkʰḯ-ne* **M** *bókki-no*
Hp *mé-re-de* **Hn** *mé-re-de* **Hr** *me-re-de*

338 'dull (embotado)' **PBM** **tsïïꞓꞓxíβa-tḯ-
ne, (gíꞓi-ne)* **B** *tsʰïꞓꞓxíβa-tʰḯ-ne*
M *sííxeβa-ti-no, gíꞓi-no* **Hp** *há.i-ni-de*
Hn *hái-ni-de* **Hr** *hai-ni-de*

339 'sharp (afilado)' **PBM** **tsïïꞓꞓxiβá-ne*
B *tsʰïꞓꞓxiβá-ne* **M** *sííxéβa-no*
Hp *ha.í-re-de* **Hn** *hái-re-de*
Hr *hai-re-de*

340 'dirty (sucio)' **PBM** **xiin(ḯ)-βá-ne,
*(bïï)-βa-ne, *(mïꞓïni)-βa-ne,
*ïdiikk(o-ne), *ïdííkk(ïï), (neꞓni)*
B *iinʸḯ-βá-ne, ḯtíïkʰyïï, neꞓni* **M** *xííni-
βa-no, béé-βa-no, míꞓini-βa-no,
ídíkku-no* **O** *áã́ma, aβóóꞓxo, ñááꞓḯ*
Hp *ï.áï-re-de* **Hn** *ï.áï-re-de*
Hr *he.a-re-de*

341 'rotten (podrido)' **PBM** **tóókï-ne,
(nókókoo-ne, nékékoo-ne), (rááraá),
(cáxaaβé-né)* **B** *tʰóókʰï-ne, rááraá,
čʰáxaaβé-né* **M** *túúki-no, núkúkuu-no*
Hp *θabí-de, rḯpai-de* **Hn** *θabí-de,
rḯɸai-de* **Hr** *θabi-de, rïɸai-de*

342 'smooth (liso)' **PW **dï(t)ï()**
PBM **(p)(ai)rïïkḯ-ne, *mééβa-ne,
rï(tḯ)rḯ(tï)-(ko-ne), (tḯꞓtḯ-ríβa-tḯ-ne)
PHO *(díhï-de-te)* **B** *pʰïrïïkʰḯ-ne,
mééβa-ne, rïꞓhïrïꞓhï {shiny}, tʰḯꞓtʰḯ-
ríβa-tʰḯ-ne {bump-?-not-}*
M *párʸíіki-no {261}, móóβa-no, rírí-
ku-no* **O** *ɸíɸyi* **Hp** *rḯ.ï-re-de*
Hn *rḯ.ï-re-de* **Hr** *rïhï-re-de*

343 'straight (recto)'
PW ?**(t)a(t)ḯꞓkï() **PBM** **tsa-tḯkkeβe*
PHO *(ha(h)íkïna)* **B** *tsʰatʰïxkʰe-βe,
ímiáá-ne {see 344}* **M** *sá-tíkkoβo
{straight ahead}, tíkkóβo-no*
O *ɸóóꞓꞓʸa* **Hp** *ha.íkïna-de*
Hn *ha.íkïna* **Hr** *atona*

344 'correct (correcto)'
PW ?**(t)a(t)ḯꞓkï()-be **PBM** **(tḯkkeβe-
be) {343}, *(í)miáá-ne {343}*
PHO *(ha(h)íkïgobe)* **B** *ímí
tʰeꞓtḯxïkʰo, tsʰaímiyé* **M** *tíkkóβo-bo,
míyáá-no {see 343}* **Hp** *ha.íkïgobe*
Hn *ñu.éra* **Hr** *mare*

345 'left (izquierdo)' **PW ?** **PBM** **náni-
(ꞓïge), *náni-(nékkï)*

PHO *(h)(ai)díˀ-p(aití) B nání-
nʸéxkʰï M náni-ˀigo O ïrooˀ-ɸatí
Hp harí-pene Hn harí-ɸene
Hr harï-ɸebehï

346 'right (derecho)' PBM *(í)mía-
(nage-ne), *(í)miá-(nekkï)
B ímiá-néxkʰï M ímíyanago-no
O ɸóóˀtʸa {straight?} Hp nabé-ne
Hn nabé-ɸene Hr nabe-hi

347 'old (viejo)' PBM *tsïk(íxeˀï)-ne,
*tsïk(áa)-ne, *kéeme-(be) {246,47},
(kiJaˀo-te), (amia-te) B tsʰïïkʰáane,
kʰeéme M síkíxeˀï-no, kóomo-bo {old
age}, kiJaˀu-to {old-people-pl}, amïya-
to {old-pl} O ïroo-hï
Hp háka-ra Hn hái.ai.e, háka-ra
Hr hakaï.e

348 'rub (fregar (frotar))'
PBM (pákígáikkï), (tákiyóˀkó),
(tákaixáro), (pítsítsiˀíkï, píčičiˀíkï),
(píkiïˀkï), (pígáβáraïkï)
B tʰákʰiyóˀkʰó, tʰákʰaxʸáro,
pʰíčʰíčʰiˀyïkʰï, pʰíkʰiïˀkʰï,
pʰíkʷáβáraïkʰï M ɸákígáikkɨ-ˀi
O tsoo-, xïïrï Hp mo.í-de Hn gï-te,
meJé-no-te Hr bïga

349 'pull (jalar, halar)' PBM *giiïkï,
(táJári(ˀx)íkï) PHO ?*tō() B čiïkʰï,
tʰáčári(ˀxʸ)íkʰï M gíɨyiki-ˀi, gíki-ˀi
O ááˀti, tsōōˀmï {see 364}
Hp tonó-de Hn θonó-de Hr θono-de

350 'push (empujar)' PW ?
PBM ?*(káínááko), (čímóko, číméko),
(píβóroˀxáko), (gaáo), (píkóriïkï),
*(k)átí(kkaáí)ro, *(g)átï(xi)ro,
*ká(βïïˀx)áako, *ká(bóy)áako
PHO (inoiˀtá-te) B kʰátʰïxkʰaáyo,
kʰáβïïˀxʸákʰo, pʰíβóroˀxákʰo, kʷaáo,
pʰíkʰʸóriïkʰï M gátíxeru-ˀi, kábúyaaku-
ˀi, káñááku-ˀi, čímúku-ˀi O haaJa
Hp ñui-dá-de Hn ñui-tá-de
Hr ñui-ta-de

351 'throw (echar)' PW ?**gain(ãï)
PBM *piko, (gáino), (xïkko), (gaáo),
(gaagóo), (íččiβétso, íttsiβétso),
(kaˀpíní) PHO *(bï-ˀtá-te),
*(ai)nãï-() B pʰikʰʸo {put down},
kʷaáo, kʷaakóo, íxčʰiβʸétsʰo {cause
to leave}, kʰaˀpʰínʸï M ɸíkú-ˀi
{store}, gáñú-ˀi, xíkku-ˀi O ïïtsa,
anãātʸo Hp bï-dá-de {put}, dai-dá-de,
paï-de Hn bï-tá-de, ba-tá-de, ñáï-te
Hr bï-ta-de, ni-ta-de, kuaï-ta-de

352 'hit (golpear)' PBM *íJaáyo, *gá-
(βíríko), *gá-(níïkï), *gá-(póóβi),
*gá-(paákko), *gá-(iáko), *gá-
(píxïˀxáko), (eˀnéní), (káitéiteˀxíko)
PHO (bo-ˀtá-te), (adzï) B íčaáyo,
kʷápʰaáxkʰo, kʷáiákʰo,
kʷápʰíxïˀxákʰo, eˀnéní,
kʰátʰʸétʰʸeˀxíkʰo M íJáyu-ˀi, gáβíríku-
ˀi, gáníïkɨ-ˀi, gáɸúúβe-ˀi {ref} O aadzi
Hp bu-dá-de Hn bu-tá-de, ɸa-te
Hr bu-ta-de, ɸaro-de

353 'split (hender)'
PW ?**(gai)taide(ako)
PBM *gá(č)ére(á)ko PHO ?*(bo)-ˀtá-
(de) B kʷáčʰéreákʰo M gáJéréku-ˀi
O taarï Hp bo-dá-de Hn bo-tá-de
Hr bo-ta-de

354 'pierce (punzar)' PW ?**(ka)pai()
PBM *kápáitïkkï-nï, (gáˀexïro)
PHO ?*(paiˀ), *tō-ˀ(tá-te)
B kʰápʰátʰʸïïkʰï-nï {sprout},
kʷáˀexïro M káɸáttʸïkkɨ-ˀi {punch}
O ɸaaˀ, haara, tʸōōˀɸo Hp Ju-dá-de
Hn Ju-tá-de Hr Ju-ta-de

355 'dig (cavar)' PW ?**(t)aïˀde
PBM *tseeˀdi, (kanokko), (ganókko)
PHO (dáïˀ-te) B tsʰeˀti, kʰanoxkʰo,
kʷanóxkʰo M séédi-ˀi O ɸïïso
Hp ráï-de Hn ráï-te Hr raï-te

356 'tie (atar)' PBM *tsíttsi, *doˀxín(ï)
B čʰíxčʰï, toˀxíní M sísi-ˀi, dúxéne-ˀi
O okáápï, gãã Hp kuiná-de
Hn kuiná-de Hr kuina-de

357 'sew (coser)' **PW** ? **PBM** *(pájóó)*,
(gikko) **B** *tsɨxkʰo* **M** *ɸájúú-ʔi*
O *mõõtʸo* **Hp** *tɨpó-de* **Hn** *tɨɸó-de*
Hr *tɨɸo-de*

358 'fall (caer)' **PW** ? **PBM** **aakí(t)te*,
(áipɨ, áipe) **PHO** *(piti)* **B** *aakʰɨtʰʸe*
M *áákétte-ʔi* *{inanimate}*, *áiɸe-ʔi*
{animate} **O** *ooʔo, hooβï, ɸaati*
Hp *baï.í-de* **Hn** *baï.í-de, u.ái-de*
Hr *kai-de, u.ai-de*

359 'swell (hinchar)' **PW** ? **PBM** **xoorii-*
(ne), *(gaaméne)*, *(ɨbatsïíβe)*
PHO *(tïdi-te)*, *(púʔboko-te)*, *(hiiʔka)*
B *oóri, kʷaaméne, ɨpatsʰííβe* **M** *xúúri-*
ʔi **O** *hïʔxa* **Hp** *uaháti-de, pí.iɓuku-de*
Hn *ɸái-de, ɸí.ipuku-de, θïrí-de*
Hr *θïri-de*

360 'think (pensar)' **PBM** **íttsam(áá)i*,
*ítts(í-kɨnï), **itts(o)* **PHO** **komékï*
paʔká *{heart measure,34}*
B *ɨxtsʰaméi, ɨxtsʰï-kʰïnï, ɨxtsʰo*
M *ésámááí-ʔi* **O** *xomïïxoʔyáji, ɸaaʔxa*
{test,measure} **Hp** *komékï paká-de,*
du.énai-de, merïdaidï-de **Hn** *komékï*
ɸaká-de **Hr** *komekï ɸaka-de* *{heart*
measure}

361 'sing (cantar)' **PW** ? **PBM** **mattsí-*
βa, (gáníkkaméi) **PHO** *(doʔ-te)*
B *maxtsʰí-βa, kʷánɨxkʰʸaméi*
M *másíβa-ʔi* **O** *ñoomï* **Hp** *ró-de*
Hn *ró-te* **Hr** *ro-te*

362 'smell (oler)' **PW** ? **PBM** **xɨgíkk(o)*,
*ottsó-ʔi, (nïnïïkkï), **xïgi(íkï)*,
(tsïïʔxïkï), *(aráʔko)* *{tr}*, *(βoβókkï)*,
(kïβa), *(áipïxakóóβe)* *{intr}*
B *ɨcïxkʰʸït̶, oxtsʰó-ʔi* *{to smoke}*,
ïcïïkʰï, tsʰiiʔxʸïkʰï, aráʔkʰo *{tr}*,
βoβóxkʰï, kʰïβa, ápʰʸïxakʰóóβe *{intr}*
M *xígíkku-ʔi* *{sniff}*, *úsu-ʔi, nínïïkki-*
ʔi **O** *dʸooro* **Hp** *hajé-de* **Hn** *hajé-de*
Hr *haje-de* *{intr}*, *ñïta-de* *{tr}*

363 'puke (vomitar)' **PW** ?
PBM **ígí(bámáai)*, **ígí(mïtïʔxáko)*

PHO **kïʔkóe* **B** *ici, ícímítʰïʔxákʰo*
M *ígíbámáai-ʔi* **O** *xooʔxï* **Hp** *kïkúe-de*
Hn *kïkúe-de* **Hr** *kïkue-de*

364 'suck (chupar)' **PW** ? **PBM** *(gɨini,*
geeni, gɨine), *(mogini)*, *(noiʔ-noi)*,
(noíʔ-ko), *(pïʔxa)*, *(ïïʔa)*, *(tsɨïʔi)*,
(tsoóʔko) **PHO** *?*()tō()*, **()gō* **B** *nʸoʔ-*
nʸo, nʸoíʔ-kʰʸo *{milk}*, *pʰïʔxa*
{caramels}, *ïïʔa, tsʰïïʔi* *{... the juice*
out of something}, *tsʰoóʔkʰo* *{...*
something dry into mouth} **M** *gééne-ʔi*
{fruit}, *múgini-ʔi* *{milk}* **O** *tsõõʔño*
{see 349}, *gōō* **Hp** *jïjó-de, moní-de,*
mugú-de **Hn** *hanó-de,*
čičó-de, jibá-de **Hr** *haro-de,*
hakono-te, jiba-de *{fruit}*

365 'blow (soplar)' **PW** ***poonoʔ*
PBM **íbáts(ï)(ʔxáko)*, **boottsó-(kï)*,
*gittsí-(kï), *(poonï)*, *(gibó)*, *(βoβókkï)*,
(iókko), *(βooíkï)*, *(áápïïkï)*, *(číyoáko)*,
(ïïbo) **PHO** **poo(noʔ-te)*, *(hainó-te)*
B *ípátsʰïʔxákʰo, poxtsʰókʰï, čixčʰïkʰï,*
βoβóxkʰï, ióxkʰo, βooíkʰʸï, áápʰïïkʰï,
čʰíyoákʰo, ïïpo **M** *ébásu-ʔi* *{light*
fire}, *búúsu-ʔi* *{fan}*, *gísɨ-ʔi* *{blow-*
gun} *{35,96}*, *ɸúúni-ʔi* *{mouth}*,
gíbú-ʔi *{wind}* **O** *ɸooɸo, hïïʔxa*
Hp *haiñó-de, pú.uno-de* **Hn** *haiñó-de,*
ɸú.u-de **Hr** *ɸuri-de, hï.í-de*
{witchcraft}, *ɸirai-de* *{etc}*, *θaïrïri-de,*
betari-de

366 'fear (temer)' **PBM** *?*ígí,*
*(ai)n(ó)ï?(i)kko(), **nïʔ(néβe)*,
(ápiitsóge, ápiičóge), *(áábiméi)*,
(ámítsáraʔkóge), *(nóïʔkóge)*
PHO *(hakïdoʔiʔ-te)* **B** *ici, ičí-rʰʸe,*
nïʔnéβe, ápʰïičʰóče, áápimʸéi,
ámítsʰáraʔkʰóče, nóïʔkʰóče **M** *ígi-ʔi,*
ñïʔikku-ʔi **O** *tïïro* **Hp** *hakïru.i-de,*
jï.i-de **Hn** *hakïru.i-te* **Hr** *hakïnai-te*

367 'squeeze (apretar, exprimir)'
PW ***ïni(neko)* **PBM** **(m)aámï,*
*aamí-tsó, ((ai)n(ai)nɨko), (gátiaini),
(páítsïïʔxáko, páčíïʔxáko), (...)
PHO *?*(aiʔtá-te)*, **ta(ʔtai-te)*, *(ïni)*

B *aámï, aamí-tsʰóⁱ, pʰácʰïïʔxákʰo,*
tʰákʰíríʔxákʰo, kʰopʰéxtsʰo,
tómïmïʔxákʰo, tʰámootʰáro, iʔto
M *máámɨ-ʔi, áámɨsu-ʔi {make hit},*
ñéñéku-ʔi, gátiañɨ-ʔi O *tsaaka {com-*
pressed} {borrowed?}, ááñi {squeeze out
of} Hp *omíǐ-de, ïdúi-de, aidá-de, dáḍai-*
de Hn *omíǐ-de, ïdú.i-de, na.ïtá-de*
Hr *omï-de {hand}, ïdui-de*
{machine}, ïigue-de, kïmai-de

368 'hold (sostener)' PBM **ikka(ne),*
(gááyïkkïnï), (kátóroʔxáko), (teʔme),
(maittsótso, maččótso) B *ixkʰʸa*
{exist}, kʰátʰóroʔxákʰo, tʰeʔme,
maxčʰótsʰo {feed} M *ikka-ʔi {be},*
gááyɨkkɨnɨ-ʔi O *aнaaβïta* Hp *motí-de*
Hn *moθíño-te* Hr *moθi-de, duba-de*

369 'down (abajo)' PBM **gií-ne, *baári*
PHO **āna* B *čiínʸe {below}, paá(ri)*
M *gíi-no, báari {on the ground}* O *āā,*
āāнa, ñooñi, ñooñihó Hp *ána* Hn *ána*
Hr *ana*

370 'up (arriba)' PW ***kai(), **(k)aime*
PBM **kaame* PHO **kaipo), (aime)*
B *kʰaame* M *káamo-βɨ {up-in}*
O *aaнihó, aaнi, bïнōō, bïнōóʔ*
Hp *káipo* Hn *ká.iɸo* Hr *a.aɸe*

371 'ripe {294} (maduro)' PW *?*
PBM **nááme-ne, (tïpai-ne),*
(kéémene) PHO **hïāí(hī) {red},*
*hee(), *(e)hiʔtï B *náámene,*
kʰéémene M *náámo-no, tíɸai-ño*
{red} O *hāāhī {red}, aaa, hïïʔto*
{dark} Hp *hí.aï-de {red}, hé.e-de,*
murí-de Hn *hi.áï-de {red}, hé.e-de*
Hr *hi.aï-de {red}, e.iθï*

372 'dust (polvo)' PW ***xáénïʔ-()*
PBM **pá-giixï {57,164,171},*
*(xíínï)-giixï {72} PHO **aenïʔ-hiβóda*
B *pʰá-čixʸï, -čixʸïí, íínʸï-číxʸï* M *-gíixɨ*
{powder classifier} O *ahooʔïβóra,*
ahóóʔï, añōōʔïβóra Hp *enǐ-čoma,*
ïmúitaï Hn *enǐ-čoma {ʔpowder,164}*
Hr *hi.ora, imuikï*

373 'alive (vivo)' PBM **bóʔɨɨ-(beke),*
(gáxánékkíǐ-beke), (ménǐnékkíǐ-beke)
B *póʔɨɨ-pekʰe, kʷáxánéxkʰǐǐ-pekʰe,*
ménǐnéxkʰíǐ-pekʰe M *búʔée-no*
O *hiitʸóra* ïī Hp *ká.a-de, hí.ere-de*
Hn *ká.a-de* Hr *kahe-de*

374 'rope (cuerda)' PW ***(i)gaï(baï)*
PBM **gáaibaï, (dóoxɨ-yï), (pádoʔxɨ)*
PHO *(igaï)* B *kʷáápʸaï, pʰátoʔxɨ*
M *gáaibaɨ {of hammock}, dúuxe-yɨ*
O *ñííʔoɸe, mõãʔšaʔóɸe* Hp *íga.ï, ra.o*
Hn *íga.ï, ra.o* Hr *igaï, ra.o*

375 'year (año)' PW ***pï(e)*
PBM **pí(k)kaba, (meeméʔe)*
PHO *(pïemóna)* B *pʰíxkʰʸapa,*
meeméʔe M *ɸikába* O *dʸoʔōōhī*
Hp *pïmóna* Hn *ɸïmóna* Hr *ɸï.emona*

376 'dent (abollar)' PBM *(gáinaaʔíyo),*
(táinaaʔíyo) PHO *(tíʔbekai-te)*
B *kʷánʸaaʔíyo, tʰánʸaaʔíyo*
Hp *číbekai-de* Hn *cípekai-de*
Hr *čipekai-de, čipeno-te, ǰibeno-te*

377 'small house {75} (casita)' PBM *(iʔ-*
xá-gíǐ) PHO **(ho)pó-tïʔb(i) {suffix*
doubtful} B *iʔ-xʸá-kʷíǐ* O *ɸohoo-tsiβo*
Hp *hopó-čuбi* Hn *hoɸó-čupi*

References

Agnew, Arlene, and Evelyn G. Pike. 1957. Phonemes of Ocaina (Huitoto). IJAL 23:24–27.

Allin, Trevor R. 1975. A grammar of Resígaro. Ph.D. dissertation St. Andrews University (Scotland).

Barnes, Janet. 1984. Evidentials in the Tuyuca verb. IJAL 50:255–271.

Burtch Scaife, Bryan. 1975. Fonología del idioma huitoto murui. Datos Etnolingüísticos No. 9. Microfiche. Yarinacocha, Peru: Instituto Lingüístico de Verano.

Burtch, Shirley. 1983. Diccionario huitoto murui. Yarinacocha, Peru: Instituto Lingüístico de Verano.

Crothers, John. 1976. Areal features and natural phonology: the case of front rounded vowels. Proceedings of the second annual meeting of the Berkeley Linguistics Society; 124–38.

———. 1987. Typology and universals of vowel systems. In Joseph H. Greenberg (ed.), Universals of human language 2:93–152.

Greenberg, Joseph H. 1970. Some generalizations concerning glottalic consonants, especially implosives. IJAL 36:123–45.

———. 1987. Language in the Americas. Stanford University Press.

Grimes, Barbara. 1984. Ethnologue: Languages of the world, 10th edition. Dallas: Summer Institute of Linguistics.

———. 1988. Ethnologue: Languages of the world, 11th edition. Dallas: Summer Institute of Linguistics.

Hock, Hans Henrich. 1986. Principles of historical linguistics. Berlin: Mouton de Gruyter.

Kaufman, Terrence. 1990. Language history in South America: What we know and how to know more. In Doris L. Payne (ed.), Amazonian linguistics: Studies in lowland South American languages. Austin: University of Texas Press.

Kaye, Jonathan D. 1971. Nasal harmony in Desano. Linguistic Inquiry 2:37–56.

Key, Mary Ritchie. 1979. The grouping of South American Indian languages. Tübingen: Gunter Narr Verlag.

Labov, William, Malcah Yaeger, and Richard Steiner. 1972. A quantitative study of sound change in progress. Philadelphia: The U.S. Regional Survey.

Ladefoged, Peter. 1971. Preliminaries to linguistic phonetics. Chicago: University of Chicago Press.

Leach, Ilo M. 1971. Vocabulario ocaina. Lomalinda, Colombia: Instituto Lingüístico de Verano.

Loukotka, Čestmir. 1968. Classification of South American Indian languages, Johannes Wilbert, ed.

Mason, J. Alden. 1950. The languages of South American Indians. In Julian H. Steward (ed.), Handbook of South American Indians 6:157–317. Washington: U.S. Government Printing Office.

Minor, Eugene E. 1956. Witoto vowel clusters. IJAL 22:131–37.

———. undated A. (probably mid-1970s). Comparative Swadesh-Rowe wordlist of the three Huitoto languages (Muinane, Minica, and Murui). (Last page missing.) Ms. in the archives of the Summer Institute of Linguistics, Colombia.

———. undated B. Incomplete Swadesh-Rowe wordlist of Andoke (items 1 through 86 only), not phonemicized. Ms. in the archives of the Summer Institute of Linguistics, Colombia.

——— and Dorothy Hendrich de Minor. 1971. Vocabulario huitoto muinane. Yarinacocha, Peru: Instituto Lingüístico de Verano.

——— and ———. 1976. Fonología del huitoto. Sistemas fonológicos de idiomas colombianos 3:59–67. Lomalinda, Colombia: Instituto Lingüístico de Verano.

——— and ———. 1987. Vocabulario bilingüe huitoto–español español–huitoto (dialecto Minica). Lomalinda, Colombia: Instituto Lingüístico de Verano.

Payne, David L. 1985. The genetic classification of Resígaro. IJAL 51:222–31.

Stolte, Joel A. 1980. La nasalización en las lenguas tucanas orientales. Artículos en lingüística y campos afines 7:1–27. Lomalinda, Colombia: Instituto Lingüístico de Verano.

Smith, Wayne. 1990. Lista de palabras Swadesh-Rowe en miraña. ms.

Tax, Sol. 1960. Aboriginal languages of Latin America. Current Anthropology 1:430–36.

Thiesen, Eva. In preparation. Diccionario bora–español español–bora.

Thiesen, Wesley. 1978. Bora. In Eugene Loos (ed.), Materiales para estudios fonológicos 1:7–24. Yarinacocha, Peru: Instituto Lingüístico de Verano.

———, and Eva Thiesen. 1975. Fonemas del bora. Datos Etnolingüísticos 1. Microfiche. Yarinacocha, Peru: Instituto Lingüístico de Verano.

Thráinsson, H. 1978. On the phonology of Icelandic preaspiration. Nordic Journal of Linguistics 1:3–54.

Tovar, Antonio. 1961. Catálogo de las lenguas de América del Sur. Buenos Aires: Editorial Sudamérica.

Van Otterloo, Roger and James Peckham. 1976. Miraña Survey Report, including wordlist obtained from Miraña speaker Juan Miraña. Ms. in the archives of the Summer Institute of Linguistics, Colombia.

Walton, James W. In preparation. Diccionario muinane–español español–muinane.

———, Grace Hensarling, and Michael Maxwell. In press. El idioma muinane.

——— and Janice Walton. 1972. Fonemas del muinane. Sistemas fonológicos de idiomas colombianos 1:41–52. Lomalinda, Colombia: Instituto Lingüístico de Verano.

Waltz, Nathan and Alva Wheeler. 1972. Proto Tucanoan. Comparative studies in Amerindian languages; 119–149. The Hague: Mouton.

Wheeler, Alva. In preparation. Western Tucanoan linguistic comparisons.

Witte, Paul. 1981. Características del discurso en la lengua andoke. Estudios en andoke y muinane; 1–104. Lomalinda, Colombia: Instituto Lingüístico de Verano.